John
& Paul

ALSO BY IAN LESLIE

Conflicted: How Productive Disagreements Lead to Better Outcomes

Curious: The Desire to Know and Why Your Future Depends on It

Born Liars: Why We Can't Live Without Deceit

JOHN&PAUL

A Love Story in Songs

IAN LESLIE

CELADON BOOKS NEW YORK

www.celadonbooks.com

Designed by Jonathan Bennett

Library of Congress Cataloging-in-Publication Data

Names: Leslie, Ian, 1972– author.
Title: John & Paul : a love story in songs / Ian Leslie.
Other titles: John and Paul
Description: First U.S. edition. | New York : Celadon Books, 2025. |
    Includes bibliographical references and index.
Identifiers: LCCN 2024052410 | ISBN 9781250869548 (hardcover) |
    ISBN 9781250869531 (ebook)
Subjects: LCSH: Lennon, John, 1940–1980. | McCartney, Paul. | Beatles. |
    Male friendship. | Rock music—1961–1970—History and criticism. | Rock
    music—1971–1980—History and criticism. | Popular music—1961–1970—
    History and criticism. | Popular music—1971–1980—History and criticism. |
    LCGFT: Biographies.
Classification: LCC ML421.B4 L45 2025 | DDC 782.42166092/2
    [B] —dc23/eng/20241105
LC record available at https://lccn.loc.gov/2024052410

Our books may be purchased in bulk for promotional, educational, or business use. Please contact your local bookseller or the Macmillan Corporate and Premium Sales Department at 1-800-221-7945, extension 5442, or by email at MacmillanSpecialMarkets@macmillan.com.

Originally published in the United Kingdom in 2025 by Faber

First U.S. Edition: 2025

10 9 8 7 6 5 4 3 2 1

For Alice, Io, and Douglas

CONTENTS

Prologue: December 9, 1980 1

1. Come Go with Me 7

2. I Lost My Little Girl 23

3. What'd I Say 35

4. Will You Love Me Tomorrow 47

5. Besame Mucho 55

6. Till There Was You 69

7. Please Please Me 73

8. She Loves You 87

9. If I Fell 99

10. I Don't Want to Spoil the Party 107

11. Ticket to Ride 115

12. Yesterday 121

13. We Can Work It Out 131

14. In My Life 141

15. Tomorrow Never Knows 149

16. Eleanor Rigby 161

17. Here, There and Everywhere 169

18. Strawberry Fields Forever 173

19. Penny Lane 187

20. A Day in the Life 195

21. Getting Better 203

22. I Am the Walrus 209

23. Lady Madonna 225

24. Yer Blues 229

25. Look at Me 239

26. Hey Jude 243

27. Julia 259

28. Martha My Dear 267

29. Get Back 271

30. Two of Us 279

31. Don't Let Me Down 287

32. The Ballad of John and Yoko 291

33. Oh! Darling 299

34. The End 307

35. God 319

36. How Do You Sleep? 327

37. Dear Friend 335

38. Jealous Guy 339

39. Let Me Roll It 347

40. I Saw Her Standing There 357

41. Coming Up 363

42. (Just Like) Starting Over 371

43. Here Today 379

Acknowledgments 389

Notes 393

Bibliography 423

Index 427

John
& Paul

PROLOGUE

Paul McCartney emerges from the recording studio in which he has been working all day to face a group of reporters holding microphones toward him under blinding lights. They ask for his reaction to John Lennon's murder, the night before. McCartney is chewing gum. His answers are short, laconic. "Er, very shocked, you know. It's terrible news."

"How did you find out about it?"

"I got a phone call this morning."

"From whom?"

"From a friend of mine."

"Are you planning to go over for the funeral?"

"I don't know yet."

"Have you discussed the death with any of the other Beatles?"

"No."

"Do you plan to?"

"Probably, yeah."

"What were you recording today?"

"I was just listening to some stuff, you know, I just didn't want to sit at home."

"Why?"

McCartney visibly loses patience. "I didn't feel like it."

The reporters run out of new questions.

"It's a drag, isn't it? Okay, cheers," McCartney says, and makes for his car.

☙

More than half a century after they stopped making music, the Beatles continue to permeate our lives. We listen to their songs while driving and dance to them in clubs and in kitchens; we sing them in nurseries and in stadiums; we cry to them at weddings and funerals and in the privacy of bedrooms. They are not likely to be forgotten anytime soon; if anything of our civilization is remembered a thousand years from now, there is a good bet it will be the chorus of "She Loves You" and an image of four men crossing a street in single file.

We've barely begun to recognize or understand the wild improbability of the achievement. In 1962, nobody could have foreseen that America's cultural hegemony was about to be rudely disrupted, or that the hegemon would surrender so blissfully to the disrupter. The heist was sprung from a gray island at the edge of the Old World whose glories were behind it. Great Britain seemed stuck in some long-gone era of top hats and dirty chimneys, all vitality spent. But from its damp soil sprouted a life force so vigorous that it jump-started a new epoch. It didn't come from the country's capital, either, but from the suburbs of a provincial city in industrial decline, streets forlorn with war damage. Here two teenage boys invented their own future and, in doing so, our present. Neither John Lennon nor Paul McCartney studied music; they couldn't even read the notes. They schooled each other, and then they schooled the world.

When Peter Jackson's documentary *Get Back* was released in 2021, many viewers commented on how strangely modern the Beatles seemed, as people. The footage showed us London streets populated by gents in pinstripe suits and hippies in afghan coats, everyone time-stamped by the historical moment. But when John, Paul, George, and Ringo were in frame, we felt as if they could walk out of our screens, into our living rooms, without missing a beat. It wasn't so much how they dressed as their demeanor: how they talked to one another, the way they sat, the jokes they made. That isn't a coincidence. The critic Harold Bloom argued that we recognize ourselves in Shakespeare not just because he captured something eternal in human nature, but because he wrought our very idea of what a person *is*—an intro-spective, self-fashioning individual. Similarly, the Beatles were crucial to the creation of a post-1960s personality: curious, tolerant, self-ironizing, unaf-fected, both feminine and masculine. Timothy Leary declared, "The Beatles are mutants. Prototypes of evolutionary agents sent by God, endowed with a mysterious power to create a new human species." The microculture of the Beatles, which had such a decisive impact on our culture, germinated in the many hours that John and Paul spent in Paul's front parlor or in John's bedroom, guitars on laps, making songs, poetry, and laughter.

This is a book about how two young men merged their souls and multi-plied their talents to create one of the greatest bodies of music in history. The partnership of Lennon and McCartney was responsible for 159 of the Beatles' 184 recorded songs, and they were the dominant creative decision-makers within the group. "There is no doubt in my mind that the main talent of that whole era came from Paul and John," said George Martin. "George, Ringo and myself were subsidiary talents." This is also a love story. John and Paul were more than just friends or collaborators in the sense we normally understand those terms. Their friendship was a romance: passionate, tender, and tempestuous, full of longing, riven by jealousy. This volatile, conflicted, madly creative quasi-marriage escapes our neatly drawn categories, and so has been deeply misunderstood.

We think we know John and Paul; we really don't. A popular narrative about the group and its central partnership emerged in the wake of the Bea-tles' demise in 1970. It was drafted by John Lennon in a series of dazzlingly articulate interviews, and fleshed out by a generation of rock critics who idol-ized him. In the 1970s, John was the hero the world wanted: ostentatiously antiestablishment, charismatically tormented—a figure who matched not just the moment, but also much older ideas of genius. Paul was deemed a "straight," a bourgeois poser with no substance. A dualism took hold that has persisted ever since, with John presented as the creative soul of the Bea-tles, and Paul as his talented but facile sidekick. After Lennon's untimely end in 1980, this narrative became canonical. Somehow it survives, albeit in a moth-eaten form, even though it says more about the cultural and political preoccupations of a bygone era than about what actually happened. "John versus Paul" is still the polarizing shorthand by which fans and writers discuss the Beatles. But as the protagonists themselves often acknowledged, there was no "John" without "Paul," and vice versa. Their collaboration, even at its most competitive, was a duet, not a duel.

The standard narrative has distorted the true personalities of Lennon and McCartney, and impoverished our understanding of the Beatles' music. We need a new story, not least because recent years have seen the emergence of important sources of evidence that definitively undermine the old one. Releases from the Beatles' record label have included hours of demos, outtakes, and studio chatter, which throw new light on the band's relationships and creative processes. Peter Jackson's documentary *Get Back*, for which he updated the extensive footage of the band shot in January 1969 for Michael Lindsay-Hogg's documentary *Let It Be*, proved revelatory. These new primary sources give us access to the band as it actually was, rather than as subsequently reconstructed by critics and biographers—or by its members, whose memories, like everyone else's, are flawed and biased.

This book tells the story of John and Paul's friendship, from when they meet until John's death. It does so by way of the richest primary source of all: their songs. Each chapter is anchored in a song that tells us something about the state of their relationship at the time, either in its words or in how it was created or performed. In 1967, John Lennon said, "Talking is the slowest form of communicating anyway. Music is much better." From the moment they began writing, Lennon and McCartney conceived of the pop song not just as a tune with words, but as a way of processing overwhelming pain or joy, or both, and as a means of communication. They saw the song this way because they needed to. They were both deeply emotional men who had the fabric of their world ruptured at a young age, and they longed to connect—with each other, with audiences, with the universe. When they couldn't speak what they felt, they sang it.

⊛

"'A drag' isn't how the world will see it," says an ITN reporter, sententiously, after a clip of McCartney's reaction to Lennon's murder is played on the *News at Ten*. As millions reel at the sudden, violent death of one of the most famous and loved men in the world, that mean and paltry phrase hits the headlines: "It's a drag." McCartney's apparently emotionless demeanor seems to confirm what many already suspect: that Lennon and McCartney fell out years ago and no longer had any affection for each other. Amid the sadness, this news arrives like another little death. The infectious joy the two of them took in each other's company had been so plain, onstage, on-screen, and, above all, in music. Now one is gone while the other chews gum and makes glib remarks.

Whatever happened to John and Paul?

1   COME GO WITH ME

They met on a hot day in July 1957—twelve years after the war, ten years before *Sgt. Pepper*—amid the homespun pageantry of a suburban English garden party: brass band, fancy-dress parades, cake stalls and hoopla games, police dogs jumping through rings of fire. Paul McCartney, fifteen years old, was a tourist that day, over from Allerton, a mile or two across the golf course. He didn't hang out in Woolton much—it was a posh neighborhood, a little prissy—but his friend from school, Ivan, lived there, and Ivan had suggested they go to the fete. There would be girls, plus Ivan had this local friend, John Lennon, whom Paul might like to meet, or at least see play with his group.

The church committee in charge of Woolton's annual fete had decided to host a skiffle band this year—something for the youth—and they'd invited John Lennon's group, the Quarry Men, to play (in Britain, skiffle was a more polite forerunner of rock and roll). Ivan knew Paul was a music nut, a sharp-fingered guitarist and an impressive singer. He was not a Teddy Boy like John—he wasn't as flamboyantly rebellious—but he was a devotee of Elvis Presley and Little Richard. At around 4 p.m., he and Ivan arrived at St. Peter's church, and handed over threepence each to the lady at the gate (half price: the children's price). The noise of Lennon's group was billowing through humid air from the field next to the church. Paul sweated in his white sports coat and tight black trousers.

He had seen John around, on the bus, in the chip shop, and he was already fascinated by him. Paul was an intellectually hungry boy who was unconvinced by school and unimpressed by the prospect of an office job. Here was this older lad, nearly seventeen, a leather-jacketed, sideburned, vulpine rocker who seemed to have already made an irreversible break from workaday life. John Lennon was not someone you wanted to be seen paying attention to until you were ready for it to be returned. He carried a reputation for verbal and physical combat and was usually surrounded by a schoolboy entourage.

Now, as Paul and Ivan approached the makeshift stage, Paul McCartney was afforded a legitimate chance to gaze at John Lennon. To hear him, too. It must have been an awful, muddy, glorious racket. One lad scrubbing a washboard, another grabbing at a tea-chest bass, a drummer dutifully thumping. And up front: Lennon, the opposite of bashful, staring down the crowd and blasting out, in his rude, powerful voice, songs that Paul knew by heart.

Later Paul remembered that he was struck by how good Lennon looked, and how good he sounded. He was also intrigued by what Lennon got wrong. Lennon played his guitar oddly, his left hand making simple but unfamiliar shapes on the fretboard, and he messed up the words in a way that Paul found almost inexplicably thrilling.

The first thing to note is that this was not a meeting of equals but fundamentally lopsided. For teenagers, age gaps are magnified: every year is a generation. John was not just older; he was already a big figure in the small world of southeast Liverpool teenagers. He had glamour, a gang of mates, and a skiffle group of which he was the undisputed leader. He was, according to those around him at the time, magnetic, unignorable. Girls fancied him, boys feared him. Standing before that stage, looking up, Paul knew that if he wanted to be friends with John, or join him up there one day, he was the one who would have to make the effort. John Lennon didn't care.

Paul also knew that he had a shot at propelling himself into John's orbit through their shared love of rock and roll—a love of listening to *and* playing it. Indeed, this was the reason he wanted to meet John in the first place. Paul was seeking out partners who were as crazy about music as he was. What started on his dad's piano had become a full-blown obsession after he aquired a guitar. He would play it on his bed, in the living room, on the toilet, every minute his hands were free. He learned the chords for skiffle and rock and roll songs and sang along. He got pretty good, and he knew it. For all that he was looking up to the older boy that day, he was also auditioning him.

Other than music and a pronounced suspicion of authority, John and Paul shared something else: they were walking wounded. Each, in his short life, had experienced jarring, alienating, soul-rending events that left permanent scars.

By the time he met John Lennon, Paul McCartney's mother had been dead for eight months. Mary Mohin came from Catholic Irish stock and was raised in poverty, the second child of four. Her own mother died in childbirth when Mary was nine. Mary's father, who was from County Monaghan, took the family back to Ireland, tried and failed to make a living in farming, and returned them all to Liverpool, this time broke, and with a new wife and stepchildren, with whom Mary and her siblings did not get on. In Mary, this chaos seems to have instilled a steely self-reliance. She threw herself into a nursing career, specializing in midwifery. At thirty she was a ward sister, and unmarried. Mary Mohin had been friendly with the McCartneys, a Protestant Irish family, for years, and had recently moved in with her friend Ginny McCartney. Gin's older brother Jim, a cotton salesman, handyman, and former leader of a semiprofessional jazz band, was still single, despite being in his late thirties. Whether it was late-blooming love, loneliness, or some mixture of both, it's impossible to know, but in April 1941, Mary and Jim married. Their first child, James Paul, was born fourteen months later. Peter Michael ("Mike") arrived eighteen months afterward.

As a young child Paul was good at getting what he wanted, usually without anyone minding or even realizing what had happened. In 1953 he passed the eleven-plus and gained entry to a prestigious grammar school, the Liverpool Institute. It was one of the last times that Paul did just what his parents wanted. After observing how much he liked playing on the piano they had in the living room, Mary and Jim found a teacher for Paul, but Paul abandoned the lessons after a few weeks. He didn't want to learn scales and dots on a page; he wanted to get straight to playing what he loved. His parents encouraged him to audition for the choir at Liverpool Cathedral—he could sing beautifully—and Paul deliberately flubbed it. His school years would be marked by this kind of self-sabotage. It wasn't that he had any difficulty learning; quite the opposite: he was a remarkably quick study. Nor was it that he didn't like his teachers or fellow pupils—he was a socially supple, unfailingly charming boy. It was just that he was very clear on what interested him and what bored him, and he had a stubborn aversion to being told what to do.

Mary was the engine of family life. Jim McCartney was genial, dapper, and funny, but it was Mary who set standards of dress, cleanliness, and manners, and insisted they were kept to. She was warm, too, a liberal dispenser of hugs and kisses. As an adolescent, Paul guarded his independence from her—even Mary could not make Paul do piano lessons if he didn't want to. Still, he admired her. He saw how hard she worked, for one thing. A midwife and a health visitor, Mary, who had responsibility for families on their estate, was a highly respected local figure who received presents from grateful new parents. She created happiness! It was also Mary to whom Paul looked for comfort when he was anxious (he later wrote a song about this, "Let It Be"). On Sundays, Mary made roast dinner, while Paul lay on the carpet and listened to his father play songs at the piano—"Lullaby of the Leaves," "Stairway to Paradise." The piano was at the heart of the home and the heart of social life—wherever the wider McCartney clan gathered, at home or in the pub, a singsong usually ensued, often with Paul's father leading proceedings. The association of music-making with love and happiness became ingrained. Paul lived inside the ordinary miracle of a loving family and, like everyone else who does so, took it for granted. Until it was taken away.

The McCartneys were not well off. The cotton industry was in a bad way, Jim's job did not pay well, and he was said to be overly fond of a flutter on the horses. But thanks to Mary taking extra shifts at the hospital, the family did well enough to move out of their house on a poverty-stricken, often violent estate in Speke, to a similar but newer house on Forthlin Road in Allerton, on the southern edge of the city. Paul was nearly fourteen. He loved the house and how on leaving it he could quickly find himself in another world of fields and meadows and cows. Within a year, though, he crossed another kind of borderline. When Mary McCartney felt a pain in her breast she put it down to the menopause. Doctors told her to forget it, but it got worse. She went to see a cancer specialist, who recommended immediate surgery, but by then it was too late. Mary was forty-seven when she died. It all happened within a month. Paul and Michael knew almost nothing about it until their mother went into the hospital for a mysterious reason, while they were shipped out to their aunt and uncle's house. Gathered in the living room to be told the news by their dad, Mike cried, while Paul asked, "How are we going to get by without her money?" It sounds cold, and it troubled Paul for years afterward, but to me it is heartbreaking: the sound of a hyperactive young brain going into overdrive in order to evade a shattering psychological blow.

Much of McCartney's mature personality can be traced to Mary's life and the fact of her death: his work ethic, his devotion to family, and his need to help others enjoy the experience of being alive. Her death also inculcated a determination to project invulnerability. Mike recalled that it had a far bigger impact on Paul than was obvious. It drove him into himself, and for a while he pushed others away, even his family. As Paul later put it, "I learned to put a shell around me." As an adult, when Paul felt pain, or sadness, or anger, he usually hid it (although it came out in his music). That sometimes made it hard for people to fully trust him, or to feel like they really knew him.

Paul and Mike were told next to nothing about their mother's death. "We had no idea what my mum had died of," said Paul. "Worst thing about that was everyone was very stoic, so nobody talked about it." The extended family rallied around Jim rather than the children. In 1965, Mike McCartney recalled he and Paul staying at Auntie Gin's for the first Christmas without their mum. Seeing them looking miserable, Gin said, "Listen, loves, I know the way you're feeling . . . but you've got to try and think of other people. You've got to think of your father. I know this has been a great shock but we all get great shocks and we have to get over them. Now you'll really have to pull yourselves together."

Gin wasn't being cruel or heartless. Pulling yourself together was a necessary coping tactic for anyone who had lived, as she had, through poverty and war. But now it meant that the McCartney children were excluded from their own loss, made to seal up their pain (psychologists today call it "grief disenfranchisement"). Paul learned to maintain an appearance of perfect emotional competence no matter what strain he was under. Bereavement also forced him to consider urgent existential questions in a way that most of us do not until much later, if at all. In the days after Mary's death, Paul prayed for her to come back. "Daft prayers, you know. If you bring her back, I'll be very, very good for always," he recalled. "I thought, it just shows how stupid religion is. See, the prayers didn't work, when I really needed them to."

☙

In July 1957, John Lennon's mother was very much alive, almost painfully so. Around this time, Julia Lennon was both central to John's life and outside it: an intimate who remained just out of reach. It wasn't that she didn't love him, or that he didn't love her; it's that she didn't seem to want to be his mother, and this broke his heart.

In 1929, a seventeen-year-old boy called Alf Lennon met a fifteen-year-old girl called Julia Stanley in Sefton Park, Liverpool. Alf was working-class, Irish Catholic, short and irrepressible: a charming chancer, a talented drinker. Julia, who came from a Protestant family, was middle-class, slender, and idiosyncratically beautiful, with striking red hair and a fine-boned, noble face. So began an enduring but deeply erratic relationship. Alf joined the merchant navy and began to spend months at a time at sea. Julia had already left school and worked as an usherette at the cinema. The two lovers would see each other when Alf came back to Liverpool, but she never bothered replying to his letters and treated him coolly when he was home, which may have suited both parties. They married in 1938, the result of a dare that escalated: she told him he'd never propose and so he did. Julia accepted in the spirit of adventure, and because everyone told her it was the wrong thing to do.

Julia was the fourth of five sisters raised in a cultured and proudly self-improving home. Her father taught her the banjo and she learned to play popular American songs, picked up from sheet music, films, and records. Among her sisters, Julia was known as the freest spirit: the rule-breaker and mischief-maker with no interest in settling down. The oldest, Mimi, eight years Julia's senior, was in some ways her opposite: ambitious for social advancement, fiercely conscious of responsibilities, a believer in self-betterment through hard work. Yet Mimi had a sense of humor, too, and while she was judgmental, she was also forgiving. The two sisters stayed close, despite repeated clashes of will.

Their biggest clash came over the welfare of Julia and Alf's son, John, born on October 9, 1940. Mimi was present at the birth. Alf was away at sea. Julia and John lived with Julia's parents and sister Anne, and various lodgers. Julia, twenty-six, was not ready to give up on her youth. She took a job as a barmaid in a local pub and began a relationship with a Welsh soldier she met there called Taffy, whom John would later remember being around. Mimi and her husband, George, who did not have children of their own, often looked after John in their house in Woolton. In 1944, Alf returned after eighteen months at sea, to be told by Julia she was pregnant with Taffy's child. John, who witnessed his parents rowing, must have been horribly confused. Alf then took John away to stay with his brother and sister-in-law, ten miles away. John stayed with this couple for at least a month. He was well looked after, but never saw his mother. When Alf returned to sea he deposited John back with Julia, although John spent much of his time at Mimi's house. (Julia gave birth to her second child in 1945; she gave it up for adoption.)

Mimi felt increasingly strongly about what she perceived to be the neglect of her nephew and, in the spring of 1946, took decisive action. Julia had started going out with a door-to-door salesman called Bobby Dykins and moved in with him to a tiny one-bedroom flat. She and Bobby shared a bed with John, who was five. Mimi was appalled. She informed the council, which sent an official to inspect the home. The official agreed with the boy's aunt that the child was not being properly cared for. Mimi was licensed to be John's primary carer. She and George took John into their house, on Menlove Avenue, for good.

The disruption to John's early life didn't end there. A few weeks later, Alf turned up while on leave and stayed the night at Mimi's. The next day he told Mimi he was taking John to the shops, and didn't come back. He whisked John to Blackpool, where they stayed with a friend of Alf's called Billy Hall, and his mother. (Hall: "He was only five but he seemed much older—you could talk with him almost like an adult.") Alf had a vague plan to immigrate to New Zealand with John. His immediate problem was that he needed to go back to sea, and Billy's mother wasn't keen on looking after John for the months he was away.

Julia now arrived in Blackpool, with Dykins, to retrieve John. An argument ensued in the Halls' living room. John remembered his father demanding that he choose which parent he wanted to be with. Alf later claimed that John said he wanted to be with him, which is quite possible, since they had been together happily for the past few weeks. Julia, in tears, walked away, which made little John beg her not to go. She picked him up and took him with her to Liverpool. John did not hear from his father again until he was an adult. Once in Liverpool, though, Julia, who was pregnant again, handed her son back to Mimi, instilling a lifelong sense of hurt, puzzlement, and betrayal in John.

Under the care of Mimi and her husband, George Smith, John became a member of Woolton's genteel community: he enrolled at the local school and at Sunday school at St. Peter's church, where he sang in the choir. Mimi and George were not well off—George managed two small dairy farms—but lived in a semidetached house with a spacious garden. It even had a name: Mendips. John loved his uncle George, a kindly man who bought him his first mouth organ, left sweets under his pillow, and taught him how to ride a

COME GO WITH ME 15

bike. Mimi was a voracious reader, and the house was full of novels, poetry, and biographies, which John devoured. He and Mimi would read the same book and argue about it afterward. He liked to read the household's two daily newspapers, sometimes on George's knee.

Mimi was not affectionate; she didn't hug. She was strict, demanding, scolding, sardonic, snobbish. But she was never cruel. She did not hit John, despite it being common for parents to do so (Paul was occasionally beaten by his father). Above all, Mimi was present. When she took John in, she promised that he'd never return to an empty house and never be left in the care of a childminder. She kept her word. Mimi walked John to primary school and collected him every day. She always turned up.

At school, John was a star pupil, inquisitive and articulate. He had no problem passing his eleven-plus to win a place at Quarry Bank High School for Boys. At home, Julia visited him for a while, but then the visits stopped. Mimi told Julia they were unsettling for the boy. John spent much of his childhood under the impression that his mother had moved far from him, without understanding why (in reality, Julia lived just a couple of miles away). He did see her now and again. The only known photo of him with his mother is from a family gathering at Aunt Anne's house in 1949. Julia has her hands under John's armpits, tickling him.

At Quarry Bank, things started to slide. John did well in art but badly in most other subjects, finishing near the bottom of his year while racking up multiple detentions. He hit puberty early, becoming distracted by girls and by the need to dominate his peers. "I wanted everybody to do what I told them to do," he remembered. "To laugh at my jokes and let me be the boss." John was torrentially articulate and very funny, cracking up his classmates and annoying his teachers. He was always alert to the possibility of violence, occasionally using his fists, but more often finding a way to psychologically intimidate boys he couldn't take on physically. Ever since he was a baby, Lennon had been passed around among adults, almost none of whom seemed prepared to take him in for good. He learned to be wily, watchful, and manipulative when he needed to be. Richard Lester, the director of *A*

Hard Day's Night, said of John, "I noticed this quality he had of standing outside every situation and noting the vulnerabilities of everyone, including myself. He was always watching."

When he was fourteen, John suffered his first bereavement: his beloved uncle George died suddenly from liver disease. Around this time, John began seeing more of Julia, of his own volition. He turned up at her front door one day, emboldened by a cousin down from Edinburgh who wanted to visit her. He was welcomed in, and from then on, John would often bunk off school and hang out at Julia's house. At first he kept these visits a secret from Mimi. It must have been an oddly illicit thrill, making clandestine visits to his own mother. It was certainly disorienting—he wasn't sure if Julia felt like his mother, or his aunt, or a big sister, or something else; in later life he talked about a sexual attraction to her.* Julia, who was in her early forties, loved pop music. She introduced John to American folk songs and Doris Day records, a pleasure he later shared with Paul. She taught him to play the banjo and sing along. Later on, she bought him his first guitar; he played banjo chords on it. Julia was the most outrageous, the most reckless person John knew. She flirted with his mates, wore stockings on her head, and danced in the kitchen. In 1956 she shared John's excitement about Elvis. When he decided to form a skiffle group, she was all for it. As John's relationship with Julia deepened, his schoolwork suffered, and his love for rock and roll became all-consuming. He and Mimi rowed more incessantly and bitterly than before. He spent an increasing amount of time at his mother's, staying for weekends in the home she shared with Dykins and her two daughters.

---

* From an audio diary Lennon made in 1979: "I was just remembering the time I had my hand on my mother's tit in Number 1 Blomfield Road . . . I was about fourteen. I took the day off school, I was always doing that and hanging out in her house. Oh we were lying on the bed and I was thinking, I wonder if I should be doing anything else, you know. I always think whether I should have done it, presuming she would have allowed it." There's no evidence that Julia invited or encouraged any such transgression; the story is significant insofar as it lingered in John's mind for the rest of his life. According to Lennon's biographer Philip Norman, John told the story to Yoko Ono, and to the therapist Arthur Janov. Oddly enough, Paul has spoken of having sexual feelings toward his mother, too: "At night there was one moment when she [Mary] would pass our bedroom door in underwear . . . and I used to get sexually aroused." (Quotations from Philip Norman, *John Lennon*; Barry Miles, *Paul McCartney*.)

John's close friends could sense that underneath the schoolboy bravado was mental turmoil. And no wonder: a bereavement is awful for a child but does at least provide a degree of negative certainty. John's mum wasn't dead; she just lived somewhere else, with other children, and, worst of all, this was seemingly through choice. Julia reappeared intermittently, shimmeringly. When she visited Mendips, she would hug him, tickle him, and vanish; later on, when he started visiting her, he was made to feel at home without ever feeling truly at home. Julia was loving and magnetic and always just out of reach. It was a relationship that blurred the lines between parent, sister, friend, and lover. He adored Julia in part because she did not act like a mother, but at some level, he dearly wished her to be one. John's childhood left deep flaws in his psyche: a nagging need for all-consuming love, and a terror of abandonment and betrayal.

When John played at the Woolton village fete, he wore a checked shirt Julia had bought for him. Julia came to see him, with her two daughters. Mimi was there, too, and she was appalled. "Mimi said to me that day that I'd done it at last. I was now a real Teddy Boy," he said later. It was not a compliment. It's tempting to say that John was inspired by Julia and had to overcome Mimi, and indeed that's how the story is often told. In fact, he and Mimi stayed in affectionate touch right up until the end of John's life. She was his only constant. It is true to say, however, that these two women, who between them were the biggest influences on John's formative years, offered diametrically opposed models for how to live. One represented hard work and self-discipline: the importance of making something of yourself, of learning how to play the social game and winning at it. The other represented freedom, self-expression, and the need to break out of society's prison to seek higher, purer truths of art and experience. In 1957 it must have felt to John Lennon that life was about choosing between these two paths—between two ways to be a person.

Then along came Paul.

⊛

Years later, when Paul recalled how John chewed up and spat out songs onstage that day, the one that came to his mind was not "Hound Dog" or "Be-Bop-a-Lula," but "Come Go with Me." It wasn't skiffle or rock and roll, it was doo-wop. Elvis Presley led the invasion of America into the lives of British teenagers, but behind him came battalions from different cities playing different genres. On pirate radio, alongside rock and roll, you could hear the plangent twang of country and western, the dirty and seductive grooves of R&B, the suave harmonies of doo-wop. If you were really into music, as John and Paul were, you recognized all these different sounds, even if you didn't bother much about classifying them.

Passionate, joyous, and playful, doo-wop was a glimpse of heaven from the street. A style developed by the gospel quartets of the 1940s, it was adopted by groups of young African and Italian Americans who wanted to sing somewhere other than a church and about something other than Jesus. Although largely male, it was decidedly non-macho, and later became the basis of the girl-group sound. Doo-wop retained a strain of spirituality, a sense of secular prayer. If rock and roll embodied kinetic desire, doo-wop was the sound of longing—for sex, sure, but also for something more elevated. There was a seeking, childlike quality to it. It was the sound of young adults, or old children, making pleas and asking questions: "I Wonder Why," "Tell Me Why," "Why Do Fools Fall in Love?"

"Come Go with Me" was a song by the Del-Vikings, a mixed-race group of US Air Force servicemen who met at a base in Pittsburgh. They released this, their first single, early in 1957. It was a sensuous and dreamy invitation to elope. When the Quarry Men bashed through it, it became something else. In the original, the singer pleads with his darling to run away with him, and begs her not to leave him languishing: "Please don't let me / Pray beyond the sea." When John sang it, said Paul, it became, "Please don't send me down to the penitentiary." John must have picked up the word from a skiffle or blues song. By throwing it into "Come Go with Me" he semi-accidentally made it a song about freedom and imprisonment. Years later, McCartney looked back in wonder at this: "It was *amazing* how he was making up the words . . . he didn't know *one* of the [actual] words. He was making up every one as he went along. I thought it was great." Why was McCartney so blown away by this? For one thing, "Come Go with Me" wasn't a song that any casual fan of skiffle or rock and roll would know. It was a rarity, the kind of tune you would know only if you were listening to Radio Luxembourg, as they both were. If you knew it, then you really knew. More important, by improvising his own words, John was showing Paul that you could be enthralled by American music without deferring to it; that you could make it your own rather than pretending to be someone you were not; that you could get it wrong in a way that felt right.

Doo-wop and the music that grew out of it, from girl groups to Smokey Robinson–style soul, formed an underacknowledged but crucial influence on the Beatles. You can hear it in their painstaking attention to harmonies and love of vocal blending, in their use of backing vocals as sonic coloring, and in a plethora of details, like the way John hangs on a falsetto in "In My Life" ("in *m-ah-ahy* life") or Paul sings the bass part on "I Will." Lennon uses doo-wop's innocence as a backdrop for dark humor in "Revolution" ("*shoo-bee-doo-wop*") and in the final section of "Happiness Is a Warm Gun" ("*bang bang shoot shoot*"). Paul rips his vocal cords to shreds over a doo-wop chord progression on "Oh! Darling." Lennon drew on doo-wop, this time affectionately rather than ironically, in "(Just Like) Starting Over," which turned out to be the last single he released. Doo-wop bookends the John-and-Paul relationship, present at its beginning and at the final parting of ways.

⊕

After the Quarry Men finished their set, a period of hanging around ensued— the kind of hanging around that teenagers do a lot of, listless and tense at the same time. The group had been booked to perform again that evening, for a dance in the church hall. There seemed little point in going home, and given that the day was hot and sticky, they wandered over to the hall, which was being prepared for the dance. They gathered by the stage, in a room off to the side with a piano.

John and Paul had been introduced briefly outside, but it was in the church hall that each began to assess the other at close quarters. The conversation turned to music. Paul, who must have run through this moment in his head, asked John for a go on his guitar, and John said yes. Paul had to retune it, since John had tuned the strings in a funny way. The others noticed that Paul held the guitar upside down, which was odd, although even just in the act of tuning up he looked like someone who knew what he was doing. Then Paul knocked out a stunning version of "Twenty Flight Rock," an Eddie Cochran rocker familiar only to aficionados. He knew every word.

Paul then took to the piano to sing Little Richard's "Long Tall Sally." He had honed his Little Richard impression at home. When he first tried to emulate a Little Richard *whooo*, he couldn't escape his self-consciousness. What was a well-brought-up boy from Liverpool, England, doing trying to imitate a wild-sounding Black man from America? Then one day he forgot himself and just *did* it, and it felt amazing, like he had jumped out of his skin. So he did it again, and again. Now he did it for John Lennon, his screams and whoops reverberating through the hall.

McCartney later recalled sitting at the piano and smelling beery breath over his shoulder, before realizing it was John. Looking back, it's tempting to imagine Paul as the center of attention, everyone crowding around him, mouths agape. But one of those present—Pete Shotton, a Quarry Man, and John's best mate at the time—said he barely remembered Paul being there at all. I suspect that Paul didn't seek to dominate the occasion and was quite happy for others to drift in and out. He had an audience of one.

He hit his target. Lennon was struck by how well this lad could play, and by how handsome he was ("He looked like Elvis. I dug him"). He was also impressed and a little unsettled by Paul's lack of fear. Lennon looked to dominate any group of boys, including his group. Up until then, the Quarry Men had been an irregular, slightly half-hearted affair, months of inaction lightly punctuated by gigs. Members came and went, turning up or not turning up, staying in only until John turned on them. "I'd been kingpin up to then," he recalled. "Now I thought, if I take him on, what will happen?"

⊕

Shortly after the fete, John sent Pete Shotton to ask Paul if he wanted to join the Quarry Men. Paul pretended to think about it before saying yes. There's a photo from November that year of one of John and Paul's first appearances onstage together. It was taken at New Clubmoor Hall in north Liverpool. The Quarry Men have smartened up: they're wearing white shirts and thin black ties. John and Paul are the only two wearing dinner jackets, and they take the front of the stage, with neither at the center. It would not be true to say they were equals—not yet—but Paul was already much more than just another member of John's group.

At Woolton fete each of them heard the other say, *Come go with me.* And when Paul reached across to take John's guitar—retuning it, reversing it, turning it on its owner like a weapon—the twentieth century tilted on its axis. Two damaged romantics with jagged edges that happened to fit began to fuse into something new and packed with energy. "That was the day," John Lennon said, ten years later, "the day that I met Paul, that it started moving."

2   I LOST MY LITTLE GIRL

In Peter Jackson's *Get Back*, we watch the Beatles at work in 1969, as they attempt to put together both a new album and some kind of TV show, as yet unspecified. The sessions are beset by uncertainty over the project and the future of the group. In muted conversations, the Beatles acknowledge the possibility of an imminent split. Between takes, they run through dozens of songs that they learned years before in Hamburg and Liverpool. Some are covers, some are songs that Lennon and McCartney wrote before they were famous. John or Paul will sing an opening phrase and the other will pick up on it, his face lighting up with a grin. There is a loose plan to make the album about the band's musical roots, but the most important role of these run-throughs seems to be emotional. The songs remind them of what they have loved about playing together. The songs are sustenance.

At one point, Lennon launches into a song called "I Lost My Little Girl." It is about as simple as a song can be. It uses three basic chords, the first chords anyone learns on the guitar. The words are trite: the singer says he woke up this morning, his head in a whirl, and only then did he realize he'd lost his little girl. There is another verse, in which we learn that her clothes were not

23

expensive and her hair didn't always curl. Then it's back to the title phrase, followed by *Oh, oh, oh*. The clip in *Get Back* is short, but on the bootlegged audiotape of the sessions we can hear the band spin this elementary song out for over five minutes. Lennon cycles through the three chords over and over again, repeating the verses, adding his own embellishments. The others join in: George adds bluesy lead guitar; Paul harmonizes and calls back to John, echoing his lines in a cheesy American accent. There is no attempt at developing the song. It doesn't go anywhere. It just is. Those pulsing, repetitive chords go around and around until the song begins to sound less like the Beatles than their minimalist peers, the Velvet Underground. It's a fascinating moment, particularly because John is singing a song by Paul—the first song Paul ever wrote on a guitar.

⊛

We can almost pinpoint the moment that John Lennon first heard "I Lost My Little Girl." At his first gig with the Quarry Men, Paul botched a guitar solo so badly that they all remembered it for years afterward. Paul was deeply embarrassed—he had been brought into the band on the basis of musical competence and now he was the one exposing them as amateurs. It marked the end of his brief tenure as lead guitarist, and the start of something else. Soon afterward—possibly later that evening—Paul did something he hadn't done before: he played John one of his own songs. Perhaps he felt the need to redeem himself. The song he played was far from a masterpiece. But it was a song.

In interviews, McCartney sometimes refers to "I Lost My Little Girl" as his first song, because it was the first rock and roll song he wrote. Actually, by the time he was fourteen he had already been trying his hand as a songwriter, composing songs at his dad's piano, influenced by the music that wafted around the house: big band jazz, show tunes, music hall. One of his compositions from this period was "Suicide," a jaunty but dark Sinatra-style song about women who put themselves at the mercy of smooth-talking men. Another was a music hall–style number, later titled "When I'm Sixty-Four." After Elvis—then Little Richard, Chuck Berry, and Buddy Holly—erupted into McCartney's world, rock and roll became his primary obsession, as it did for John Lennon, and the object that represented it was the guitar. In July 1957, soon after meeting Lennon, McCartney won his father's consent to trade in his first instrument, a trumpet, for a guitar. "The minute he got the guitar, that was the end," said his younger brother, Mike, ten years later. "He was lost. He didn't have time to eat or think about anything else."

McCartney, left-handed, was learning an instrument designed for a right-handed person to strum or pick the strings with their stronger hand. Given the primacy of rhythm in rock, that meant he had trouble making songs come alive. Rather than accept this hindrance as an unfortunate fact, he made the guitar fit him. At first this simply meant turning it upside down, as he did when he grabbed hold of John's guitar in St. Peter's church hall. But playing a guitar upside down changes its sound: the strings ring out in reverse order, top notes first. McCartney took the strings off and put them back the other way around so that he could attack them with his left hand from the correct direction.

Lennon also approached the guitar from an unusual angle: he had been taught to play the banjo by his mother and transferred these lessons directly to the guitar. Lennon realized he needed someone of McCartney's caliber at least as much as McCartney needed him. He rationalized the Quarry Men, weeding out members he didn't consider good enough, rarely firing anyone directly but finding ways to make them go. Pete Shotton had been Lennon's closest friend since the age of six. He didn't play an instrument, so he was given the washboard to play. In the autumn of 1957, Lennon engineered a row while they were out on their bikes, then finished the job by smashing the washboard over his head at a party. "Well that takes care of that problem, doesn't it, Pete?" said John, brutal and amicable all at once (they stayed friends).

Around the time he heard Paul's song, John came up with what he later regarded as *his* first song: "Hello Little Girl." It had the melodic zing of Buddy Holly, who first entered the British charts the month before that gig at New Clubmoor Hall. As skiffle faded, Buddy Holly and the Crickets became Lennon's guiding inspiration. Holly's songs were catchy yet based on a handful of chords. Holly himself was not stunningly handsome like

Elvis, exotic like Little Richard, or swaggering like Gene Vincent. He was a normal-looking guy with glasses (for John, nearsighted and self-conscious about it, this was significant). Holly's singing style was different, too: intimate, almost conversational, and decorated with little vocal hiccups. "Hello Little Girl" is a more fully formed song than "I Lost My Little Girl." It stayed in the repertoire of the Quarry Men and then the Beatles for years; it was one of the songs that caught George Martin's attention when Brian Epstein first played him a disc of the group. There is an echo of Paul's song in its title: a suggestion that even at this stage, the two were borrowing and building on each other's ideas.

As 1957 turned into 1958, the friendship deepened at an accelerating rate. Lennon was now attending art college. John had failed all his O levels, even art, and seemed to have squandered any hope of betterment through education. But his headmaster, who, despite everything, rather liked Lennon, agreed with Mimi to recommend him to Liverpool College of Art, which accepted him. Lennon was soon bored by classes on printing and architecture, and fitted awkwardly into the college's bohemian milieu. Among the tweed jackets who discussed the finer points of typefaces while sipping ale and listening reverentially to jazz, this lilac-shirted, leather-jacketed Teddy Boy stood out. Lennon projected attitude: he had a baleful stare and always looked ready to launch or repel an attack. This was partly a habit from school and partly accidental: he preferred not to wear his glasses.

Liverpool College of Art was on Hope Street, not far from the city center, and it happened to adjoin Paul's high school, the Liverpool Institute. Paul had another year of school to go, but he was thoroughly disaffected. He'd already taken two O levels and failed one; the school expected him to take more, progress to the sixth form, and train to become a teacher. Paul did not believe in that plan. He had his own. His intelligence was not in question—his teachers had always commented on how quickly he learned. Jim McCartney recalled how he seemed to be able to dash off his homework while watching TV and yet retain information from both. Paul didn't hate authority so much as refuse it. He didn't dress outrageously or insult his teachers. He would listen to them, and smile, and do the opposite of what they said.

John and Paul now spent their weekdays divided only by walls. They met frequently and illicitly, skipping their respective classes, exiting their respective buildings, and meeting up on Hope Street. John would have his guitar. They'd walk to the bus stop and catch a double-decker to the southern suburbs. Up on the top deck they would smoke, strum, and talk. Half an hour later they would be inside Paul's house, usually empty during the day. Paul would grab his guitar, and the two of them would sit in the small living room, or "front parlor," face-to-face. John wore his glasses, the better to see what Paul was doing. Paul pointed out that John's banjo chords were different from guitar chords, and showed him the right shapes to make. Paul's reversed guitar meant that the two of them could act as mirrors for each other. (Years later, Paul recalled that John had beautiful hands.) There was a gramophone in the living room and they would play a record, attempt the song themselves, then lift the needle to hear it again until they figured it out. Lennon's humor, savage and silly, cracked Paul up, and John realized that in Paul he had not just an audience, but a foil.

They went to John's house, too, though less often because it was rarely empty, and Aunt Mimi was rather strict. Although Paul could walk from Allerton to Woolton, John's house, full of novels and poetry, felt like another world: a world of intellectuals. Mimi, who could be sharp with John's visitors, didn't mind this one. She would patronize Paul ("Your little friend's here"), which he interpreted as a sign that she liked him. Although Mimi did not object to the boys playing their guitars, she didn't welcome noise inside the house and insisted they stood in the front porch, or vestibule. The porch's high roof and tiled floor endowed their voices with an Elvis-like echo. They worked out harmonies, John taking the lower part. One boy stood with his back to the outside, the other with his back to the house, close enough to feel the other's breath.

They were playing the rock and roll songs they loved, but they were also doing something extraordinary: coming up with songs of their own. Neither Paul nor John knew anyone who wrote songs; it was not common practice even among rock and roll fans with guitars. Songwriting was for Americans. It was Americans who created classic songs sung by Bing Crosby and Frank

Sinatra, and Americans who made rock and roll. John and Paul vaulted this psychological barrier together, assisted by Buddy Holly, who wrote his own songs, using a few simple chords. After "I Lost My Little Girl" the songs began to flow, in bedroom, parlor, and porch. John or Paul might come to the other with a scrap of an idea, a chorus or a title, and together they would try to make it into something. This meant overcoming another barrier. Anyone who has created something knows how exposed you feel when showing someone your unfinished work. Yet these two trusted each other enough to do so, even when the work they shared was full of feelings. The more they shared, the closer they became.

Sometimes John and Paul would get together at Julia's house for their writing sessions. Like John's other friends—like John—Paul was dazzled by Julia, and quite fancied her. "I always thought she was a very beautiful woman, with long red hair . . . a very spirited woman." Whenever they left Julia's house, Paul noticed a tinge of sadness about his friend. Julia loved American songs from the 1920s and 1930s. Paul knew plenty of these himself and they became an ingredient of his and John's shared enthusiasms. They admired the intricacy of these songs, their elegant structures and well-crafted melodies, and for both of them, these songs invoked their parents.

Songwriting became a competition, but not a competition of egos so much as ideas. They made the *songs* compete. They were ruthless critics of each other's work, but not of each other. After they were famous, Paul put it like this: "We never argue. If one of us says he doesn't like a bit, the other agrees. It just doesn't matter that much. I care about being a songwriter, but I don't care passionately about each song." (By which he means not that he doesn't care about the song being good, but that he doesn't care if *he* is the reason it's good.) Each was just as capable of dismissing his own idea.

They were already taking this work seriously, and shared an unspoken recognition that there was no time to waste. With one foot out of the education system, they were effectively betting their futures on music. Paul appropriated an exercise book from school in order to record and catalog their songs. Each song was given its own page. There was no musical notation, since neither could read music: just lyrics and chord names and occasional vocal instructions ("Ooh ah, angel voices"). At the top of each page was the song title and above it the phrase: "ANOTHER LENNON-McCARTNEY ORIGINAL."

John and Paul made an agreement to take shared ownership of each other's talent. If one wrote a song by himself, he would bring it to the other and the credit would always be the same, effacing its origin. "We decided on that very early on. It was just for simplicity, really," said McCartney, "and—so as not to get into the ego thing—we were very pure with it." The decision to put Lennon's name first was made relatively straightforward by the alphabet (although it is hard to imagine the older boy would not have taken precedence). They had in mind the songwriting pairs who made American songs famous before rock and roll came along: Rodgers and Hammerstein, Lerner and Loewe, Gershwin and Gershwin.

They were not replicating the classic model of a songwriting partnership, however, but creating a new one, whether they realized it or not. By the time Rodgers and Hammerstein met at university, they were already musical sophisticates, and they did not write a show together until each had established successful careers. Lerner and Loewe were twenty-four and forty-one respectively when they met. George and Ira Gershwin didn't start writing together until they were in their early twenties, after George had studied composition in Paris and Ira had a musical under his belt. In every case, there was a clear division of labor between composer and librettist: Hammerstein, Lerner, and Ira Gershwin did the words; Rodgers, Loewe, and George Gershwin did the music. Leiber did words, Stoller music.

The Lennon-McCartney partnership was a very different creature. It entailed the two of them educating each other in the art of songwriting and doing so from scratch, or, if not from scratch, then from whatever was lying around: records, TV, books of guitar chords, a few tips from experienced musicians like Paul's dad. And there was no division of labor. "Who writes the words and who the music? So people ask endlessly," wrote Brian Epstein, in his memoir. "The answer is that both write both." Words and music were intuitively understood by both as a single compound. Music created meaning, words made rhythms and sounds. As they were learning how to write songs they were learning about each other, molding each other, at an age when personality is at its most malleable and porous.*

⚙

Paul's disastrous turn on lead guitar meant that the Quarry Men had a vacancy, and by early 1958, he was confident enough in his relationship with Lennon to make a risky suggestion: that they give a tryout to a boy he knew from school. George Harrison had been in the year below Paul at the Liverpool Institute and they used to get the same bus to school. When Paul was set back a school year, in the autumn term of 1957, he began to see more of George, and noticed how accomplished a guitarist the younger boy had become. George had been taught guitar by someone his dad was friends with from his merchant seaman days. He picked it up quickly. Like Paul, he was an intelligent boy who resented school and loved rock and roll. Like Paul also, he came from a stable and loving family (in George's case, with both parents present throughout his childhood). George was overtly rebellious. He grew his hair long and sculpted it into an Elvis quiff. He took great care over clothes, wearing a bright yellow waistcoat under his school blazer. Paul and George visited each other's home to play guitars, and while they never formed the intense connection Paul had with John, they became good friends, despite the age gap.

Introducing him to John was another matter. George was a kid, after all, even younger than Paul, not quite fifteen. He was slight in build and might have been taken for thirteen. Still, the three of them hung out. Nobody is quite sure who broached the topic of George joining the group, but they all remembered an encounter on the top deck of a bus, coming back from a night out. George had his guitar and Paul urged him to play a tune called "Raunchy." "And Little George—he was always little—he got his guitar out of his case and by golly he played it. And we all fell about. He's in, you're in, that's it!" The three of them quickly became the core of the Quarry Men,

---

* Their collaboration wasn't restricted to songwriting. When Paul arrived at Mendips one day in October 1958, John was at a typewriter, hammering out a story called "On Safairy with Whide Hunter" [sic]. Paul joined in. It went into the book as another Lennon-McCartney original. John later published it in a book of his poetry, with the note "Written in conjugal with Paul."

playing gigs as a trio at private parties and wedding receptions, sometimes rehearsing at George's home in Speke.

John's relationship with Paul was unchanged by George's addition to the group. It was accepted by George that Paul was closer to John than he was, and he seems to have been unbothered by this. He wasn't quite as voluble or antic as the other two: his pulse was slower, his sense of humor almost lugubrious. There was a stubborn confidence to George; he never seemed intimidated. He could soak up John's derision or Paul's condescension and return either with interest. George did not write his own songs. Rather than disrupting or changing the Lennon-and-McCartney friendship, he re-inforced it.

By early 1958 the Quarry Men had shed their identity as a skiffle group to focus on rock and roll. They sometimes played with a school friend of John's called Duff Lowe, who remembered: "I never took it that seriously. But Paul and John always gave it 120 percent. It had to be perfect." That summer they even made a professional recording, having discovered a local studio and record press for hire. On July 12, 1958, in a suburban living room with a microphone hanging from the ceiling, they recorded two sides of a single: a rather breathless version of the Buddy Holly song "That'll Be the Day" for the A side, and a Paul song called "In Spite of All the Danger." John sang both. Seventeen years later he said, "I was such a bully in those days I didn't even let Paul sing his own song."*

At art college, John formed a close friendship with a fellow student from the year above him. Stuart Sutcliffe was regarded as an exceptional talent by his tutors. Physically he was small and unimposing, but like George Harrison he had a quiet charisma, projecting the introverted cool of James Dean. The friendship seemed unlikely to fellow students, but John adored Stuart. He liked that Sutcliffe was not passing through art college on his way to a day job but was a true artist, driven to create, committed to his craft. Sutcliffe

---

* It's usually misleading to assign exclusive authorship of a song to either John or Paul, at least while they were in a group together. So when I refer to a "John song" or a "Paul song," what I mean is that John or Paul originated the song, and oversaw it to completion, rather than that the song was his alone.

had left home and lived in glamorous squalor with fellow artists. For his part, Stuart was, in the words of a female friend at college, "carried away" by Lennon.

On Tuesday, July 15, 1958, John was at his mother's house on Blomfield Road when Julia left in the evening to visit Mimi at Mendips, less than two miles away. She didn't tell him the purpose of her visit. A couple of weeks previously, Julia's partner, Bobby Dykins, had been arrested for driving while drunk, on his way back from the restaurant where he worked as a waiter. He received a heavy fine and was banned from driving. He also lost his job, since he was no longer able to get home from the city late at night. When the household's straitened situation became apparent, Dykins told Julia that they could no longer afford to have John around to stay. However she felt about it, Julia's purpose that evening was to convey the message to her sister. Julia left Mimi's house shortly before 10 p.m. As she was saying goodbye at the gate, John's friend Nigel Walley approached to see if John was home. Mimi told him he was out. Julia, with her customary charm, said, "Oh Nigel, you've arrived just in time to escort me to the bus stop." They walked down Menlove Avenue together. As they neared the bus stop, which was on the other side, they said goodbye. Julia turned left to cross the road; Nigel turned right toward his home. He heard a terrible skidding and a thump. When he turned around he glimpsed Julia's body flying through the air.

John recalled a policeman knocking on the door of Blomfield Road and asking if he was Julia Lennon's son, before informing John and Dykins that Julia was dead. John was seventeen. Later, he recalled: "I thought, fuck it, fuck it, fuck it. That's really fucked everything. I've no responsibilities to anyone now."

In the months after Julia's death, John seemed numb on some days, drunk and vitriolic on others. Mimi, in shock herself, saw it as her role to maintain order rather than tend to his emotional needs. Alf Lennon, who found out a couple of months later, did not get in touch. John was left alone with his grief.

Perhaps not completely. Paul, George, and John would get together and play guitars, often at George's house (George's mum was keen that the boys keep John busy). John did not talk about his mother's death with Paul, but the event cemented their bond. It's common for someone who is bereaved to want to be with someone who knew and liked the one who has passed away, and John knew that Paul understood something of what he was going through. McCartney later said: "Each of us knew that had happened to the other . . . at that age you're not allowed to be devastated, and particularly as young boys, teenage boys, you just shrug it off." It *shattered* them, he said, but they had to hide how broken they felt. "I'm sure I formed shells and barriers in that period that I've got to this day. John certainly did."

Shells and barriers are defensive fortifications, but for John and Paul this shared trauma also blasted open an underground tunnel through which they were able to communicate in secret from the rest of the world, and even from themselves. In music they could say what they felt without having to say it.* The songs they wrote and sang together were not "about" their feelings—they *were* their feelings, including those for each other. At least in their early years, those feelings were refracted through the idiom of rock and roll. It was not a conscious strategy. *I lost my little girl*—only much later did McCartney reflect that he wrote it in the wake of his mother's death.

⊛

The 1969 group rendition of "I Lost My Little Girl" that was captured in Jackson's *Get Back* happened toward the end of the January sessions, in a studio the Beatles built for themselves at the headquarters of their then-new record label, Apple, on Savile Row in London. Earlier on we see the group sitting in a circle, discussing Paul's dream of making an album that culminates in a spectacular theatrical show of some kind. But he hasn't overcome either his own vagueness about what the show ought to be or the reluctance of the others to play live. The mood is downbeat. Paul chews his thumb while rocking gently back and forth on his chair. He looks tired and glum. Lennon tells him, gently but firmly, that he isn't going to get what he had in

---

* In 2016, McCartney told *Rolling Stone*: "Music is like a psychiatrist. You can tell your guitar things that you can't tell people. And it will answer you with things people can't tell you."

mind when he initiated the project. Addressing George, but talking to Paul, indirectly, John says, "Say it's his number, this whole show. Well, it's actually turned into our number more than his number, that's all. It's just that, really." Paul sounds resigned. "Yeah, I know, it is the majority decision and all." Paul can feel life seeping out of the project and out of the band itself. He says to John, "We're in a recording studio again, in London, making another album . . . It's just funny to realize that after this is all over you'll be off in a black bag somewhere, at the Albert Hall."* The mildly derogatory reference to Lennon's peace tour with Yoko Ono hints at how McCartney feels about where his partner's attention is now focused. He knows that what John and Paul make together is no longer the central concern of John's life, and although he does not admit it, he is hurting. John can tell; he feels it, too. Shortly after this conversation he launches into "I Lost My Little Girl." It's a balm.

---

* The Albert Hall event took place the previous month. It was actually a white bag.

3   WHAT'D I SAY

By the autumn of 1959, the Quarry Men were a trio. At various times, Eric Griffiths, Rod Davis, Pete Shotton, Bill Smith, Len Garry, Colin Hanton, and John "Duff" Lowe were lost or pushed out. This left an odd, lopsided group: Lennon, McCartney, and Harrison all played the guitar. Drummers and bass guitarists were in short supply, and Lennon's eccentric little band found it very hard to recruit any, partly because they found it hard to tolerate anyone except one another. ("The rhythm's in the guitars," they told skeptical promoters.) They almost ceased to exist for a while; Harrison played briefly with another group.

More and more beat groups were springing up in Liverpool's suburbs, playing American-style rock in café-bars and informal clubs: Rory Storm and the Hurricanes, Cass and the Cassanovas, Derry and the Seniors. As their names suggest, these groups followed a format—a front man and singer, backed by an instrumental group. The Quarry Men didn't have a front man, since Lennon did not want to be one or be subordinate to one. The group pottered around the edges of the scene, playing family parties and art college dances, and eventually landed a regular spot at a club called the Casbah, run by a local woman called Mona Best in the basement of her home. They picked up some fans here, although in the scene at large they remained something of a curiosity, almost a joke.

John and Paul were still meeting at each other's home and writing songs, but less often than in their first flush. Paul was studying harder. Having been placed in a remedial class with younger boys, he had stepped up his efforts, and achieved good-enough O levels to join the sixth form. Under a new English teacher, Alan Durband, Paul found himself reading—and actually enjoying—Chaucer, Shakespeare, Oscar Wilde, Tennessee Williams, and others (he particularly liked reading plays, and wondered if he might become a stage director).

Early in 1960 Lennon moved into a flat on Gambier Terrace with Stuart Sutcliffe and another art college friend. Harrison and McCartney, who still lived at home, became frequent visitors to this citadel of adult bohemia, where they could smoke and play guitars and listen to American records as much as they liked. Having left behind the broken Menlove Avenue–Blomfield Road nexus of his childhood, Lennon was even more dependent on his friends for emotional succor, and when Sutcliffe sold one of his paintings for £90, Lennon encouraged him to buy a bass guitar and join the group, even though Stuart could not play bass or anything else. Paul wasn't happy about this: it broke what he took to be an inviolable rule of the group, that any new addition should be able to play. He later admitted that he was also jealous of Stuart's closeness to John. Still, in the absence of alternative bass players, he agreed to Stuart joining. Even if Paul and John were seeing less of each other, they were still tight. During the 1960 Easter holiday, the two of them hitchhiked down to Caversham, Berkshire, in the south of England. They took their guitars and stayed for a week with Paul's cousin Bett and her husband, Mike, who ran a pub. John and Paul worked behind the bar and played a gig at the end of the week, billing themselves as "the Nerk Twins."

Sutcliffe helped the group solve the problem of its name. Now that Lennon was no longer at Quarry Bank, there was no reason to persist with the "Quarry Men," and the group experimented with a few names without settling on any. In a half-hearted attempt to conform to beat scene norms, they tried "Johnny and the Moondogs," but they were never comfortable with having a designated leader. In homage to Buddy Holly and the Crickets, Sutcliffe suggested another kind of insect. John decided it would be better if "beetles" was spelled wrong, to make a pun on beat music. Although they tinkered with it a few times, it stuck.

John and Stuart hung out at an Italian-style espresso bar near the college. The Jacaranda was run by Allan Williams, an entrepreneurial Welshman who had formed a business relationship with the London pop impresario Larry Parnes. The raw energy of rock and roll's first phase was fading now, as a new generation of more carefully packaged singers took over. Britain's leading star was Cliff Richard, a smooth-voiced singer who adopted some of Elvis's mannerisms while making them more palatable to older generations. Observing Richard's success, Parnes hit on a successful formula: find a pretty boy who can hold a note, give him an emotionally evocative name, dress him up like Elvis. Tommy Hicks became Tommy Steele; Ronald Wycherley became Billy Fury. In May 1960 Parnes asked Williams to help him find a backing band at short notice for one of his lesser stars, Johnny Gentle, for a weeklong tour of Scotland. Williams asked four groups, none of whom could take the time off. So he asked the Beatles.

Lennon and McCartney hated the new breed of pop stars. They had already formed an aversion to the artificial and synthetic. Even Elvis, back from military service, was making sappy movies. Their other heroes were dead or missing: Buddy Holly had been killed in a plane crash; Little Richard had renounced the devil's music (for now); Chuck Berry was in trouble with the authorities. In 1957 they had been, in their own minds, at least, at the vanguard of a revolutionary moment. Now they found themselves at a tangent from their peers, a subculture within a subculture, gazing backward as much as forward. Still, they could hardly afford to be purists, and this was a big deal: a whole week of paid engagements and a chance to impress a big-time London promoter. As usual, they had no drummer, so they enlisted a stolid twenty-eight-year-old called Tommy Moore, rented a van, and set off. The tour was shambolic. They played to half-empty halls in small Scottish towns. They crashed the van, injuring Moore, who was already miserable, since he didn't share the sense of humor of his young, bewilderingly garrulous co-workers.

He had to go to the hospital, but there was a gig that evening. Lennon, displaying the kind of ruthlessness he reserved for anyone he didn't regard as an equal, corralled Moore into playing.

Still, with a professional tour under their belt, Williams was able to find the Beatles more gigs over the summer of 1960. They were not regarded as anything like a first-rate act, even by Williams, but they would play anywhere they were asked to. They played bleak clubs in out-of-the-way towns, facing down marauding Teds who threatened to duff them up. For a while they were the resident band at a strip club run by Williams, where they had to play unobtrusive instrumental tunes. John and Paul were still writing songs—a tape of the group playing at Forthlin Road in spring 1960 includes six new Lennon and McCartney originals. But as they did more performing, they did less songwriting.

A bigger break came in August. On a trip to London, Williams met with a German promoter, Bruno Koschmider, who was in England to find beat groups to play in his Hamburg nightclub. Williams offered Koschmider one of his successful bands, Derry and the Seniors, who went to Hamburg in July 1960 and immediately proved the viability of Koschmider's plan. Koschmider got back in touch with Williams to see if he could find him another group for a second nightclub he owned. Williams asked Rory and the Hurricanes, but they had a residency at a Butlin's holiday camp for the summer. So he turned once more, with trepidation, to the Beatles, promising Koschmider he would work on finding him a better option. The Beatles leaped at it. For one thing, they would be earning a proper wage—even Mimi was impressed when John told her how much. For another, it would be an adventure—a month overseas, when none of them had ever spent time abroad. There was still one hurdle to clear: Williams stipulated they find a drummer. Tommy Moore was not an option. Paul and George knew Mona Best's son Pete, a handsome, taciturn eighteen-year-old. Pete Best had been playing drums in a group for a year or so. He was competent enough, and he had his own kit. So it was that in late summer 1960, five Beatles loaded themselves and their gear into a minibus owned and driven by Williams. After an arduous journey they arrived in Hamburg, in the early hours of August 17, 1960.

In some ways, Hamburg was similar to Liverpool: a west-facing port, heavily industrial, cosmopolitan, very much not the country's capital and proud of it. It had been devastated by bombs, though unlike Liverpool it had been handsomely rebuilt. Fifteen years after the war, it was prosperous and thriving with well-organized activity that extended even to the city's red-light district, where Koschmider's clubs were located. In St. Pauli, just behind the dockyards, merchant seamen and dockers went looking for music, gambling, sex, fights, and beer-induced obliteration. The district's main drag, the Reeperbahn, and principal side street, Grosse Freiheit ("Great Freedom"), constituted a twenty-four-hour, multicolored neon carnival of desire, crammed with nightclubs, cafés, gay bars, drag shows, peep shows, strip joints, transvestite bars, brothels, and sex shops, peopled by hookers, pimps, sharks, and gangsters, and guarded by belligerent bouncers. Violence was an ever-present undercurrent, and often an overcurrent.

For John, Paul, and George, perhaps nothing—Beatlemania, Shea Stadium, LSD—ever lived up to the thrill of arriving in Hamburg for the first time. The place must have felt exhilarating and terrifying all at once. Picking through crowds on the garishly lit Reeperbahn, they were in a city where they didn't speak the language, a world away from families and schools; from friends working factory jobs or diligently preparing for careers in offices; from the people who cared about them but who also surveilled and judged them. There was nobody to rag them for playing at being pop stars. They *were* pop stars: almost unbelievably, they were here because somebody was paying them to be a rock and roll group.

The group met Koschmider at his club, the Kaiserkeller, an impressive venue, where Derry and the Seniors were in residence. Koschmider whisked them to the smaller, grottier of his two clubs, the Indra, a former transvestite cabaret joint on Grosse Freiheit. The Beatles were booked to play there six nights a week, four to six hours a night. Koschmider, a war veteran with a crippled leg, alighted on British beat bands as a USP in St. Pauli's competitive marketplace. Live music in most clubs meant mediocre jazz. Rock and roll attracted a younger crowd who stayed out later and drank more beer.

That was the Beatles' job: to sell beer. When sailors and tourists strolled down Grosse Freiheit, their decision on whether to enter a club would be determined by the music spilling out of doorways. The Beatles had to make enough noise to pull them inside and then be sufficiently entertaining to keep them there.

Koschmider was dissatisfied at first. For one thing, the Beatles were playing so loudly that local residents were complaining; when he told them to turn it down, they ignored him. (Koschmider recalled: "You couldn't talk to the Beatles. They were so cocksure of themselves.") For another, they were not dancing. The Beatles had never put much effort or thought into stagecraft, which they associated with showbiz phoniness. Through a mixture of nervousness and principle, they tried to project an air of beatnik cool. Sutcliffe wore shades and sometimes turned his back on the audience while playing. Koschmider was dismayed. Customers were wandering in, taking a look, and wandering out. He complained to Williams, who wrote a sternly worded letter to the group from Liverpool, which they more or less ignored. Then one night, Koschmider's day-to-day manager, Willi Limpensel, started yelling at them: "MACH SCHAU! [Make show!] MACH SCHAU!" To the Beatles it sounded hysterically funny, like a member of the Goons doing a Nazi impression. But it worked.

We can regard what happened next as the true birth of the Beatles. John Lennon was first to respond to the absurdity of the situation. Taking Limpensel's instruction as a goad, he started diving around the stage as they played, lurching toward the mic, duck-walking like Chuck Berry. He sang lying on the floor, and pretended he had a bad leg like Gene Vincent (or Bruno Koschmider). Paul picked up on John's wild spirit, raising the neck of his left-handed guitar to engage in a fencing match. George stamped his feet. A Rubicon had been crossed. The Beatles had answered the German's demand in their own way rather than by attempting to emulate the bland professionalism of acts like Derry and the Seniors. They were doing stagecraft, and doing it wrong. "We did 'mach schauing' all the time from then on," said John.

They worked hard at it. In Liverpool, the teenagers could be rowdy, but they were at least there to see a band. In Hamburg the Beatles faced customers who weren't sure if they wanted to be there and had no reason to pay attention. The group learned what kind of noise made people stay and buy beer, how to get applause, what made people dance, how to detect boredom, what to do when people are too tired or too drunk to pay attention. Once customers were inside, the Beatles conscripted them. Breaking the fourth wall became a defining characteristic of their act. They asked for requests, bantered with some regulars and genially insulted others, and kept up running jokes. One musician who watched them play said, "All the other bands said, 'Thank you, the next song is . . .' But the Beatles made jokes on stage." Sometimes John and Paul would face each other across the same microphone as they sang, Paul's left-handed guitar mirroring John's right-handed one. As Icke Braun, a Kaiserkeller regular, put it: "The audience saw them sideways, and there was such a wonderful symmetry in it that also suited their music."

In Liverpool, the Beatles had been used to playing twenty-minute sets; now they had to play for hours at a time. They were not short of material, even then, but since they had so much time to fill, they would sometimes take one song and spin it out for twenty minutes or even an hour. They loved to do this with "What'd I Say," a call-and-response Ray Charles number, sung by Paul. They played it every night, and every night it was different. They would substitute new words for the lyrics, take off in different directions on the bridge, pull and push the song in every direction to the verge of collapse. After a few weeks, the Indra Club was regularly jammed with smoking, dancing, beer-drinking customers.

☙

In a foreign land, the Beatles turned themselves into a sovereign principality. John and Paul had already created their own microculture back home, drawing from songs, radio comedy, nonsense poetry, and playground slang. Now, in a place where they could barely make themselves understood, they developed a densely self-referential group vernacular, with the two of them its most fluent speakers. They regarded themselves as artists, drinking in experience. Paul: "I had been reading Shakespeare, Dylan Thomas and Steinbeck, so that when we came to this Hamburg experience . . . we saw it differently from the other groups."

The five Beatles shared squalid living quarters: dingy storage rooms, backstage at a run-down movie theater called the Bambi Kino. As Paul recalled it, "No heat, no wallpaper, not a lick of paint, and two sets of bunk beds, like little camp beds, with not very many covers." German movie dialogue boomed through the walls. Their rooms were next to the toilets, which they shared with customers. John, Stuart, and George were in one room, Paul and Pete in a second, smaller adjoining room. Conditions forced a rough intimacy. They would be onstage together all night, crash out together in their cells, sometimes with girls, then manage a couple of hours of daylight before returning to the club for the next show. On nights off, they would go drinking together, visit strip joints and brothels, and share sexual adventures. They were growing up on fast-forward deep inside one another's lives, melding into a single organism. Only Pete Best did his socializing away from the group. He was the odd man out, although it makes more sense to see him as the only normal bloke in a group of oddballs.

☸

In October, Koschmider moved the group to his main club, the Kaiserkeller, which they would share with Rory Storm and the Hurricanes. The Hurricanes had played a season at Butlin's, which put them well above the Beatles in the rock-group hierarchy. They wore suits and executed well-honed stage routines. The Beatles noted their professionalism but did not rate them; in a letter home, George described them as "phoney." The only person in the group who was any good, he said, was the drummer, Ringo Starr.* Now that the Beatles were in direct competition with the Hurricanes, they increasingly defined themselves against them; the slicker the Hurricanes were, the more anarchic the Beatles became.

Lennon was the wildest. He performed his tasteless "cripple" impressions (since his teenage years, he had had a fascination with the physically

---

* There is almost an hour of live and home demo recordings of the Hurricanes from around this time, which shows us what Harrison meant: they perform a smooth pastiche of American pop, without bringing anything of themselves to it.

handicapped or deformed; the characters in his drawings often sported gro-
tesquely long necks or two heads). If he felt that a crowd was unresponsive to
the group he might shout, "Go on, you fucking Krauts, you fucking ignorant
German bastards." This was partly to get a reaction from the audience but
also to amuse and scare his bandmates, who were, after all, almost the only
people in the room capable of understanding him. If an audience member
did get provoked, Lennon relied on the club's truncheon-wielding bouncers
to head off the threat. Just as at school, he would raise the possibility of
physical confrontation while finding ways to avoid it. When he was drunk,
however, which was often, he seemed capable of anything.

Kaiserkeller sessions were nine to twelve hours long, with the Beatles and
the Hurricanes alternating every hour or ninety minutes. The Beatles were
fueled on free beer and Preludin ("Prellies"), a variety of amphetamine
popular with St. Pauli musicians. The Kaiserkeller was crowded, unventi-
lated, and frenzied. A member of Rory Storm's band recalled:

> The whole place just shook . . . a solid mass of bodies. You couldn't
> see through the smoke. Fights would break out on the dance floor
> or on the seats, and these huge glasses would be flying every which
> way . . . If there was a sailor on the floor you'd see [the bouncers]
> lay into him, kicking him.

St. Pauli clubs were owned and patronized by mobsters with fearsome
reputations. If they bought you a drink, you drank it; if they requested a
song, you played it. The Beatles, engaged in amicable enmity with everyone around them—rival bands, Koschmider, Germans in general—had to
be smart to survive. At the same time, they exuded a spirit of childlike fun
by which the Germans found themselves carried away, almost despite themselves. One day, the Beatles began a leapfrogging contest in the street that
ended in a long line of Germans leapfrogging behind them, cops holding up
traffic to wave them through. Another night, they started a strawberry fight
with the audience.

John, Paul, and George all strove to get better at playing and singing. Stuart Sutcliffe, though artistically ambitious, did not share this commitment to self-improvement, which became problematic. (Neither did Pete, but the Beatles had learned that if you have a competent drummer, you stick with him.) As the others developed their techniques and extended their range, Stuart's deficiencies became more apparent. Paul, the most committed to self- and group betterment, needled him about it. Had they been in Liverpool, Stuart's awkward fit would have generated only acrimony; Hamburg transformed it into something more creative. Shortly after the Beatles started playing at the Kaiserkeller, a young graphic artist called Klaus Voormann wandered in. Riveted by the boisterous leather-jacketed Englishmen onstage, he returned the next night with his girlfriend, Astrid Kirchherr, a photographer's assistant, and a friend, Jürgen Vollmer. Voormann, Kirchherr, and Vollmer became regulars. They stood out from the crowd of sailors and mobsters. Most Kaiserkeller customers talked among themselves; these three observed the band closely, from a table near the stage. One night, Voormann approached Lennon during a break to show him a record sleeve he'd designed. Lennon put him on to Sutcliffe, "the artist in the band." Sutcliffe was captivated by the Germans, who had met at art college in Hamburg. They were unembarrassed intellectuals, engaged in a quiet rebellion against stolid postwar German society. Their cultural touchstones were French: films, novels, fashion, philosophy. Stuart and Astrid, at twenty-two a couple of years his senior, fell in love. Within weeks, she parted amicably from Voormann to be with him.

Lennon dubbed them "Exis" because of their affinity with existentialist intellectuals such as Sartre and Cocteau. The Exis were more likely to listen to jazz than rock and roll, but the raucous wall of sound generated by the Beatles converted them. As with everyone who fell for the band—then and since—it was the people as much as the music that compelled them. Astrid said, "They looked absolutely astonishing . . . my whole life changed in a couple minutes. All I wanted was to be with them and to know them." As far as we know, nobody ever said this about Rory and the Hurricanes. The fascination was mutual: Astrid, in particular, made a strong impression.

She dressed in black, wore her blond hair boyishly short, and conveyed firm opinions on art and design in broken English.

Crucially, she took the Beatles seriously as artists, rather than just kids having fun with guitars. Not long after their first meeting, Astrid invited the Beatles to a deserted fairground for a photo shoot. Instead of aiming for show-business glamor, Astrid presented the Beatles as pensive, scruffy rebels. She had them pose among shuttered carnival booths and empty rides: the structures that remain when all glitz is stripped away. A group of young men who loved to clown around returned solemn gazes to the camera. Up onstage, blasting out "What'd I Say," the Beatles were a wild, whirling fairground ride. Astrid saw that they were not just that.

4   WILL YOU LOVE ME TOMORROW

In November, with the Beatles' contract at the Kaiserkeller running out, a rival of Bruno Koschmider's, Peter Eckhorn, made them a good offer to play at his club. When Koschmider found out, he was furious, sabotaged the deal, and played a hand in getting McCartney and Best arrested and deported on a trumped-up charge of arson (they had been working illegally without permits anyway). Harrison left for home, too (at seventeen, he was too young to work in Hamburg's clubs and since the start of November had been playing only until the 10 p.m. curfew). A week later, Lennon, now without bandmates or a source of income, made his way back to Liverpool, alone and miserable. Sutcliffe stayed in Hamburg with Kirchherr.

Dispirited by this humiliating end to the best time of his life, John took a while to reconnect with Paul and the others, who were not even sure if John was back in Liverpool. It might have been the end of the Beatles. Paul got himself a Christmas job as "second man" on a lorry delivering parcels. The group got back together after the intervention of a friend of Allan Williams, called Bob Wooler. Wooler, thirty-five, was a disc jockey and compère on the dance-hall circuit. After talking to a despondent

Lennon in the Jacaranda, he lined up a few gigs, and squeezed the Beatles onto a bill with three other groups at Litherland Town Hall, in the north of Liverpool. The group started rehearsing again, recruiting a temporary bass player in Sutcliffe's absence.

The Litherland gig took place on December 27, 1960. Few in the audience had heard of the Beatles, who came from the other side of the city. Since Wooler billed them as "direct from Hamburg," many assumed that the group with the odd name was German. If anyone remembered them, it was as a shambolic, drummerless group who didn't seem much interested in putting on a show. Wooler had barely seen them play himself, but they intrigued him as people. "I just trusted my instinct that they would go down in an unusual, important way," he said. He was right. When the curtains opened and Paul McCartney ripped into the opening of "Long Tall Sally," the city shook. Nobody had ever seen a band like this. The Beatles did not play dainty pop tunes; they played rock and roll, hard and fast and direct. The two frontline singers, sometimes joined at the microphone by a third, combined roars and howls with sweet balladeering and soaring harmonies. They looked different from other bands, too—they dressed in black leather jackets and cowboy boots, which they stomped to the beat. Instead of dance routines, they clowned around. And it turned out they were not German. They bantered in Liverpudlian accents; they were funny and rude. When Lennon stepped up to the mic and said "Get your knickers down," the crowd erupted with delight. The Beatles ended their set with a rollicking half-hour version of "What'd I Say."

This was the band that Allan Williams sent to Hamburg because none of his good bands could make it. What happened? It wasn't just practice. "Hamburg didn't change anyone else the same way," said Chris Huston, a rock guitarist from Liverpool. "When [the Beatles] came back from Germany it was like they knew something we didn't. They had this *arrogance*." The Beatles historian Mark Lewisohn notes that when Rory and the Hurricanes returned from Hamburg, they found it hard to get work and went on the dole (their drummer, Ringo Starr, considered becoming a hairdresser). Only the Beatles came back transformed. After Litherland, they went from almost total obscurity to being the undisputed leaders of the Liverpool beat scene. While they were away, local guitar groups had proliferated. Most modeled themselves on Cliff Richard and the Shadows: they wore matching suits and performed neat little step routines. The Beatles seemed from a different world entirely; a spectator recalled that while most Liverpool bands performed in "a polite, orderly way," the Beatles "attacked the crowd." A guitarist with Rikki and the Redstreaks recalled, "We'd been pussyfooting around . . . The Beatles just came straight at you." At gigs, people who had been paying only partial attention to the bands onstage would be suddenly transfixed by the Beatles: "Everybody who was anywhere in the hall . . . stopped and came forward, straight to the front of the stage. They stood there with their mouths open." Violence often followed, as crowds of drunken men obscurely perceived a threat. Lennon liked to wind them up, performing a theatrically exaggerated wink to the girls in the audience, and it was left to McCartney to calm things down. This was already an established dynamic: John would push things as far as he dared, knowing that Paul would be there to pull him back.

Rock and roll remained at the core of what the Beatles did, but they were not content to be an oldies band, playing only Chuck Berry and Little Richard. They ransacked musical genres—country and western, rhythm and blues, instrumentals, ballads—for songs they could make their own. They sought out obscure songs nobody else knew about: B sides and rarities dug up from the NEMS (North End Music Stores) record department on Whitechapel. They could listen to a song one or two times and not just remember it but swallow it, digest it, absorb it into their bloodstream. Every song they played became a Beatles song; they stole but never copied. Being different was a marketing strategy but above all an expression of voracious musical curiosity.

A natural extension of the imperative to be different would have been to play their own songs, but while John and Paul had dozens of Lennon-McCartney originals under their belts, they rarely played them. Lewisohn notes that "no one around the Beatles in 1961 . . . was aware of [their songwriting]." Perhaps they felt their songs weren't good enough to perform, although several became part of their repertoire or hits for other bands later on. More likely, they saw the group as separate from the songwriting they did together. One was public, the other was private and personal, something between them. On the rare occasions they did play a Lennon-McCartney song, like "One After 909," they failed to mention it was one of their own. For now, songwriting was a secret they kept to themselves.

☿

The Beatles had nearly ceased to exist after Hamburg came to an end. They now came close to breaking up again, this time because of an intragroup dynamic that was to recur throughout their career. Early in 1961, Paul took a full-time job as an electrical apprentice in a factory called Massey & Coggins. His father had been insisting that he start a professional career rather than rely on the Beatles to work out. McCartney made an effort in his new job, winning the respect of the manager, Jim Gilvey ("He was a very polite young man"). He got on with his colleagues, who called him "Mantovani" after finding out he sang in a group. He says he considered the possibility that his father was right about the Beatles: "The group had got going again but I didn't know if I wanted to go back full time." Lennon was furious. He thought it was mad not to commit to the group just as they were gaining momentum. Later on, John said: "Paul would always give in to his dad. His dad told him to get a job and he fucking dropped the group, saying, 'I need a steady career!' We couldn't believe it." Perhaps Paul did want to please his father, but perhaps he also wanted to establish his independence from John. It's hard to believe that Paul was serious about pursuing a factory-based career. He later said of his decision to leave the job, "I never liked bosses," which goes directly to one of McCartney's defining traits: a powerful aversion to being controlled by anyone or anything, and to the feeling of being bossed. Paul used his job as capital in an unspoken negotiation with John over status. He wanted John to recognize him as an equal, his closest partner, the one he could not do without. If John wanted Paul to commit to the band, then he would have to commit to Paul.

A turning point arrived after the Beatles landed a gig at the Cavern, a former jazz club in the middle of town. Its new owner, Ray McFall, hired Bob Wooler as a talent booker and Wooler suggested the Beatles for the lunchtime slot. The Cavern was a step up from their usual venues. It was housed in a cellar on a street in the middle of the city's business district. McFall culti- vated a smart crowd: no alcohol, no jeans. The lunchtime clientele consisted of secretaries, shop assistants, runners, boys in suits, and girls in nice dresses. McFall served food so that customers would stay for a whole hour or more.

Only a handful of bands were able to play at lunchtime, since the mem- bers of most groups had day jobs. The Beatles were free of such quotidian concerns—except, that is, for Paul. On the day of the booking, February 9, 1961, Lennon and Harrison went down to Massey & Coggins to persuade Paul to join them. After putting up a show of reluctance, Paul sneaked out of work and went with them. When the scruffy, jeans-wearing Beatles first arrived McFall was uneasy, but when he heard them play, he was smitten. McFall's description conveys a sense of their triple threat: "John started, then Paul, then George, and they alternated. Then there'd be a number with two of them—Paul and George or John and Paul—and I couldn't get over the quality of the music."

The question over Paul's membership in the group was still unresolved, however. It came to a head when McFall booked the Beatles for another lunchtime slot. This time, according to their friend Neil Aspinall, Lennon offered McCartney an ultimatum: "John said to Paul on the phone, 'Either fucking turn up today or you're not in the band anymore.'" McCartney pas- sively resisted, until turning up at the last minute. Lennon recalled this as a personal victory: "So he had to make a decision between me and his dad then, and in the end he chose me." *In the end he chose me.* It is striking how Lennon frames McCartney's decision as a struggle with his father—not how McCartney himself characterized it—and as a choice between his father and John Lennon. Paul didn't choose the Beatles, or rock and roll; he chose John. It's as if Lennon wanted McCartney to come and be an orphan with him.

McCartney left his job, without breaking from his father. With the band's central relationship functioning once more, the Beatles continued to get bet- ter and busier. The Cavern became a regular gig. Half-empty at first, the club was packed within weeks. There was no language barrier here, and even more than in Hamburg, they became closely attuned to their audience.

There wasn't much of a backstage at the Cavern. The stage was low, the space cramped. Even if they had wanted to, the Beatles could hardly have pretended to be who they weren't. They pulled the audience into their weird world. Paul and John bounced off each other; George made dryly funny interjections. John pretended to have a club foot. Someone in the audience would be asked onstage to do a number. Being in a basement enhanced the sense of a refuge from reality, as did the lunchtime slot: going to see the Beatles in the middle of a weekday must have felt like walking into someone else's daydream.

Musically, the Beatles kept widening their scope. In early 1961, when Paul had his job, John became the group's primary hunter of new music (the roles would be reversed later on), and his taste was as multifaceted as he was. Motown became a major influence, and so did girl groups. These new forms of Black American music taught the Beatles how to put a wider range of feelings into their music.

The advent of rhythm and blues (R&B; later "soul") resulted from a structural change in the American music industry: for the first time, Black artists, Black producers, and Black entrepreneurs addressed themselves directly to white teenagers, confident that they could exploit what was now an established mass market for pop. Berry Gordy's Detroit production house, Motown, led the way. Gordy met his primary artist and business partner, William "Smokey" Robinson, then a seventeen-year-old doo-wop singer, in 1957, the same year that John met Paul. The Beatles, and John in particular, loved Robinson's group, the Miracles, before they knew the name of the singer whose angelic voice on "Who's Lovin' You" cracked at just the right moments, turning an elegant pop song into a heady lament. R&B rhythms were beguiling and sinuous, the chords cleverly structured, the lyrics literate and urbane: this was singing and playing beyond the reach of the Beatles, for now, but they began incorporating Motown songs into their act, while John sought to emulate the emotional intelligence he heard in Smokey's voice.

You can see why the Beatles were attracted to records by the Cookies, the Shirelles, the Ronettes. These were *groups*, not an entertainer with a backing band. At the heart of their sound was a blend of voices, which now became central to the Beatles' sound, too. John and Paul were strongly influenced by the intimate harmonizing of the Everly Brothers, but their incorporation of George into a three-part chorus, and their use of "ahhs" and "oohs" to support the lead line, owed more to doo-wop and to girl groups. The singers were not always "professionals," and their delivery was all the more affecting for it. Girl groups liberated Lennon to open up his throat and bare his soul. He might never be able to float and glide like Smokey, but he could emulate the almost occult hormonal energies called forth by the lead singer of the Chantels (Arlene Smith, sixteen) on their hit single "Maybe." Girl-group songs were created by a new generation of pop songwriters on Tin Pan Alley who created heat-seeking missiles aimed at the hearts of America's fastest-growing record-buying audience: teenage girls. This was music full of longing, hurt, and high drama. Jealousy was a major theme, one to which Lennon was naturally drawn. So was rebellion.

There are five girl-group cover versions on the first two Beatles albums—far more than any other single influence—and they performed many more onstage, some of which we know of only through contemporary accounts. If there's one of these lost cover versions I would love to hear, it's "Will You Love Me Tomorrow," a Shirelles song Lennon liked to sing at the Cavern. I imagine him allowing his voice to catch and crack in the middle section (*tonight with words unspoken . . .*). "Despite all his mucking around," recalled Lindy Ness, a Cavern regular, "whenever John sang . . . he delivered complete emotional intensity." Lennon understood, in his bones, the emotion that animates "Will You Love Me Tomorrow": wanting love and not trusting it to stay. What he learned from Smokey and from Black teenage girls was how to communicate the feeling rather than just feel it.

Stuart Sutcliffe returned to England in January and rejoined the band. Astrid flew out later. The pair dressed in matching tight black leather trousers and sometimes swapped clothes, making for an exotic sight on Liverpool's streets. The other Beatles were already wearing their hair longer than other men of their age, something for which Paul was ribbed by his workmates at the factory. Stuart and Astrid emboldened them.

Despite success at home, the Beatles were keen to return to Hamburg. John and Paul wanted to be away from Mimi and Jim asking questions about what they were doing with their lives. They yearned to be on an adventure again. In Hamburg, they had rarely been apart. In Liverpool, they had other calls on their time. Lennon had a steady girlfriend, Cynthia Powell, a student at his art college. Paul had a serious girlfriend, too: Dot Rhone, a girl he met at the Casbah. In 1960 he got a shock when it turned out that Dot was pregnant with his child. They agreed to be married, which threatened to end Paul's pop career, except that Dot suffered a miscarriage. Hamburg was simpler, and spring brought good news: Peter Eckhorn had secured pardons for McCartney and Best. Harrison had turned eighteen. At the end of March the Beatles traveled to Germany to begin a stint at the Top Ten Club.

5   BESAME MUCHO

This time around, the Beatles stayed in attic rooms above the Top Ten Club—spartan, but an improvement on the Bambi Kino. The digs were shared with the singer Tony Sheridan and his girlfriend. Sheridan was the biggest British rock and roll act in Hamburg. He had some success back home but never quite made it due to being notoriously difficult to work with. Sheridan took a shine to the tricky and obstreperous Beatles. They played as his backing band at the Top Ten, and he sometimes joined them during their own sets. Musically accomplished, he encouraged the Beatles to use bluesy dominant seventh chords, and not to take any shit from anyone.

Years later the Beatles would remember the Top Ten as their favorite Hamburg venue. It was larger and smarter than the Kaiserkeller, with a better sound system. Paul played the club's battered upright piano and, typically enough, got very good at it. Eckhorn made the Beatles work even harder than Koschmider had. At the Kaiserkeller they had one night off a week; at the Top Ten Club they played seven nights a week until two or four in the morning, with a fifteen-minute break every hour. They used more drugs than ever. Lennon remembered taking pill after pill to get through a night's work, sleeping for two hours, then waking up and taking another one, because it was time to go onstage again. They had to fit in sex, too, a problem of space as much as time, given that they were in communal rooms with bunk beds. Harrison recalled losing his virginity as the others pretended to sleep, before applauding the consummation. Almost by default, the group became ever closer, although Pete Best kept mainly to himself, as before. Stuart was no longer part of the core group either, for different reasons. He was now engaged to Astrid, and on this trip lodged with the Kirchherrs in their comfortable home. He was taking painting seriously again, under the tutelage of the eminent Scottish artist Eduardo Paolozzi, at Hamburg College of Fine Arts. He also had health problems, including terrible headaches.

Sutcliffe faced relentless ragging from McCartney, and one night, during a performance, he snapped, walloping Paul off his piano stool. The two proceeded to "beat the shit out of each other" onstage in front of an amused audience of German gangsters. Shortly afterward, Sutcliffe and the other Beatles confronted the inevitable and decided to part. McCartney was later blamed for pushing him out, but in truth Sutcliffe was increasingly focused on a career in art. Astrid explains Paul's perspective:

> Let me ask you this: what would you do if you were in a band, and were a brilliant artist, and one of your best friends is just fiddling around and doesn't even practice, but is content to just look great—to look rock and roll? I know what I'd do, I would go crazy . . . I think Paul was very brave, putting up with Stuart for so long.

Stuart lent Paul his bass guitar until Paul acquired his own: a violin-shaped Höfner from a Hamburg store.

Paul wasn't thrilled at becoming the group's bassist. Playing bass was generally regarded as the most unglamorous, least interesting role in a rock and roll group: the average bassist just stood there playing two notes per bar: *dum, dum.* John and George immediately ruled themselves out. Yet once McCartney allowed himself to be cajoled into the job, he warmed to it: "I started to realize the power the bass player had within the band . . . even though the whole band is going along in A, you could stick in E. And they'd say: 'Let us off the hook!' You're actually in control then—an amazing thing." Just as he had with the guitar, he would play the bass his way, rather than let the instrument or convention dictate. He quickly developed a melodic flair that became a hallmark of the group's sound, and mastered the skill—one that has confounded generations of bass players—of playing relatively complex bass lines while singing the song's melody, which allowed him to retain his share of the frontline spotlight.

The Beatles recorded their first professional tracks as a backing group for Tony Sheridan. They cut five tracks with Sheridan and two of their own, one a cover, "Ain't She Sweet," one an instrumental: "Cry for a Shadow." Once again, John and Paul declined to share a Lennon-McCartney original with the world. The record label asked the Beatles to write individual biographies: in his, Paul said that he had written "around 70 songs" with John. John's, meanwhile, said he had "written a couple of songs with Paul." The recordings show that all the Beatles were competent instrumentalists now, but it's McCartney's bass playing, fluid and lithe, that sounds advanced. He makes his presence felt in another way, too. You can hear him, faintly—he is nowhere near a mic—*whooping* during the intro to "Cry for a Shadow." McCartney's vocal exclamations, his whoops and screams, are dotted throughout Beatles' recordings and form a crucial aspect of their musical personality. They seem to burst out of him unbidden, like the ecstatic yelping of a dog at play.

After three months in Hamburg, the Beatles returned to Liverpool in July 1961, and resumed their residency at the Cavern. They were still the most popular band in Liverpool. As a contemporary put it: "At nights, a buzz used to go around the Cavern when the Beatles were arriving—*they're here, they're here*—and we all used to turn around to see them come in." One of the numbers they played at this time was Paul's arrangement of "Besame Mucho," a Latin American standard that had just been covered by a doo-wop group, the Coasters. The original song is romantic and steamy; the title, which means "kiss me a lot," makes a kiss out of the mouth (try saying "mucho"). It was not a hit, but Paul was captivated by the melodrama of its minor-to-major chord change, and the Beatles turned it into a raucous comedy set piece, complete with *cha-cha-booms*. If John was more likely to import brooding R&B numbers into the repertoire it was Paul who brought in these wild cards, which were adored by their fans, even if they made the group harder to categorize or understand for anyone who wasn't already in on the secret.

Bob Wooler was now the group's adviser and sometime press officer. He was fourteen years older than John Lennon, who called him "Dad"—one of those Lennon jokes that seem to be doing some hidden work. A closeted gay man, Wooler was sensitive to Lennon's barbs. He christened John "the Singing Rage." Wooler wrote a perceptive article for *Mersey Beat* that presented the Beatles as a series of paradoxes: self-assured yet vulnerable, rugged yet romantic, calculating yet naive. Although they were difficult to pigeonhole, their live act was undeniable—"from beginning to end, a succession of climaxes." The Beatles had "resurrected original style rock 'n' roll music," by which Wooler didn't just mean that they played Little Richard and Chuck Berry. He meant the *spirit* of rock and roll: its rebelliousness, and its direct bid to the heart and body. John singing "Will You Love Me Tomorrow" was as much a part of the Beatles' rock and roll revivalism as Paul singing "Long Tall Sally."

Wooler noted that they appealed to both sexes. The Beatles disrupted the gender binary in audience appeal and in sensibility and appearance. The English journalist Malcolm Muggeridge dropped into the Top Ten Club when the Beatles were playing, completely by chance while on a night out in Hamburg. In his diary, he describes the group he came across as "ageless children, sexes indistinguishable . . . Long-haired; weird feminine faces . . . like Renaissance carvings of saints or Blessed Virgins."

☙

The summer of 1961 brought another impasse for the band, this one born of success. The Beatles were popular and well paid and had as much work as they could handle, but John and Paul were bored. They were playing the same venues to crowds who knew them well. Rather than ascending to a greater peak they were stuck at the top of a small one. Lennon recalled, "The group was in debate, about whether it would exist or not." According to Wooler, "[The Beatles] were *definitely* going to collapse as an entity unless something happened for them." The only real participants in this debate were Lennon and McCartney (neither Best nor Harrison was unsatisfied). Both had an allergy to repetition. Other groups learned a set and repeated it efficiently. The Beatles played an endlessly changing repertoire of songs, frequently refreshed by trips to NEMS. This need for variety and evolution applied to their career as well as their music. Lennon and McCartney knew they could keep being successful at what they were doing, and this was precisely what they found dispiriting. They were kings of their hometown and prisoners of it. They believed they were better than the acts on TV, but the people who put acts on TV didn't come to Liverpool.

In September 1961, ahead of his twenty-first birthday, John came into a substantial sum of money: £100, equivalent to about £2,000 today. According to Julia Baird, John's half sister (daughter of Julia Lennon and Bobby Dykins), this was an inheritance from his mother, although he seems to have told Paul it was a coming-of-age gift from an Edinburgh aunt. He could have invested this windfall in new equipment for the band. He could have put it toward a deposit on a flat with his girlfriend, Cynthia, now living as a lodger at Mendips. He could have splurged on records and beer. Instead, he planned a monthlong holiday with Paul. Wooler advised against it: "I thought this was disastrous because they would be away from the scene too long and lose their fans." George didn't want them to go. John and Paul agreed to compromise on a two-week break. Even so, George was furious. When Stuart heard about their plan, he took it to mean the band was breaking up.

Those who knew Lennon and McCartney marveled at how close they were. Bernie Boyle, a Cavern regular who did some work for the Beatles as a roadie, observed their eerie mental connection: "They were so tight it was like there was a telepathy between them: on stage, they'd look at each other and know instinctively what the other was thinking." People were drawn to them, and also wary of them, for both were capable of shriveling outsiders with wit. Together, they had an aura of unbreachable self-assurance. This was partly the arrogance of the damaged. The psychiatrist Bessel van der Kolk observes: "After trauma the world becomes sharply divided between those who know and those who don't." Bob Wooler said, "At times, they reminded me of those well-to-do Chicago lads Leopold and Loeb, who killed someone because they felt superior to him. Lennon and McCartney were 'superior human beings.'" A fellow musician, Johnny Gustafson, bumped into the pair on the day they left Liverpool for Paris, on Saturday, September 30. "They both had bowler hats on, with the usual leather jackets and jeans. They said they were off to Paris, so I walked down to Lime Street station with them and watched them go."

☮

Stepping off the train at Gare du Nord, they had no plan except to find Jürgen Vollmer, one of the Exis, who was staying on the Left Bank. Vollmer took them to Montmartre, a glamorously seedy district populated by artists and night workers, a Parisian St. Pauli. They found a small hotel room. Their original plan had been to move on to Spain, but they ended up staying in Paris for the full fortnight. They visited the haunts of Hemingway and Sartre. They didn't go up the Eiffel Tower because it cost too much, contenting themselves with lying on the grass underneath and gazing up. They sat in cafés and drank milkshakes. They went to see some French rock bands and tried to play themselves, persuading Jürgen to talk to the manager of one club, but there was no interest. When John turned twenty-one, Paul treated him to a hamburger and Coke for his birthday dinner.

Paul took a camera, and several photos of the trip survive. The two of them look touchingly young and touchingly happy, in leather jackets, bowler hats, and sunglasses, grinning in a bar, posing in the street, larking about in their hotel room. There are more photos of John than of Paul. My favorite is a blurry image of John, fast asleep in bed.*

In Paris they had Jürgen restyle their hair. They had been sporting

---

* We couldn't secure the rights to publish these photos, but they are widely available online. See also any other photos I mention but which aren't included.

greased-back quiffs, a legacy of first-wave rock and roll. Now they wanted the more natural-looking, floppier style favored by Parisian hipsters. Jürgen cut their hair in his hotel room and they let it grow out. On their return to Liverpool they were teased about this girly new hairstyle, but kept it.

Ever after, Paris was John's favorite city in the world. He said later, "All the kissing and holding was so romantic . . . the way people would just stand under the tree kissing. They weren't mauling each other, they were just kissing . . . I really loved it." He and Paul returned to Liverpool with ambition renewed.

✠

The Beatles needed a manager yet resisted being managed. Wooler: "They were strong willed. They had their own ideas. Whoever took on the Beatles had to knuckle down to the Beatles—and the breed of person who will submit to that sort of control is rare." Within a year they somehow managed to locate two members of this rare breed—or rather, Brian Epstein located them, and then located the second on their behalf.

Epstein, twenty-seven, was a local businessman, the eldest son of one of Liverpool's most prominent and successful Jewish families. His father, Harry, ran a group of furniture businesses. His mother, Queenie (originally Minnie), was the daughter of a major furniture manufacturer from Sheffield. Harry and Queenie's second son, Clive, had completed National Service and was already proving his value to the family business. Brian still lived with his parents and had yet to find his métier. He had been sent to a succession of private schools without being happy at any of them. In his autobiography, he wrote, "Throughout my schooldays I was one of those out-of-sorts boys who never quite fit. Who are ragged, nagged, and bullied." He acquired the accent and manners of the English upper classes at school but little else; despite his intelligence and privilege, he left at sixteen with no qualifications. He went to work at one of his father's stores as a sales clerk and at this proved unexpectedly adept. He enjoyed serving customers and sharpening the store's presentation. In 1952, at eighteen, he was called up for National Service, and discharged a year later after a psychiatric report determined that he was unfit for service. He rejoined the family firm in 1954 to help his father expand the business. North End Music Stores, NEMS for short, sold pianos, radios, and record players.

An undercurrent of misery flowed through Brian's life. Bullied at school for being Jewish, he later realized he was attracted to men, in a society that condemned and despised homosexuality. Like many gay men of his era, his life was split in two. While living with his parents in a well-to-do suburb, he kept a flat in one of the town's most deprived areas, to which he took ostensibly straight working-class men for casual, anonymous, often violent sex. If his pleasures were dark and subterranean, his dreams were perfectly lit. Brian dreamed of being onstage. While at NEMS, he became a patron of the Liverpool Playhouse and loved to socialize with the actors. "There was a sort of wistfulness about him," recalled one of its members, the actress Helen Lindsay. "He wanted to belong to what he perceived as a charmed circle . . . a magic world." He won a place at London's RADA (Royal Academy of Dramatic Arts) but was as unhappy there as he was at school.

In the autumn of 1957 he returned to Liverpool to open a new branch of NEMS, specializing in records. His new job coincided with the explosive commercial growth of rock and roll. Brian and his brother Clive made the store a big success, and in 1959 opened a second on Whitechapel, in the center of Liverpool, where John and Paul were to spend many hours. By 1961 the Epsteins had a chain of five stores and NEMS was one of the biggest record retailers in the North of England. Brian was busy, successful, but unsatisfied. He still longed to join a charmed circle. "I fancy Rome," he wrote in his journal. "I want to live in luxury, learn the language, live Italian, and just add myself to that very attractive, utterly ridiculous little group that calls itself the International Set." (Patricia Highsmith's thriller *The Talented Mr. Ripley*, about a man of ambiguous sexuality faking entry to a charmed circle of rich Americans in Italy, had recently been a bestseller.) *Mersey Beat*, the magazine devoted to Liverpool beat groups, was on sale at NEMS, and Brian noted how quickly it sold out. He started to contribute record reviews himself. He may well have read about the Beatles in it. Then, toward the end of October, a few customers requested "My Bonnie" by the Beatles, even though it was available only in Germany—it was the single from the sessions with Tony Sheridan in Hamburg. Epstein asked Bill Harry, the editor of *Mersey Beat*, where he could see this act, and Harry told him about the Cavern lunchtime sessions. The Cavern was just around the corner from the Whitechapel store.

So it was that on November 9, 1961, Brian Epstein, briefcase in hand, walked down the steps into the Cavern, accompanied by his assistant, Alistair Taylor. It must have been like descending into his own id. A dark and smoky room, claustrophobically low ceiling, sweaty walls, a crush of bodies. A throbbing noise that gradually revealed itself as music. And there onstage, a group of skinny young men giving a show that was the opposite of show business. "I had never seen anything like the Beatles on *any* stage," Epstein said later. "They smoked as they played and they ate and talked and pretended to hit each other. They turned their backs on the audience and shouted at them and laughed at private jokes." To Brian, a connoisseur of stagecraft, the Beatles did everything wrong. They were undisciplined, unprofessional, and seemed to be entertaining themselves as much as the audience. Yet he found himself transfixed. Three years later, he talked about that night as a deeply personal revelation:

"Everything about the Beatles was right for me. Their kind of attitude toward life, and their humor, and their own personal way of behaving—it was all just what I wanted. They represented the direct, unselfconscious, good-natured, uninhibited human relationships which I hadn't found and had wanted and felt deprived of. And my own sense of inferiority evaporated with the Beatles because I knew I could help them, and that they wanted me to help them, and trusted me to help them."

The Beatles spoke directly to the conflicts in Brian's soul. Here were oddballs who exuded a shameless candor; here were rough-looking young men with the blithe arrogance of a charmed circle. It was as if Brian's nocturnal life and daylight fantasies had met and fused on the Cavern stage. Epstein's enthusiasm for the Beatles has been glibly explained by his sexual attraction to them, and to Lennon in particular. This rather begs the question of who, in that club, regardless of gender or sexuality, *didn't* fancy the Beatles— they were polymorphously captivating. It is true that Epstein was sexually magnetized by Lennon, but it's also true that he fell in love with the Beatles as a group, and it was this that led him to offer them a style of management unprecedented in the pop industry: one based on devotion rather than profit-seeking.

The Beatles agreed to a meeting with Epstein at his Whitechapel store, on Wednesday, November 29, after a lunchtime session. They regarded him as a serious player, a successful businessman with music industry connections—an "expert," as Lennon put it. They knew Epstein was "queer," too, which didn't bother them much, although McCartney was alert to what it might mean for the balance of power within the group. The Beatles agreed that Epstein would act on their behalf on a see-how-it-goes basis. That Friday he traveled to London for meetings with the two biggest record companies, EMI and Decca. The executives, who didn't wish to offend the young man from NEMS, agreed to take a look at this group from Liverpool.

Epstein fixed a follow-up meeting with the Beatles for Sunday, at 4:30 p.m. This one was nearly disastrous. John, George, and Pete arrived on time; Paul did not. Half an hour went by. The small talk ran out. Finally, Brian suggested George call Paul at his home. George returned with news from Jim McCartney that Paul had just got out of bed and was in the bath. Brian was angry now and only somewhat mollified by the others' good humor. ("He may be late," said George, "but he's very clean.") Eventually Paul turned up. Brian told the group about the interest from London record companies. He also told them they should be charging higher fees for gigs, and promised to see to it. Crucially, he conveyed an ambition not just commensurate with their own but beyond it. Brian was already thinking of America as well as Britain. "You're going to be bigger than Elvis," he said, a prophecy they found outrageous and thrilling. They agreed to be represented by him. John later claimed to have made the decision himself, over Paul's objections: "I make a lot of mistakes, character-wise, but now and then I make a good one . . . and Brian was one."

We should be wary of John's retrospective tendency to present himself as the driving force of the band, but Paul's lateness to the Epstein meeting is well attested. Why did he throw a spanner in the works? He seems to have been uneasy about what Brian's appointment would mean for him. Paul, who like John was a close reader of people, could see that Epstein was besotted by Lennon. He understood what that felt like. As he put it later, "I'm sure Brian was in love with John. We were all in love with John, but Brian was gay, so that added an edge." What worried him was John's power over Epstein, and therefore his power over the group if Epstein became their manager. His concerns were not groundless. In his first months as manager, Epstein treated John as the most important Beatle, running any proposed changes by him before talking to the others. Lennon reveled in this role. He later said, "I was pretty close to Brian because if someone's going to manage me I want to know them inside out." He got Brian to confide in him about his sexuality: "And there was a period when he told me he was a fag and all that. I remember him saying, 'Don't ever throw it back in my face that I'm a fag.' Which I didn't." He does seem to have kept his word on that point, although he taunted Epstein about his Jewishness.*

As for McCartney, he had given up school and the prospect of becoming middle-class for a career in music, against the advice of his father. He would have felt responsible for his family's economic security. He was ambitious. Given how much was at stake, the idea he might become a backing musician for John Lennon was not worth contemplating. In the contract that the Beatles signed with Epstein there is a clause that says the manager may split up "the Artistes . . . so that they shall perform as separate individual performers;" Epstein's assistant, Alistair Taylor, claimed that this was inserted at Paul's request. Taylor recalls Paul saying, in an early meeting, that if the group didn't work out, he would pursue a solo career.

Despite his initial hostility, and one occasion when he sorely tested Epstein by skipping a show, Paul's problem with Brian—or John and Brian—largely resolved itself. Brian learned to consult Paul, and his efforts on behalf

* The two of them enjoyed, if that's the word, a mildly sadomasochistic relationship. Tony Barrow, who worked for Epstein, recalled John walking in on a meeting in Brian's office: "Beaming broadly he walked toward me and shook my hand, an unusual thing for him to do. Brian then extended his hand but at the last moment John's hand plunged down to Epstein's groin and he grabbed tightly hold of his testicles. Epstein gasped in pain as John, gripping relentlessly, simply said 'Whoops!'" (Tony Barrow, *John, Paul, George, Ringo and Me*, 66.)

of the group began to pay off. Epstein secured an audition with Decca, in London, on New Year's Day 1962. John and Paul thought this was it—they couldn't fail. But Decca rejected them. The audition tapes survive. It's not that the Beatles' performances are terrible—they sound professional, albeit nervous—it's that they convey little of the spirit of the Beatles. Without the joyous, disarming, funny yet intense personality the Beatles projected on-stage, they did not yet seem so special.

They faced an uphill struggle anyway. Epstein later quoted Decca's A&R manager Dick Rowe as saying that groups with guitars were "on the way out"; really, guitar groups had never been in. Cliff Richard and the Shadows were the sole precedent. Other than that, it was mainly solo performers on the charts (it's notable that Lennon said, "We dreamed of being the British Elvis Presleys"). Decca must have believed that there was potential for another Shadows, but the Beatles in no way fit the Shadows' model. Having decided they could sign only one guitar group, Decca chose Brian Poole and the Tremeloes instead. Poole's group had a lead singer, wore smart suits, had short hair, and played a narrow repertoire of polite pop songs while per-forming dance routines. They were from London, and shared mutual friends with Decca's A&R man. It probably wasn't a hard choice.

The Beatles were shocked when they found out. Lennon wondered if it meant the end for the group and for his career. He thought he might be too old to make it now, which wasn't unreasonable—pop stars often broke through as teenagers. Epstein's belief and resilience kept the group going. He gently persuaded them into changes designed to broaden their appeal. He got them to stop eating, smoking, and swearing onstage. He encouraged them to give George more turns at the mic, as he saw that their lack of an on-stage leader could be turned into a selling point. He liked the Parisian-style haircuts John and Paul had developed and employed a stylist to cut their hair in a way that emphasized them. Rather than trying to make them conform to the competition, Epstein was good at noticing what made the Beatles differ-ent and amplifying it. "I didn't *change* them," he later said. "I just projected what was there." Most famously, he encouraged them to swap their leathers for suits. Lennon later described this as "selling out" but in truth the suits were no more or less authentic than the leathers, which now felt rather parochial and old-fashioned. And the suits that Brian helped them choose were nothing like the pink or silver lamé follies sported by the Shadows and the Hurricanes. They were tailor-made, in dark blue mohair; single-breasted, narrow-legged, sharply cut; cool.

Epstein drew up a contract offering unusually reasonable terms. He raised their prices with promoters and gave them a weekly account of income and expenses. The Beatles were now a business, albeit a small one. Epstein broadened the geographical reach of their gigs and secured their first radio broadcast, on a regional BBC program called *Teenager's Turn*. He convinced them that they were no longer kids playing at being pop stars, or struggling artists, but professionals on the verge of stardom. At their second meeting, Epstein learned—probably at the pub afterward—that John and Paul had written some songs. One can imagine them mentioning this sheepishly, as something he might like to know. Epstein was enthusiastic. He saw potential for a new income stream: money from publishing rights as well as shows (only the very biggest stars made money from record-sale royalties). In the last months of 1961, John and Paul introduced a few of their own songs to the Cavern.

Epstein, who knew the Beatles wanted to return to Hamburg, had negotiated a deal, much improved on previous contracts, for a seven-week stint at a new venue called the Star-Club, owned by Manfred Weissleder. John, Paul, and Pete arrived in Hamburg in April 1962, this time by plane. George, who had been ill, followed the next day with Brian. John, Paul, and Pete were taken for a look at the new venue, a huge and opulently appointed theater that held up to two thousand people. Weissleder treated them to drinks and steaks. Brian had arranged decent accommodation. This was progress.

Lennon had not contacted Sutcliffe yet, although he doubtless had plans to. Unbeknownst to him, however, Sutcliffe died that day, of a brain hemorrhage. By the time George and Brian boarded a plane to Hamburg, they knew: the news had reached Stuart's mother, Millie, by telegram from Astrid Kirchherr. Stuart had been back to Liverpool only recently, for a visit.

Everyone who saw him remarked that he seemed unwell, but this was, nevertheless, a terrible, juddering shock. George cried when he found out.

When John, Paul, and Pete went to greet Brian and George off the plane from England, they hadn't heard the news yet. Delivered to the airport by Weissleder's driver in a Chevrolet with a turntable and a cocktail bar, they finally felt like pop stars. At the terminal, they were surprised to bump into Astrid and Klaus (who had come to meet Millie). When Astrid broke the news,

> Paul tried to be comforting; he put his arm around me and said how sorry he was. Pete wept . . . John went into hysterics. We couldn't make out, in the state we were both in, whether he was laughing or crying because he did everything at once. I remember him sitting on a bench, huddled over, and he was shaking, rocking backwards and forwards.

For Lennon, it was the bitterest joke. First Uncle George, then his mum, now Stu. Each dear to him, each ripped away, brutally, inexplicably, nonsensically. It was like an implacable law: the people he loved would leave him or die or both. Astrid captured something important when she said he did "everything at once." In Lennon, laughter, anger, and pain were coiled tightly together.

Two days later the Beatles played their opening night at the Star-Club. John clowned around onstage. He dressed up as a cleaning woman, pretended to be a cripple, and went knocking over microphone stands.

6   TILL THERE WAS YOU

There are few songs more important to the Beatles' early career than "Till There Was You." It took a spot on their second LP. It was one of four songs they played at the pivotal Royal Variety performance in 1963 and the second song they played on their debut *Ed Sullivan Show* appearance in 1964. It entered their repertoire in 1961, by which time Paul had developed a reputation as the group's balladeer. At the Cavern or the Star-Club, he would gaze over the heads of the audience toward some imaginary paramour (or camera) and assume the role of romantic lead in a musical. A female lead, perhaps; the ballads McCartney liked to sing, in his most mellifluous voice, were often associated with women. He sang "Falling in Love Again" by Marlene Dietrich (for which he wrote his own English lyrics), and "Over the Rainbow," made famous by Judy Garland. McCartney knew "Till There Was You" from Peggy Lee's version, to which he was introduced by his cousin Bett.

The young women in the Beatles' audience adored Paul's ballads. Cavern-goer Bernadette Farrell recalled: "Girls used to say his eyes were like mince pies . . . He had long eyelashes and he would deliberately flutter them, and though you knew he was always aware of himself, he was so friendly to everybody that you couldn't help but like him." The rock and roll purists in the Beatles' audience did not feel the same way. Rock and rollers were not meant to be into 1940s torch songs. These songs were coded feminine and so was their singer. Paul's fluttering eyelashes, his "pretty" face, even his charm, blurred a gender boundary that, in postwar Britain and Germany, was vigilantly policed.

McCartney's passion for music did not begin with Elvis. He loved the songs his dad played on the piano and his mum sang when she was making Sunday lunch. He loved sing-alongs at family gatherings and in the pub. He loved songs from musicals at the pictures and variety shows on TV. He grew up imbibing folk, music hall, jazz, and show tunes. One of his most important contributions to the Beatles was to ensure these older songs were infused into the group's musical bloodstream. McCartney said:

> I could never see the difference between a beautiful melody and a cool rock 'n roll song. I learned to love all the ballady stuff through my dad and relatives—"Till There Was You," "My Funny Valentine." I thought these were good tunes. The fact that we weren't ashamed of those leanings meant that the band could be a bit more varied.

As well as female fans in Liverpool, McCartney's ballads later helped win over older generations. But the ballads were more than a marketing tactic. By playing songs that were, as McCartney put it, "to the left and right of rock n' roll," he was giving himself and the Beatles permission to play anything. There is a direct line between "Till There Was You" and songs like "Eleanor Rigby" and "Strawberry Fields Forever." McCartney has made this point himself: "We went on from 'Love Me Do' to writing deeper, much more intense things. So it was just as well someone didn't come up and tell us how uncool 'Till There Was You' was."

Except, of course, people did let him know how uncool it was—among them, John Lennon. Lennon was an atheist of a distinctly religious bent. When he found something to believe in, he did so zealously. He converted to the church of rock and roll in 1956, which meant renouncing everything that came before it. He seemed to associate the classic songs his mother taught him with the vulnerability of childhood; in his 1970s interviews, whenever he was at his most insecure, he returned to the notion that he only ever liked rock and roll.

Lennon was conflicted over McCartney's balladeering. On the one hand, he could see it was popular, and he liked those songs, too; on the other, he wanted to be with the Teds, the purists—the real men. He was jealous of Paul's appeal to girls, too. Cilla Black recalled, "[John] liked women, but was always a bit uncomfortable, a bit nervous in their company—always a man's man. Paul was beautiful . . . and I know John thought, 'God, with him around, I don't stand a chance.'" John's mixed feelings manifested themselves in teasing—taking the piss. When Paul sang "Somewhere over the Rainbow" at the Cavern, face tilted upward, luxuriating in the song's extravagant melody, John would lean on the piano and heckle: "God, he's doing Judy Garland!" Or he might make his "cripple" face, or do a hunchback impression—he had an array of monsters—or shout "SHUT UP TALKING!" at the audience with mock sternness. This double act was all part of the Beatles experience, but it was also how John expressed his discomfort.

The ballad that triggered John's unease the most was "Till There Was You." Late in 1962, someone happened to make a crude recording of the Beatles playing at the Star-Club. Though the sound is indistinct and muddy we can hear so much: heckles from drunken audience members, and sloppily played but utterly scalding rock and roll. We can also hear Lennon using humor to process his feelings about his partner and himself. When Paul sings "Till There Was You," John repeats Paul's lines in a parodic echo ("*There were birds*; THERE WERE BIRDS . . . *No, I never heard them at all*; NO, HE NEVER HEARD THEM"). Paul chuckles, but doesn't stop.

7   PLEASE PLEASE ME

The Beatles returned from their third Hamburg stint in June 1962 after a month and a half during which Lennon was wilder, angrier, and drunker than ever. While they were there, Brian Epstein traveled back and forth to London pitching to anyone who would take a meeting. It was soul-sapping work. Decca's rejection was final; EMI's most prestigious labels, Columbia and HMV, showed no interest; a string of smaller companies said no. A&Rs (artists and repertoire), the record-company executives responsible for finding talent, were nonplussed by the idea of a group without a leader; of a group whose members played *and* sang *and* wrote songs; of the very idea that the next big thing might come from the provinces. Everyone scoffed at the group's name. But Brian kept going, armed with an acetate of the Decca audition. One day, through a serendipitous series of events—not all of which he knew about—he found himself in a room with the head of a small subsidiary of EMI: George Martin, of Parlophone Records. The meeting took place at EMI's head office, in Manchester Square. Epstein played Martin some of the group's material, highlighting the self-penned numbers. Martin was polite but not terribly impressed. Epstein left for Liverpool, and that might have been that, had it not been for office politics.

Martin, like Epstein, was well spoken and impeccably mannered, and, also like Epstein, not quite what he seemed. His effortless urbanity was effortfully achieved, and concealed a restless, nonconformist temperament. Martin had grown up in north London in a small flat with no bathroom; the communal toilet was shared with three other families. His parents struggled to maintain middle-class respectability; at one point his father sold newspapers in the street. Martin won a place at a grammar school, and in 1943, aged seventeen, he joined the Royal Navy. Both institutions were engines of social mobility. He developed a love of classical music—he sang in the Royal Navy choir, where he met his first wife—and won a place at the Guildhall School of Music and Drama in London to study piano, oboe, and orchestration. By this time, all traces of his lower-class upbringing had been erased. He married on his twenty-second birthday, and fathered two children. But at EMI, which he joined in 1952 after a stint at the BBC, he began an affair with his secretary, Judy Lockhart-Smith. In late 1961, a few months before meeting Epstein, he left his family home in Hatfield and moved into a small flat in London he shared with his father. (Martin married Lockhart-Smith in 1966; they were together for forty-nine years.)

When Epstein met him, Martin was thirty-six, and under a lot of strain: he had broken up his family, and he was clashing with his bosses. His contract with EMI was about to expire and he was unsure whether he wanted to extend it. Martin had produced several hits for Parlophone, generating significant revenue for EMI, but didn't feel adequately rewarded or recognized. Although he produced some classical records, he was drawn to the growing pop market. He was a brilliant producer of novelty songs, featuring the hippest comedians of the day, such as the Goons and Peter Sellers (favorites of John and Paul). Martin took comedy seriously. His records were not gimmicks, as far as he was concerned, but little works of art, full of clever musical ideas and unexpected sound effects created with the adroit use of technology. Martin resisted pressure from his bosses to make a record if he didn't think it had creative potential.

By turning it into a home for eccentric talents who didn't fit in elsewhere, Martin made Parlophone EMI's most creatively dynamic label. In early 1962, when the young journalist David Frost wanted to interview a producer about the the record industry, it was Martin he sought out. Since Martin played such an important creative role in his records, he wanted to be awarded "points"—royalties on hits—and told EMI he would take a salary cut in return. But his employers had no truck with such innovations and the very fact that Martin asked did not go down well. His immediate boss, Leonard Wood, came to believe that this talented but rebellious and wayward producer needed to be put in his place. He decided to stamp on Martin by instructing him to carry out a task nobody would relish: making a record with an oddly named pop group from Liverpool.

The Beatles had come to Wood's attention through the managers of EMI's publishing arm, Ardmore and Beechwood. A&B were on the lookout for intellectual property they could acquire cheaply, and they saw potential in the Lennon-McCartney track "Like Dreamers Do" (originated by a seventeen-year-old McCartney). If EMI made a record of it, A&B could own the copyright. They tried to persuade their A&R colleagues to make the record but none were interested, so they took the idea to Leonard Wood. At first, Wood ignored the request. But now he changed his mind. This would be Martin's problem.

When Epstein received a letter from Parlophone proposing another meeting, he knew none of this. His second meeting with Martin, in May, was relatively brief. The two men, who had a respectful rapport, agreed on the essentials of a contract. It was unlikely to earn the Beatles any money—recording contracts rarely did in those days—but it meant they would make a record, maybe score a hit, and then who knew? A recording date was set for Wednesday, June 6, 7–10 p.m. This was, as Epstein later said, "the greatest thing that could happen." He came out of his meeting at EMI Studios, crossed the road to the post office, phoned his parents, and sent a telegram to the Beatles in Hamburg:

CONGRATULATIONS BOYS EMI REQUEST RECORDING SESSION
PLEASE REHEARSE NEW MATERIAL.

He received messages in return:

[John] **WHEN ARE WE GOING TO BE MILLIONAIRES**

[Paul] **PLEASE WIRE TEN THOUSAND POUND ADVANCE ROYALTIES**

Crucially, John and Paul now interpreted Brian's instruction to "rehearse new material" as a sign to revive their songwriting partnership. It had been lavishly prolific in the years after they met, generating dozens of Lennon-McCartney originals, but once the Hamburg era began it went into hiatus. Writing songs was an alternative route to riches, an insurance policy for failure, and when the group was going well, they had less reason to pursue it. The pause was also connected to the evolution of their friendship, so intense in that early stage: all those sessions in the front porch and front parlor, face-to-face, heart-to-heart. Songwriting may have been a slightly uncomfortable reminder of their early intimacy. But now they got to work. By the time they returned to Liverpool, three weeks later, they had rehearsed two new songs with the group: "Love Me Do" (originally written in 1958) and "P.S. I Love You." These would become the two sides of their first single.

The Beatles left England as local heroes; they returned as EMI artistes. On Tuesday, June 5, they traveled to London to make the single. Brian met them at the Royal Court Hotel, where the four Beatles were booked into two twin-bed rooms, an arrangement they were to follow for years to come. On Wednesday, Neil Aspinall, the Beatles' friend, roadie, and all-round assistant, drove the group to EMI Studios in St. John's Wood, north London.* EMI's commissionaire, who wore a uniform with war medals on it, guided them through the gates. He later recalled his impressions: "They pulled into the car park in an old white van. They all looked very thin and weedy, almost under-nourished." When Aspinall announced them, the commissionaire thought, "What a *strange* name."

---

* It later became known as "Abbey Road," which is how I'll refer to it.

The Beatles were led into Studio 2, a very large, windowless, high-ceilinged room. On one side, a staircase led up to the control room, from where engineers and producers surveyed the musicians on the shop floor. McCartney recalled how intimidating Studio 2 felt: "[It had] great big white sight-screens like at a cricket match towering over you, and up this endless stairway was the control room. It was like *heaven*, where the great gods lived, and we were down below. Oh God, the nerves." George Martin was not yet present; he delegated the first part of the session to his assistant and engineers, who were wary of these shaggy-haired Scouse young men. There was an awkward period of getting the right gear in place as the Beatles' amplifiers were revealed to be inadequate and replacements had to be found. The group then ran through the songs they had prepared while Martin's team tried to identify which songs should be on the single.

Unbeknown to the Beatles or Epstein, it was certain that one of the songs chosen would be a Lennon-McCartney original, to please Ardmore and Beechwood. The EMI team settled on "Love Me Do" as the leading candidate over "P.S. I Love You" and "Ask Me Why." As one of the EMI team put it, "all of a sudden there was this raunchy noise which struck a chord in our heads." "Love Me Do" originated with Paul, back in 1958, under the influence of Buddy Holly. When it was revived to prepare for this session, John helped Paul work out a bridge section ("Someone to love . . .") and added a bluesy harmonica riff. In its original form the song was perkier and poppier; John and Paul now brought to it a musical sensibility soaked in everything they had been into since 1958, including the grit of Black R&B.

The engineers invited Martin to join them and he watched from the control room without the Beatles knowing he was there. Martin agreed with his colleagues about "Love Me Do." He liked how Lennon's harmonica sliced rudely through the stolid groove. But he spotted a problem. John sang the verse, with Paul harmonizing, Everly-style—notably on that elongated, beseeching *please*. John sang the refrain (*Love me do-oo . . .*) unaccompanied, which brought focus to it. But then he had to cut his line short so that he could play the harmonica riff. Martin descended the steps from the control room and introduced himself to the young men. He suggested that

McCartney sing the refrain. John and Paul agreed. McCartney was terrified but sang it well.

George Martin's first direct interaction with the Beatles had resulted in what was to be a recurring feature of the band's songs and a vital part of their musical personality: the swapping of vocal lines between Lennon and McCartney. John and Paul both had exceptionally wide vocal ranges for pop singers, but John was more comfortable in the lower part of his range, while Paul was more comfortable in the upper range; almost every time we hear them harmonize, it is McCartney on the high line. That *Love me do-oo* refrain is relatively low, which may be why Lennon took the lead on Paul's song, but since the harmonica was Lennon's instrument they had this problem, which they seem to have ignored until Martin pointed it out. Perhaps they assumed that if the lead singer is the narrator, the "I" of a song, he cannot very well change places with someone else. But if Martin didn't care about first-person consistency, why should they?

From then on this swapping of the narrative voice between John and Paul would often occur when the vocal melody cut across their respective ranges. John sings the verse of "A Hard Day's Night" ("I've been workin' like a dog") and Paul takes over on the bridge ("When I'm *hooome* . . ."). The same thing happens on "Any Time at All" and "I Don't Want to Spoil the Party." A technical necessity resulted in the distinct and thrilling aesthetic effect of two men who share the same "I"—the same consciousness. It became an expression of the group's camaraderie that also evoked how two people can slip in and out of each other's subjectivity: the way we internalize the voices of those we know and love. John and Paul played with its possibilities in "We Can Work It Out" and, most spectacularly, "A Day in the Life."

When the recording session was over the Beatles were invited up to the control room: the locus of power. They crowded in with Martin and his team, amid the machines. After playing back the recordings, Martin delivered a lecture on the technicalities of studio recording. When he finally paused to ask if there was anything they didn't like, Harrison replied, "Yeah—I don't like your tie." There was a beat of silence—then everyone laughed, including

Martin. Although he had not been overwhelmed by their music, he fell for the young men themselves. "It was their charisma, the fact that when I was with them they gave me a sense of well-being, of being happy . . . I thought, 'If they have this effect on me, they are going to have that effect on their audiences.'"

Once the Beatles left, Martin pondered a problem he suddenly found himself very interested in solving. He didn't think the drummer was up to scratch, but the others could play well enough, and at least two of them had strong voices. He was jealous of the hits his more successful rival at EMI, Norrie Paramor, had produced for Cliff Richard and the Shadows. "*Still* I was thinking, 'Is it John Lennon and the Beatles, or Paul McCartney and the Beatles?'" Martin said later. "I knew it wasn't George." Since he couldn't decide, he decided to make a virtue of it. The Beatles did not fit any template, but what had Martin built at Parlophone if not a home for talented misfits? He wanted to find them another song, though. Martin didn't think any of the recordings they made at that session would be a hit and he wasn't convinced by the Lennon-McCartney songs he heard. He instructed an assistant to find a suitable song for the single. "Love Me Do" could go on the B side.

John and Paul detected George Martin's coolness toward the original songs they played him, and, determined that their first record should feature their own material, got to work. Within forty-eight hours of returning from London, John had a new song ready: "Please Please Me," written in Aunt Mimi's spare bedroom and finished "with a lot of joking and messing about" in the McCartney front parlor. It was a ballad in the mode of Roy Orbison, the American singer whose tremulous tenor conveyed a mixture of vulnerability and defiance. Songs like "Crying" built inexorably toward a climactic phrase and note that pierced the listener's heart. At Aunt Mimi's, Lennon wrote a melody that hits a similar peak on the title phrase. "Please Please Me" is then revealed to be about reciprocity: ". . . like I please you." In the love songs that Lennon wrote over the next few years, a sense of grievance recurs, sometimes subtly, as here, sometimes hot with anger. The other inspiration for "Please Please Me" was a hit from before John was born, a Bing Crosby

song called "Please," the kind of song Julia had taught him to play on the
banjo and ukulele.

☿

Over the summer the Beatles were in limbo, waiting on EMI. They stuck
to a relentless schedule, playing to audiences who were now excited to see
the band with a record deal. It was during this period that John, Paul, and
George decided to eject Pete Best from the group. Martin had made it clear
to Epstein that he did not think Best was up to it, and that he would em-
ploy a session drummer on any recordings. Ringo Starr, the drummer with
Rory Storm and the Hurricanes, had played with the Beatles a little when
Best was not available. When he did, he confirmed what John, Paul, and
George already suspected: that he was a much better drummer, with more
technical command and flair. And the Beatles didn't just like playing with
him; they really liked *him*. Starr was laconic like Harrison, but with an idiosyncratic sense of humor all of his own. He was firm in his preferences,
but not opinionated, and happy to support his bandmates. The other three
were grammar-school kids; Lennon and McCartney in particular prided
themselves on their cultural literacy. Starr had grown up poorer than any of
them. He spent much of his childhood on sickbeds at home and in hospital,
suffering from stomach problems, at times close to death. His schooling was
severely disrupted. But he didn't lack for intelligence or wit.

Epstein had wanted to keep Best on and was initially unenthusiastic about
Starr. "I thought he was rather loud," he said, by which he meant uncouth
and working-class, but the others insisted. Ringo did not take much persuading. He soon became a kind of anchor for the group, the individual
member most able to put his ego aside for the greater good, a vital, stabiliz-
ing element among willful and often headstrong personalities. He did, however, find it hard to penetrate a group of friends who had known one another
since school days and been through so much together over the previous four
years. He later admitted it took him a long time to feel accepted as an equal.

The task of breaking with Pete might have fallen to John as the band's de
facto leader. But Lennon could not bring himself to tell Pete, and the others
did not want to either. As George put it, "Being unable to deal with the

emotional side of that, we went to Brian Epstein and said, 'You're the manager, you do it.'" In August, Epstein invited Best to a meeting and delivered the news. Best was shocked and hurt, but that was that.

☿

At the start of August, John's girlfriend, Cynthia, discovered she was pregnant. When she told John, "I watched his face drain of all its color, and fear and panic creep into his eyes. He was speechless for what seemed like an age. 'There's only one thing for it, Cyn, we'll have to get married.'" Lennon felt that he was losing his dream just as it seemed to be within reach. Married pop stars with children were . . . well, it wasn't even a thing. In that context, John's proposal of marriage, unromantically delivered, was an act of considerable resolution. John and Cynthia were married on August 23 in a minimal ceremony that wasn't attended by Aunt Mimi, who disapproved. The couple moved into Epstein's flat on Falkner Street, in town, which he lent to them until they could afford their own.

In August, Epstein received an acetate with a demo of a song called "How Do You Do It." The song had been shopped to Parlophone by its songwriter, Mitch Murray. George Martin thought it could work as an A side for the Beatles, and shared his plan with the music publisher Dick James, a former singer who had recorded for Parlophone. Now in his thirties, bald and bespectacled, James had retired from singing to become a music publisher with the rare quality of being enthusiastic about music. When Martin told James about the group from Liverpool, James said, "Liverpool? You're joking." Martin had to spell out their odd name. When Murray was told his song was going to be recorded by a group, he didn't get it. "What do you mean, *group*? . . . Dick had to explain to me that they sang and played at the same time."

Pop artists who had not released any records were expected to do what they were told, but the Beatles were different in this way, too. When they heard the acetate, they were horrified. "We hated it," said Paul. "How Do You Do It" is not a bad song; Lennon and McCartney might even have written it in their early days. But that's why they despised it. Their tastes had already been transformed by R&B, and to their ears "How Do You Do It" sounded too cute, too white. Paul said, "We felt we were getting a style, the

Beatles' style, which we were known for in Hamburg and Liverpool, and we didn't want to blow it all by suddenly . . . becoming run of the mill." This attitude might sound unremarkable, now that we're used to the idea of pop artists wanting to stay true to their musical instincts. But Lennon and McCartney somehow rigged up their artistic integrity out of nothing.

Still, refusing to record the song point-blank would have been rash, and with a second recording session booked for September 4, John and Paul showed willingness by at least trying to make it their own. They wrote a new intro and changed some of the chords so that it sounded less glib; they didn't polish the song so much as roughen it. At EMI for the new session, they played it to Martin along with five of their own, including John's ballad, "Please Please Me." That "How Do You Do It" was the only non-original song shows just how hard they were now pressing to record their own material. Martin was not impressed by their songs, however, and he was pleased with what they had done with Murray's.

The Beatles now approached Martin to voice their disquiet, with Lennon as spokesman. It was a brave move, even if we assume that Lennon was less unequivocal than he later recalled: "We said, 'We'd sooner have no contract than put that crap out!'" In the meeting, Martin did not budge, but a week or so later he decided that "Love Me Do" should be the A side after all. The Beatles took this to be a sign of Martin's humility; in fact, he had been forced into it. The men from Ardmore and Beechwood wanted a song they owned on the A side. Murray and his publisher felt "How Do You Do It" was too good for a B side. The single would therefore feature two Lennon-McCartney numbers. The Beatles came back to Abbey Road for a third session. They rerecorded "Love Me Do," and recorded "P.S. I Love You." (To Ringo's chagrin, a session drummer, Andy White, played on that session, since Martin, who had only just met Starr, wasn't yet comfortable with him.) Finally they had a single, and a release date: Friday, October 5.

John and Paul now made a decision that would shape the future of the Beatles. In business terms, the group had up until this point been a single entity, with the income they received from performing split four equal ways. But they were about to release a single that featured songs written by Lennon and McCartney, which meant that the two of them were presented with a publishing agreement from Ardmore and Beechwood for "Love Me Do" and "P.S. I Love You." Brian showed John and Paul the contract at the Falkner Street flat. To the standard clauses, he added an extra one: that when it came to "sheet music, records, publicity etc.," credit will be given to "LENNON/ MCCARTNEY." From now on there would be two streams of income to the band: one going to the group, and one going to Lennon and McCartney. John and Paul agreed to split the songwriting income with each other, fifty-fifty, regardless of which of them came up with a song. They were formalizing the pact they had made as teenagers, in their first flush of mutual creativity: agreeing to be bound together in the eyes of the law.

The conversation at Falkner Street extended beyond the imminent single. The three of them agreed there and then that Brian should be the manager and agent for Lennon and McCartney, as well as the Beatles, with a separate contract. John and Paul were now a group within the group. They had always been so, in personal terms; now they were in economic terms, too. The decision required a certain ruthlessness. George often contributed musical ideas to songs; it was not obvious that he shouldn't share in their partnership. "It was an option to include George in the songwriting team," said Paul later on. "I remember walking up past Woolton Church with John one morning and going over the question, 'Without wanting to be too mean to George, should three of us write or would it be better to keep it simple?' We decided we'd just keep to two of us."

That walk, past the place where they first met, was a momentous one. From now on, John and Paul had a clear and compelling economic reason to create songs together. This flipped them into a permanently creative mode. The professional marriage strengthened the personal bond, enhancing their sense of themselves as a pair of connected minds on which the Beatles depended. It's not clear that George and Ringo were even told about this second contract. George certainly noticed its effect. About this period, he said: "An attitude came over John and Paul of 'We're the grooves and you two just watch it.'"

Contrary to Martin's misgivings, "Love Me Do" was a modest success, hanging around in the middle of the top fifty for several months. Meanwhile the Beatles maintained a hectic schedule. In November they returned to Hamburg for the first of a pair of two-week stints at the Star-Club (overlapping with none other than Little Richard). In between, they returned to London to record a second single. This time, Martin and the Beatles were agreed on what it should be.

At their second EMI session, John and Paul had played him "Please Please Me" in its original, Orbisonesque form. Martin found it dreary but suggested it might work speeded up. After the session, Lennon and McCartney worked on a more high-energy arrangement. When Martin heard the demo of it, he was delighted, and worked with the band in the studio to refine it. An introductory riff played on lead guitar was doubled by John's harmonica as a point of continuity with "Love Me Do." Unlike previous sessions, which had been tense and protracted, this one, Martin recalled, was "a joy." At the end of it, he allowed himself a touch of drama. Over the intercom from the control room, he said, in words that must have landed on the Beatles like the prophecy of a sky god, "Gentlemen, you've just made your first number one record."

If John and Paul had followed "Love Me Do" with songs of similar quality the Beatles might have scored another hit or two, before slipping back to merely regional celebrity. As it was, they leaped forward, beating not only their own mark but also that of everyone around them. "Please Please Me" is impatient, lusty, playful, and reproachful. On the opening line Lennon sings the descending melody while Paul hangs on the top note, a trick they picked up from "Cathy's Clown" by the Everly Brothers. Listeners had heard vocal harmonizing on country-style pop or on vocal-group records but they hadn't heard it done like this before. The words would have sounded new, too. The opening line ("Last night I said these words to my girl") is a framing device: the narrator letting us into a story from his life. There is an almost shocking directness to the accusation that Lennon then makes, or recounts himself making—that his girl never even *tries*. It isn't nice, but it feels honest and authentic, and its aggression is leavened by the music's ecstatic bounce. Once the song takes its grip it does not let go. What might have been a dip in interest at the end of the verse's first line is filled with a punchy, three-step turnaround into the second. When it moves from verse to pre-chorus, the song jumps from one surprising chord to another, spinning the listener around, as Lennon growls "*Come on*," mixing sexual frustration with sly humor. Ringo makes sleazy drum rolls and Paul and George engage John in call-and-response.

All of the pressure this section builds is released on the second word of the title phrase—"Please *please* me, whoa yeah"—which Lennon sings in doo-wop-style falsetto. The middle eight has a girl-group flavor, Paul and George chiming in on the last three words of the first line ("in my heart"). It leaps up another falsetto peak ("with *you*") and uses an extra bar—it is a middle *nine*: all wrong, yet absolutely right. McCartney's bass powers the song from beneath. In the middle section he walks down the scale as the vocal line moves up, an early example of his ear for the contrapuntal. "Please Please Me" is a model for how McCartney would impose himself on his partner's songs. Through his talents for arrangement, singing, and playing, he helped to turn a somewhat maudlin, aggrieved ballad into a cruise missile carrying a payload of joy. The song ends with Lennon repeating his reminder that *he* has played *his* part—"like I please *you*, oh yeah"—until, with a final falsetto "you," we're spun around one more time and abandoned, less than two minutes after the story began.

Scientists call it a phase shift: an abrupt transformation that has been building for some time; heated water suddenly becoming steam. The Beatles underwent one in Hamburg; "Please Please Me" was another. Before recording it, they were an exciting live act who performed other people's songs onstage but struggled to convey the same energy in the studio. Afterward, songwriting, performing, and recording were integrated into a sleek new machine. "Love Me Do" had hinted at this shift, but the song simmers without ever coming to a boil. "Please Please Me" is a series of climaxes: the mouth organ's clarion call; the opening harmony; the call-and-response; the sweet release of the chorus; the final *oh yeahs*. It combines Bing Crosby, the Everlys, Little Richard, girl groups, and Motown, yet instead of sounding patched together, it is utterly itself, unified by force of collective personality.

On Martin's recommendation, the publishing rights to "Please Please Me" and its B side ("Ask Me Why") were sold to Dick James rather than Ardmore and Beechwood. James proved his worth as a marketer by getting on the phone in front of Epstein and booking the Beatles onto their first national TV show, *Thank Your Lucky Stars*.

ⓐ

Britain endured a brutal winter in early 1963. The Beatles spent it on the road in a freezing van, lying on top of one another to keep warm. Toward the end of February, they returned to the Cavern, where they received a telegram with news that Martin's prophecy had been fulfilled. "Please Please Me" was number one. When Bob Wooler announced this to the crowd, the response was silence. "Everyone was stunned," said a regular. "That was the end of it as far as we were concerned." The Cavern fans were right: it *was* the end of something. The Beatles played at the Cavern well into 1963. But what had begun just over five years before as a connection between two minds had developed into a force too powerful to stay underground. *We decided we'd just keep to two of us.* Lennon-McCartney originals had made their way from the periphery of the Beatles' mission to its center.

8   SHE LOVES YOU

The Beatles started 1963 as Liverpool's top band and ended it as the biggest pop stars Britain had ever seen, with four number one singles and two number one albums. Fast as this ascent was, it was not instant. As "Please Please Me" climbed the charts, the group toured more intensively than they ever had. In January and February they played a week of gigs in Scotland, taped BBC radio and TV appearances in Birmingham, Manchester, and London, and joined a package tour, headlined by the teenage pop star Helen Shapiro, that took them around the whole of England. They played ballrooms, theaters, cinemas in coastal towns. The days of long, sprawling, semi-improvised shows were over; now they played an efficient thirty-minute set, two or three times a night.

John and Paul were writing more than ever, despite, or rather because of, this frenetic schedule. A crucial factor in their collaboration was sheer physical proximity. Before, the Beatles had traveled to gigs in Merseyside and returned home at the end of the night. Now they were either on the road or staying in hotels. When John and Paul were together—in hotel rooms, dressing rooms, the van, the coach—they would share whatever melodies or lines they had in their heads, inviting the other to help finish the song. In this way, the songwriting partnership caught fire.

We're used to the idea that mastery of a complex skill requires years of practice, but Lennon and McCartney's stop-start songwriting history suggests another lesson. Had they focused on creative outputs, rather than inputs, earlier on, they might have become stuck in a narrower range of expression. The years that they spent listening, in the deepest sense—learning and playing songs by other artists—meant that by the time they had sufficient incentive and opportunity to write their own songs, they had a profound grasp of pop's clichés, musical and lyrical—clichés they loved but loved to turn upside down and back to front, so that their own work felt surprising and unignorable and fresh. They were bursting with ideas for songs, and ideas for every *part* of a song—what to do for an intro, how to transition from verse to chorus (and back again), how to create a dramatic climax and a sparkling middle section, how to arrange the vocal harmonies.

They were able to develop ideas very fast. "From Me to You" was written on the tour bus, on the way from York to Shrewsbury. As Lennon remembered it later, they were messing around on guitars when one of them alighted on a melody. John came up with the first line. By the time they reached Shrewsbury, they had a song. This was typical of their working method. They would strum and chatter in a dreamy, seemingly aimless state until the germ of an idea emerged, at which point they went to work. Their creative zone was thus one of overlapping realms: personal and professional, conscious and unconscious. They would draw from whatever materials were on hand, particularly newspapers and magazines. These materials would sometimes make their way into songs without them willing it. Lennon said that after "From Me to You" was released, he and Paul couldn't remember how they hit on the title phrase. Then one day he picked up a copy of the *New Musical Express* and opened it at the letters column, "From You to Us." Only then did he recall that there had been a copy of the magazine on the coach that day.

Even before "Please Please Me" reached number one, George Martin decided that the group should make an album. The Beatles paused from touring to record ten new tracks, all drawn from their Cavern repertoire. Since their schedule did not allow any more time, they had to record everything in one marathon session, on February 11, starting at 10 a.m. and ending just before 11 p.m. Four of the new songs were self-penned, including "I Saw Her Standing There," which was chosen as the album opener. Paul came up with the melody while driving home from a gig on October 22, 1962. Shortly afterward he went on a day trip to London with one of his girlfriends at the time, Celia Mortimer. She recalls him working out lyrics as they wandered through London squares.

He took it to John, and the two of them completed the song in the front parlor of Forthlin Road. The second line was originally "never been a beauty queen" (McCartney was thinking of beauty queen competitions at Butlin's). After John laughed it away, they searched for another rhyme for "seventeen," settling on "you know what I mean." As McCartney remarked later, that was better precisely because "you *don't* know what I mean." They were learning to value ambiguity, to trust in the listener's imagination.

The *Please Please Me* album closes with a cover of an Isley Brothers song that the Beatles had started performing in 1962 at the Cavern: "Twist and Shout." The Beatles turned this pleasant pop song into a carnal joyride, using every ounce of their stage-learned expertise in evoking visceral reactions. Its musical centerpiece is the consecutive layering of "ahhs." John, then George, then Paul, construct a bluesy A7—the fifth, or "dominant" chord of the song—which begs to be resolved to the tonic. Lennon recorded the lead vocal with a heavy cold and his shirt off at the end of that thirteen-hour session at Abbey Road, knowing that this was his and the group's only chance to nail the song before the studio closed. It's the sound, he later said, of "a frantic guy doing his best." John's intensity is matched by his partner: that wild, animalistic scream you hear as the "ahhs" collapse into the chorus is Paul.

The album was released in March 1963, and progressed steadily up the British charts until it reached the top, where it stayed for thirty consecutive weeks—from early May to late November—a feat equaled by nobody before or since. At the same time as it reached number one, "From Me to You" hit number one on the singles chart. "From Me to You" wasn't even on the album. It was a sort of gift for their fans. This became a habit of theirs, to release singles that weren't on the LP, as if drawing from a bottomless well.

The Beatles had become a national news story, albeit a relatively minor one for now (the Profumo scandal was unfolding on the front pages). An early interviewer was the *Evening Standard*'s Maureen Cleave, who became a friend. In February, after meeting Lennon and McCartney, she wrote a short, closely observed introduction to the group, headlined, "Why the Beatles Create All That Frenzy." Cleave first has to explain to readers that the Beatles are a new kind of act: "They are a vocal-instrumental group, three guitars and drums, and they don't sound a bit like The Shadows, or anybody else for that matter." She remarks in passing that they write their own songs, and notes they are unusually well educated for pop stars. She emphasizes how different they look: "Scruffy, but scruffy on purpose . . . their shirts are pink, their hairstyles are French." She quotes a Liverpool housewife: "They look beat-up and depraved in the nicest possible way." On stage, they are full of confidence, and remarkably funny: "They know exactly what they can get away with, and their inter-song patter is in the Max Miller-music hall tradition, with slightly bawdy schoolboy overtones." She summed up their attitude: "They like each other and everybody else."

Cleave was unusual: most of the journalists the Beatles encountered treated them as the latest product from the teen entertainment machine, albeit an intriguing one. Celebrity entertainers were expected to engage in a formal dance with the media, mixing bland expressions of gratitude to fans with tributes to showbiz peers and cute personal anecdotes. The Beatles did not defer to these conventions. They were polite and charming, but they also gave the appearance of being *honest*—of refusing to be anyone but themselves.

> PAUL: Cliff and the Shadows invited us to this great kind of party. I mean all I could say was, "Oh wait till I tell the girls back home." Mind you, I knew it was a soft thing to say.

> JOHN: Yeah, you're supposed to make things up, like, er, "What a great job you're doing in the industry . . ."

PAUL: Because we've never been fans of Cliff's . . .

JOHN: We've always *hated* him. He was everything we hated in
    pop. But when we met him we didn't mind him at all . . . we
    still hate his records, but he's really very nice.

It was all wrong, a public relations nightmare, except it was the opposite.
Note how John and Paul nudge each other on through degrees of candor. Paul
admits that they don't like Cliff's music, and John leans into it. John and Paul
were the most talkative in these group situations, with George chiming in
with dry, sarcastic lines, and Ringo dispatching jokes like drum fills ("Why do
you wear all those rings on your fingers?" "Because I can't get them through
my nose"). The Beatles took what we later learned to call a postmodern
attitude to their own fame, providing an ironic commentary on it as they
went, gently satirizing the journalistic charade, inviting the fans into what
had hitherto been a private club. They broke the fourth wall, just as they had
onstage, in Hamburg and Liverpool.

"I mean, we don't believe in our fame the way Zsa Zsa Gabor believes
in hers," Paul told Cleave. "We're kidding everyone, you see." John told a
reporter, in early 1964: "We're kidding you and we're kidding ourselves. We
just don't take anything seriously." In a 1963 BBC radio interview with Lennon, the interviewer complained, half-jokingly, "This is going wrong. I want
to get a nice 'personality' bit." Lennon replied, "I haven't *got* a nice personality." Underlying the mockery of show business was a gentle but firm
insistence that they be taken seriously as artists. Asked what he would do
after pop stardom, Lennon said, "I'm not going to change into a tap-dancing
musical . . . This isn't showbusiness. It's something else. This is different
from anything that anybody imagines. You don't go on from this. You do
this and then you finish." We are used to pop acts who think of themselves
as artists, but at the time such talk was almost incomprehensible. Lennon
and McCartney projected themselves with such confidence that it was as if
they had been preparing for this for years, and in a sense they had. Half a
decade of shared laughter, trauma, failure, squalor, and delight meant that

they emerged into the spotlight with an uncannily sure sense of who they were and how much they were prepared to compromise in order to meet the world's expectations—that is, not at all.

During this crazed activity, Cynthia Lennon gave birth to a boy, on April 8. John came to see the two of them in hospital a few days after the birth, once he was able to find time between engagements. According to Cynthia, he was overjoyed to hold his baby, and "consumed with happiness and awe." But she also noted that he chose that moment to tell her he would soon be going on holiday, and not with her and their new son, but with Brian Epstein. Lennon's ambivalence toward his family—loving them, but not wanting to be tied to them—would persist. The boy was called Julian, after John's mother.

⊛

On July 1 the Beatles went back to Abbey Road to record the first single of a renewed contract from EMI. John and Paul had plenty of original songs to choose from now, but they brought one they'd finished just four days before, perhaps because they realized it was the best thing they'd ever written. On June 26, 1963, when John and Paul were sharing a twin-bed hotel room in Newcastle, they found themselves with time to spare before the evening's show. So they picked up their guitars, lit cigarettes, and started playing. Paul had been wondering if it was possible to write a love song in which the protagonist was neither the lover nor the loved but a third party who wanted to bring them together. He was fascinated by film and liked the idea of a song as a narrative or mise-en-scène in an unfolding drama. Sitting on their beds, he and John worked out the logic of his idea, before completing it the next evening, at Forthlin Road.

"She Loves You," released in late August, became the bestselling single of 1963, indeed of the decade. The Beatles' performance of it on *Sunday Night at the London Palladium* alerted the whole nation to Beatlemania. It was the perfect expression of this group of boyish, girlish men, who apparently took the devotion of young women in their stride while reserving their primary affection for one another. "She Loves You" leaped out of radios and TV sets, mugging anyone in the vicinity. Lennon and McCartney accepted Martin's suggestion that they begin with the chorus, so the song explodes into being before you're ready for it.

The musical genius of "She Loves You" is easy to miss because its effect is so immediate. Lennon and McCartney make a symphony out of the simplest unit of language. The three "yeahs" are repeated three times in that opening chorus and each time over a different chord: the same story told from three different perspectives. Conventional pop songs start on the home chord so that the listener knows immediately where they are. "She Loves You," which is in G major, begins on the relative *minor* chord, switches quickly through two major chords, and only arrives at the tonic on a fourth, elongated "yeah." The effect is dizzying and disorienting, like tumbling down a hill without being sure when you've hit the bottom. The landing is luxuriously carpeted: on that final "yeah" the three singers unfurl a rich harmony that evokes the pre-rock-and-roll era. In the first twelve seconds of the song we're spun through at least three different eras of pop, and it all happens so fast that the only option is surrender. The track ends on another jazzy chord. George Martin suggested cutting it, on the basis that it sounded old-fashioned, but Lennon and McCartney insisted. They didn't care about sounding current; they cared about sounding new.

John and Paul sing "She Loves You," weaving in and out of unison and harmony. Although the lyrics are spoken by a single narrator, it sounds like a conversation between friends who have bumped into each other in the street, an effect created by the pauses between lines: "You think you've lost your love" is answered, melodically, by "Well, I saw her yesterday." "She Loves You" is infused with the spirit of girl groups. One of the appealing things about girl groups is that they are groups of girls. The singer and her backing vocalists are addressing not just a lover, or a heartless universe, but also one another, and part of what moves the listener is this sense of friends talking to friends: testifying, affirming, consoling. What these girls talk about, mostly, is boys. Discussing relationships was seen, back then, and may still be seen now, as a distinctively female activity—girl talk—and dismissed as gossip by men who prefer, or say they prefer, to talk work, or politics, or sport. Well, John and Paul never had much time for sports, and they loved talking to girls.

"She Loves You" is a boy-girl love song and a song about friendship between boys. The narrator of "She Loves You" addresses his prideful, difficult friend and implores him to count his blessings. The song pauses on the line "with a love like that" (its three beats echoing the three words of the chorus) in order to throw a spotlight on the words "be glad." The scenario "She Loves You" describes would be reproduced in real life, eleven years later, when McCartney acted as a go-between for Lennon and Yoko Ono. That wasn't just coincidence; it arose out of a consistent feature of the Lennon-McCartney relationship: Paul's desire, verging on a need, to steer his wayward friend toward safe harbor.

Pop songs work on several different frequencies at once. Written down, they might suggest one story, but in sonic motion they throw off meanings and feelings like sparks from a Catherine wheel, beyond the conscious intention of their creators. "She Loves You" vibrates with the glorious confusion of being young. The narrator presents himself as a detached and rational friend but is more deeply invested in this triangular story than he knows. "She Loves You" secretly wants you to notice how much *I* love you.

☿

Paul McCartney met and fell for Jane Asher when she was seventeen, in April 1963. Jane was already a show business veteran. She was in her first film aged five, had recently appeared in a Disney movie, and had taken leading roles in critically acclaimed plays. Paul knew her from TV: she was a regular guest on *Juke Box Jury*, a BBC show on which a panel judged new singles a "Hit" or a "Miss." Jane was well-spoken, forthright, and funny. She met the Beatles backstage following a pop concert called *Swinging Sound '63*, at the Royal Albert Hall. Since they were all fascinated by her, they invited her to join them at a friend's house in Chelsea for after-show drinks. Jane, uncharmed by John's inappropriate questions about her sexual experience, ended up chatting mostly to Paul, who impressed her by quoting from Chaucer's *Canterbury Tales*, in Middle English: "Ful semly hir wympul pynched was." In the early hours of the morning Paul dropped her off at her family home on Wimpole Street, central London. McCartney was entranced by Jane's poise, intellectual confidence, and cultural nous. He seems to have considered her a potential wife from the beginning of the relationship, rather than as someone suitable for one of his many flings. He took her to meet his family at his twenty-first birthday party in Liverpool, a month after they met.

By the end of the year, the Asher house was his home, too. The Beatles had been living in hotel rooms and then a rented London flat—crash pads, really—and Paul yearned for a home. Late in 1963, after he had been dating Jane for several months, Jane's mother invited him to stay the night in a little room at the top of the house. He ended up staying for more than two years. Paul's room was about the same size as his bedroom at Forthlin Road, with space for a single bed, a wardrobe, and, just about, a piano, so that he could fall out of bed and start working out an idea. He was a star and soon-to-be millionaire, living in a garret, and very happy.

For Paul, the Ashers were like a fantasy alternative family. They were posh and rich and lived in a grand house; they were also cultured and warm and eccentric. Jane's younger sister, Claire, had performed in a radio soap opera series; her older brother, Peter, was an actor, too. Jane's father, Richard, was an eminent physician who combined deep empathy for suffering—he suffered from depression himself—with a mischievous sense of humor (he coined the term "Munchausen syndrome" to describe a medical condition he identified: patients whose chief symptom is the fabrication of symptoms). The Ashers enjoyed talking about novels, ideas, and history and playing word games. They enjoyed one another, too; Paul loved the love in the house as much as its books and pictures.

The Ashers were very musical. Jane's mother, Margaret, had been George Martin's oboe teacher at Guildhall. Peter was a budding pop singer. Crucially, they were inclusive enthusiasts rather than snobs. "It was the assumption that you were reasonably intelligent that I liked. They didn't talk down," said McCartney. They introduced Paul to music, ideas, and experiences that enriched his mind and fed into his work. "I often felt the guys were sort of partying, whereas I was learning a lot; learning an awful lot." The Ashers boosted McCartney's confidence as a social actor in London, and as an artist.

☸

After being allowed a holiday in September, the Beatles went straight to work on a follow-up album. EMI wanted it in time for the Christmas market, and for what might be their last chance to milk the cash cow before it died. Nobody expected or needed the Beatles to improve on *Please Please Me*, and any other act, given so little time, would have produced a mediocre retread. Indeed, a mediocre retread would have been perfectly fine. Instead, the Beatles got *better*. *With the Beatles* included seven Lennon and McCartney originals, plus one from George, who had seen what his bandmates were doing and decided to try it, too. The group's playing is more accomplished and expressive than before, and the instrumentation more varied, even if some of the songs bear the mark of being made in a rush. The album includes "All My Loving," an important song for Paul, who recalls hearing it singled out on a BBC radio show one day and thinking, *Hey, I can write hits*. While every track bears McCartney's imprint, Lennon's voice is more prominent. His cover of "Please Mr. Postman" by the Marvelettes, at once jokey and desperate, is a highlight.

Perhaps the most remarkable thing about *With the Beatles* is that the strongest track they made in late 1963—the one that was, along with "She Loves You," one of the twin peaks of their year—isn't on it. By the autumn of 1963, John was living with Cynthia and Julian in a rented Kensington flat. He and Paul didn't have anywhere private and peaceful to work when they were in London, and so Margaret Asher offered them the use of her basement and the piano in it (she gave oboe lessons there). This is where they wrote "I Want to Hold Your Hand," Paul sitting at the piano, searching for the next chord, John either next to him or pacing the room. After about an hour or so, they had a song.

Even more than "She Loves You," "I Want to Hold Your Hand" was a collaboration, in which nobody, including John and Paul, knew where one man's contribution began and the other's ended. The next day, John and Paul took it to the group, and to Abbey Road, where it became a powerhouse. "I

Want to Hold Your Hand" was released as a single about six weeks after John and Paul composed it. It knocked "She Loves You" off the number one spot.

It begins with a stutter: a guitar riff that starts and restarts, like someone so excited about what they want to say that they can't bring themselves to speak. The masterstroke is the transition from its earthy, hard-driving major-key verse to a gentle and intimate interlude beginning on D minor (*And when I touch you . . .*). With the instrumentation suddenly stripped back, we feel like we're walking on air, hand in hand. "I Want to Hold Your Hand" displays John and Paul's acute empathy with their teenage female fans. Like other songs from this period ("Please Please Me," "From Me to You," "Thank You Girl"), it directly addresses an imaginary listener which every girl imagined was her. Its chorus makes a modest and reassuringly specific appeal from which no girl or girl's mother would recoil, allowing listeners to revel in the rest of the song's tantalizing ambiguity (touch me . . . how? Where?). "I Want to Hold Your Hand" also shows us the child in the man; there is a plaintive quality to John's vocal that evokes a boy's need for his mother's touch.

Until the autumn of 1963, the Beatles were primarily of interest to pop fans and only vaguely noticed by everyone else. But in early November, the Beatles performed at the Royal Variety Show in front of the Queen Mother and more than twenty-one million viewers on TV. Lennon's preprepared line ("For the people in the cheaper seats, clap your hands. And the rest of you, if you'll just rattle your jewelry") struck just the right balance of irreverence and charm. From then on, they were truly national figures. The teenage girls who created Beatlemania were derided as psychologically disturbed by older generations, but there was as yet no vocabulary up to the task of describing this group, or capturing the magnitude of the earthquake. Screaming was the most appropriate response.

9   IF I FELL

On November 22, 1963, a gash was ripped in America's soul when President Kennedy was assassinated. In December, as their parents wept, shocked and bewildered teenagers glued themselves to a song on the radio. An enterprising disc jockey in Washington, DC, had got hold of a copy of "I Want to Hold Your Hand" from an airline stewardess, and his listeners went crazy for it. Other DJs soon found it had the same effect.

The Beatles had released three singles in America: "Please Please Me," "From Me to You," and "She Loves You." The records got almost no promotional support (it was assumed by just about everyone in the industry that pop music was an American export, never an import), and all of them flopped. In early November, Brian Epstein flew to New York to persuade Americans that his group could be as popular in the US as they were in Britain. Although he didn't make much progress with record labels, he did secure a February spot for the Beatles on the TV host Ed Sullivan's popular Sunday-night show. In light of this, Capitol Records, EMI's American partner, committed to release "I Want to Hold Your Hand" in mid-January.

But after the song went viral, Capitol moved to rush-release it on December 26, backed by a major marketing campaign complete with Beatles wigs. "I Want to Hold Your Hand" sold 640,000 copies in the first week; sales grew throughout January and didn't stop. American teenagers fell upon the Beatles with something close to desperation, as if they had been starved of them; never has the word "release" been more appropriate.

America's first glimpse of the Beatles was not on Sullivan's show, but on that of his rival, Jack Paar, who hosted a Friday-evening show. In the first week of January 1964, Paar played a clip of the Beatles performing "She Loves You" to screaming fans in Britain. He treated it as an amusing curio ("It's nice to know that England has finally risen to our cultural level"). But the teenagers who saw it and later watched the Beatles live on *Ed Sullivan* knew better. Here, in the midst of national trauma, was a scream of joy, and instead of jarring it felt undeniably right.

Meanwhile, the Beatles were in the middle of an eighteen-day engagement at the Olympia Theatre in Paris, a city that had not yet taken to them. The workload was almost Hamburg-like: two or three shows a day, with two days off in total. The hall was not always full. The audiences were composed mainly of older Parisians in evening dresses and tuxedos. The Beatles were disappointed at the lack of girls. Still, unlike in Hamburg, they were staying in a fancy hotel, the George V, where they spent a lot of time listening to music, including one record that got played over and over after Paul borrowed it from a French Europe 1 radio DJ: *The Freewheelin' Bob Dylan*. In fact, they spent more time in one place here than they had done anywhere since Hamburg. As usual, John and Paul spent a lot of time songwriting. At McCartney's request, a piano was moved into one of their suites, and this is where they created some of the songs that would feature on the *Hard Day's Night* album later that year. In Paris they also made a new single, "Can't Buy Me Love," recorded at a local studio.

It was at the George V that a telegram arrived with the news that "I Want to Hold Your Hand" was number one in America. On February 7 the Beatles flew to New York to be introduced properly. McCartney was pessimistic, at least outwardly. "They've got their own groups," he said on the plane over. "What are we going to give them that they don't already have?" He may have been thinking of the Beach Boys, a group of Californian brothers who sang about surfing and cars and who had their first US top ten hit in the spring of 1963. In some ways the Beach Boys were like the Beatles: they had no obvious front man and wrote their own songs. Like the Beatles, they blended rock and roll with doo-wop and girl groups, putting even more emphasis on vocal harmony.

The Beatles landed at the newly renamed JFK Airport, to be met by a sea of fans. They were amazed but went straight to a press conference at which they were their usual, cheerfully insouciant selves. (Q: "How do you account for your success?" John: "Good press agent." Q: "What do you think of Beethoven?" Ringo: "Great. Especially his poems.") They were asked a *lot* of questions about hair; it is positively odd to see quite how obsessed male journalists were by it. From there, they were driven to the Plaza Hotel, in Cadillacs. On the car radio they listened to live commentary on their journey. Inside the hotel they watched themselves on television and read about themselves in the newspaper. There is footage, filmed by a documentary crew, of the group in their suite, meeting the press. The Beatles are amused by the length of the film crew's microphone and McCartney insists that the cameraman turn his lens on it. "Go *on*," he says, smilingly, "defy convention!" From the moment that McCartney stepped up to the microphone on Ed Sullivan's show and sang "Close your eyes . . . ," every pop act in America was flailing in the Beatles' wake. By April, the first five positions on the US pop chart were occupied by the group from England.

The Beatles returned to the UK in triumph toward the end of February. The months that follow are a blur of implausible productivity. In their first week back they recorded much of what would become the *Hard Day's Night* soundtrack and LP: the first Beatles album to include only original songs. Then they spent six weeks in London shooting the film. Lennon published a book of his poetry and sketches, which he called, at Paul's suggestion, *In His Own Write*. There is something delicious about a third-person title being suggested by a second person who co-created the first person's sensibility. *In His Own Write* is full of the verbal rigmarole that Lennon and McCartney loved, a riot of Edward Lear and Spike Milligan and playground slang. A pop star publishing a book of poems was yet another first for the press to come to terms with. Lennon was hailed as "the literary Beatle," a title he savored. The book included the phrase "a hard day's night" (said to have been coined by Ringo), and this replaced the working title of the film, *Beatlemania*, to general relief.

The film's producer asked Lennon and McCartney if they could write a song of the same name to open and close the movie. John, determined to beat Paul to the A side of the next single, came up with one more or less immediately. "A Hard Day's Night" has two parts. The verse ("It's been a hard day's night . . .") is sung by John; the middle eight ("When I'm home . . .") by Paul; they share the first-person narration. Like many John songs, the melody of the verse is horizontal and straight-ahead. Sung over a hard-charging rhythm, it sounds like someone driving, eyes on the road, determined to get home. It's only when Paul comes in on a high harmony ("But when I get home to you . . .") that the singer remembers *why* he's traveling—to see the person who makes everything all right. The moment that Paul launches into the middle eight is one of the most exciting in all of the Beatles' music. The song becomes, emphatically, a celebration rather than a complaint, and the group becomes, emphatically, a group. It's as if Paul (or John and Paul's joint subjectivity) is saying, *Wait a minute, let's revel in that thought about home. Isn't it* good, *feeling her holding you tight?* John's and Paul's voices dovetail thrillingly. After the repeat of Paul's section, John overlaps him with a hoarsely sensual *hmm* to start the last verse, showing the tenderness that lay just beneath his hard-man front. The track fades out on a dazed, arpeggiated version of the opening chord, a beautiful touch, designed as a kind of fade-in to the action of the movie.

After a monthlong vacation, the Beatles embarked on a global tour that included nearly three weeks in Australia and New Zealand. On the other side of the world they were greeted like gods. In Adelaide, a city of half a million inhabitants, 250,000 people turned out to cheer their motorcade from the airport. The Beatles made the most of the sexual opportunities that presented themselves everywhere they went. Lennon later compared the Beatles' aftershow scene to *Fellini Satyricon*, a Bacchanalian riot of depravity. No sex scenes were featured in *A Hard Day's Night*. Despite the avidity with which they pursued sex in private, the Beatles did not project sexuality as overtly as their heroes Elvis and Gene Vincent, or Mick Jagger of the Rolling Stones. It is not that the Beatles had to suppress their sexual side in public; it's that they never could take themselves seriously as objects of lust. They knew that their performances incited desire, but like so much else about stardom, they found the idea of being sex symbols essentially comic.

The director, Richard Lester, and his screenwriter, Alun Owen, were tuned in to the Beatles' sensibility, and created a movie that was several levels above the usual vehicles for teen idols, which the Beatles had been keen to avoid. (Throughout, nobody utters the words "the Beatles.") After spending three days with the band on tour in Ireland and London, Owen was struck by how much their existence was confined to hotel rooms and cars. He proposed a film about the Beatles as "prisoners of success." The movie riffs on this theme with wit and verve. The dialogue is funny and self-aware, playing with the clichés of Hollywood musicals ("Why don't we do the show right here?" says Lennon). The musical performances, however, are sincere and free of clowning. The movie captured the double nature of the band's public image: the way the Beatles poked fun at themselves yet also took themselves seriously. They were kidding and they really, really meant it.

The best-known scene comes toward the end, and contains no dialogue. To a soundtrack of "Can't Buy Me Love," the four Beatles escape from a TV studio and run out into a field where they clown and dance and spin around like children as the camera chases dizzily after them. It is an exhilarating release from the stuffiness of small rooms and train carriages, the joyless spaces of adult life. The childhood freedoms of friends and bodies and music were what the Beatles had sought since they were teenagers. That was why they turned their faces against school, against offices, against lorries and shop floors. But they now found themselves drawn into a different kind of confinement, days regimented almost to the minute, amid constant demands to feed the machine. In an interview, McCartney likened being in the music industry to working in a factory. Lennon, in particular, was finding his new life tougher to cope with than was apparent from the outside. It wasn't just the constriction; it was having to play a part. In interviews, at receptions, and even at private parties, he was expected to be "Beatle John," and it had reached the stage where he wondered who he really was.

McCartney's sense of himself was rooted in the home he grew up in and a childhood that teemed with aunts and uncles and cousins. Lennon didn't have that kind of psychological ballast. At Mendips and at Julia's he had been at home without ever quite feeling at home. He was friendly with his half siblings, and his schoolmate gang, but he had very few intimates outside of the Beatles. There was Cynthia, but it was hard for him to sustain his bond with her or to develop one with Julian, because he was away so much. His letters to Cynthia, sent from foreign cities, are full of love for both of them. But he was never faithful, and when he did live with Cynthia and Julian for brief periods in their rented flat, his mood was erratic, sometimes playful and caring, other times irritable and distant.

Being with Paul in a hotel room, strumming a guitar, or hanging out with all the Beatles—that was a kind of home. Of the thirteen originals on *A Hard Day's Night*, nine are originated by John (George sings "I'm Happy Just to Dance with You," written by John). Lennon's songs on the album are full of anger at women ("You Can't Do That") and self-pity ("I'll Cry Instead"). Yet they do not *sound* as bitter or truculent as the lyrics might suggest. Filtered through the group, John's negativity is subsumed into some deeper sense of gladness for being alive. On the page, "Tell Me Why" is a furious accusation of betrayal (it sounds like it is directed, consciously or otherwise, at Julia: "Tell me why you cried and why you lied to me"). To the ear, it is utterly joyous.

A Hard Day's Night also shows the extent to which John's self-expression is supported and inflected by Paul. The two partners often swap the lead vocal, and Paul's voice features prominently on John's tracks—particularly on "If I Fell." In some ways this is one of John's most Paul-like songs: classic in form, melodically expansive. Its introductory verse is typical of the pre-rock-and-roll songs that Paul loved and John cherished, too, albeit covertly. The intro isn't just ornamental; it shapes the mood and meaning of the whole song. From the moment John sings the title phrase and the opening question ("Would you promise to be true?"), a lurching chord change makes us uncertain where we stand within the song's harmonic world. John's voice leaps up ("and help *me* . . .") to a note that's so high in his register that he almost breaks on it, before coming back gracefully down the scale, via each syllable of "understand." The intro to "If I Fell" makes us *feel* Lennon's uncertainty as well as hear it in his words. Falling in love, it shows us, starts with falling.

At the end of the intro, John says he's been in love before and now knows it to be "more than just holding hands." (Throughout the Beatles' career, and beyond, both John and Paul would often use their own songs as emotional shorthand.) As John sings that phrase we exit the intro, and the song finds its harmonic footing, in the sunshine of a major key: the home key. The song goes soaring over the rooftops ("If I give myself . . ."), and now the singer is no longer alone: Paul has joined in, taking the melody, while John sings a lower harmony. "If I Fell" becomes a duet. As the writer and musician Jonathan Gould points out, John's and Paul's vocal lines do not move in parallel, like a couple holding hands, but perform an intricate courtship dance, moving apart and then closer again as the song unfolds, like birds weaving in and out of each other's flight path, alternately shielding and leading the other. There's a heart-piercing moment after the word "pain," sung over the dominant major chord, which then shifts to its parallel minor ("and I . . ."). It feels like defiance dissolving into vulnerability, as the singer confesses to fear that his love will be unreturned.

The subtlety of Lennon and McCartney's harmonizing was a little dumbfounding to musicologists. Toward the end of 1963, the classical music critic William Mann wrote an essay for the London *Times* that anatomized their songs through the lens of music theory. It has been much mocked, since it is dense with technical terms like "aeolian cadence," and blind to much of what made the Beatles' music powerful—its sonic world, its rhythms and timbres. But at a time when barely anybody took pop music seriously, Mann's piece was visionary. He recognized that Lennon and McCartney, though unschooled, were nonetheless operating at a high level of musical sophistication. He also saw that they were doing things intuitively that conventionally educated composers would not have tried. "One gets the impression," wrote Mann, eyebrows almost visibly raised, "that they think simultaneously of harmony and melody." What did Mann mean by that? Conventionally, a composer thinks in terms of a leading melodic line and a supporting one, but Lennon and McCartney composed music in which both melodies are of equal status. On "If I Fell," it's the interplay between the two voices that creates the song's meanings and emotions. John sounds uncertain, hurt, and vulnerable, Paul hopeful, yearning, romantic; together, they sound everything at once.

McCartney later stated, "Sometimes the harmony that I was writing in sympathy to John's melody would take over and become a stronger melody. Suddenly a piebald rabbit came out of the hat!" Accidentally, though not coincidentally, this is a beautiful description of the Lennon-McCartney relationship. At different times, each partner would become its dominant voice, while the other receded; occasionally they were in perfect unison.

> *If I give my*—both rise
> *heart*—John rises, Paul falls
> *to you*—Paul rises, John falls
> *I must be sure*—in unison

Just as the sound of a singing voice can be modulated and sometimes transformed by another, each partner was influencing, almost creating, the other's personality and sensibility as they went along. The interweaving also created a third part, a separate entity. This is Paul's rabbit out of a hat, neither black nor white but piebald: a magical creature.

10   I DON'T WANT TO SPOIL THE PARTY

A Hard Day's Night definitively fulfilled Brian Epstein's pre-
diction: the Beatles were bigger than Elvis. In August 1964,
the Beatles returned to America for a hectic monthlong tour of
thirty-two concerts in twenty-four cities, to build on the movie's
spectacular success. Touring was beginning to feel rather routine.
They would arrive in a town, take a press conference, play an
increasingly perfunctory set to thirty thousand screaming teenagers, escape in a car to their hotel, and hit the road in the morning. This relentless schedule was finally starting to take its toll on
Lennon and McCartney's output. "Material's becoming a hell of
a problem," Lennon told a reporter.

The most creatively significant moment of the US tour took
place in a New York hotel suite, where they met the singer they
had been listening to since the beginning of the year. Bob Dylan
was by now a star in both America and Britain. For his part, he
had quickly perceived that there was more to the Beatles' sound
than met the ear. "They were doing things nobody was doing," he
later said. "Their chords were outrageous, just outrageous, and
their harmonies made it all valid." As college students acclaimed
him for providing a serious alternative to the teenybopper Beatles,

Dylan started writing love songs and experimenting with a poppier, group-based sound. Still, he was not the type to openly admire a contemporary, and his first meeting with the Beatles was somewhat cagey. It relaxed a little after he introduced them to marijuana.

That the Beatles got stoned for the first time together courtesy of Bob Dylan is historically piquant and somewhat surprising, given that pot smoking was hardly unknown among British musicians and club-goers. The Beatles had gobbled Preludin pills in Hamburg but had so far drawn a line at recreational drugs, as opposed to drugs that helped them to work. Now all four of them embraced pot. It came along at the right time for Lennon and McCartney, who were struggling to keep the grind of touring from deadening their inspiration. When everyone in the world wanted a piece of the Beatles, pot became the park into which they could all escape. It intensified their tendency to communicate with one another on an exclusive wavelength, and soon became as important to John and Paul's songwriting as the pills had been to performing.

After returning from America in late September, the Beatles managed to record six original songs, adding to two they'd recorded before the trip. Then they had to go on the road again, on a British tour. With no time to write a full quota of new songs, they recorded a bunch of cover versions for the new album, which they decided to call, rather pointedly, *Beatles for Sale* (there was already no question who was in charge of album naming and design). The ironic distance that the Beatles had maintained from their fame now darkened into something more downbeat, evident in the cynical joke of the album's title, and the cover photograph, shot by Robert Freeman in Hyde Park. Pale and weary, the Beatles stare back at their audience through foliage, like deer caught in a hunter's sights. After a movie that presented them as almost cartoon-like figures, it served as a reminder that at the heart of Beatlemania were four human beings.

The songs they chose to cover were not by soul or girl-group artists but by their earlier, original influences: Buddy Holly, Chuck Berry, Little Richard. This was probably because they knew those songs so well that they were easy to do quickly, and indeed most were knocked out in one or two takes.

But there was also a sense of reaching back to a time when they were free to do whatever they wanted: to the childhood of the group. Among the original songs, the dominant styles are country, folk, and rockabilly. Bob Dylan's influence is apparent. John, in particular, took from Dylan the idea that he wasn't just an expert craftsman but an artist: someone who consciously communicated feelings and ideas to the world. For him, that didn't mean protest songs, but writing more personally.

Whereas the previous two albums had kicked off with a blast of positive energy, the first three tracks on *Beatles for Sale* are brooding and reproachful, at least lyrically. John's opener, "No Reply," tells a story of romantic betrayal and jealousy. It's sung with Paul, in Everly Brothers mode. The economy of narration, the imagery (the love object peeping from her lit window), and the sheer drama that the Beatles wring from moments like "I nearly died" show how fast they were progressing as songwriters and arrangers. It's followed by two more Lennon songs that supercharge the strain of self-pity in country and western music: "I'm a Loser" and "Baby's in Black."

"I Don't Want to Spoil the Party," the twelfth track on the album, is in the same vein. Lennon later described it as "very personal." Although he enjoyed being the center of attention and making people laugh, John didn't have Paul's natural ease with people who weren't already close friends. Like the narrator of the song, struggling to hide his unhappiness, John leaned on alcohol to mask his social discomfort, and when drunk, he could become boorish and provocative. This created difficult, sometimes chaotic situations, from which Paul had to extract or save him. The "legendary" Hamburg stories of Lennon doing mad things while drunk no doubt bury many occasions when his inebriation was merely sordid or embarrassing. This dynamic carried over into their days of fame, most notably in the ugliest incident of the Beatles' career, which took place the year before.

✲

Toward the end of April 1963, Lennon went on an eleven-day holiday with Brian Epstein to Barcelona—the one he informed Cynthia about at the hospital. It's not clear why he chose to go with Brian rather than staying with Cynthia and Julian ("what a bastard I was," said John in 1970, recalling this), or why, if he was determined to go away with friends, he didn't go with Paul, George, and Ringo, who all went to Tenerife. His decision may have been about consolidating his status as the Beatle who was closest to the manager. That was Paul's theory: "John was a smart cookie. Brian was gay, and John saw his opportunity to impress upon Mr. Epstein who was the boss of the group."

John was curious about Epstein's sexuality and perhaps his own. Years later, he said, "We used to sit in a cafe in Torremolinos looking at all the boys and I'd say, 'Do you like that one, do you like this one?'" According to his friend from childhood, Pete Shotton, Lennon confessed to having had a sexual encounter with Brian on the trip. John told Pete, when they met in Liverpool shortly after the holiday, that Brian said that he didn't want to have penetrative sex with him: "I'd really just like to touch you, John." (This has given rise to a whole theory about "I Want to Hold Your Hand," by the way.) Shotton also reported that Lennon was very worried, after the holiday, about rumors he and Brian had had an affair. Lennon said so himself, in 1970: "It was terrible. Very embarrassing," he told the editor of *Rolling Stone*, Jann Wenner. On June 18 his anxiety, or shame, erupted into violence at Paul's twenty-first birthday party.

☥

A pop star might have been expected to hold a glittering party in London. McCartney held his in the back garden of Aunty Gin's house, on Dinas Lane in Huyton. His father and brother, uncles, aunts, and cousins were there, together with his new girlfriend, Jane Asher, the other Beatles and their partners, and a few other pop stars, including the Merseybeat singer Billy J. Kramer, and two of the Shadows, who were playing a summer show in nearby Blackpool. So was Bob Wooler, loyal promoter of the Beatles in their pre-fame days.

When John arrived at the party with Cynthia, he was already drunk. At some point, he became enraged by a joke that Wooler made about Lennon's holiday with Brian. Whatever the joke was, it's unlikely to have been malicious; Wooler was not a malicious man. It may have been as light as referring to John's return from his "honeymoon" in Spain. Yet Lennon attacked

Wooler in a blind fury, punching him and kicking him on the ground until he was pulled away. (According to Billy J. Kramer, Lennon also assaulted a young woman who was part of a group of guests standing outside.) An appalled Cynthia dragged Lennon away from the party. Wooler was rushed to hospital.

The next day, John was terrified he had destroyed the group's career. His most immediate fear was that Wooler would die, a concern that was not unreasonable, though he did recover. The Beatles had to be in London the next day to perform in front of a live audience for a BBC radio show. One can only imagine the atmosphere between John and Paul: John scared and ashamed, Paul furious at him for spoiling his party, both too hungover to confront it directly. The four-song set opened with "Some Other Guy," an R&B cover that John and Paul sing in unison. It's a blistering performance.

Epstein went into action, enjoining Lennon to send a telegram to Wooler. Sent two days after the incident, it read: REALLY SORRY BOB TERRIBLY WORRIED TO REALISE WHAT I HAD DONE STOP WHAT MORE CAN I SAY? Wooler was paid £200 and dissuaded from suing for assault. The group's press officer, Tony Barrow, took a proactive approach, feeding a version of the story to the *Daily Mirror*, along with a suitably regretful quote from Lennon. The *Mirror* ran Barrow's story, and nothing more was heard about it.

"I must have been frightened of the fag in me to get so angry," John said of the incident, speaking in 1971. Lennon was, in his observed behavior, vigorously heterosexual, but it seems he sometimes felt an attraction to men that he didn't know how to process, like one of the violent dockers that Epstein used to pick up at night. Indeed, Lennon's assault on Wooler, a gay man, might be seen as a delayed and displaced assault on Epstein. There's also a more prosaic reason for Lennon to unleash his fury on Wooler. Wooler was friendly with Epstein, and John probably blamed Wooler for spreading the rumors about him. It's likely that Lennon turned up at the party *already* simmering with anger, and that Wooler's remark, whatever it was, was merely the trigger. John didn't relish parties or family gatherings the way Paul did. In his mind, the success of the Beatles was down to the choice that he and Paul had made to break with ordinary life; to acknowledge that the two of them were of a different, superior species. Playing the part of the good lad who had done well for himself made him feel fraudulent. So he drank and drank, nurturing a secret desire to spoil the party.

In general, we've underestimated the extent to which Lennon's mental instability created problems for those around him. In other circumstances his membership in a professional band simply wouldn't have been viable. The group stayed together because John was brilliant but also because everyone close to him recognized it was the band that was keeping him together. John wasn't derailed by the rock and roll lifestyle, but saved by it. Paul understood this better than anyone.

☿

The Beatles' last single of 1964 was "I Feel Fine." It was not on *Beatles for Sale*, and would have sounded almost comically out of place on it. Inside its two and a quarter minutes, it's pretty much impossible *not* to feel fine. A Lennon-initiated song, to which McCartney seems to have contributed the bridge, it was recorded on the same day in October as many of the covers from *Beatles for Sale*.* "I Feel Fine" was another big step forward. It was built around a guitar riff Lennon adapted from a 1961 R&B song by Bobby Parker called "Watch Your Step." The Beatles had barely used riffs—repeated lead guitar figures, which act as a focal point for the song. But Lennon, perhaps inspired by the Kinks, had got interested in using them for singles. The riffs he created were sinuous and melodic, a very different flavor to the Kinks' "You Really Got Me." The riff of "I Feel Fine" snakes through three different chords. Ringo provided a Latin-style beat borrowed from Ray Charles's "What'd I Say" and John sang simple words ("Baby's good to me . . . you know"), stringing them along a characteristically flat, bluesy melody line. George doubles up the riff. The resulting groove is irresistible. On the bridge, John, Paul, and George sing "I'm so glad" in Technicolor harmony and it feels like the sun coming out. It seems odd that while he was writing "I'm

---

* In a sign of how at ease the Beatles felt in the studio now, the finished track begins with a whine of feedback, the first time such a noise was deliberately featured on a record. It was the result of a plugged-in acoustic guitar being propped up against a live amp; they liked how it sounded.

a Loser," "No Reply," and "I Don't Want to Spoil the Party," John should create a song that feels as weightless as sunshine, but it was really the flipside of the self-doubt and alienation those songs describe. John was truly happy only when making music with the other Beatles.

Even in Lennon's downbeat songs, the mood was consistently leavened by McCartney's singing and playing. It's often in the bridge or middle eight that Paul asserts his optimism, as on "A Hard Day's Night." The Beatles used middle eights to evoke new perspectives; to show the song's narrator a way out of his predicament. In the middle section of "No Reply," the heartbroken singer issues an admonishment to the girl that's really a pep talk to himself; a reminder that the only reason he feels so bad is because he loves so hard.

One of the most spectacular moments in the Beatles' entire repertoire comes in "I Don't Want to Spoil the Party." The middle eight is repeated twice so that it's almost a chorus. The singer is feeling miserable because the girl he loves isn't at the party. Out of the dark minor-key verses springs a suddenly hopeful major-key passage in which the singer anticipates feeling *glad* to be reunited with her. McCartney's high vocal line becomes so prominent that he effectively takes over the story. The section culminates in a drawn-out, jointly delivered declaration: "I . . . STILL . . . *LOVE* . . . HER!"

11   TICKET TO RIDE

"Ticket to Ride" resembles a stoned "I Feel Fine." Like that track, it is based on a guitar riff. When we first hear it, it sounds straightforwardly sunny. But then the drums enter like a roll of thunder and a disjointed beat, rather than giving flight to the riff, drags it back. The song hangs on its opening chord for slightly longer than is comfortable as a droning bass roots us to the spot. When Lennon begins to sing, he sounds weary, rueful, dazed: "I *think* I'm gonna be sad . . ."

The Beatles had never sounded like this before. Nobody had. "Ticket to Ride" was born from a mélange of influences without sounding much like any of them: the drum pattern has a similarity to the one on "Be My Baby" by the Ronettes (and "Cathy's Clown" by the Everly Brothers); the long hang on the tonic chord sounds like "Dancing in the Street" by Martha and the Vandellas; John's mood of bemused hurt sounds a little like the Dylan of "I Don't Believe You." It was longer (the first Beatles single to exceed three minutes), heavier, and stranger than anything they had done before, yet felt utterly immediate. "Ticket to Ride" is a masterpiece: a complex emotional statement that is also a killer pop song.

John had written several songs featuring women who betray and abandon him. This time, his anger is submerged into the song's booming, marshy soundscape. Paul lights up key phrases with his high harmonies ("I think it's *today*, yeah"). On the middle section, the stuttering, hesitant beat suddenly becomes a tambourine-fueled canter, as the singer (John and Paul in harmony) tries to work up some resolve: the girl ought to "think twice" and "do right by me." But he doesn't really sound like he believes it. In fact he, or they, sounds sympathetic to the girl's need to be free. A whole new section begins on the fade-out (an innovation suggested by McCartney). Over a rockabilly beat, Lennon repeats, "My baby *don't care*," and by now, his tone is almost admiring, like he's waving goodbye to this liberated girl as she rides away on a mystery train.

"Ticket to Ride" is a Lennon idea, a Lennon and McCartney song, and a McCartney production. John later claimed the song as almost entirely his, but it was Paul who suggested to Ringo that broken drum pattern, so crucial to the feel of the track. It's Paul's bass that creates its doomy undertow. It's Paul's backing vocal that electrifies the melody. It's also Paul who plays lead guitar, including the anguished, bluesy fill that joins the bridge to the verse.

At this point, Lennon was the more prolific song originator. Paul had written big hits, but he exerted much of his influence through John's songs. John sometimes made decisive musical contributions to Paul's songs—for instance, his rhythm guitar triplets on "All My Loving"—but less often. This isn't because John cared less about Paul's songs; it's because John was more likely to take partially worked-out songs to Paul and the others, and then flesh them out in collaboration. His ideas were platforms for the creativity of the group. McCartney's ideas tended to be more fully formed, which left less scope for Lennon and the others. He had the ability to hear a song—melody and counterpoint, key changes and instrumentation—in his head, like an aural hallucination, together with a clear idea of how to make it real in the studio. Paul was also an instrumental all-rounder and the most accomplished musician in the group. As his confidence in his abilities rose, he began taking a greater share of the group's creative decisions. This wasn't yet a source of tension with Lennon, since John was taking the lead on so many tracks.

"Ticket to Ride" was the first song the group worked on when they met in February 1965, to begin recording tracks for their new film, *Help!* Once the song was finished, it was instantly agreed on as the next single. In April, it went straight to number one in the UK. That same month, the Beatles recorded their next single. They had just returned from filming on location in the Bahamas and the Austrian Alps. Together with Richard Lester, who was directing again, they settled on *Help!* as the name of the film; it sounded like a pop-art speech bubble. Lennon, as he had done with *A Hard Day's Night*, and eager to continue his run of singles, seized the opportunity to write the title song.

While the movie's title might have been a joke, Lennon took it as a cue for a song about the perilous state of his mental health. "I *meant* it," he declared, in 1970. In 1980, he said, "It was me singing 'help . . .' You see the movie: he—I—is very fat, very insecure, and he's completely lost himself." John talked a lot about his being fat around this time; he wasn't, really, except perhaps by comparison with the others. John felt uncomfortable with his marriage and with fatherhood, and worried about how long he could sustain his creative hot streak. He relied on his bandmates, Paul in particular, to ease his mind. One of the Beatles' aides told the journalist Phyllis Battelle, who spent three days with the group on location in the Bahamas, "Lennon needs the others to bring him out of his moodiness. The one who does it best is Paul." The wife of a film crew member said: "Paul and John have a way of tuning out the others. When they're 'on' George and Ringo sometimes sort of wander away." (Battelle said she had observed this, too.)

Supported by Paul and the others, Lennon had the wherewithal to turn his anxieties into great music. He wrote "Help!" as a ballad but was persuaded, as with "Please Please Me," that it would work better speeded up. John later said he regretted this decision, but a song that could have been lachrymose gained a compellingly frantic urgency. Lennon's literate lyrics ("self-assured," "independence vanished in the haze," "I've changed my mind, and opened up the doors"—the latter a reference to drugs and to Aldous Huxley) might have sounded self-conscious in a slow song; in the context of high-energy pop they sounded excitingly different.

"Help!" was the first Beatles single that is not obviously a love song. Who is the "you" John is asking for help from? Even more than usual, the backing vocals are crucial to the song. They are arranged in a countermelody, contributed by Paul. As John's lead vocal virtually reaches out and grabs the listener by the shoulders, Paul and George *anticipate* him, telepathically, singing the start of each of his phrases before he does. The emotional effect is of a man who's able to be honest about his anxieties because he knows that his friends are listening.

☯

The film *Help!* did not live up to *A Hard Day's Night*. It lacked the latter's delicate balance of irony and sincerity, and the Beatles' performances are not as convincing, not least because they were all stoned. Still, there is at least one enduring visual idea in it. We see the Beatles going home to adjoining houses in a suburban terrace. Once we're taken inside we realize that the houses are all joined up into one residence. The notion that the Beatles were an inseparable gang was central to the band's public image. It worked so well because it was true. Fame only pushed this already tight group further together. At parties full of dignitaries and celebrities they would congregate in the bathroom to smoke a joint.

The movie's fantasy of a group of friends who lived together in suburban bliss was almost literally the case. In the summer of 1964, after years of staying in rented flats, John and Cynthia Lennon made a home in Weybridge, a suburb in Surrey from where besuited bankers and accountants commuted to London. The Lennons acquired a mock-Tudor mansion, with more than twenty rooms, called Kenwood. It was a place to escape the capital's hothouse and raise their son away from swarms of fans and journalists, and the kind of upwardly mobile move of which Aunt Mimi would have approved, as indeed she did. Still, John felt uneasy about leaving London. In 1965 he told an interviewer: "I really wanted to live in London but I wouldn't risk it."

He was keen the other Beatles be near him. George had already moved into a bungalow called Kinfauns, a short drive away. Ringo and his family moved into another mock-Tudor house, less than a mile from John's. Only Paul held out. He loved being part of the Asher family and was energized by

London's social and artistic scenes. The decision wasn't taken lightly. Paul said later, "I talked to the others about it since, and we both—we've all decided that it would be silly for me to buy a house in Weybridge that I wasn't keen on, just to, sort of, go along with the whole thing." Paul said he was happy to drive to Surrey to see John. John learned to drive; he passed his driving test on the same day that the band recorded "Ticket to Ride" and bought a top-of-the-range Rolls-Royce (he was a terrible driver and soon hired a chauffeur). Inevitably, however, he began to worry that he was out of touch, not just with London, but also with his principal creative partner.

"Ticket to Ride" glints with meanings; you can walk around it forever and see different shafts of light bouncing off its surfaces. It's about a breakup, viewed through a haze of pot smoke. It's about a generational shift in the balance of power between men and women. It's about a shift in the balance of power between John and Paul, as John comes to suspect that Paul doesn't rely on him quite as much as he relies on Paul.

12   YESTERDAY

Paul awoke late in his bedroom at the top of the Asher house one morning with a tune running around his head. He wondered what it was. It didn't sound like something he would have written, but like some wistful jazz melody from his childhood, something his father used to play: "Stairway to Paradise," "Lullaby of the Leaves." He went straight to the piano in his room:

> I just fell out of bed, found out what key I had dreamed it in, and it seemed near G, and I played it. I said to myself: I wonder what it is, you know. I just couldn't figure it out at all, because I'd just woken up. And I got a couple of chords to it. I got the G, then I got the nice F sharp minor seventh, that was the big waaaahhhh. That led very naturally to the B which led very naturally to the E minor. It just sort of kept tumbling out with those chords. I thought: well this is very nice, but it's a nick, it's a nick [from another song].

Paul played it to John, who did not recognize it. He played it on the piano at a party at the home of the singer Alma Cogan, a pop star since the early 1950s. Cogan liked the song but did not recognize it. At one point, her mother walked in and asked if anyone would like some scrambled eggs, and McCartney instantly worked this suggestion into a scratch lyric: "Scrambled eggs / Oh my baby how I love your legs." He hummed it to Lionel Bart, the composer of *Oliver!* Bart did not recognize it. McCartney played the song to his old English teacher, Alan Durband, on a visit to his home. Durband didn't recognize it. Paul eventually came to believe that he had, in fact, written the tune. Still, he kept it to one side, almost as if he was scared of it.

In April 1965, the Beatles spent four weeks at Twickenham Studios in west London shooting scenes from *Help!* There was a piano on one of the stages, which the director, Richard Lester, remembered McCartney sitting at between shoots: "He was playing this 'Scrambled Eggs' all the time. It got to the point where I said to him, 'If you play that bloody song any longer I'll have the piano taken off stage. Either finish it or give up!'"

Immediately after the shoot for *Help!* was completed, on May 27, 1965, McCartney flew to Portugal with Jane Asher for a holiday. They were borrowing a villa owned by the Shadows' guitarist, Bruce Welch. During a long cab ride from the airport, Asher fell asleep, and when McCartney closed his eyes, the problem of the song's words returned to him. During this half-awake state he hit upon the idea of starting each verse with a single, three-syllable word—*yesterday*, *suddenly*. On arrival at the villa, he asked Welch, about to leave for home, for a guitar. He sang the whole song to him (having turned the guitar upside down). Welch admired the song's unusual chord progression. McCartney said he needed to polish up the words. He finished it during his stay.

The origin story of "Yesterday" is often told as an example of divine inspiration, because it came to McCartney in a dream. But it is also an example of what the science writer Steven Johnson calls a "slow hunch": an idea that takes its time to ripen and requires a lot of work to realize. For all that Paul and John liked to knock off hit songs within two or three hours, they sometimes sweated over them. In 1964, John told a reporter, "And if we don't like a number we've written we damned soon start knocking it about until we've got it right and we can say that we DO like it. We've had one on the go for four months and have only just got it so we like it." (We don't know which song he was referring to.) The long gestation of "Yesterday" was related to McCartney's uncertainty over whether it was suitable for the Beatles. It felt a very long way from rock and roll. He offered it to Marianne Faithfull, but she didn't get around to recording it until later.* It's not clear at which point it was decided that the song should be a Beatles track, but on June 14, 1965, McCartney took it to the second set of recording sessions for the *Help!* album. He played it to John, George, and Ringo, who approved, but didn't think it required them to play on it. "Yesterday" would be a Beatles song with only one Beatle on it.

George Martin suggested a string section, which made McCartney nervous: "Are you *kidding*? The Beatles is a rock n' roll group!" he remembered saying. But in truth McCartney had never seen the Beatles as just a rock and roll group, and he was happy to let Martin persuade him. When they sat down at the piano and Martin ran him through the string voicing he had in mind, McCartney suggested only one change, that the cello play a bluesy E flat after the second time he sings "she wouldn't say." Martin later acknowledged how well McCartney's suggestion worked: "I wish it had been me. John Lennon fell in love with that particular sound when he first heard it."

Ⓟ

In the first year or so of their professional songwriting partnership, Lennon and McCartney shared a joint creative personality as Beatles, albeit with different inflections. From 1964 onward they began to evolve more distinct songwriting styles. John's was quickest to develop. Taking cues from Dylan, he became introspective, literate, self-lacerating, and sometimes other-lacerating in song.

Paul's songwriting personality had been relatively simple: sheer exuberance and joy in being alive, allied to a romantic, reflective side. In 1965 he began to expand his range of expression. Musically, he ransacked the vast store of styles that he had been absorbing ever since he was small, while

---

* Since 1963, Paul and John had been shopping songs to other artists; a McCartney song called "Love of the Loved" went to Cilla Black.

taking on new ones from the flourishing of pop and rock that was happening all around, as well as from more recondite sources—avant-garde music and modern art. He kept improving his technical abilities.

Crucially, he found a wider range of emotional expression, too, and here his principal influence was his partner. You can hear this on a track from the *Help!* album: "The Night Before." Until now, we haven't heard *Paul* upset, wounded, and accusing girls of lying to him. But now he is, supported by John and George on backing vocals ("Ahh—the *night before*"). He's using a different physical voice, too: more chest-driven, forceful, masculine. He wouldn't always use it: he was molding his voice to the song, something he would specialize in, as he began trying on new styles and sentiments. On another *Help!* track, "Another Girl," he finds a new girlfriend who will love him "till the end" and "always be my friend." But instead of singing to her, he addresses the girl he's leaving behind—who he's totally over, of course—to let her know how happy he is: another Lennonesque twist. It features a bluesy, buzzing lead guitar, which Paul recorded the next day after deciding George's previous effort wasn't what he wanted.

By mid-1965, then, McCartney's mature artistic talent was trembling on the launchpad. If we could pinpoint a day it takes off, it would be that Monday, June 14, session, the first day of the last week of recording sessions to complete the *Help!* album, before the band goes to Paris to start a European tour. The Beatles convene at Abbey Road in the afternoon, and go to work on three Paul songs. The first is "I've Just Seen a Face," a country-style song based on a tune that Paul developed at the piano at Wimpole Street, which became a particular favorite of Aunty Gin—it was briefly called "Aunty Gin's Theme." "I've Just Seen a Face" starts with a trail of braided triplets on acoustic guitar that seem to be taking us somewhere, but then we're plunged into the gallop of the song itself, a song about being taken by surprise. The melody and the words trip over themselves in a breathless enactment of love at first sight. When the singer runs out of words halfway through a stanza, he sings the rest of the line wordlessly; the effect isn't of someone forgetting the words but forgetting themselves. The chorus ("falling, yes I am falling . . .") is happy and wistful at the same time, as if the singer is already nostalgic for the moment he's experiencing.

The Beatles crack it in only six takes, then move on to "I'm Down," which would become the B side of the "Help!" single. It's hard to imagine a more extreme switch of mood. McCartney wrote "I'm Down" as an alternative show-closer to his rendition of "Long Tall Sally," and it is clearly a Little Richard homage. But instead of trying to emulate his idol's gleeful sexual innuendo, McCartney makes it about himself—or a version of himself, modulated through Lennon. "I'm Down" is indignant and reproachful and somehow touchingly vulnerable. Paul's vocal has such furious, ragged energy that it borders on a nervous breakdown. John and George affirm the opening statement ("I'm *really* down"), but then interject in a way that suggests they're part of the singer's consciousness: "How can you laugh . . . ," they ask, and Paul finishes the question: ". . . when you know I'm down?" John's Hammond organ and George's guitar are both wonderfully unhinged. Ringo makes it a controlled explosion.

After it's done (in seven takes), the Beatles disperse. Later in the evening, Paul returns to Abbey Road to record "Yesterday." As the sole Beatle performing on the track, he is the only one needed, but he seems to have been joined by at least one other (there is an outtake of him in the studio, explaining to either George or John that the song is played with the guitar tuned down a full step). He does two takes, before going to meet Jane Asher at a bar in Kensington, the day's work done.

Three songs, in three wildly divergent styles and moods, each sung with total command. After June 14, it must have become apparent to both John and Paul that McCartney was operating at a new level.

⚐

The closer you look at "Yesterday," the odder it gets. Let's start here: what happens when you try to sing it? Unless you have practiced it, this tune that you think you know so well will evade you. That is because it is a more unusual song than it seems. When McCartney woke up that morning in Wimpole Street, he didn't only have a tune in his head, but a whole harmonic world. It has echoes of American jazz standards but there is also something premodern about it, as if McCartney had tapped into an underground river of English songs flowing from John Dowland. The musicologist Wilfrid Mellers described "Yesterday" as a "small miracle." It was also admired by the British composer Peter Maxwell Davies, a specialist in early music; when he picked it on *Desert Island Discs*, the BBC radio show, he remarked on how harmonically strange it is. Its opening melody line is seven bars long; conventionally, it would be eight, and that's what the ear expects. McCartney cuts a bar out and lands too soon on "Suddenly . . . ," making you feel the singer's disorientation. There is a childlike quality to "Yesterday"; Mellers described its tone as one of "frail bewilderment."

Later, and partly because of the success of "Yesterday," McCartney gained a reputation for sentimentality, yet his execution of "Yesterday" is deliberately unsentimental. His choice of briskly strummed acoustic guitar, rather than piano, was the first in a series of decisions designed to avoid any hint of mawkishness. When the string quartet recruited by George Martin came to the studio, McCartney insisted they play with minimal vibrato. Vocally, his tone is more Northern folk than crooner, phrasing clipped to the point of brusqueness, hinting at emotions that lie too deep for tears. What are those emotions? Regret, obviously, but also grief. She has left and he has no idea why, except that it must be his fault.

The question of where "Yesterday" fitted into the Beatles' output remained an awkward one. George Martin suggested to Epstein that it should be released as a McCartney solo record, but Epstein refused. So "Yesterday" ended up as just an album track on *Help!* (It was recorded too late to make the movie.) On August 1 the Beatles played in a Blackpool theater for a live TV broadcast, to promote the album. They performed six songs and the penultimate one was "Yesterday." This involved some awkward stagecraft. After finishing "Ticket to Ride," George Harrison stepped up to the microphone as John left the stage. He said, "We'd like to do something now that we've never, ever done before . . . And so, for Paul McCartney of Liverpool, opportunity knocks!" (a mischievous allusion to a popular TV talent show). Harrison scampered off and Paul sang "Yesterday" alone with his guitar, on a darkened stage, under the spotlight, with accompaniment from a string orchestra in the pit. The audience was hushed. It was the first time the song had been heard in public. When McCartney finished, the lights came up and the other Beatles returned. Lennon carried a bouquet of flowers. He jokingly handed the stems to Paul, before saying, "Thank you, Ringo, that was wonderful."

In mid-August the Beatles went on another North American tour. They played fewer cities but bigger venues—bigger than anyone had ever played: sports stadiums and arenas. Provided with inadequate amplification, they could barely hear themselves over the screaming. At Shea Stadium in New York they played to more than fifty-five thousand fans, a new record. The concert was filmed for a documentary. The Beatles close the set with "I'm Down," during which, wreathed in sweat and grins, they all go totally nuts. John laughs maniacally and plays the organ solo with his elbows. Paul laughs and pirouettes and belts out his song. The Beatles look as though they think it's all insane and glorious, a collective fever dream in which they have enlisted the whole wide world. Years later, when Lennon bumped into the show's promoter, Sid Bernstein, he said, "Sid, at Shea Stadium, I saw the top of the mountain."

The Beatles did not play "Yesterday" on that tour and it did not receive much radio play or attention in Britain. It almost passed into Beatles history as an interesting anomaly ("I think we all regarded it as a filler on the *Help!* album," said McCartney, later). Then the Americans intervened. Capitol, the Beatles' North American record label, was owned by EMI but acted independently of it. In Britain, the Beatles, together with Martin, had taken artistic control over their output ever since the success of "Please Please Me," deciding what went on the albums and which tracks would be singles. Capitol had its own ideas, putting out different versions of the albums with different titles, and sometimes choosing different singles. This was infuriating for the Beatles and Epstein, but they had no legal recourse. Now Capitol decided that "Yesterday" would be a single, and released it in mid-September. It sold a million copies in its first week, reached number one on the *Billboard* chart and stayed there for four weeks.

The cover versions started immediately. Matt Monro gave it the easy listening treatment it invited. He was followed by countless others, many from genres other than rock and pop, including jazz (Sarah Vaughan, 1966), more easy listening (Perry Como, 1966, and Frank Sinatra, 1969), and country (Tammy Wynette, 1968). Two of the best versions were by Black artists who were direct inspirations to the Beatles: Ray Charles (1967) and Marvin Gaye (1969). "Yesterday" was received as a striking departure from the Beatles' previous work. No pop group had made a record like this before. It affected the Beatles' image in two significant ways. First, it was taken as proof that they were "real" musicians rather than teenage sensations. Second, it marked a moment when the individual musical personalities of Lennon and McCartney became more apparent to critics, and to fans. It began a process of public differentiation in which McCartney came to be regarded as the sentimental balladeer, Lennon the abrasive rocker.

"Yesterday" brought Lennon's run of singles to an end and contributed to the internal shift in the group's balance of power. It was a huge hit in the US, their biggest market ("Ticket to Ride" had reached number one but fared less well than previous singles). This aggravated John's insecurity that he was losing his creative primacy within the group, which was bound up with a fear that his partner didn't need him. "Yesterday" began to make it seem like Paul was the star—and if he was the star, he could do without the group. As Paul put it later, "The old bugbear had come back," meaning the unwritten rule that neither John nor Paul should step out and assume the role of front man. In 1965, Paul was certainly not about to demand top billing, or go solo, but his rise in status made John uncomfortable. McCartney: "I got up to his level . . . We grew to be equals. It made him insecure. He always was, really."

John would make mildly snide remarks about "Yesterday" repeatedly in years to come. After the breakup of the Beatles, he worked it into the lyrics of his solo songs, most notably in his bitterest attack on McCartney, "How Do You Sleep?" When asked about "Yesterday" in 1980, he said, "Beautiful—and I never wished I'd written it." He criticized its lyrics: "You don't know what happened—she left and he wishes it was yesterday . . . it doesn't really resolve."

"Yesterday" played into an emotional fault line in the Lennon-McCartney relationship. Although John liked to present himself as a rock and roll purist, Paul knew better:

> One of his favourite songs was "Girl of My Dreams" [a hit for Bing Crosby and Perry Como]. And he loved "Little White Lies" [a 1930s song that was a hit for Betty Johnson in 1957]. He also went on to write the lullaby "Goodnight," which Ringo sang. That side of John he'd never dare show, except in very rare moments.

Music, for John and Paul, was never just about music, though we could invert that: for them almost everything was understood through music. McCartney associated Lennon's secret love of "granny music" with the tender, loving man who lived inside the tough, sardonic one.

If John scorned old-fashioned ballads it was because they were tied to his own desperate need for love. If he tried to cut Paul down to size now and then, it was because he feared Paul might not need him anymore. There are reports of the two of them rowing loudly during this period. This was not so much a sign of the relationship's deterioration as of its vitality, the best evidence for which is the music they made together over the years to come. "Yesterday" was a decisive victory for McCartney's conviction that the Beatles should play in any musical field they liked, however far from rock and roll. Whatever Lennon's fears, it didn't lead Paul seriously to consider a solo career; rather, it boosted his conviction that he could make the Beatles even better than they were. He asserted his musical ideas even more strongly than before. For all that he was confident of his talents, taking such creative leadership must have been a little scary, too. If Paul was cautious about developing "Yesterday," that's because it represented superpowers—his own.

13   WE CAN WORK IT OUT

The Beatles' phenomenal success finally led EMI to accept that if they wanted studio time, they should get it. Until now, Abbey Road, like all the major recording studios, had been run like a factory, the aim being to maximize output, with producers, engineers, and arrangers trained to work at speed. Studio time was booked in blocks of three hours, deemed enough time to record a single and its B side. These strictures were now relaxed for the Beatles, who were allowed to use the studio as an R&D department rather than just a manufacturing facility. This enabled them to explore the potential of four-track recording machines, introduced to Abbey Road at the end of 1963. Multitrack recording meant the band didn't have to perform everything "live" but could record their parts separately. These could then be individually manipulated, and rerecorded when necessary, creating many new possibilities. It meant less emphasis on the moment of performance and more opportunity to dwell on details. It was easier to add instruments from outside the group's repertoire, like the flutes on Lennon's "You've Got to Hide Your Love Away."

Within the group, this change played to McCartney's strengths in particular, since he was both the most dexterous and versatile musician—able to add parts on guitar, bass, or keyboard—and the most relentless. One of the first fruits of the new regime was a McCartney-originated song called "We Can Work It Out." The Beatles took nearly eleven hours of studio time, on two different days, to record it, the most time they had taken to complete any one track. The song also marked a new phase in Lennon and McCartney's songwriting: one in which John and Paul put their differences to work.

"We Can Work It Out" was inspired, at least in part, by Paul's arguments with Jane Asher. Paul wrote love songs for Jane—"Things We Said Today" was written on holiday with her—but she was a muse to McCartney in several ways. She was more into classical music than pop, spurring McCartney to show her that pop needn't be as simple as she imagined—that it could convey the nuanced sentiments of "Things We Said Today" or accommodate a string quartet. McCartney was a romantic; Jane less so. On a TV game show, she was asked if she believed in love at first sight and said no ("So she doesn't like the Beatle," purred Zsa Zsa Gabor; Jane was unamused). You can think of "I've Just Seen a Face" as McCartney's playful case for romance, in all its dippiness.

McCartney and Asher were both willful and had plenty of heated arguments. Asher was not an easy person to flatter, seduce, or persuade, which was partly why McCartney, used to having his way, was so compelled by her. She put her acting career at the center of her life, rather than him, something he found hard to accept (in "And I Love Her," a ballad he wrote while living with the Ashers, he declares his love will never die "as long as I have you near me," an ominously conditional clause). "Wait," written in early 1965, is a minor-key plea to a lover to be there for him when he returns from a long trip. McCartney was serially unfaithful to Asher when he was on tour, and also when she was away. We don't know how much, if at all, she knew about this, as she's never spoken about her relationship with McCartney. But there's a delicate acknowledgment of his infidelities in "Wait": "I'll be good, *as good as I can be.*"

If "We Can Work It Out" is about Jane, it's also about John. In common with other McCartney-initiated songs from the same year, like "Tell

Me What You See" and "You Won't See Me," the verse of "We Can Work It Out" evokes a tense, eyeball-to-eyeball dialogue. Paul took his unfinished song to John for completion (interesting in itself, since he was not usually short on ideas for middle eights). When he played "We Can Work It Out" to John, it's hard to imagine that they weren't put in mind of their own relationship. "We Can Work It Out" does sound a little more like an address to a working partner than a lover: *get it straight or say good night.* Lennon contributed a middle section that uses the phrase "my friend."

John's voice is prominent in this section, which has the effect of making the song a dialogue with two different perspectives. Listeners have tended to interpret the two parts according to a simple model of each partner's personality: Paul's section is optimistic, John's pessimistic. Lennon himself said this, in 1980: "You've got Paul writing 'we can work it out, we can work it out,' real optimistic, y'know, and me impatient: 'Life is very short and there's no time for fussing and fighting my friend.'" But it's actually Paul who sounds more impatient. Does he have to keep on talking until he can't go on? He keeps asking the other to see things *his* way, without suggesting he will return the courtesy. The subtext is that "we can work it out if you'll just agree with me." There's even a threat: we might fall apart. The bright major key, Ringo's propulsive beat, and the casualness of McCartney's delivery prevent the verse from sounding negative, although the suspended chord adds tension, as does the seasick harmonium. Lennon responds to McCartney by swooping up to take an aerial view, gazing down at the petty conflicts of everyday life. Paul has noted that relationships do not always last; John points out that life itself is finite. In the rhythm of his words as much as in what he says, John suggests that Paul slow down and stop obsessing over everything.

The two halves of the song fit together musically thanks to Harrison's brilliantly inventive idea of returning to McCartney's verse from Lennon's section by way of a dreamlike, German-flavored waltz. The slower tempo is anticipated, or led, by Lennon's stresses, which put the brakes on: fuss-*sing*, fight-*ting*.

"We Can Work It Out" invites us to look at life in two opposing ways and believe in both: let's solve every problem we can; let's not worry about what we can't control. The Beatles were able to communicate a philosophical dialectic inside a three-minute pop song because John and Paul were developing distinct individual worldviews and pitting them against each other in their work.

⊛

LSD was already influencing the Beatles' music in 1965, not directly, but through the effect that it had on John and Paul's relationship. Lennon first tried acid with Harrison, Cynthia, and Harrison's girlfriend, Pattie Boyd, in the spring of 1965, without choosing to. They were attending a dinner at the home of Lennon's fashionable dentist, who thought it would be cute to spike their coffee with it. Freaked out, the friends piled into George's Mini Cooper and drove to a nightclub (yes, this story could not be any more 1960s). At the club, they sank into a collective reverie, which continued back at George's home in Esher. For John and George, the episode was profoundly stirring. "In ten minutes I lived a thousand years," said George.

John and George took the drug again at the party the group hosted in Los Angeles, on Benedict Canyon Drive, in August 1965. They invited the others to join them. "John and I had decided that Paul and Ringo had to have acid," Harrison said, "because we couldn't relate to them anymore . . . acid had changed us so much." Ringo agreed, but McCartney resisted. He said he'd heard "It alters your life and you can never think in the same way again. I think John was rather excited by this prospect, but I was rather frightened by it." He worried he would "never get back home again." Lennon and Harrison were frustrated by McCartney's refusal, which represented a breach of the internal group norm that they should all be on the same wavelength.

The divide over LSD increased a sense of distance between Paul and the other Beatles. Between professional engagements, Lennon, Harrison, and Starr spent downtime in their suburban cocoon. McCartney, in central London, was in perpetual motion, going to gigs, galleries, and movies, and making friends. The NEMS publicist Tony Barrow told a journalist:

> Paul is now leading a very organised life. The other three don't
> know what they're doing. They wait for others to tell them. But

Paul always knows—you ring him up and he will say, "No, not Thursday, I am dining at eight. Not Friday, because I have got to see a man about a painting. But Saturday's okay . . ." Out of all of them, he has developed the most.

When John saw Paul it was usually to work, according to Cynthia: "The time they spent working together was intense, and when it was over they needed to let off steam and relax apart. John spent less of his free time with Paul than with either of the others."

Pot had a positive influence on John overall, not least because it substituted for alcohol, which brought out the worst in him. He became less aggressive, less angry, more reflective; in short, he mellowed. But pot, and, more infrequently at first, LSD, also exacerbated his predilection for doing little unless he had to. We can imagine Paul turning up at Kenwood, full of plans, asking Lennon whether he had any new material, or whether he'd been lying on the sofa watching TV for three days. We can also imagine John telling him to light a joint and stop fussing. The Abbey Road engineer Norman Smith recalled that, around this time, "the clash between John and Paul was becoming obvious." This highly productive conflict accelerated the already fast artistic development of the partnership and the group. Evidence for this is the remarkable output of their October to November sessions: sixteen tracks that make up a double-A-side single and the *Rubber Soul* album (in Europe, anyway; in America, Capitol released a different version, which included tracks from the *Help!* sessions). The Beatles were undergoing another phase shift.

Rubber Soul's drugs are pot, Dylan, and Motown. The album's punning title was chosen out of mild embarrassment that the group was drawing on contemporary Black R&B and soul (the term "plastic soul" was current; Paul can be heard using it jokingly after an outtake of "I'm Down"). But what's striking about *Rubber Soul* is how much the results sound like nobody else. McCartney's songs showcase his ever-expanding range of styles and emotional palette. The album opener, "Drive My Car," is a delirious, funny, Motown-ish slice of dance pop, propelled by a riff on which McCartney and

Harrison double up. It features a female protagonist (who else at this time would think of asking a girl what she wanted to *be*?) and embodies the spirit of McCartney's London life, fizzing with random encounters with creative, busy, hungry people. In "Michelle," a very early McCartney song that he revived and refurbished, he plays the part of a French chanteuse. The chords and melody show McCartney at his most musically sophisticated. Lennon, inspired by Nina Simone's "I Put a Spell on You," suggested the cry of "I love you, I love you, I love you" for the middle section, which makes "Michelle" heartfelt as well as pretty.

McCartney's darker songs are about the frustration of trying to communicate or connect with someone. In "You Won't See Me" he complains he "can't get through" to someone who is refusing to give him the time or attention he deserves. In "I'm Looking Through You," McCartney fully inhabits his emergent, Lennon-influenced persona. You can hear Dylan, too, in its mingling of hurt pride with imperious contempt, his gruff vocal delivery perfectly calibrated to the song. "You've changed," he repeats, as if processing the fact that Asher was no longer the ingénue he met (insofar as she ever was). But the song is really about how *he* has changed. He has "learned the game" yet his lover still thinks of him the *same old way*. You were once above me, he says, but *not today*. This makes sense in the context of McCartney's relationship with a woman from a higher social class. It can also be read as a demand that Lennon recognize the majesty of his unfurling talent. McCartney was coming into his own, as an adult and as an artist, and demanding to be seen.

At the same time as the Beatles recorded "We Can Work It Out," John brought "Day Tripper" to the group, a sunny song that refers obliquely to people who only dabble in drugs without committing to a change of mindset. He hadn't admitted publicly to taking LSD, but he was hinting at it in his songs, perhaps to signal he was hip to the emerging counterculture. The increasing abstraction and allusiveness of Lennon's lyrics might have been a way to protect his privacy (in "Norwegian Wood" he sings about an affair by transforming it into a kind of fable), but it was more than that. He was using words to communicate feelings that can't be clearly articulated.

Lennon's songs from this period don't have the blood and thunder of earlier albums. He doesn't complain about betrayal (save for "Run for Your Life," an Elvis pastiche that he doesn't really seem to have his heart in). In fact, John's contributions to *Rubber Soul* are, for the most part, mellower than Paul's. "Girl," "The Word," "Nowhere Man," "Norwegian Wood," and "In My Life" are rueful, playful, ironic, and tender. They are full of strange, inspired ideas: the insidious, awkwardly beautiful melody of "Norwegian Wood"; the decision not to continue the vocal line after the one-word refrain of "Girl," but to simply breathe in. A combination of pot-induced dreaming, a desire to best Dylan, and a need to keep up with Paul was bringing out the best in John.

Lennon and McCartney continued to tap the vein of creativity established by "We Can Work It Out": turning their personal differences into arguments about life. "Nowhere Man" is often interpreted as John chiding himself to shake off his torpor, but it can also be taken as a sly rebuke to busy people— the people who tell you to stop wasting your life. When Lennon tells "Nowhere Man" he doesn't know what he's missing, we shouldn't assume he means the thrills of London's social scene; he could mean the riches of the mind, as explored from the couch. The ambiguity about where life really is—out there, or in here—is what gives the track its resonance.

Rubber Soul might seem like an explicable advance in retrospect, even an inevitable one. But it's almost incomprehensible. The Beatles spent fifteen days in the studio, between other engagements, making their new album and its accompanying single. That was longer than other artists were taking and it was the longest the Beatles had spent on one, yet it's a fraction of the time it takes to record most modern albums, and frankly, it's just not enough time to do what they did. *Rubber Soul* includes the Beatles' first songs not in the mode of romantic love (other than "Help!"), and songs that are about love but in new ways. They used a sitar brought to the studio by Harrison; a harmonium to underlie "We Can Work It Out"; tape manipulation to make familiar instruments sound strange: a sped-up piano that sounds like a harpsichord; a fuzz bass layered over a bass guitar. Above all, though, it's the harmonies, two- and three-part, that make *Rubber Soul* float on air: harmonies painstakingly worked out in all the time they didn't have. There were some signs of strain. John and Paul struggled to finish a full quota of songs. Sessions booked at the end of October were used for mixing because of a lack of new material. Both Lennon ("What Goes On") and McCartney ("Michelle") retrieved songs they'd written years before. "Wait" had been intended for the *Help!* album. At one point, they allowed the engineer Norman Smith to pitch a song to them. But this evidence of fallibility just deepens the mystery of what they achieved.

When *Rubber Soul* came out, the reviews were positive but, to our eyes, almost comically inadequate to the task of capturing how impressive it is. The *NME* deemed it "altogether a good album with plenty of tracks you'll want to hear again and again." "Norwegian Wood" was a "folksy-sounding bit of fun by John"; "In My Life" was "a slow song, with a beat . . . Song tells of reminiscences of life." It is hard for us, looking back, to grasp just how much the Beatles had to invent a whole new category of music in order to be seen for what they were. They were at a huge disadvantage to everyone who came after them, since they didn't have the example of the Beatles to follow. Even by 1965, they only had a small community of like-minded peers: the Rolling Stones, the Who, the Beach Boys, Dylan. They were the biggest act in the country, and an anomaly. The bestselling single of 1965 was "Tears" by the comedian Ken Dodd, which could have come from the 1950s. Other top hundred bestsellers included ersatz folk ("I'll Never Find Another You," the Seekers, number two), instrumentals ("Zorba's Dance" by an Italian bouzouki player, a possible inspiration for the guitar solo on "Girl," number forty-one), country ("King of the Road" by Roger Miller, number eighteen) and pre-Beatles pop ("The Minute You're Gone" by the durable Cliff Richard, number nineteen). Beatles records were loved by fans and admired by similarly minded musicians, but poorly understood by the media and the entertainment industry.

In no time at all, the Beatles had transformed themselves from performers who made LPs to recording artists who worked with sound to make album-length artistic statements. It took a long time for critics, used to analyzing music in terms of structures and words, if at all, to grasp how important was the unique *noise* they made. As much as John and Paul loved songs, they were always entranced by the sounds of the records they adored: the guitars and the drums and the voice as much as the chords, melody, or lyrics. Lennon recalled what it was like to hear "Heartbreak Hotel" for the first time:

> I could hardly make out what was being said . . . we'd never heard American voices sing like that, they'd always sung like Sinatra, or enunciated very well. Suddenly there's this sort of hillbilly hiccup on tape echo and all this bluesy background going on, and we didn't know what the hell Presley was singing about, or Little Richard, or Chuck Berry . . . to us it just sounded like a noise that was great.

Once in the recording studio themselves, he and Paul set about making noises that were great. The deepest truth and greatest beauty of a Beatles song is found in Paul's bass, John's and George's guitars, Ringo's drumming; in the ensemble and the arrangements; in technological innovations and happy accidents; in the wash of sound achieved by Martin and his engineers; and in the grains of the Beatles' voices.

"We Can Work It Out" became, appropriately enough, the subject of a disagreement. John wrote "Day Tripper" specifically to be a single, but "We Can Work It Out" was immediately recognized as a potential hit. Lennon argued strongly for "Day Tripper." He wanted to showcase the rockier side of the Beatles at a time when they were facing serious competition from the Rolling Stones. Unsettled by "Yesterday," he may also have wanted to reassert his dominance over the Beatles' singles. In the end, they made the single a double A side—the first ever. In the US *Billboard* Hot 100 (which measured popularity by radio airplay as well as retail sales), "We Can Work It Out" reached number one, while "Day Tripper" peaked at number five, two weeks later.

14   IN MY LIFE

Given the many songs they wrote, and the fluidity of their process, it's surprising that Lennon and McCartney didn't disagree more on who wrote what. In their post-Beatles interviews, there are only two or three songs about which they had definite and conflicting recollections. The best-known example is "In My Life." In 2019, computer scientists used a machine-learning program to determine, at least to their satisfaction, that the song's primary author is Lennon. But "In My Life" is a problem that exposes the limits of binary intelligence.

There isn't any disagreement over who conceived "In My Life" or wrote its words: Lennon. The song started as a set of lyrics without music, unusual for both Lennon and McCartney. John's initial idea was to write about the bus journey from Aunt Mimi's house into town. The result was a rather literal itinerary of a journey to Penny Lane, via Church Road, past the old tram sheds and the site of the Dockers' Umbrella (an overhead railway, dismantled in 1956), on the number five bus. John realized, as all writers must, that his first draft was terrible, and rewrote it, weeding out all the specific references and making it more about his feelings for these places. He wanted to match his partner's success with "Yesterday" and write a song with lyrics into which anyone could pour their own lives.

The disagreement comes over how John's words were set to music. Lennon says that McCartney came up with the middle section, where the melody points downward in symmetry to the verse ("Though these places have their moments . . ."). But McCartney recalls writing the entire melody, and the chiming guitar riff that opens the song. He recounted a visit to Kenwood, where John showed him his lyrics:

> My recollection, I think, is at variance with John's. I said, "Well, you haven't got a tune, let me just go and work on it." And I went down to the half-landing, where John had a Mellotron, and I sat there and put together a tune based in my mind on Smokey Robinson and the Miracles . . . I tried to keep it melodic but a bit bluesy, with the minors and little harmonies . . . So it was John's original inspiration, I think my melody, I think my guitar riff. I don't want to be categorical about this, but that's my recollection . . .

McCartney's language is painstakingly diplomatic, almost mandarin. I tend to believe his story, since it is so detailed. Lennon's memory is detailed, too, but only when he talks about writing the lyrics, and though he was happy to take credit for the melody, he never made direct claim to it. The expansive tune does sound more typical of McCartney, although the chord changes are ones Lennon often used. In a sense they were so far inside each other's musical mind that it doesn't matter. Paul knew that Smokey Robinson was one of John's favorites, which is why he had Smokey in mind when he sat down at the Mellotron (an electric keyboard) or picked up a guitar (the riff is similar to one on the Miracles' track "My Girl Has Gone," known to have been part of George Harrison's singles collection at the time). John was learning from Paul about how to write a ballad; Paul was writing a tune he knew John would love to sing. Somewhere between the two of them, "In My Life" emerged.

It was a given that if a pop act discovered a winning formula, it should be repeated. The Beatles did not agree, which made them a puzzle. It was also a given that pop fame was ephemeral. At every press conference, the Beatles were asked, "When will the bubble burst?," and while they casually batted it away, it was hard to ignore. For John and Paul, their songwriting partnership represented a sustainable future. Since journalists did not have the vocabulary or critical apparatus to conceptualize the Beatles' music, McCartney made it his mission to explain to others, and perhaps to himself, what he and John were up to. In November 1965, shortly before the release of *Rubber Soul*, he gave a long interview to a small magazine called *London Life*, in which he made clear the extent of their artistic ambitions.

McCartney, at this time, was a man with his mind on fire. He consumed cultural and intellectual stimulation like a jet plane guzzling fuel. His London circle included the Ashers, the countercultural entrepreneur Barry Miles, the art dealer Robert Fraser, John Dunbar and his wife, Marianne Faithfull, and Tara Browne, a twenty-year-old aristocrat who threw extravagant parties. In the *London Life* interview, Paul refers to Dylan and the Who but also to Handel, the painter Francis Bacon, the playwrights John Osborne and Eugene O'Neill, the actors Tom Courtenay and Albert Finney, and the poet Robert Graves. He said he identified with what Graves said about the imperative of creativity: "I write poems because I damn well must."

In the wake of "Yesterday," McCartney was increasingly willing to draw a contrast between himself and John as individual songwriters. To *London Life*, he said, "Mine are normally a bit soppier than John's. That's because I'm a bit soppier than John." Around the same time, he told another interviewer, "John doesn't like to show he's sentimental. I don't mind." This became a theme of McCartney's commentary on the partnership for years. There is some truth in it. On *Rubber Soul*, McCartney had "Michelle," which instantly became very popular. But he also had "I'm Looking Through You." And John was perfectly capable of writing emotionally sincere love songs, as he noted later on, citing "If I Fell" and "In My Life." Both of those and "Nowhere Man" use a particular chord change that had an emotional significance for John in particular—a melting transition from major IV to minor

IV (in "In My Life" it falls on the second line of the verses: for example, on "no one" in "There is no one compares with you." The minor IV then recurs, to great effect, on the elongated "my life" of the title phrase). That change derives from pre-rock-and-roll traditions: it was, famously, used by Cole Porter in "Ev'ry Time We Say Goodbye." It's also in "Till There Was You." You might call it soppy.

Paul's self-deprecation was partly a call to John to locate his own soppiness and partly a way of diminishing himself in public so that his partner felt strong. He knew that he was winning the musical argument (explicit or otherwise) over how far from rock and roll the group should be prepared to go—Paul's answer being very far indeed.

☙

Before Christmas 1965, Granada Television broadcast a tribute to the Lennon-McCartney songwriting partnership called *The Music of Lennon & McCartney*. The Beatles performed both sides of their single "Day Tripper"/ "We Can Work It Out," but the show consisted mainly of other artists covering Lennon-McCartney songs, with the two songwriters themselves delivering scripted links. John and Paul were wary of the idea when it was proposed to them, since they did not want to be seen as putting themselves above the other Beatles, something George was already sensitive to. But they agreed to take part because the producer, Johnnie Hamp, had championed the Beatles in their early days.

The show was recorded in Manchester in early November. John and Paul took a break from the *Rubber Soul* sessions to participate. Paul invited a journalist he and John liked, named Keith Altham, to join them for lunch. The lunch turned into a freewheeling conversation over several hours, continued in the Lennon-McCartney dressing room. Despite being guest of honor on a show that featured musicians interpreting Lennon-McCartney songs, John embarked on a rant about how nobody was any good at covering Beatles tracks. "There are only about 100 people in the world who really understand what our music is all about," he said. "Ringo, George, and a few others scattered around the globe."

John went on to articulate a theory of songwriting that he and Paul had evidently discussed or at least converged on intuitively (McCartney made a similar point in an interview a few months later):

> We try to give people a feeling—they don't have to understand the music if they can just feel the emotion. This is half the reason the fans don't understand but they experience what we are trying to tell them. Lack of feeling in an emotional sense is responsible for the way some singers do our songs. They don't understand and are too old to grasp the feeling. Beatles are really the only people who can play Beatle music.

When they began songwriting together, John and Paul vaguely aspired to be the new Rodgers and Hart, but this was only for lack of precedents. Nobody longed to hear Rodgers and Hart perform "Bewitched" or "My Funny Valentine." Similarly, nobody much cared that Elvis Presley didn't write his own songs. Lennon and McCartney wrote songs for themselves to perform, first and foremost. Of course, they also believed in the song as an entity in its own right: from 1963 onward, they were giving songs to other artists, including "I Wanna Be Your Man" for the Rolling Stones. They didn't disapprove of all Beatles covers—they asked for Esther Phillips, an R&B singer, to be flown over from America for the Granada show because they loved her version of "And I Love Her." But they did not have the craftsman's detachment from his work, because they instinctively believed in Tolstoy's definition of the artistic calling: "to transmit that feeling that others may experience the same feeling."

There was a variation in emphasis between the two of them. It's not coincidental that it was Lennon who expressed such disdain for Beatles covers. He, most of all, believed in music as an extension of the self. There are few successful covers of, say, "Strawberry Fields Forever" or "Julia." McCartney was a little more circumspect about self-expression, partly because he was at least as interested in others' selves as his own, and also because he was so fascinated by songcraft—by the structure of a song as an almost physical entity, sculpted out of music and words. The five most-covered Beatles songs are all by him ("Yesterday," "Hey Jude," "Eleanor Rigby," "Michelle," "Let It Be").

But as with everything else to do with the partnership, both did both. "In My Life" is one of John's most-covered songs. He succeeded in creating a universal song that is also deeply personal. When John claimed, after the Beatles broke up, that "Yesterday" didn't "resolve," he was referring to an idea from the tradition of songcraft, that a song should wrap up at the end with an insight, like the final couplet of a sonnet. As Lennon himself showed many times, this isn't always necessary, and it can be merely trite. But he achieved it beautifully in "In My Life." The song's opening lines create an emotion of wistful nostalgia for the places and people (some dead, some living) he has known. He declares his love for them all. Then the story takes a turn. Lennon declares his love for a particular person—for "you." Memories lose their grip on him, because he has found a new kind of love, different from conventional love, which makes him better able to cope with death and decay. His affection for the past is undimmed, but his love for *this* person makes him happy to live in the present.

In interviews given after Lennon's death, McCartney repeatedly returned to the idea that his friend wore "a suit of armor"—that he hid his real self behind the bravado and the scathing wit. "The thing about John," Paul told the journalist Ray Coleman in 1994, "is that he was all upfront. Most people stayed up late and got drunk with him and thought they were seeing John. You never *saw* John! Only through a few chinks in the armour did I ever see him." He said there were "moments when I actually saw him without the facade, the armour . . . which I loved as well, like anyone else. It was a beautiful suit of armour. But it was wonderful when he let the visor down and you'd just see the John Lennon that he was frightened to reveal to the world." But McCartney rarely acknowledged his own suit of armor. This is someone of whom a close collaborator, Denny Laine of Wings, said, "He is the best person I've met in all my life at hiding his feelings." McCartney has often complained that Lennon rarely complimented him on a song, but he doesn't mention any examples of him complimenting his partner, and there are no credible third-party accounts of him doing so. McCartney sought the approval of his older, brilliant friend, without imagining that his friend might desire the same from him.

Musically, "In My Life" is a descendant of "If I Fell," and is as wrapped up in the Lennon-McCartney relationship as that song is. Many of Lennon's songs from this period—"Day Tripper," "Girl," "Norwegian Wood" (and later, "And Your Bird Can Sing")—are about someone glamorous and emotionally distant, tantalizingly out of reach. These songs are not "about" Paul directly, but they do have a flavor of his golden progress through London society as seen through the eyes of a socially awkward suburbanite. Paul needed John to trust in him—he wanted to *get through* to John, to convince him that he was committed to their partnership, and worthy of his trust. What he didn't quite see is that John wanted an acknowledgment of love, since love and trust were for him almost synonymous. Of course, neither of them could say so. In "In My Life," John told Paul just how much their shared history, and shared present, meant to him. The visor was down and I doubt Paul even noticed.

15   TOMORROW NEVER KNOWS

Paul McCartney's Christmas present to the other Beatles at the end of 1965 was a mixtape he put together at home and transferred to an acetate disc. It featured Paul doing links in the style of a New York DJ. It was, he later said, "something left-field, just for the Beatles . . . like a magazine programme full of weird interviews, experimental music, tape loops and some tracks that I knew the others hadn't heard." He titled it *Unforgettable*, after Nat King Cole's 1951 hit, the first song of the mix.

Generally, the Beatles did not sit around and discuss what kind of music they wanted to make or what their next album should be like. As George Harrison put it, "Everyone gets our records and says, 'Wonder how they thought of that?' or 'Wonder what they're planning next? . . .' But we don't plan anything . . . All we do is just keep on being ourselves. It just comes out. It's the Beatles." They didn't plot next steps partly because the next step was always in front of them, but at the end of 1965 the Beatles made it clear to Brian Epstein that they needed more time to themselves before going back to work. Epstein obliged, and after the end of their British tour in late autumn, the Beatles entered their longest period of professional inactivity so far. They had three months before starting on a new album.

The Beatles had lived more life than most people of their age—more than most people ever live—and now they were pondering what it all meant, and who they wanted to become. They might have got lost in stoned introspection. McCartney's mixtape was a way of setting a course for what came next, a gentle assertion of the leadership he had already assumed in the studio and a nudge down the road that led to *Revolver*. It was typical of him, and them, to communicate in songs and jokes rather than speech. The message was clear enough: *Let's steal from everywhere.* The tape made a significant impact. Harrison said: "John, Ringo and I played it and realized Paul was on to something new."

George's phrasing here hints at how the group now functioned. John, George, and Ringo were in and out of one another's houses on a daily basis. Paul lived in London, where he had his own set of friends and acquaintances. After George married Pattie in January 1966, only Paul remained unmarried. Unlike John and Ringo, who had his first child with his wife, Maureen, in September 1965, Paul had no children. John, Ringo, and George and their partners ate together, smoked together, took acid together. Paul was a visitor, bringing news from the outside. Maureen Cleave, who wrote a penetrating series of profiles of the Beatles from this period, after spending time with each of them in turn, described Paul as "half Beatle and half not."

Looking back on this time, John said of their songwriting relationship, "It got false." Even if we don't take Lennon's retrospective narrative at face value, it's true that their sessions became less spontaneous. Paul had to drive down from London for a songwriting session, which introduced an edge of formality to a working relationship that had in previous years been seamless in its flow from personal to professional. In 1969, McCartney mused on how the end of touring had changed things: "We lived together when we played [toured] together—we were in the same hotel, up at the same time every morning . . . just as long as you're this close all day, something grows, you know. And then when you're not this close, then just physically something goes." To understand why this distancing made the partnership more, not less, creatively combustible, we need to take a closer look at what Paul and John were up to at this time.

PAUL

By early 1966, McCartney's participation in the musical, artistic, and intellectual life of London had speeded up into a whirligig that even in retrospect is hard to comprehend. The best we can do is catch glimpses of him as he whizzes around. Here are a few spaces in which we know Paul McCartney spent time during this period:

Indica Books and Gallery in Mason's Yard, Mayfair. Indica was intended as a hub for avant-garde ideas, art, and literature. It was set up by his friends Barry Miles, Peter Asher, and John Dunbar. They opened it in January. Paul threw himself into it: he helped erect bookshelves, painted the walls, designed and printed a thousand sheets of wrapping paper.

The drawing room of a house on Hasker Street, Chelsea, occupied by the philosopher and peace campaigner Bertrand Russell, then in his nineties. McCartney went to visit with Jane. They took tea and discussed the Vietnam War.

The basement of the Royal College of Music, in Kensington: a participatory music event hosted by the composer Cornelius Cardew, a disciple of John Cage. About twenty people attended. Cardew sat at the piano and tapped on its leg, or plucked one of its strings without playing any notes. Others improvised on violin, saxophone, and percussion. Transistor radios emanated static. Paul ran a coin along a radiator and tapped out beats on a beer mug. Afterward he told his companion Barry Miles, "You don't have to like something to be influenced by it."

A Cliff Richard concert.

The Scotch of St. James nightclub, where he saw a new Motown artist perform: fifteen-year-old Stevie Wonder.

A ski lodge in Klosters, Switzerland, with Jane. Here McCartney wrote "For No One," a song about a broken love affair.

John Dunbar and Marianne Faithfull's flat in Lennox Gardens, Mayfair. A frequent visitor, he smoked pot and listened to modernist jazz (Albert Ayler, Sun Ra, Ornette Coleman) and classical music (John Cage, Karlheinz Stockhausen), and jammed with other musicians.

The West London flat of the guitarist John Mayall, where he listened to American blues: B.B. King, Buddy Guy, J. B. Lenoir.

His car. Most cars did not have cassette players; Paul had one installed. Driving down to Weybridge to see John, he would listen to compilation tapes he had made.

The Italian Cultural Institute in Belgravia. A lecture given by the avant-garde Italian composer Luciano Berio, who presented his latest work, *Laborintus 2*, a collage of cut-up tapes, instruments, and voices. McCartney sought him out for conversation afterward.

A temporary studio in a flat in Montagu Square (recently vacated by Ringo) that Paul used to make demos. He shared the space with William Burroughs, who was experimenting with cut-ups—cutting tapes of electronic music at random intervals and splicing them back together. ("Nice-looking young man, fairly hardworking," said Burroughs.)

His room at the top of the Asher house, where Paul used reel-to-reel tape machines to create tape loops, combining music, found sounds, and reversed tapes. Once he'd made something he would take it to John, or use it as a soundtrack to one of Dunbar's soirées.

He was also finishing his new home, a Regency town house on Cavendish Avenue, in St. John's Wood, close to Abbey Road. He bought it the previous April and had it renovated. Paul instructed the architect to design the ground floor so that smells from the kitchen would waft into the living room, as they had at Forthlin Road. He filled it with modern art and traditional furniture ("I like it to be comfortable").

The Bayswater flat of the DJ Alan Freeman. When Paul arrived for an interview, the first thing he did was sit down at Freeman's piano, at which he stayed for half an hour, working on a song (possibly "Eleanor Rigby").

When McCartney finally talked to Freeman, he conveyed the sense of a man burning with curiosity. He slips between the Beatle "we" and "I":

We've got interested in things that just never used to occur to us.
I've got thousands, millions of new ideas myself. What I really want
to do now is to see whether I could write all the music for a film . . .
I want to read a lot more than I do. It annoys me that so many millions of books came out last year and I only read twenty of them.

He talked about how much he liked modern classical composers:

Then I play them to John and he says "What a drag! All these millions of records coming out all the time and we've not been getting
on to them." Then we rush out and buy loads of modern compositions. The only thing is to listen to everything and then make up
your mind about it.

Before and after this period, McCartney rarely spoke so expansively about
art or music. He tended to keep his musings almost defensively simple, out
of the English and particularly Liverpudlian concern not to be seen as pre-
tentious. In 1966 he didn't care about that. In an interview with Barry Miles,
he said:

With any kind of thing my aim seems to be to distort it . . . To take
a note and wreck it and see in that note what else there is in it . . .
It's all trying to create magic. It's all trying to make things happen
so that you don't know why they've happened.

In another interview he said, "I can hear a whole song in one chord. In
fact, I think you can hear a whole song in one note if you listen hard enough."
He also said, "Melodic songs are in fact quite easy to write. To write a good
song with just one note in it—like 'Long Tall Sally'—is really very hard."

JOHN

In Liverpool, John had been the one at the cultural cutting edge, talking
surrealism and existentialism with Stuart and other art-school friends. John

now observed Paul's hectic social life with amusement and a little envy. He was self-conscious about his relative passivity yet perversely proud of it: "I just sort of stand there and let things happen to me," he said. As Paul scoured London for inspiration, John traveled further inside his own mind, assisted by LSD. In early 1966 he took his third trip, alone at Kenwood. He became fascinated by what the drug did to his sense of self, the way it gently unraveled him. Even more than pot, LSD made John's anxieties and frustrations disappear, at least temporarily.

Maureen Cleave painted a picture of John's dreamy, almost childlike existence. Kenwood was crammed with paraphernalia and curios picked up on tour, including a gorilla suit and a (literal) suit of armor. John didn't know what day of the week it was. He ate at no particular times except when he felt like it. He did not say much to Cleave about Julian, except to mention that he was thinking about sending him to boarding school. He fretted about being out of the cultural action: "I'm dying to move into town. I'm waiting to see how Paul gets on . . ." In a 1964 interview John had talked of an ambition to buy a detached house "standing in its own grounds." That way, he said, "I can get away from everyone when I feel like it. No distractions at all. Then I think I could write more." That was what Kenwood was meant to be, but he felt distracted there, too. Cynthia describes him at home, moving restlessly among notebook, guitar, piano, and television. Paul had always been the one able to help him focus. Now that Paul was around less than he used to be, John used LSD to stimulate his mind.

Lennon owned a copy of *Man and His Symbols*, a collection of essays edited and contributed to by Carl Jung, who argued that childhood required the development of a socially adaptive persona, a mask, which the adult must cast off in order to become fully himself. The authentic self could be glimpsed in fantasies and dreams, which should be examined for hints and messages as to the true purpose of one's life. "One must surrender consciously to the power of the unconscious," wrote one of his co-authors. Jung called this the quest for "individuation." To John, this idea was very suggestive. He was impatient with his Beatle identity even though he loved being in the group. "We've never had time before to do anything but just be the

Beatles," he told Cleave. Lennon was glad not to be a *Beatle* all the time, constantly in front of an audience or a camera, but he was, if anything, more fond of being a *beatle*: part of a group of friends and collaborators, and one half of a creative partnership that stimulated him more than ever. Cleave said this of John and Paul: "Obviously, they were the most important part of the group. They were, I think, very, very fond of each other." They constantly made each other laugh, and would excitedly share discoveries. "Paul and I are very keen on this electronic music," John told another interviewer.

All of the Beatles were, paradoxically, learning to be themselves in tandem. Of the four, Lennon's need for the group may have been the greatest. He was always mercurial, oscillating between "extremes of frivolity and shyness, arrogance and humility," as the photographer Robert Freeman put it, shifts of mood that confused him as much as anyone else. Being a beatle made sense of his disjointed self; it helped him feel whole. In 1970 he recalled the night of his first LSD trip. "I did some drawings at the time," he said. "I've got them somewhere—of four faces saying, 'We all agree with you.'"

When John talked to Maureen Cleave in early 1966, he was looking for something without knowing what it was. "You see, there's something else I'm going to do, something I must do—only I don't know what it is. That's why I go round painting and taping and drawing and writing and that, because it may be one of them. All I know is, this isn't it for me." He conflated the idea of his incomplete self with the house he was in. "Weybridge won't do at all. I'm just stopping at it, like a bus stop. Bankers and stockbrokers live there . . . I think of it every day—me in my Hansel and Gretel house. I'll take my time; I'll get my real house when I know what I want."

The others seemed to know what they wanted and to be pursuing it. Ringo loved being a father and home-builder. George was burrowing ever further into Indian music and philosophy. Paul was pinballing around London. John didn't feel as paternal as Ringo, he didn't have George's capacity for single-minded obsession, and he lacked Paul's kinetic energy and gregariousness. And so, at Kenwood, under the influence of television and acid, he explored the seabed of his own mind, relying on Paul to haul him back from the depths and help him discover what he had found. Uncertainty and insecurity spurred him on—nowhere more so than in the creation of "Tomorrow Never Knows."

☿

On April 6, the Beatles returned to Abbey Road to start on the new album. Despite their long break, they, and John in particular, had relatively few songs to work with. In an interview from early March 1966, John said, "Paul and I ought to get down to writing some songs for the new LP . . . there's been too much messing 'round." There was a determination to break the boundaries of pop but not much to show for it. The paucity of output obscured a vast increase in stored energy. John had heard one of Paul's new songs, which told a story about loneliness and the end of life. John had a knack of exploding into action when put under pressure—as he had at the Indra Club when the group had to *mach Schau*, or recording "Twist and Shout"—and now, at the last minute, he conjured up a song that would become the most audacious musical statement the group had ever made.

A week or so before, John and Paul had been together in London, and they visited the Indica bookshop to forage for new thinking and new ideas. John asked Barry Miles if he had any books by "Nits-Ga." Miles eventually worked out that John meant Nietzsche. It was an autodidact's mistake. Miles found him a copy of *The Portable Nietzsche*. John continued to browse the shelves, with, we might imagine, cheeks burning a little. He picked up a copy of *The Psychedelic Experience* by Timothy Leary, sat down on a sofa, and began turning its pages. *The Psychedelic Experience* combined Jung with a popularized version of Eastern philosophy to offer a psychological and spiritual justification for LSD. Leary had been a clinical psychologist at Harvard University. In the early 1960s he discovered LSD and became a passionate advocate for it, leading, indirectly, to the termination of his university position. He now promoted what he regarded as the drug's world-changing possibilities, encouraged by conversations with Aldous Huxley. In *The Psychedelic Experience*, Leary paraphrased and glossed an ancient text, *The Tibetan Book of the Dead*, the purpose of which is to help those close to death let go of life and prepare for rebirth.

Leary presented LSD as a shortcut to transcendence of the self, the oceanic state of ego loss that Hindus and Buddhists seek to achieve via meditation. LSD users often experienced a kind of loss of self or personality, a feeling of insignificance in the vastness of the universe. In Leary's terms, it offered a glimpse into "the Void": the blissful nothingness that lies beneath everyday perceptions and emotions. John found this promise deeply appealing. He had been reflecting on the nature of consciousness since his first experience of acid in early 1965, after which he wrote "Help!" (when he sang "I've changed my mind," he didn't just mean changing his opinion). Since childhood he had been roiled and buffeted by rage, jealousy, shame—diseases from which he dearly wished to be set free.

Of course, a neurologically active drug with unknown side effects is not the same thing as millennia-old traditions of practice and meditation, and *The Psychedelic Experience* is, in reality, a mishmash of Eastern-sounding platitudes and pseudoscience. But at the Indica bookshop, sitting on that sofa, John was ready for it—and when John was ready for something, he went all in. In the days after the Indica visit, he started work on lyrics for a new song.

John saw an opportunity to prove that even if he was not an urbane cultural maven like Paul, he was still the Beatle best able to channel the culture's most radical currents. He found creative inspiration in the book's mode of address. Leary and his two co-authors wrote the book as a guide through a psychedelic trip, and *The Psychedelic Experience* has a calmly evangelistic tone, telling the reader it is going to be OK. Lennon repurposed this voice: an instructor, or guide, imparting wisdom to an anxious novice. "Whenever in doubt, turn off your mind, relax, float downstream," wrote Leary in his introduction. John virtually lifted this sentence, after its first clause, for the first line.

He did put his own stamp on it, though: he added an "and" ("*and* float downstream"). That seems like a trivial change, but as the musicologist and Beatles scholar Walter Everett points out, it turns the rhythm of the line into iambic pentameter, the main metric vehicle of English poetry and drama. Whether or not John would have named it as such is beside the point: he acquired a feel for iambic pentameter at Quarry Bank, reading Shakespeare and Milton, and in his reading of books from Aunt Mimi's shelves. It was part of his verbal muscle memory. The verses of "Tomorrow Never Knows" repeat a pattern: a line of iambic pentameter, followed by an answering phrase based on a gerund (*being, knowing, believing*), a structure that echoes and inverts the pattern of "Yesterday" (even the title is an inversion: from "yesterday" to "tomorrow"). From a handwritten manuscript of the lyrics, we can see he used the same pattern in his discarded lines. This was the first time that the Beatles had used iambic pentameter, and probably the first time it had been used in pop. In fact, it's blank verse, since it doesn't rhyme—an innovation in itself, since nearly all pop songs, including Beatles songs, used rhyme schemes.

Leary had written, "The light is the life energy . . . Do not fear it. Surrender to it . . . Beyond the restless flowing electricity of life is the ultimate reality—The Void." In the book, Leary described the Void as "unobstructed, shining." Lennon adapted some of Leary's phrases and coined his own, like "the colour of your dream." The phrase "ignorance and haste" is not in Leary's book and seems to be adapted from a proverb in the King James Bible (in an interview around this time John said how grateful he was to Aunt Mimi for sending him to Sunday school).

John took his as yet unnamed song to Paul and George Martin at a planning meeting for the new LP, held at Brian Epstein's house. Musically, it was sketchy and conceptual, more of an idea than a song. Two or three key elements were in place: the hanging on one chord, like a tambura drone (Lennon had been driving toward this for a while now: "Ticket to Ride," "The Word," and "Norwegian Wood" all dwell for an unusually long time on the root chord, as if Lennon was trying to cut away everything superfluous and decorative, Bauhaus-style); the philosophical lyrics, which were nothing like anything the Beatles had written before; and an ambition to make the song sound like the *experience* of a psychedelic trip.

Lennon and McCartney were learning how to get even more out of Martin, though they went about it in different ways. Paul, with his ability to hear everything in his head and his technical know-how, would come to Martin with a plan of action for him to execute or improve upon. Lennon was more likely to approach him with the feeling he wanted to convey: Martin recalled him saying he wanted a song "to sound like an orange." Lennon's approach was inherently collaborative. When he said that, for this track, he wanted "to sound as though I'm the Dalai Lama singing from the highest mountaintop"—disembodied and godlike—Martin was stimulated rather than merely baffled. John suggested swinging from a rope suspended above the microphone so that the clarity and volume of his singing would fluctuate accordingly. That proved impractical, but the Abbey Road engineers ran his voice through an oscillating Leslie speaker cabinet, usually used for an organ, to achieve something close to the effect he wanted.

On the first attempt at recording, the group used a heavily treated loop of drums and guitars for the backing track, combined with live drums played by Ringo. A gentle six-note melody was repeated over the beat. Even this sounded too tame, somehow. They decided to play the whole thing live, this time using an off-center drum pattern suggested to Ringo by Paul, similar to the one on "Ticket to Ride." They also introduced a series of tape loops created by McCartney. These included loops of an orchestral chord, a passage of sitar, and a Mellotron—a primitive synthesizer that replicated instrumental sounds—on its flute setting. The most striking loop was one McCartney created out of his own laughter, which he distorted until it sounded like seagulls. The finished track feels like standing in a full-force gale as the rubble of history blows by us. Lennon's voice surfs serenely above an unearthly concatenation of noises and Ringo's stuttered, pulverizing drumbeat. John commands the chaos and subdues its terrors, inviting us to consider "the meaning of within" and to play the game to "the end of the beginning," a phrase that John Winston Lennon borrowed not from Leary, but from Churchill, who had died the year before.

What they were now calling "The Void" was by far the strangest-sounding track that the Beatles, or any pop group, had ever recorded. There was no girl or boy, no verse or chorus, just a continuous flow that loops around, toggling between two chords, and fades out on the word "beginning." It brought together McCartney's experiments in sound with Lennon's desire to communicate truths about the meaning of life. It blended Indian music with Stockhausen, psychedelic philosophy with English poetry and comedy. The Beatles created it not much more than two years after their first appearance on *The Ed Sullivan Show*.

The closing section of the track features McCartney vamping away at an old piano, Goons-style. Neither Lennon nor McCartney was comfortable with unalloyed seriousness. Lennon decided that "The Void," as a title, was too "heavy." During a televised press conference in 1964, Ringo had expressed the unpredictability of the group's career by saying "tomorrow never knows"; in the footage you can see Lennon cracking up behind him. Like most of Ringo's jokes, it had its own wisdom, and John stored the phrase away. As soon as "Tomorrow Never Knows" was finished, the Beatles knew it would go last. The new album would end on its beginning.

16   ELEANOR RIGBY

In the early months of 1966, whenever McCartney sat down at a piano, wherever it was, he would start tinkering with a song he called "Miss Daisy Hawkins." From the moment he found its first five syllabic notes, the song seems to have found its themes: loneliness, futility, the end of life. McCartney was twenty-three.

Without discussing it, both John and Paul came back from their break with songs about death, written from a detached, omniscient perspective. In "Tomorrow Never Knows" John dispenses instruction from the mountaintop. In two minutes, "Eleanor Rigby" captures the entire lives of two individuals in a series of stark images. Musically, both songs are stripped down to a few parts in order to distill and intensify some essence. "Eleanor Rigby" confines itself to a narrow melodic range and the song has minimal harmonic development: like "Tomorrow Never Knows," it alternates between just two chords. Set in a minor key, its tightly wound, almost claustrophobic verse plays out over an accompaniment—a string section arranged by George Martin—that sticks close to the tonic, except when the cellos burst into a galloping run up the scale. This section is joined to a refrain in which the singer asks where all the lonely people come from while the cellos play a Bach-style descending line. Paul is joined by John and George for a second refrain—"Ah, look at all the lonely people"—in which the melody soars up before tailing off. In the final section, the two refrains come together in contrapuntal harmony. The mood throughout is tense and austere.

As a teenager, Paul used to run errands for an elderly woman in his neighborhood. He wondered what it was like to be her. In Hamburg, he befriended the old woman who ran the bathroom at the Kaiserkeller and sold pills to the customers. He was curious about those left on their own, unmoored from family. Still, it's hard to explain "Eleanor Rigby." Nobody had created a pop song like this before. Its cultural ubiquity has stopped us from noticing how strange it is—at least as radical, in its way, as "Tomorrow Never Knows," which John came up with after hearing Paul play "Eleanor Rigby." Both John and Paul were living up to Arthur Schopenhauer's definition of genius: unlike talent, which hits a target nobody else can reach, genius hits a target nobody else can see.

☙

Since Lennon became known as "the literary Beatle" McCartney's talents as a lyricist have been overlooked. His feel for words is essentially musical and sensual rather than semantic. As a boy, he drank in the ecstatic rhyming in classics like "The Honeymoon Song," one of those pre-rock-and-roll songs that he insisted be part of the Beatles' repertoire early on. In a performance of it the Beatles made at the BBC you can hear him reveling in lines like "The skies are as bright as your eyes / The horizon is open." Internal rhymes and half rhymes abound in his lyrics—little irruptions of pleasure.

As a singer, he rolls around in word-sounds like a cat in a pool of sunshine. From the reprise of the *Sgt. Pepper*'s title track: "Sergeant Pepper's *one and only lonely* hearts club band." In "Mother Nature's Son" there is the ravishing line "Swaying daisies sing a lazy song beneath the sun." McCartney's own favorite line in "Penny Lane" is about the fireman: "He likes to keep his fire engine clean / It's a clean machine" ("machine" rhyming with "clean" twice over). Walter Everett notes that McCartney knew, instinctively, how to write lines that enact their meaning in sound. In "She's Leaving Home," "She goes downstairs to the kitchen / clutching her handkerchief" conveys the snuffling of someone struggling to suppress their sobs. Like John, he loved wordplay (in "What You're Doing," he rhymed "doin'" with "blue an'[d]"; "runnin'" with "fun in"), but he rarely tried to emulate John's sophisticated vocabulary or densely surrealistic imagery. He preferred to write lyrics that seem simple on the surface but which pulsate with meanings, like the overtones surrounding a single note. He knew how to communicate an idea with almost brutal economy, as in "For No One" ("The day breaks / Your mind aches"). He also liked to be suavely witty, as in "Lovely Rita" ("When it gets dark I tow your heart away") and "Back in the USSR" ("Let me hear your balalaikas ringing out").

In "Eleanor Rigby" McCartney uses the sounds of words as connecting fibers; Everett points to how "Paul grabs a sound and hangs on to it." In the same place in each verse, we get "rice" paired with "face," "church" with "dirt"—not rhymes so much as matching colors. There is a discipline to McCartney's structure. Each line of the verse opens with a five-syllable phrase in which the fourth syllable is stressed ("Eleanor Rigby / Waits at the window / Father McKenzie / Look at him working"). These opening phrases are mirrored by the closing phrases of each line in "Tomorrow Never Knows"—you can sing "it is not dying" or "it is believing" in their place. Paul ends each line of "Eleanor Rigby" with a little commentary or question on what has preceded it—"Lives in a dream / Who is it for? / No one comes near"—similar to the God's-eye mode of "Tomorrow Never Knows." The two songs speak to each other.

In "Tomorrow Never Knows," however distant Lennon's voice sounds, the message is ultimately a soothing one. "Eleanor Rigby" offers no comfort. It turns an unflinching, even acerbic gaze on its characters. A woman picks up rice in a church, tidying up after a wedding. Oblivious to joy, she lives in a dream and wears a face that nobody sees. In the second verse, we meet Father McKenzie, writing his sermon for nobody. In the third and final verse, they are brought together without coming together. He buries her in a perfunctory ritual. Everything is concise, economical, and devastating: *no one was saved.*

Around this time, both John and Paul were dwelling on the decline of

Christianity. In Cleave's interview, John contrasted it with the rise in popularity of the Beatles, a relatively mild observation that came back to haunt
him. But in "Eleanor Rigby" Paul slid a knife into the bone. This was something of a pattern. When Lennon was outspoken, everyone noticed. Paul's
scorn and aggression were either subtly disguised, or direct but overlooked.
In his Cleave interview he described America as "a lousy country" for the
way it treated its Black citizens. In 1966 he told David Frost, "Americans
seem to believe that money is *it*" and "They believe in it all the time . . . [It's]
frightening." To Cleave, he was contemptuous of America's pretensions to
morality:

> There they were in America, all getting house-trained for adulthood
> with their indisputable principle of life: short hair equals men; long
> hair equals women. Well, we got rid of that small convention for
> them. You can't kid me the last generation were any more moral
> than we are. They hid it better.

The Beatles were due to visit America later that year. Brian Epstein was
concerned that John was being too political when he said he worried about
the war in Vietnam. McCartney blithely disparaged the moral character of
America and Americans—and nobody minded.

After *A Hard Day's Night* the Beatles had distinct personas in the minds
of the public: vividly drawn but crude cartoons. Ringo was the doleful
clown, George quiet but deep. John was the Beatle with the sharp tongue
and scathing wit, Paul the cute and charming one. The Beatles conspired to
create these masks but by 1966 they were weary of them. The year before,
the journalist Ray Coleman asked Lennon how he felt about being known as
"the cynical one." He replied:

> When I meet intelligent and hip people, I have to be on my toes
> not to disillusion them. The people who have fallen for my image
> and publicity go to Paul . . . Paul can be very cynical and much
> more biting than me when he's driven to it. 'Course, he's got more

patience. But he can carve people up in no time at all, when he's pushed. He hits the nail right on the head and doesn't beat around the bush, does Paul.

That McCartney's harsh side went unnoticed had a lot to do with how he looked. Lennon's aquiline nose and narrow eyes (often narrowed because he couldn't see far) made him *look* sharp and judgmental. McCartney's winsome eyes and neatly arranged features made him look like a baby, or a cartoon of a little girl. It was hard to believe anyone so cute could be callous. Paul was also more socially facile. This wasn't just a front—he did genuinely like people and wanted them to feel at ease. In private, though, he could be demanding of aides and associates, and blunt to the point of rudeness. Epstein, in his memoir, describes Paul as "temperamental and moody and difficult to deal with . . . he is a great one for not wishing to hear about things." Maureen Cleave highlighted his "shrivelling wit" and "critical intelligence."

In pre-fame letters and in the group's first interview, in November 1962, McCartney explicitly identified Lennon as the leader. Journalists habitually referred to Lennon as the "Chief Beatle." But if Lennon was the group's founder and figurehead, it was McCartney who propelled it forward; who taught Lennon how to play the guitar properly; who recruited George; who did the most to push Stuart out; who chased, harried, and wheedled promoters; who set the bar ever higher in the studio; who insisted that the group keep moving. Harrison told Tony Barrow that when he joined the Quarry Men in 1958, Paul already seemed to be the decision-maker: "I knew perfectly well that this was John's band and John was my hero, my idol, but from the way Paul talked he gave every indication that he was the real leader, the one who dictated what the Quarry Men would do and where they would be going as a group." Cleave described Lennon's presence as regal, comparing him to Henry VIII. We may imagine McCartney as Wolsey or Cromwell: chief diplomat or consigliere, directing affairs of state from beside the throne.

The *Hard Day's Night* personas had some truth to them: Lennon *was* scabrously witty; McCartney *did* know when to smile and charm, and he did write heartfelt love songs. But you only have to change the angle of view by an inch or so to see them very differently. For certain people, Lennon's heart swelled uncontrollably. His vituperation was the flipside of a tendency for headlong infatuation. McCartney was emotionally intense: anger, jealousy, and resentment bubbled away underneath his pleasant exterior. "Yesterday," for which McCartney gained a reputation as a romantic balladeer, is a song of despair. "Eleanor Rigby" is often described as melancholy, but there is a cold fury to it, too. You can hear Paul's latent anger at the meaninglessness of his mother's death, and at the false consolations of a religion he did not believe in. When McCartney asked Martin to give the song a "biting" string arrangement, the model they turned to was the violins in *Psycho* (1960).

Ⓟ

"Eleanor Rigby" was another of McCartney's slow hunches: it took him at least three months to write. A dinner party hosted by Cynthia and John at Kenwood proved to be a staging post on the way to its completion. After dinner, McCartney played his song on guitar to a few Beatles intimates, including John's friend Pete Shotton, and invited suggestions for how to finish it. He had the first two verses with their two characters, Eleanor Rigby and Father McKenzie (then "Father McCartney"), but hadn't yet worked out a third verse. Shotton (according to his memoir) said, "Why don't you have Eleanor Rigby dying and Father McKenzie doing the burial service for her?" At this, Lennon blurted out, "I don't think you understand what we're trying to get at, Pete." He said it with such vehemence that the gathering broke up.

Shotton's account is indirectly corroborated by a story told by Lennon in 1980 that sounds like it was about the same incident, recalled slightly differently.

> By that time, he [Paul] didn't want to ask for my help, and we were sitting around with Mal Evans [the Beatles' faithful roadie and assistant] and Neil Aspinall, so he said to us, "Hey you guys, finish up the lyrics." Now, I was there with Mal, a telephone installer who was our road manager, and Neil who was a student accountant, and I was insulted and hurt that Paul had just thrown it out in the air.

He actually meant he wanted me to do it, and of course there isn't
a line of theirs in the song because I finally went off to a room with
Paul and we finished the song.

The first verse was Paul's, he said, "and the rest are basically mine." Lennon persistently laid claim to at least half the song without much apparent
justification. In a 1970 interview, he said he'd written "a good half of the
lyrics or more"; he repeated the claim in a letter to *Melody Maker* in 1971.
In 1972 he told the journalist Ray Connolly he'd written 70 percent of the
lyrics and said the same to another journalist in 1980. Connolly, despite being sympathetic to Lennon, didn't believe him for a moment. Pete Shotton—
John's friend—said John's contribution was "virtually nil." McCartney put
it at about 20 percent.

Lennon's urge to exaggerate is understandable. As soon as the world
heard "Eleanor Rigby," it was hailed as a masterpiece, specifically for the
poetic quality of its lyrics. But *John* was meant to be the "literary Beatle."
So whenever John was at his most insecure—in the wake of the breakup,
and in 1980, when he stepped back into the limelight after several years
out of it—it became important to lay claim to "Eleanor Rigby." Note how
insulted he is by the idea that someone ordinary—a telephone installer, an
accountant—might contribute to a Lennon-McCartney song. McCartney's
willingness to accept ideas from others felt like a repudiation of his own
genius.

For years, McCartney gave a pretty detailed account of how "Eleanor
Rigby" got its name. He landed on "Eleanor" first, borrowing it from the actress Eleanor Bron, who played the female lead in *Help!* Next, he cast around
for a surname with two syllables. In February 1966 he drove down to Bristol
to see Jane Asher perform in a play, and while there he noticed a sign on a
wine merchant's storefront that read, "Rigby & Evens Ltd." So that was how
it happened. Except, in the early 1980s, somebody pointed out that there
is a gravestone in the cemetery next to St. Peter's church in Woolton, Liverpool, that bears the name Eleanor Rigby. Paul knew that church well: it
was where he first met John Lennon. He and John had walked through that

graveyard many times. When McCartney found out about this, he dismissed it, at first. Later on, he conceded that he may have subconsciously picked up the name from the gravestone. (The gravestone in question isn't even for Eleanor Rigby herself, but her grandfather; her name is farther down.) I can understand his reluctance—he knew his own story—but the idea that he coincidentally landed on the name, for a song about a woman who "died in the church," seems implausible. However deeply in his mind her name was buried, it had been saved.

17   HERE, THERE AND EVERYWHERE

My favorite pictures of John and Paul together were taken in Obertauern, Austria, the location of the skiing scenes in *Help!* On the evening of March 18, 1965, the two of them took part in an impromptu jam session in the lounge bar of their hotel, the Edelweiss. A group from Berlin called Jacky and the Strangers was the entertainment. Lennon and McCartney had supposedly met Jacky Spelter in Hamburg, and at some point Spelter invited them onto the small stage. That's about all we know, apart from what we can see, which is that John and Paul are a little drunk or high and sweatily, joyously into it. John is playing Jacky's electric guitar, Paul is on the drums.

George and Ringo had gone to bed. This was John and Paul, the Nerk Twins, as seen in Caversham. The manager of Marietta's lounge put an end to their impromptu gig. As he told a journalist later, he had booked Jacky Spelter and the Strangers, not the Beatles.

In the 1990s, McCartney told a story that seems to refer to that evening.

> I remember one of my special memories. We were in
> Obertauern, Austria, filming for *Help!* John and I shared

a room and we were taking off our heavy ski boots after a day's filming, ready to have a shower and get ready for the nice bit, the evening meal and the drinks [I find it touching that they shared a room, and that they took pleasure in each other's company—"the nice bit"]. And we were playing a cassette of our new recording and my song "Here, There and Everywhere" was on there. And I remember John saying, "You know, I probably like that better than any of the songs on my tape."

McCartney recalled it being one of the few times Lennon ever said anything nice about one of his songs. "He was not the kind of guy who would say: 'Hey, my mate's written 'Here, There and Everywhere . . .' He didn't dare let you see that nice side. So it was always rock n' roll, rock n' roll, rock n' roll . . ."

What's interesting here is that his memory is both very specific (the hotel, the boots, the tape) and flawed. "Here, There and Everywhere" was not written or recorded until the following year, 1966. Paul clearly remembers that evening in Obertauern with a special fondness, and also recalls John saying something generous about "Here, There and Everywhere," and seems to have conflated the two incidents. Whatever happened, the result is that Paul associates "Here, There and Everywhere" with the soft-hearted, generous side of his friend.

☮

Revolver splits sunlight into a rainbow. It is not just the variety of songs, sounds, and ideas that astonishes, but the way its prismatic glories cohere. That the album feels like a unified artistic statement is down to the personal bonds among the Beatles. Without having to worry about whether they could perform these songs live, or whether their fans would disappear if they didn't rush an album out, they had made space to discover themselves, and one another. On previous albums, the artwork showed the four Beatles gazing out at us, the audience. On the back cover of *Revolver*, they face one another. If John and Paul were more insecure about their relationship than previously, that was because it was more important to them than ever.

McCartney contributes the only love songs on *Revolver*, although one of them, "For No One," is about the end of love. A somber exercise in anti-sentimentalism, it features an unusual mode of address—the singer narrating his own life in the second person as if scripting a film about himself: *your* day breaks, *your* mind aches. (The idea of an aching *mind*, rather than the more conventional heart, is inspired.) The mood of despair is barely held at a distance by the second-person address. "For No One" probably arose from his difficulties with Jane Asher, although they remained a couple until 1968. Paul wrote "Here, There and Everywhere" shortly after, as if gripped by two competing visions of the relationship. Taken together they suggest an emotional extremist, closer to John in temperament than one might guess.

"Here, There and Everywhere" is very much a songwriter's song. McCartney has mentioned "Cheek to Cheek," the Irving Berlin song made famous by Fred Astaire in the film *Top Hat*, as inspiration, along with "God Only Knows," by Brian Wilson of the Beach Boys. Both songs reach for heaven. In "Cheek to Cheek," the end of the middle section and the start of the verse are indistinguishable. McCartney loved that: "It's so neat the way it just wraps itself up . . . I always thought wow, that's a great trick." (One imagines the teenage McCartney enjoying *Top Hat* on the telly at Forthlin Road while his analytical brain simultaneously crunched through its harmonic structure.) As with "Yesterday," Paul found a way of joining together the verses with the first word of each, although here the trick is more sophisticated since the three initial words are each taken from the internally rhyming title phrase, sung in full only at the end of the song. The last word of the bridge is the first word of the third verse—*everywhere*—so that melody and lyric fold seamlessly back into the body of the song.

There is something inviolable about a pop song with such a carefully patterned, self-referential structure; its completeness wards off more unsettling emotions. McCartney allows the merest hint of something darker in the middle eight, with its chromatic, sharking guitar line over a minor chord. There is a trace of desperation in the singer's plea for his lover to be here, beside him, everywhere (the way a mother is for a small child), a state of bliss Paul was very much not achieving with Jane. The feel of the track is close to Smokey Robinson and the Miracles—like John, Paul loved the ethereal beauty of Smokey's voice. McCartney achieves weightlessness with his lead vocal, singing impossibly softly. He floats inside a voluptuous envelope of doo-wop harmonies, sung by Paul, John, and George over Ringo's minimalist drumming. Structurally, the Beatles song that "Here, There and Everywhere" most resembles is "If I Fell." Like that one, it has an introductory verse, in the style of those romantic prewar songs. John might have noticed that "Here, There and Everywhere" also has a similar chord progression to "If I Fell": one that climbs, stepwise, toward the stars.

18   STRAWBERRY FIELDS FOREVER

The Beatles finished recording *Revolver* on June 22, 1966, and flew to West Germany the next day, to start a global tour. They were not happy about going back on the road. John told Maureen Cleave, "We have been Beatles as best we ever will be—these four jolly lads. But we're not those people anymore. We are old men." Touring was lucrative for them, and for a global machine of promoters, venue owners, and merchandise sellers. Brian Epstein wanted them to continue, partly because he feared he would be left without a role if they stopped. Then there were the fans, who wanted more chances to see their heroes in the flesh, even if they couldn't actually hear them. But for John, Paul, George, and Ringo, the experience of this tour would be so abysmal, and so harrowing, that it virtually made the decision to stop touring for them.

In Munich, Essen, and Hamburg, they played no songs from the new album. The set list was based on early hits, and rock and roll numbers from before they were famous. Unusually for them, their playing was erratic, their singing could be out of tune, lyrics were forgotten or fluffed. The audiences screamed everything down anyway. German police used draconian measures to control the crowds. The Beatles witnessed fans being manhandled and beaten. They answered asinine questions from the press with what good grace they could muster, which was increasingly little.

In Tokyo they were kept in virtual lockdown at the Hilton Hotel. The building crawled with police, every exit and entrance under constant surveillance. They were only allowed to leave their room at the precise moment that they needed to get a car to the concert venue. Younger Japanese welcomed the Beatles as avatars of modernity; for others the group represented a threat to civilized values. Protesters in trucks paraded banners that said "GO HOME BEATLES," while playing martial music. From Japan the Beatles flew to the Philippines, where they unwittingly caused a diplomatic storm. On the day of their two concerts in Manila, President Ferdinand Marcos and his wife, Imelda, had arranged a reception at the presidential palace, but nobody had told the Beatles, or Epstein. Officials in military uniform arrived at the hotel to summon the Beatles to the palace. "This is not a request," they said. "We have our orders." Epstein refused. The heads of police arrived. The British consulate in Manila entered a plea. The Beatles refused. They *hated* official receptions. A story began running in the local media: the Beatles had snubbed the president and first lady.

The Beatles went to the venue, a football stadium, and played two shows to eighty thousand fans. The next day, they were due to fly home via Delhi. As they waited to be picked up, they saw newspapers full of stories about the failed meeting at the palace. The staff at their hotel had turned frosty. Their security was withdrawn. At the airport, the porters refused to carry their luggage. As they struggled through a seething crowd, Marcos loyalists began shoving and hitting anyone in the Beatles' entourage. It was terrifying. When the Beatles finally made it to the plane, they kissed their seats. Epstein, in particular, was in a bad way, physically and mentally. He felt he had let the Beatles down by not taking more care over the itinerary, and he was in the early stages of glandular fever. On the flight home from Delhi, the Beatles told him that they wanted their upcoming tour of America to be their last. He took it badly.

In an interview at the airport, George Harrison said, "We'll take a couple of weeks to recuperate before we go and get beaten up by the Americans."

This proved prescient. Although the Beatles were not physically assaulted during their tour of the US, they endured a battering from the media and public more severe than anything they had ever experienced.

In his interview with Cleave, John Lennon had remarked on the decline of religion and how the Beatles might be more popular than Jesus now. His tone wasn't boastful—if anything, it was slightly wistful. In his rather haphazard fashion, Lennon had been reading and thinking about religion a lot. He had the temperament of a believer but not of a conformer, and while he had some affection for the Church he saw it as part of the past. He read a bestseller called *The Passover Plot*, a kind of nonfiction Dan Brown, which proposed a conspiracy theory about how the apostles had faked the resurrection and distorted the true message of Jesus. "Christianity will go," he said to Cleave. "It will vanish and shrink . . . We're more popular than Jesus now; I don't know which will go first—rock 'n' roll or Christianity. Jesus was all right but his disciples were thick and ordinary."

When the interview was published in London's *Evening Standard*, these remarks weren't even noticed. An American teen magazine called *Datebook* ran extracts from the interview at the invitation of Tony Barrow. *Datebook* was running a "speaking out" issue on political topics, for its young and predominantly liberal readership. Its editor, Art Unger, mailed the magazine to conservative radio DJs in the South, with the aim of sparking outrage and generating publicity for the magazine. Unger thought the DJs might bite at McCartney's remarks about America being "lousy" with racism. He put McCartney's face on the cover, next to his quote. But when a couple of DJs in Alabama read the magazine, they bypassed the McCartney quotes and snagged on Lennon's words. The DJs proposed a ritual burning of Beatles records, and the stunt was reported on by national media. Epstein, barely recovered from the last tour, was forced to fly to the US with Tony Barrow to quell the controversy. When the Beatles arrived, six days later, protests and record bans were still rumbling on. Beatles haters across the country finally had a cause to rally around. It wasn't that they found the remarks blasphemous so much as arrogant and hubristic; this was a political and cultural protest as much as a religious one. The Beatles had refused to play for segregated

audiences, which made them particularly unpopular with white suprema-
cists. Death threats were made. There were concerns of a sniper infiltrating
one of the gigs.

Before the Beatles' first press conference, in Chicago, Epstein and Barrow
took Lennon aside to brief him on what to say. They wanted him to reassure his audience that he wasn't attacking Christianity or implying that the
Beatles were gods. Lennon was under immense psychological pressure. He
felt that he had made not just himself but also his friends vulnerable to attack. "He was terrified," Cynthia Lennon told the journalist Steve Turner in
2005. "He was the one who had opened his mouth and put his foot in it . . .
he was very frightened." As Epstein and Barrow spoke, Lennon put his head
in his hands and began quietly weeping. He was worried by the physical
threats but also by the threat to the group's career. His bandmates, Paul
in particular, might finally decide that being in a group with John Lennon
was more trouble than it was worth. The Beatles' last single, "Yellow Submarine" / "Eleanor Rigby," had moved only slowly up the American charts;
its highest position was number two. There were still unsold tickets for the
tour. The Beatles were now competing with other credible and successful
artists—the Beach Boys, the Supremes, the Rolling Stones, Bob Dylan—all
of whom had hits that summer. Ringo spoke openly about the possibility
of the group splitting up ("I couldn't stand never seeing the lads again").
Lennon was also scared of becoming what he most despised: someone who
would say anything for the sake of approval. During the previous year's tour
of America, he had told a reporter, "I've reached the point in my life when I
can only say what I feel is honest. I can't say something just because it's what
some people want to hear. I couldn't live with myself."

In footage of the press conference (in Barrow's hotel suite), the Beatles
are squeezed onto a sofa in front of madly patterned wallpaper. They wear
dark, sober suits. Lennon chews gum and speaks fast. Plainly uncomfortable, he strives to be conciliatory but there is a measure of defiance, too.

I didn't mean what everybody thinks I said. I'm not anti-Christ or
anti-religion . . . I'm not saying we're *better* or *greater* or comparing

us with Jesus Christ as a person . . . I just said what I said and it was wrong, or was taken wrong, and now it's all *this* [nodding to the assembled press corps]. If I had said *television* is more popular than Jesus, I might have got away with it.

There is laughter at this, though not from John. George gently points out that Christianity is declining in England, whether one welcomes it or not. When John is asked how he feels about this decline, he says, "I was deploring it." Is he sorry? "Even though I never meant what people think I meant by it, I'm still sorry I opened my mouth." When McCartney is asked about the record burnings, he says, "It's a bit silly. It seems a bit like a publicity stunt on their part." It is the most dismissive remark any of the Beatles venture about the affair, yet somehow Paul's mince pie eyes make it sound placatory, even soothing.

As the conference goes on, you can see the Beatles converging on a theme, like a song coming together. The theme is a search for truth. Paul says, "If people ask us questions, then we could do the whole show business bit of [giving] very vague answers and doing a very dishonest thing. But you know, all we're trying to do is answer honestly." When the journalists finally turn to music, they ask about the gap between the songs the Beatles are making now, like "Eleanor Rigby" and "Tomorrow Never Knows," and the hits that made them famous. Paul links the musical question back to the controversy:

> The thing is we're just trying to move in a forward direction. And this is why we're getting in all these messes with saying things— because we're just trying to move forward. People seem to be trying to sort of hold us back and not want us to say anything that's vaguely inflammatory. I mean, if people don't want that, then we won't do it. We'll just sort of do it privately. But I think it's better for everyone if we're just honest about the whole thing.

John's questioning of Anglicanism, suggested Paul, was of a piece with his questioning of pop convention, the musical and spiritual searches intertwined.

Having survived this first post-controversy press conference, the Beatles were increasingly confident in subsequent encounters with the press. Paul was asked what the Beatles had done for pop, and he replied, in his nonchalant manner, that they had made it more truthful: "A lot of it was just insincere, I think. Five years ago you'd find men of forty recording things without meaning, just to make a hit. Most recording artists today really like what they're doing, and I think you can feel it on the records." At a second Chicago press conference, John spoke more openly about his relationship with religion and spirituality:

> By the time I was nineteen I was cynical about religion and never even considered the goings-on in Christianity. It's only the last two years that I, all the Beatles, have started looking for something else. We live in a moving hothouse. We've been mushroom-grown, forced to grow up a bit quick, like having thirty-to-forty-year-old heads in twenty-year-old bodies. We had to develop more sides, more attitudes. If you're a busman, you usually have a busman's attitude. But we had to be more than four mopheads up there on stage—we had to grow up or we'd be swamped.

Note how he moves seamlessly from "I" to "all the Beatles" as if they were one multipart brain. There is so much compressed insight in these bright, rhythmic sentences, spoken off-the-cuff and typical of Lennon's ability to capture complex thoughts in vivid phrases.

This also represented a new register for Beatle talk. Lennon was settling into a role he had stumbled into—that of a public intellectual, or at least someone who was willing to engage in philosophical and political thinking in public. He had done some of this in songs like "Tomorrow Never Knows," although he did so by letting characters speak through him. Now he was ruminating more expansively in person. McCartney elaborated on his gospel of self-development. George advocated for Indian philosophy. The American fiasco virtually pushed the Beatles into the role of spiritual guides for the counterculture generation.

For the most part, the American concerts went off without trouble, but they were tense, and most of them failed to sell out. In Shea Stadium, site of their greatest American triumph, the Beatles played to a venue one-fifth empty. In Memphis, near the epicenter of the storm, they were assigned more than a hundred police officers and private guards. Outside the venue, a handful of Ku Klux Klan members paraded in white robes. Three songs into the set, a firecracker was hurled onstage and exploded at the foot of Ringo's drum kit. The Beatles looked at one another to see if any of them had been shot, and carried on. When George Harrison said, much later, that the Beatles had sacrificed their nervous systems to the public, he was referring to moments like this. At Dodger Stadium, seven thousand fans broke through the fencing designed to separate them from the group at the end of the show. The Beatles had to be rushed away in an armored car. When it wasn't terrifying, it was exhausting, and always artistically void. Paul told an interviewer fondly about what live performing used to mean to them: "When we started at the Cavern, people listened, and we were able to develop, to grow, to create. But when the screaming started the first casualty was the humour we put into our performances. Now, of course, we are prisoners."

Paul had been the most reluctant to give up touring, but now he joined the others in deciding it had to stop. The last gig was at Candlestick Park in San Francisco. The venue was three-quarters full. On the plane to LA (from where they would fly back to London), George Harrison said to Tony Barrow, "That's it. I'm not a Beatle anymore." He didn't mean that he was leaving the group. He meant that he would no longer be a Beatle on tour, which is what being a Beatle had meant. It wasn't clear what came next. Once again, the Beatles were venturing into virgin territory. Pop stars were performers who also made records; the idea of a rock group that didn't play live was an absurdity. Art Unger sat next to Lennon on the plane. They talked ideas—LSD, music, anthropology. Unger came away with the impression that John was depressed—that he wanted to try many things but couldn't see the point of starting anything. "There is so much I would like to do, but there is no time," John told him. "In ten years, I'll either be broke or crazy. Or the world will be blown up."

In September 1966, shortly after the band's return from LA, John Lennon had his hair cut short, thereby ending the era of moptops, and making global headlines. It is typical of the dream logic that seemed to govern the Beatles' career that Lennon had reason to have a radical new haircut, within a week of the end of the group's final tour. He had been searching for new artistic activities to see if there was something he might be good at beyond rock and roll, and so when Richard Lester invited him to be in his new film, a comedy called *How I Won the War*, he accepted. Lester gave him the role of a Second World War soldier called Musketeer Gripweed. John traveled to Almeria in Spain for a two-month shoot.

Lennon was a diligent member of Lester's cast. He turned up on set every day, even when he wasn't needed. At twenty-six, he had very little experience of adult life outside of being a Beatle. "I couldn't hardly speak I was so nervous," he said later. "I don't mind talking to the camera—it's people that throw me." He was given a pair of round, wire-framed spectacles for the part. They didn't have lenses, but Lennon started wearing them on and off set. They became a prop not just for the film, but also for the new self he was piecing together.

In Almería he was joined by Neil Aspinall and later by Cynthia (Julian stayed in England with the family of the Lennons' housekeeper). He had relatively little to do and a lot of time to reflect. "That's when I really started considering life without the Beatles," he said later. "What would it be? And I spent six weeks thinking about that." His method of reflection was songwriting. He had an acoustic guitar with him and began working on a new song. He later described "Strawberry Fields Forever" as "psychoanalysis set to music."

Lennon has a reputation for being a visionary artist, and what we expect of a visionary is that their ideas arrive fully formed, thunderbolts from the blue. "Strawberry Fields Forever" began as an odd-shaped pebble that Lennon rubbed away at patiently until it began to glint. In Almería he recorded a series of demos on a portable tape recorder, making adjustments to the words and music each time, groping toward whatever it was he wanted to say. In its first iteration, he began by singing about how no one is on his "wavelength." John had always felt different, apart from others. The idea of a wavelength led him to a line about people finding it hard to "tune in" to him. Later, he altered the first line to being "in my tree" because he was wary of sounding arrogant. He used awkward, hesitant phrasing to get there: "No one, I think, is . . ." The line about tuning in no longer made sense, and a writer more concerned with sense would have changed it. Lennon left it like that, because he didn't just want a song *about* confusion; he wanted a song *of* confusion. For Lennon, it was another breaking of a fourth wall. Rather than declaiming, he would let the world in on his uncertainty. Searching for truths about himself, he sought to convey the feeling of the search. That was how to tell the whole truth.

The musician Brian Eno was once asked to explain what it is that makes some people charismatic, and said it comes from "the sense you have that not only is somebody different but they're also confident about it, committed to it, obsessed by it even." This works as a description of John Lennon. Eno went on to say, "We don't find uncertainty charismatic . . . in general the media don't appreciate people like that. I would like to cultivate a charisma of *un*certainty, a charisma of admitting that you're making it up as you go along." But this is exactly what Lennon does in "Strawberry Fields Forever" (and before that, "Help!"). Few pop stars have combined or fused two such disparate personae, the confident and the confused. When Lennon became famous, he seemed masterful, invincible, utterly himself. But when doubts churned inside him, he decided to show those to the world, too. Backed by Paul and the other Beatles, he forged a charisma of vulnerability.

Lennon soon had the opening verse we know, replete with commas— that is, you can't, you know, tune in. It concluded that even though he felt estranged from the world, that might be OK. On the demo he sings it like a child who has learned to comfort himself. Lennon had been feeling unsure of his bearings for years now—really, ever since he and Paul had stopped spending most of their days together. Taking LSD had expanded his horizons but also contributed to a sense that he wasn't *in* the world so much as floating above or through it. Increasingly, when he picked up a guitar or sat at the piano to write, he returned to his childhood, a time when the gap between action and thought was closed. "In My Life," "She Said She Said," "Yellow Submarine": all were, in different ways, about reconnecting with that time.

After a while he landed on an idea for the chorus. Strawberry Field (he added the "s" because it sang better) was a Salvation Army orphanage near Aunt Mimi's house, with big, parklike grounds. When he was small, Mimi took him there for its annual summer fete. He remembered a Salvation Army marching band. As a teenager he used to vault over the wall with his gang of friends, and it became his secret playground, away from adults. In a way that's hard for most of us to grasp, the play world of children in 1950s England was self-contained. Children were left to their own devices, free from parental surveillance, for hours at a time. In Strawberry Field, John was a king, with no adults to berate or betray him. He knew who he was and what he wanted. Now, in a dusty corner of a foreign land, away from his best friends, he listened to his own yearning for this idyll. In some iterations, he proposed taking us *back* to Strawberry Fields (he always wanted to take us—he did not want to be alone), but by deciding on *down*, he ensured that the song transcends nostalgia. "Strawberry Fields" becomes an idea, or a feeling, that can be accessed at anytime and by anyone. But it doesn't offer itself up easily. It is a place that can be glimpsed through the undergrowth, sensed dimly beneath layers of memory but never recaptured: a smudged and faded print of happiness, rather than the thing itself.

Nothing quite unfolds as the ear expects. Lennon finds notes that loosen our connection to the tonic—the "home" chord by which we, as listeners, instinctively orient ourselves. The melody drifts, unmoored, creating a mood of dreamy unreality. On the "to" of "'cause I'm going to" he plays a chord that is like a rabbit hole into another world. Lennon then sings a pair of half-rhyming phrases, separated by a harmonic lurch downward: "Strawberry Fields . . . Nothing is real." Those last four notes could exist only in this ghostly parallel world. Then the chords move down again but the melody moves *up*, as the singer realizes there is "nothing to get hung about." Here on the other side of reality, his worst fears have not been realized.

Hidden within the title phrase and the sound of "real" is the word "feel": this is a song about what it feels like deep inside Lennon's head. After the breakup of the Beatles, Lennon said he never recorded the song he had in his mind and that he regretted letting McCartney exert so much influence over it, perhaps because it was so deeply personal to him. But if he had recorded the song more or less as he played it in Spain, "Strawberry Fields Forever" would probably have been remembered as a beautiful but minor work in the Beatles' repertoire. It was with the group that the song was raised to its full majesty.

John returned to England on November 2. On November 24 the Beatles reconvened at Abbey Road for the first time since the summer tour, to begin work on a new album (the album that would become *Sgt. Pepper's Lonely Hearts Club Band*). "Strawberry Fields Forever" was the first song they recorded and the Beatles were to take longer over it than any other track they made. As he had when it was just him and a guitar, Lennon worried away at the song for weeks in the studio, changing his mind about how he wanted it to sound. Paul added a doleful, drooping melody, played on the Mellotron, to introduce the song. The group's first take was sparse, crystalline, and a little uncertain. Over the next few sessions, the Beatles tinkered with the arrangement. After experimenting with the Mellotron, Paul switched to its flute sound, which sounds uncanny: familiar yet alien. When that version was completed, it was thought to be the final take. But now Lennon returned to it again. He wanted something darker and deeper, and asked George Martin for orchestral accompaniment.

The Beatles rerecorded the song on December 8 (orchestral instruments, scored by Martin, were overdubbed a week later). The first part of the session took place in the evening, without Martin, who was at the theater. The mood in the studio was one of antic creativity, as if the children had been left to their own devices. Paul worked with Ringo to add density and complexity to John's deliberately irregular rhythms. The resulting track was faster, more frantic and intense. The Mellotron intro conjures up a whole soundscape: a kind of queasy pastoral, a haunted wood. Rolling, cross-hatched rhythms make the listener unsure which beats will be strong and which weak, conspiring with harmony to make us lose our bearings. Ringo's drums totter and thunk; reversed cymbals hiss into life. Stabbing trumpets and marcato cellos add a deranged sense of purpose to the meandering melody.

The Beatles now had two complete versions of the track recorded: the original, lighter band version, and the second, darker orchestral version. Lennon liked both. His indecision was final: he asked Martin to weld the two together. Martin told him it was impossible, since the two tracks were at different tempos and in different keys. But neither Lennon nor McCartney had ever hesitated to ask the impossible, and often they got it. Martin and his engineer, Geoff Emerick, discovered that, by remarkable coincidence, the gap in speed matched the gap in key (when you speed up or slow down a tape, the pitch changes). With some applied ingenuity, the two tracks were cut together in a way that made the join all but disappear.

Lennon's intuition was right: it worked better to start with the group version and then introduce the orchestration, as if we're traveling deeper into the forest, like Hansel and Gretel. There were serendipitous benefits, too. Since the orchestral track had to be slowed down, Lennon's voice acquired a slightly woozy quality that adds to the sense we are entering a strange world. And since the keys of the two versions are still very slightly different from each other, the track lives for a while in what Ian McDonald calls a "microtonal borderland," enhancing the mood of uncertainty. The whole song is finely poised between dream and nightmare. Its gauzy ambiguity is housed within a conventional structure—verse and chorus. The listener is oriented just enough to take pleasure in being lost.

Sigmund Freud described the purpose of psychoanalysis as to transform human misery into ordinary unhappiness. Lennon's early working title was "Not Too Bad." Instead of a cry of anguish, John made a song about how our most baleful and threatening thoughts can be tamed, if only for a while, if we tether ourselves to something—to a memory, or a memory of a memory; to friends; to music. "Strawberry Fields Forever" embodies Rainer

Maria Rilke's principle: "Let everything happen to you: beauty and terror. Just keep going. No feeling is final." After it fades out, a segment of backward music takes us by surprise, reemerging from the silence before fading out again. The effect is of being passed by a band of chattering ghouls whom we have learned to regard as harmless.

19   PENNY LANE

While John was away, Paul, among many other things, worked on soundtrack music for a film called *The Family Way*, in collaboration with George Martin. He later won an Ivor Novello award for it. Like the "Eleanor Rigby" incident, this episode exacerbated John's insecurity. Paul found out John had been hurt by it only from Yoko Ono, after John's death. Paul: "He [John] went off to make a film . . . he wrote his books. [Working with Martin on *The Family Way*] was in the spirit of all that . . . But what I didn't realise was that this was the first time one of us had done it on songs."

When John was on a break from the shoot, Paul went to meet him in Paris, accompanied by Neil Aspinall and Paul's secret— well, secretish—lover, Maggie McGivern. Maggie had been working as a nanny for Marianne Faithfull and John Dunbar. After becoming friends in 1965, they started an affair a few months into 1966. Maggie was not interested in usurping Jane, and she and Paul had a relatively uncomplicated, irregular relationship which lasted until 1968. She recalled wandering around Paris with Paul and John, and lying under the Eiffel Tower with them, gazing up through it to the sky.

In November, a few days after John got back from Spain, McCartney took off for a holiday in France. He wanted to disappear for a while. He grew a mustache and acquired fake glasses, and Vaseline for his hair. He took a leisurely drive in his brand-new Aston Martin down to Bordeaux, where he had arranged to meet Mal Evans, the Beatles' friend from Liverpool and loyal retainer. Paul and Mal headed for Spain and made it to Madrid, whereupon Paul decided they should go on a safari holiday in Kenya, because why not, and called Epstein's office to arrange it (Epstein had someone pick up the Aston Martin from Seville). In France and Kenya, Paul noticed how much he enjoyed not being "Beatle Paul McCartney." On the plane back, he misheard Mal saying "salt and pepper" as "Sergeant Pepper," which sparked an idle notion. What if the Beatles dropped "the Beatles" and became "Sergeant Pepper's Lonely Hearts Club Band"? It remained just a notion for now.

A few days after Paul's return from holiday, he and John began working on the next album. John played him "Strawberry Fields Forever." Paul knew about Strawberry Field, of course. Hearing John sing about it, not long after they made "In My Life," excited him into writing a kind of answering song about childhood—and not just his own childhood, but the one he had in common with John.

Lennon and McCartney were not alone in reaching back into childhood for inspiration. The nascent psychedelic movement involved a Rousseau-like idealization of the child's perspective on the world; LSD was said to re-create the infant mind, unfettered by the strictures of adulthood. (Paul had finally tried acid, once, but not with the other Beatles. He took it in the company of his London friends Nicky and Tara Browne.) But while psychedelia, as it developed, tended to be twee in its evocation of childhood innocence, there is something tougher about the way the Beatles treat it: a brooding quality, a sense of monsters pressing up against the window while the kids dance in the living room.

John and Paul had been interested in writing a musical about Liverpool since 1958, when they first started writing together. They had an idea for it: Jesus coming back to Earth as the inhabitant of a Liverpool slum. You can see why they might have found the idea suggestive: the sheer incongruity of

Jesus coming from Liverpool was not so distant from the idea of the next Elvis Presley coming from there. The ambition persisted. In early 1964, John
told an interviewer, "Paul and I want to write a stage musical. That's a must.
Maybe about Liverpool." In the 1965 interview with Keith Altham, Paul
mentioned the Jesus idea before saying, "I think we are resigned to the fact
that we will just not have the time to work on a full-scale musical until the
Beatles are finished."

Shortly after finishing "Strawberry Fields Forever," the Beatles began work
on Paul's song about growing up in Liverpool: "Penny Lane." Both songs
were intended for the new album but instead, almost accidentally (there was
a gap in the release schedule), they became two sides of a single, released in
February 1967. Both "Strawberry Fields Forever" and "Penny Lane" show us
Liverpool from the perspective of altered minds. While "Strawberry Fields
Forever" takes us down into the netherworld of the unconscious, "Penny
Lane" takes us up to the sky, from where we swoop into the world below.

☙

Back in the spring of 1966, McCartney had visited Paris with his friend the
art dealer Robert Fraser. He returned with two paintings by the Belgian sur-
realist René Magritte, who used the tools of realism to undo reality. Whereas
Salvador Dalí portrays the fantastical, Magritte shows us the mundane, made
strange: a bowler-hatted man with an apple floating in front of his face; com-
muters falling from a blue sky; a window that makes us question what a window is. His paintings are easy to like and superficially easy to comprehend,
yet inscrutable and unsettling at the same time. It is art of the uncanny;
the real made subtly unreal. Magritte lost his mother, to suicide, when he
was thirteen. While it's simplistic to attribute an entire artistic sensibility
to childhood experience, perhaps there is something about losing a parent
when young that makes one question what others take for granted; to notice
the contingency of background reality. McCartney seemed to identify with
Magritte: years later he acquired the artist's easel, spectacles, and palette.

"Penny Lane" can be thought of as McCartney's Magritte. Musically, it
is inspired, at least in part, by the Beach Boys, who with *Pet Sounds* had hit
a creative peak high enough to scare McCartney into proving the Beatles

could do better (Ray Davies, of the Kinks: "Paul McCartney was one of the most competitive people I've ever met. Lennon wasn't. He just thought everyone else was shit.") Their single "Good Vibrations," which came out in October 1966, was a startling mixture of arcane orchestration (a church organ, cellos, a theremin) and pure pop joy. The story of its gestation was already legendary among pop musicians by the time the Beatles entered the studio in late 1966: six months to make, endless studio hours at extravagant cost, four different studios, each chosen for its specific ambience. When the other Beach Boys thought they were finished, Wilson insisted on making the whole thing again from scratch. The success of "Good Vibrations" further emboldened Lennon and McCartney to insist on taking all the time they needed to nail a song.

Like "Good Vibrations," "Penny Lane" has no intro. It starts with Paul singing the three syllables of the title like a magician unfurling his hand-kerchief. Over a jauntily strolling bass McCartney takes us around Penny Lane—the name of a street and small district in Liverpool. It didn't mean much to most Liverpudlians, but to John and Paul it was a place that glowed with possibility: in the Quarry Men days, the Penny Lane roundabout was where John and Paul and George crossed paths and joined forces on their daily commutes into town. From there they would catch the bus to the art college (John) and Liverpool Institute (Paul and George).

In McCartney's depiction, Penny Lane becomes a toy-town diorama populated by archetypal characters: the Banker, the Barber, the Fireman. The song's home key is a bright B major, but there is an unexpected shift to B minor in the verse (in the first verse, the shift happens on the word "know"—"every head he's had the pleasure to know"). Just as with John's more obviously weird chord changes in "Strawberry Fields Forever," the ef-fect is unsettling. A sudden shadow is cast over Penny Lane's jolly mise-en-scène.* McCartney holds us inside this uncanny moment as the bass descends, step by step, until we revert to the major on "say hello." A piccolo tweets,

---

* A chill wind blows through many apparently jolly Beatles songs: "She Loves You" ("you know you should be glad"); the bridge in "When I'm Sixty-Four" ("we shall scrimp and save"); the chorus of "Fool on the Hill." Even in "Octopus's Garden" there's a hint of trouble in paradise.

and everything feels happy again. In each of the remaining two verses, this moment feels a tiny bit more ominous. At the end of every verse, Paul sings "*very* strange." Here too, the repetition makes the phrase grow in significance as the song progresses.

In the chorus, the melody leaps upward, as the singer tells us that Penny Lane is in his ears and in his eyes. But the singer is also telling us that he isn't there. He's not looking out of the barber's window on Penny Lane: he's in a sunny suburb, remembering a place that will never be as real to him as it once was. Again, McCartney uses tonality to tell the story. In the chorus, the melody moves up but the key moves unexpectedly *down* (from B major to A major), adding an undertow of longing to the exuberance. The singer-narrator has a child's enthusiasm and an adult's experience. The adult knows in his heart, as we know in ours, that "Penny Lane" is a dream of childhood rather than childhood itself. This accounts for its strangeness: the banker who steadfastly ignores the rain falling from a blue sky, the fireman who is terrified of it; everything warmly familiar yet somehow skewed. The final twist of the song is to suggest that maybe none of it was ever real in the first place.

"Penny Lane" is led by piano and brass, evocative of sing-alongs in pubs and front parlors, and of Northern brass bands. It doesn't just take us back in the singer's life, but back in history to a time long before rock and roll, like the cellos in "Strawberry Fields Forever." In the last verse, we meet a pretty nurse, like Paul's mother, selling poppies from a tray—toy flowers to commemorate fallen soldiers. It's an image that subtly evokes deaths both personal and public. "Penny Lane" hints at and subverts England's deep cultural memory, imaginary or otherwise, of an orderly, serene Edwardian world, before war and decline despoiled it.

Like "Strawberry Fields Forever," "Penny Lane" holds two contradictory ideas before us and makes each of them true at once. "Penny Lane" is real and unreal. It's a fiction, and it's a place we can visit anytime. McCartney asks the same question posed by Prospero in *The Tempest*—whether the world we think of as solid is a fantasy, an insubstantial pageant, a dream. The nurse, the only female character in the song, is more perceptive than any of the men, who live in blissful ignorance of their unreality. Standing in the middle of the roundabout, a magic circle, she has the sneaking feeling that there is more to her surroundings than meets the eye. *And though she feels as if she's in a play*: as McCartney sings this line, the brass makes stabbing accents in an echo of "Strawberry Fields Forever," a motif, in this mini-musical, for the uncanny—*she is anyway*.

Just as with the words and melody, the crystalline surface of the "Penny Lane" sound conceals layers of complexity. McCartney stacks four different pianos, each with a different timbre, on top of one another, while his bass line offers a busy counterpoint to his melody. After seeing a performance of Bach's second Brandenburg Concerto on TV, he was captivated by the sound of the piccolo trumpet, which plays an octave above a regular trumpet. In the studio, McCartney pushed the trumpeter to the top of his range and the edge of his capability. The result is a solo that is familiar, as pastiche baroque, and at the same time surreal.

As the end of the song approaches, a thunderstorm crackles and the chorus is repeated, only this time, it moves up a key. Modulating upward for the final chorus was often used in pop to intensify a song's ending. It was the kind of cliché the Beatles called "corny," but in "Penny Lane" it is used to integrate the song's two perspectives: the child's-eye view of Penny Lane in the verse, and the adult recollection of the chorus. McCartney returns us to the key in which the song began, chorus merging with verse, as the sunshine sees off the clouds. The piccolo trumpet returns, flitting and twirling like a bird at a wedding. McCartney exclaims, "Penny Lane!" and the song dissolves in a little moan of feedback.

☙

Although "Penny Lane" and "Strawberry Fields Forever" were on opposite sides of the same single, we should imagine them facing each other, deep in conversation. Radically different, umbilically connected, they form an opus. (The *New Yorker* critic Adam Gopnik has proposed this single as a contender for the twentieth century's greatest work of art.) Both songs evoke the succor we take in the past and the impossibility of returning to yesterday, but each comes from a different angle. No song is more McCartneyesque than "Penny Lane," just as "Strawberry Fields Forever" is indubitably Lennonesque. Paul created songs that felt as if they had always existed; John channeled transmissions from another planet. Paul's melodies feel like the purpose of music itself; John strains at the limits of chords and keys, trying to get past music into pure feeling or experience.

Where "Strawberry Fields Forever" offers respite from trauma, "Penny Lane" blazes with a love of life. It is touching that McCartney picked up on Lennon's aspiration to write a song about Penny Lane—a place that was, after all, more John's than Paul's (John had lived there as a small boy with Julia, before he was taken in by Mimi). Lennon helped with the words: it was his idea to replace the line about blue skies in the refrain with one about "four of fish and finger pie"—a smutty teenage joke and another way to subvert the song's innocence.

By the end of 1966, John was more disoriented than ever. He felt increasingly distant from Cynthia, who didn't take to LSD, and he played little part in raising Julian. In November he met a Japanese artist called Yoko Ono, who intrigued him. Just before that, he was hurt by the loss of a female friend, the singer Alma Cogan, an older, charismatic, gregarious woman who had drawn the Beatles into her circle. After John's death, Cynthia said she always suspected that Cogan was one of John's lovers. Whether Alma was a close friend or something more, her swift death at thirty-four, of ovarian cancer, was another entry in John's grim ledger of bereavements.

I suspect Paul wrote "Penny Lane" for John, and that those blue suburban skies are meant to invoke Weybridge. Paul is reminding John that however disconnected or lonely he might be feeling, the two of them would always be able to meet up in the middle of a roundabout.

20   A DAY IN THE LIFE

The Beatles finished work on "Penny Lane" in mid-January 1967. A few days before, Jane Asher flew to Boston to begin a four-month tour of North America with the Bristol Old Vic. Jane's long absence meant that during the first half of the year John and Paul spent more time together than they had done for a long time. At Cavendish Avenue and Kenwood they worked on songs, smoked pot, and meditated, sometimes joined by Ringo and George. When Jane returned to England, at the end of May, she noticed a difference in her partner: "Paul had changed so much . . . He was on LSD, which I hadn't shared. I was jealous of all the spiritual experiences he'd had with John."

Six days after Jane left for America, the Beatles gathered at Abbey Road and showed George Martin something they had been working on at Paul's house. John called it "In the Life Of." In its current form it had three verses—the first one featuring a news story about a man who blew his mind out in a car—and a refrain, consisting of one phrase: *I'd love to turn you on.* The mood was reflective. There was also a middle section, sung by Paul: a jaunty, piano-led story about a man waking up and catching a bus, which seemed to have nothing to do with the rest of the song. Nobody knows why Paul and John decided that this fragment belonged inside John's song. It was like an absurd challenge they had set themselves.

That day they recorded the basic backing track, with John on acoustic guitar, Paul on piano, Ringo on congas, and Harrison on maracas. John and Paul knew they wanted something interesting to happen between the verses and the incongruous middle section, but they weren't sure what yet. They left a gap of twenty-four bars, during which the group continued playing over a repeated piano chord. Mal Evans was employed to stand by the piano and count off the bars aloud so that the Beatles didn't have to do it in their heads. His voice bled through to the band's mics and can be heard on the final mix. When Mal got to the end of the twenty-four bars, he was instructed to hit a wind-up alarm clock on top of the piano, setting off the alarm, signaling the start of Paul's section, which begins with the words "Woke up."

With the backing track laid down, Lennon recorded his lead vocal, his voice treated with echo. He did take after take, late into the night. Geoff Emerick, the Abbey Road engineer, notes in his memoir that both John and Paul had excellent pitch: few vocal takes were wasted. But John was always insecure about his singing. He hated listening to his vocal takes and preferred his voice to be blended with someone else's—in harmony with Paul's, or double-tracked with his own. "Make it so I don't sound like me," he would say to Emerick. He often asked for a tape echo effect. In the studio, he'd hear the echo in his headphones and sing with or to it almost like a vocal partner. That night, he produced a performance that captivated everyone present. The next night, they recorded Paul's vocal and bass, and Ringo's drum part. Paul encouraged Ringo to impose himself on the track, which he did, adding fills like perfectly judged brushstrokes, while keeping a gentle rhythm.

The Beatles now took a fortnight's break from the track and worked on other songs. When they returned to what they were now calling "A Day in the Life," they still hadn't decided on what to do in the twenty-four-bar transition into Paul's bit—or how to make the transition out of it, back to the main song. It's not even clear why they left this long gap, although John had a very vague idea for it: he said he wanted something that started off tiny and grew and grew until it became massive. Paul argued for something tumultuous and startling—something that would leave the listener's head in pieces. He suggested using a whole symphony orchestra, something the Beatles had never done before. Martin balked at the cost but agreed to book half an orchestra. The question now became what the orchestra would play. Paul, influenced by ideas from avant-garde classical composers, particularly Cage and Stockhausen, suggested that the orchestra members play from the lowest note on their instrument to the highest, and get there randomly rather than attempting to play in unison. John loved the idea. Paul said it should happen twice, once in the transition to his section, once at the end of the song.

Martin doubted that orchestral musicians, used to playing from sheet music, could be persuaded to improvise. Lennon suggested that if they wore silly party hats and rubber noses it might loosen everyone up. So on the evening of February 10 the Beatles threw a fancy-dress party in Studio One, the biggest studio at Abbey Road, and invited a bunch of friends, including the Rolling Stones. Mal distributed party hats, rubber noses, clown wings, gorilla paws, and clip-on nipples to everyone, including the orchestra. The division between classical and pop musicians, which was also a class divide, dissolved in the general silliness. Martin and McCartney took turns conducting, with the latter driving them hard. Over the course of the evening, amid marijuana smoke and popping balloons, the musicians delivered the structured cacophony envisaged by Paul.

There was still one more part to record. John and Paul wanted something peaceful to close the song, after the screech of an orchestra at the top of its range. It was Paul's idea to have a massive piano chord reverberating on and on forever. As George Martin said, "You get a wonderful sound from a piano if you let the overtones work." Each note brings out all the ones hidden inside every other note, and the frequencies begin to speak to one another, multiplying and expanding the sound. On February 22, pianos were moved from all over the building into Studio Two: keyboards with different histories, tones, and timbres, like the combination used by Paul on "Penny Lane." Mal joined Ringo, John, Paul, and George Martin at the pianos. They stood, so as to maximize the force with which they hit the chord. They did lots of takes,

Paul counting them in every time, until they hit one in which everyone was synchronized and no extraneous noises interrupted the long, slow fade-out to nothing. With a great deal of effort and ingenuity, the engineers now put together all of the song's constituent parts into one complete mix, and "A Day in the Life" was done.

As with *Revolver*, the most mind-blowing song on what became *Sgt. Pepper* was recorded near the beginning of the sessions, and would inevitably go last on the album. Nothing could possibly follow it.

⊛

John and Paul were both articulate, but neither was terribly interested in discussing the philosophical or aesthetic rationale for their songs, with each other or anyone else. They just tried stuff out, and then tried again, and kept on making choices until what they had captured on tape resembled what they felt in their bones. It's useful to understand how "A Day in the Life" was constructed: to know about the many decisions and accidents that led to the final track. What this doesn't tell us is how it became "A Day in the Life"—a piece of music that hums with mystery and meaning. We can only guess at that.

"A Day in the Life" is part of a subgenre of Lennon-McCartney songs that includes "A Hard Day's Night" and "We Can Work It Out," where different sections are sung by each of them, so that the song feels as if it emanates from a double consciousness. But here the two parts have starkly different feels, and rather than blending into one seamless whole they are smashed together in a deliberately jarring way. In John's verses, the words suggest someone disassociated from the horrible events he reads about in the news (that "oh boy," like a stoned Buddy Holly). The singer lives in a world of mediated experience, of photographs, news stories, films, which have dulled his empathy and frazzled his nervous system. In Lennon's real life, he watched himself on screens and saw pictures of himself in newspapers every day. He was a spectator of his own life: beatle John watching Beatle John. But he hadn't stopped feeling things, not yet. If the lyrics suggest someone numbed to human tragedy, the singing is full of sensuous melancholy. John's phrase-shaping and inflections communicate what the words don't say. Paul's bass weaves restlessly away underneath, never settling into a predictable pattern. Ringo's fitful interventions are like distant rolls of thunder.

At the end of the first two verses comes the phrase "I'd love to turn you on." The last three words are sung in oscillating semitones by voices in unison, echoed by orchestral strings. Then the other voices fade out, and we just hear John, with the echo reduced. The effect is to foreground his voice, like we've zoomed in very closely on it. At the same time, the background—everything we've taken for granted—starts to crumble and disintegrate. A great unfocusing begins. Paul bangs away at the piano, hitting wrong notes, sounding increasingly frenzied. We hear muffled shouts (Mal's voice counting the bars). Ringo keeps the pulse on a hi-hat. Paul's bass (overdubbed) walks up the scale until it plateaus on an E and repeats it, at which point the orchestra enters and begins its dissonant, upward glissando like a rising panic attack. As the orchestra pushes up against its instrumental limits at the top of its climb, we're suddenly lifted out of the chaos and dropped somewhere else altogether.

Paul's section begins with someone waking up and ends with him going into a dream. We don't know who this person is or whether it's the same character who started the song. This voice is brighter and sharper; McCartney enunciates his lyrics with lip-smacking clarity. There is an oaky, smoky warmth to this section, evoking a sing-along. Then a dreamy melody sung to *ahh* sweeps away all of this quotidian business, a transformation as sudden as taking flight. The orchestra plays an unsettling sequence of chords in unison before a five-note phrase returns the song to its home key.* John returns for another verse, now set to the more vigorous tempo introduced by Paul's song. The two segments, the two moods, the two consciousnesses merge. By this point we don't know if Paul's section was a dream of John, or if John's is a dream of Paul. There is a second orchestral eruption, which sounds like

---

* In his book on *Sgt. Pepper*, George Martin recalls Paul coming to him one day to say he'd been listening to Beethoven. "I've just sussed it out. You know the beginning of the Fifth Symphony? It's only unison. There are no chords. Everyone's playing the same notes." Martin agreed. "But that's fantastic!" said Paul. "It's a great sound!" (George Martin, *Summer of Love*, 135.)

someone's head splitting apart. The cavernous piano chord that follows is like being launched into eternity.

☮

In 1968, Lennon told *Rolling Stone*'s Jonathan Cott:

> "A Day in the Life"—that was something. I dug it. It was a good piece of work between Paul and me. I had the "I read the news today" bit, and it turned Paul on. Now and then we really turn each other on with a bit of song, and he just said "yeah"—bang, bang, like that. It just sort of happened beautifully.

Note how Lennon evokes the speed at which McCartney would build on one of his ideas—*bang bang*. Twelve years later he said a bit more: "Paul's contribution was the beautiful little lick in the song, 'I'd love to turn you on,' that he'd had floating around in his head and couldn't use. I thought it was a damn good piece of work." Assuming John's recollection is right, it sounds as if Paul suggested that line and the strange, tightly undulating oscillation on which each of its last three words are hung. You can see why John might remember it fondly. For one thing, Paul was using psychedelic language ("turn on" was already associated with LSD and drug culture), which suggested that even if Paul was still wary of the drug itself, he was with John, on his journey, in spirit. But it wasn't just about LSD. Paul had discovered a rabbit hole: his beautiful little lick took John's verse to an even stranger place than where it had been. The universe of the song must have opened up to both of them at this point. Everything else followed: the decision to introduce a radically different song in the middle; the mind-jangling, unearthly transitions; the whole experience of a death-haunted dream, disjointed and disassociated, redeemed only by the possibility of creative connection between people.

John drew on the detached, weary persona he started to inhabit in the midsection of "We Can Work It Out," now imbued with sadness and surreal humor. Paul's section reflected his own energy and drive. It would be simplistic to conclude they are simply "themselves" in these segments. "A Day in the Life" is the culmination of a period in which they drew on the contrast between their two personalities in order to create avatars for different ways to be in the world—for instincts that exist within each of us. Freud proposed two fundamental and opposing drives at work in every human being: Eros and Thanatos. Eros is the will to act in and on the world: to do, to create, to produce and achieve. Thanatos is the desire to let the world wash over us: to lie down and surrender to the void. Humans have a love for life, and a longing for easeful death. "A Day in the Life" dramatizes both. When Paul runs for the bus, John does heavy breathing, like a parody of exertion. It's as if Paul, or "Paul," absorbed by his own clock-chasing busyness, is being gently teased. His relentless forward motion begins to feel like displacement activity, a way of keeping nightmares at bay.

John's final verse borrows the energy of Paul's section. The dipping and rising *ahh* that connects them shifts in mood every time I hear it. It can sound like rapture, or anguish, or a mix of both. There is a long-running debate among Beatles fans over whether John or Paul sings it. Do an online search and you will turn up countless threads, polls, and comments devoted to this precise question. On YouTube, you can hear that section of the track with the instrumental parts erased, and the vocals isolated—just the *ahh* itself, along with one of the other Beatles making a keening *whoo* sound in the background. The effect is unsettling, spooky. Many listeners think the *ahh* sounds like John, on first hearing—it seems to be his slightly nasal, ironizing tone. An engineer from the session recalls that it was John. But the singer performs a tricky little melisma, an Indian-flavored vocal twirl, at the end of the last repetition, and that sounds more like something Paul would do. Maybe the *ahh* is Paul *impersonating* John? Or is it John and Paul singing in unison? We don't know, because these were two voices capable of hiding inside each other in one moment before springing apart in another.

The decision to release "Strawberry Fields Forever" and "Penny Lane" on a single rather than to include them on the new album was a source of some frustration for John and Paul at the time and regret for George Martin. Today, fans remake *Sgt. Pepper* with those tracks included, but we could also think of "A Day in the Life" as the third track of an EP: a trilogy of songs, all recorded between November 1966 and February 1967, about psychedelic experience, childhood, and death, as refracted through the distinctive sensibilities of John and Paul. "Strawberry Fields Forever" is Lennon leaning into Lennonism. "Penny Lane" is McCartney leaning into McCartneyism. "A Day in the Life" juxtaposes both, to seismic effect.

21   GETTING BETTER

On the evening of March 21, 1967, three of the Beatles were at Abbey Road, recording backing vocals for a song called "Getting Better." John, Paul, and George were gathered around a microphone. After a few run-throughs, John took out a silver snuffbox he kept his pills in and began poking around in it, searching for an upper to keep him going. Soon afterward, he faltered and stopped in the middle of a line. He looked up to George Martin in the control room. "George, I'm not feeling too good," he said. "I'm not focusing on me."

Martin paused the session and took John up to the roof for some fresh air. The other Beatles stayed behind. But as McCartney and Harrison discussed what might be the matter with John, they figured out that he had probably taken a tab of LSD by accident— and that maybe standing on the top of a building wasn't the best place for him. They rushed up the stairs, hoping that John did not decide to see if he could fly before they got there. As it turned out, he was OK. Still, work was halted for the night, and the band dispersed.

Paul and John stayed together. With the drug exerting its effects on his brain, John didn't want to travel back to his home in

Surrey. He and Paul headed for Cavendish Avenue, a short drive from the studio. Once there, Paul decided he would take some LSD himself. Although he had tried acid for the first time in late 1965, that was with other friends. Now he wanted to "get with John," as he later put it to Martin, who interpreted it to mean "to be with him in his misery and fear." McCartney told Barry Miles: "I thought . . . maybe this is the moment. It's been coming for a long time."

That night, John and Paul did something that the two of them practiced quite a few times during this period: they gazed intensely into each other's eyes. They liked to put their faces close together and stare, unblinking, until they felt themselves dissolving into each other, almost obliterating any sense of themselves as distinct individuals. "There's something disturbing about it," recalled McCartney, much later, in his understated way. "You ask yourself, 'How do you come back from it? How do you then lead a normal life after that?' And the answer is, you don't." The Beatles' publicist and friend Derek Taylor recalled Paul enthusing about LSD: "We had this fantastic *thing* . . . Incredible, really, just looked into each other's eyes . . . Like, just *staring* and then saying, 'I *know*, man' and then laughing."

☿

John and Paul were getting toward the end of their work on what had become the *Sgt. Pepper's Lonely Hearts Club Band* album. They were working on what they called "slog songs." "The last four songs of an album are usually pure slog," Paul told Hunter Davies, around this time. "If we need four more we just have to get down and do them. They're not necessarily worse than ones done out of imagination. They're often better, because by that stage in an LP we know what sort of songs we want."

By songs "done out of imagination," Paul meant those that one or the other of them already had floating around before sessions on the album began—like "Eleanor Rigby," "Tomorrow Never Knows," or "A Day in the Life." Those songs arrived unbidden and were sometimes fragmentary or unfinished. Once the group had realized those ones in the studio they usually needed a few more, and often had a tight deadline. So John and Paul would meet up, usually around two in the afternoon, and knock out the slog songs.

It was like the difference between letting inspiration strike and trying very hard to have a new idea. On that basis, you might expect the slog songs to sound more formulaic and less interesting. But because John and Paul were so relaxed in each other's company, they were able to tap into each other's unconscious and find surprises there. In 1967 the journalist Hunter Davies got as close as any outsider did to witnessing this process. He was at McCartney's house as John and Paul worked on a song for Ringo. They had composed the melody the day before. They had a title, too: "With a Little Help from My Friends." Davies describes the two of them in a seemingly aimless, almost trancelike state. They would "bang away" artlessly on guitars, or Paul would sit at the piano. They'd throw out musical and lyrical phrases until something that one of them did or said snagged, at which point the other would "pluck it out of a mass of noises and try it himself."

As Davies watches, they land on the idea of asking a question at the start of each verse. At this point Cynthia Lennon turns up with one of their old Liverpool friends, Terry Doran. Cynthia and Terry sit down, chat quietly, suggest lines when invited to, and read out the horoscope, while Paul and John carry on doodling. Paul suddenly starts to play "Can't Buy Me Love." John joins in, "singing it very loudly, laughing and shouting." Paul plays "Tequila" at the piano, and they go crazy again. "Remember in Germany?" says John. "We used to shout out anything." John and Paul play through their song but with John shouting random words between the lines: "knickers," "Hitler," "tit," "Duke of Edinburgh." It's the kind of moment familiar to anyone who has watched *Get Back*. This period of boisterous play stops as soon as it began. They return to the song, now very focused, and speaking softly. John finds just the right words to make a line he has been working on scan. Paul nods, says "Yes, that will do," and writes down the finished verse on notepaper.

Ⓐ

Davies was also around to see how "Getting Better" came into being. McCartney had been at home with time to kill. John was meant to be coming over to work on new songs, but he was late and it was a nice day, so Paul picked up Martha, the sheepdog he had acquired the previous summer, put her in his Mini Cooper, and drove to Primrose Hill. As Martha frolicked in the park and the sun came out for the first time in a while, Paul thought, "It's getting better," and smiled. The phrase reminded him of something Jimmie Nicol used to say. Nicol was the drummer who joined the Beatles for a few weeks in 1964 when Ringo fell ill. Whenever one of the Beatles asked Nicol how he was finding it, he'd reply, "It's getting better." The Beatles found this hilarious.

When John arrived at Cavendish Avenue later that afternoon, Paul said, "Let's do a song called 'Getting Better.'" They began strumming and improvising and larking around until a song began to form. "You've *got* to admit," said Paul, after a while, "it *is* getting better"—and John started to sing that. The two of them kept going like this until two in the morning, stopping only for a fry-up, as a succession of visitors who had made appointments to see Paul were left waiting or sent away. Into this song, initiated by Paul, John poured a stream of reflections on his own life: on the anger he had carried around with him as a teenager and younger man; on the emotional and physical abuse he had inflicted on women. Since the tone of the song is lighthearted, the heaviness of the final verse is often missed.

The evening after this session, John and Paul went to the studio. Paul played "Getting Better" on a piano for George and Ringo. The group sat around and discussed what the song should sound like, before dispersing to noodle on their instruments, trying out bits and pieces to play. Paul joined Ringo at the drums and helped him work out his part. After a couple of hours, they were ready to record the backing track. George Martin took his position in the control room. The Beatles ran through seven takes, with Paul directing the group ("Once more"; "More drums"; "Less bass"). By midnight they had a satisfactory version. Twelve days later they recorded the lead and backing vocals (this was the session interrupted by John's LSD-induced freak-out). Two days after that they were back in the studio to redo the vocals, finishing when "they'd got it at least to a stage which didn't make them unhappy."

☮

People who knew John commented on a change in his personality that took place in 1966 and 1967, roughly coinciding with his use of pot and LSD.

In early 1968, Cynthia told Hunter Davies that John was quieter and more tolerant than he used to be. Pete Shotton also noticed a distinct softening of John's personality: the "cripple" impersonations stopped, the sarcasm receded. He was no longer drinking himself into oblivion and rage. His songwriting moved past the Sturm und Drang of love betrayed and spurned. He became calmer, nicer, and more childlike. He even started hugging people. "This is the new thing," John said, on hugging a friend he hadn't seen in a while. "You hug your friends when you meet them, and show them you're glad to see them." He also stopped worrying about McCartney taking leadership of the group. As Lennon relaxed, McCartney became even more driven. Although Paul had now taken LSD with John, his drug of choice during the *Pepper* sessions was cocaine. In the studio, after the others had clocked off, he would work through the night, crafting his bass lines, obsessing over every detail of each track.

John's drug-enabled placidity came at a cost. He was taking acid frequently now, sometimes with a group of hangers-on that he would invite back to Kenwood after a night out in the clubs. Cynthia and Julian got used to strangers in the house. "They'd wander round, glassy-eyed, crash out on the sofas, beds and floors, then eat whatever they could find in the kitchen," Cynthia wrote in her memoir. "John was an essentially private man, but under the influence of drugs he was vulnerable to anyone and everyone who wanted to take advantage of him." John's use of LSD put an ever-greater distance between him and Cynthia. In the spring of 1967, he invited Pete Shotton to move into Kenwood, primarily so that he would have someone to take it with. The first time they took it together was at Julian's fourth birthday party. After that, John would bring a mug of tea and a tab of acid to Shotton's room every morning.

Not surprisingly, John's productivity suffered. He had never found it so hard to create new songs. Other than "A Day in the Life," only three of the songs on *Sgt. Pepper* were initiated by him: "Lucy in the Sky with Diamonds," "Being for the Benefit of Mr. Kite!" and "Good Morning Good Morning." Even on those, McCartney was the midwife. Although John claimed "Kite" as his, McCartney remembers being at John's house, pointing to the circus poster that inspired it and helping John turn its copy into lyrics. Paul co-wrote "Lucy," too. The number of co-created Lennon and McCartney songs on *Pepper* (at least six feature significant writing contributions from both of them) is testament to their closeness at this time, but also to how much Paul was now having to coax songs out of his partner.

Nobody, not even John, believed more in John's talents than Paul, or was more deeply invested in him making the most of them. McCartney also wanted his friend to be happy. He could see that John was calmer and better-tempered than he had been. He could also see that John was unmoored. When John wasn't working, he was tripping. Left to drift aimlessly, he might lose himself altogether. By choosing to take LSD with him, Paul was giving John a chance to take the upper hand in at least one aspect of their relationship—to play the role of psychedelic guide—while ensuring that the drug's mind-expanding properties were channeled into creativity.

In "Getting Better," Paul nudged John into creating a kind of self-help narrative of his own life, sung, paradoxically, by Paul. The narrative is commented on, waspishly, by John (*fool, you fool*), playing a Greek chorus in the drama of his own maturation. The singer has been helped to put aside the self-loathing and rage of his youth by, well, someone. His realization is arrived at grudgingly, as something he *has* to admit, just as you might acknowledge a friend who often annoys you but who is busy saving you from yourself.

22   I AM THE WALRUS

On April 1, 1967, all four Beatles arrived at the studio to record
the reprise of the *Sgt. Pepper* theme. They were in high spirits.
The album was very nearly done. It was a Saturday, unusually;
despite the intensity with which they worked when recording, the
Beatles habitually took weekends off, but Paul was scheduled to
fly to the US on Monday, to be reunited with Jane Asher. Studio
Two, where they usually recorded, wasn't available, so they had to
record in the cavernous space of Studio One, where the orchestra
had recorded its part for "A Day in the Life." The engineers set
up the equipment so that the Beatles were close together and put
up screens around them to stop the sound dissipating. The four
friends sat in a secluded semicircle so that they could watch one
another as they played. Paul counted them in and they tore into
the song with ferocity.

Early in 1967, "Sgt. Pepper's Lonely Hearts Club Band" had
become the title and theme of the new album. "I thought it would
be nice to lose our identities, to submerge ourselves in the persona
of a fake group," Paul said later. He also said: "We agreed that
we weren't the Beatles anymore, [that] it wasn't 'John' singing on
this track or that. It was anyone John wanted to be." A new wave

of groups was emerging from California, along with a market for psychedelia and hippie culture. Paul conceived of the fake group as a mix of this and an old music-hall act. If the Beatles had merely adopted the mannerisms of this new scene, they would have looked like they were trying to keep up. Instead, they plumbed the English past to create something new.

The resulting album fused modern sounds with old ones. The title track is powered by Jimi Hendrix–style guitar (played by Paul, who frequently went to see Hendrix play) while the lyrics affectionately parody a variety-show compère ("you're such a lovely audience").* The psychedelic imagery of "Lucy in the Sky with Diamonds" sits alongside a song about the comforts of marriage, in trad jazz style ("When I'm Sixty-Four" may be the most radical statement on the album). McCartney has noted how much *Sgt. Pepper* sounds like radio—a radio that is being tuned through different stations, dipping into different worlds. John and Paul grew up to the ambient background of show tunes, brass bands, dance bands, classical music, comedy performances. We tend to think of electronic media as a series of successive transformations—radio to TV to the internet, records to CDs to streaming—but in the long view, what distinguishes them may turn out to be less important than what they have in common. Electronic media have the effect of folding time upon itself. The past does not pass but becomes accessible in the present. This is how the Beatles approach culture and history on *Pepper*: as a vast library of sounds and sensations to be raided at will.

Pepper reimagines the music of the past. It treats dance bands and orchestras and variety nights and harpsichords as sources of magic, mischief, and subversion, rather than as anachronisms that must be cast behind in order to start again. The album cover, designed by Peter Blake and Jann Haworth from McCartney's concept, declares this theme. It claims its figures for the *Pepper* ethos and, in doing so, changes them. Marilyn Monroe becomes somebody else inside the Beatles' tent; so do Shirley Temple, Karl Marx, and Aleister Crowley. The generosity of spirit evident on "She's Leaving Home" extends

---

* The Beatles-Hendrix admiration was mutual. Three days after *Pepper* was released, McCartney and Harrison went to the Saville Theatre in London to see Hendrix perform. Hendrix opened the show with a cover of *Pepper*'s title track.

universally: this party includes the old as well as the young, and the dead and the living. While others were demanding the older generation fade away, the Beatles invited everyone to view this culture war from both sides at once, and in doing so to transcend it. The Beatles, dressed as psychedelic Edwardian bandsmen, stand next to a waxwork of themselves as moptops in suits.

Pepper was the first Beatles album to be made with no prospect of the songs being played live. Until the Beatles, most LPs had been conceived of as, literally, records: documents of live performance. As it developed under McCartney's direction, *Pepper* gloried in being a record for its own sake:

> We realised for the first time that someday someone would actually be holding a thing they'd call "the Beatles new LP" and that normally it would be a collection of songs with a nice picture on the cover, nothing more. So the idea was to do a complete thing that you could make of what you liked—just a little magic presentation.

Pepper achieves what the art critic Clement Greenberg termed "medium specificity." Everything about its packaging and presentation—the cover, the costumes, the gatefold design, the printed lyrics, the cut-out masks—invites listeners to remember that this is a record, and that the record *is* the work. In a stroke of intuitive conceptual genius, McCartney framed the music as a live performance by this fictional band.

The songs on *Pepper* begin with everyday activities (home maintenance, parking a car) or banal sentiments (good morning, it's getting better, I like my friends) and transform them into something strange and potent. "Fixing a Hole" starts with Paul singing a jolly melody over a galumphing bass line. Then his voice goes high and floaty and the song spirals into another dimension. The singer knows he is fixing a hole, not to fix the hole but to stop his mind from wandering—that his focus on work and activity is a way to repress what lies beneath. In that, moment, as the melody rises upward like smoke, Paul becomes a little more like John, drifting through mental space. *Pepper* repeatedly traverses the line between reality and dream, the most striking example coming at the end of Paul's section in "A Day in the Life."

Pepper's songs do not consistently refer to the idea of Sergeant Pepper's band, or a live show, or to childhood. But the unruliness of its contents is the point. *Pepper* is a loose, baggy monster in which the meandering muse takes primacy over the thinking brain. In an era when art and creativity are always being commandeered in the name of something else—commerce, politics, mental health—there is something enduringly subversive about insisting on music for music's sake. The imagination, the Beatles seem to say, is irreducible to ends, impossible to corral. It may bring delight, it may bring horror. It will go where it will go.

✈

Having completed the longest and most intensive set of recording sessions that they had ever undertaken, the Beatles went back to work. There had been talk of doing a TV show around *Sgt. Pepper*, but the Beatles didn't like to linger on a completed project. In California, Paul had heard about the hippie legend of Ken Kesey and the Merry Pranksters, who in 1964 drove a multicolored school bus across America, stoned out of their minds. McCartney thought the Beatles could do something similar for a TV special, but in their own way, combining psychedelia with the English tradition of family trips to the seaside. He gathered the others, and they agreed on the new concept: *Magical Mystery Tour*.

On the evening of April 25, four days since the last session for *Pepper*, the Beatles began work on the title track. Paul had an idea but, unusually for him, hadn't written a whole song. He knew what he wanted: a vaudeville production with high-kicking brass—something that would feel like an irresistible invitation. He sat at the piano in Studio Two and sang the chorus of "Magical Mystery Tour" as the others contributed ideas. The track was put together in bits and pieces and not completed until November; the Beatles were not working with their usual level of focus, understandably enough. The songs they worked on during this period were not for an album, as such, but for soundtracks—for the envisaged TV special, and for an animated film called *Yellow Submarine*, which they had approved but otherwise had little to do with. The music sounds improvised and loose: "It's All Too Much," "All Together Now," "Baby You're a Rich Man." These tracks have a dazed and ragged charm all of their own. "The Fool on the Hill" (started in September) and "Your Mother Should Know," both Paul songs, are suffused with dreamy melancholy (the former moves from a major-key verse to a minor-key chorus; the latter features a funereal church organ). The Beatles didn't take much of a break, but they did sound like they were gently unwinding.

Sgt. Pepper's Lonely Hearts Club Band was introduced to the world at the start of June, to a euphoric reception. Its conquest was absolute. It was as if the Beatles had thrown an invisible net of delight around the world. In America, you could drive from coast to coast and the music of *Pepper* would surround you like air: "You would hear it from cars, drifting out of windows where you walked, in your friends' homes, and in your head, always," wrote the critic Ellen Sander. The philosopher Langdon Winner recalled:

> In every city in Europe and America the stereo systems and the radio played, "What would you think if I sang out of tune . . . Woke up, got out of bed . . . looked much older, and the bag across her shoulder . . . in the sky with diamonds, Lucy in the . . ." and everyone listened. At the time I happened to be driving across country on Interstate 80. In each city where I stopped for gas or food—Laramie, Ogallala, Moline, South Bend—the melodies wafted in from some far-off transistor radio or portable hi-fi. It was the most amazing thing I've ever heard.

Pepper was hailed by the critical establishment as a high artistic achievement, the moment the Beatles escaped the confines of pop altogether. In recent years, its reputation has diminished somewhat as people point to its relative paucity of truly great songs. Was *Pepper*'s spectacular impact on the world down to its framing—the concept, the costumes, the cover—as much as its music? Perhaps, but the frame is part of the picture. *Pepper* demands to be heard as a complete work, like a symphony or opera; its songs come fully alive only in the context of the album's governing fantasy. Now that we're used to streaming music in bits, in every sense, the intended experience is hard to recapture, though perhaps that's our failure rather than *Pepper*'s.

Either way, the immediate and vast success of *Pepper* affirmed the Beatles' sense that they were living in a dream. In a dream, you decide to fly and you fly, and it doesn't even seem odd that you can. The Beatles played the fool in Hamburg and the Germans hailed them for it. They did whatever they wanted onstage at the Cavern and became the biggest band in Liverpool. They got famous in Britain and then the whole world by making music they loved and making one another laugh. After getting around to writing songs for the band, John and Paul found they couldn't write a song that wasn't a hit. They made albums with sitars and tape loops and kids' songs on them; they dressed up as Day-Glo soldiers and gave themselves a different name and sang about LSD and death. And everything worked. The more that they delved into their own imaginary world, the more powerfully they seemed to connect with everyone. The Beatles spent little time marveling at this. They scooped up happy accidents like coins in the street, and the coins were everywhere they looked.

They were by now very aware of how much they meant to people, although the knowledge was not yet a burden. They had become more relaxed about fans now that the chaos of Beatlemania had subsided. John let some into the grounds of Kenwood. Paul was friendly toward the fans permanently stationed outside Cavendish Avenue, who peered into the house at every opportunity. There is a tape of him chatting to a group of teenage girls—one of them was carrying a tape recorder—in July 1967. He sounds as if he has all the time in the world, reading out dedications to their absent friends, introducing them to Martha, and rambling on about how the world is changing ("[We] don't really want to be spanked any more, thank you, Daddy . . ."). In early 1968, when the Beatles were recording "Across the Universe" at Abbey Road and decided they wanted female voices on the track, Paul simply went outside and invited a couple of fans to help out.

✆

Shea Stadium may have been the top of the mountain, yet once they stopped touring the Beatles continued rising. In the summer of 1967 they must have felt positively stratospheric. In June, right after releasing *Pepper*, they recorded a new song live on TV and released it as a single; it went to number one. "All You Need Is Love" was written to order. The Beatles had accepted an invitation to take part in an international television special called *Our World*. A joint production between the BBC and the European Broadcasting Union, the idea was to make a groundbreaking, world-uniting live broadcast over the first satellite network capable of sending a TV signal around the world. The Beatles were chosen as the star attraction from Britain. Their segment would be broadcast live from Abbey Road.

Pepper was many things, but it didn't have a big song that everyone could sing. "All You Need Is Love" became the anthem of the summer of 1967—the Summer of Love. It was written by John, and reflected his growing interest in the possibilities of mass communication. In "Tomorrow Never Knows" he channeled psychedelic wisdom to the masses. The 1966 American tour, traumatic and unpleasant as it was, reinforced his idea of himself as a quasi-political figure, and of the Beatles as a global force for good. He was fascinated by advertising, and with "All You Need Is Love" perfected the art of condensing a message into a slogan everyone could remember, repeat, and sing.

The song's uplift is inflected with deadpan wit. Its tautologies ("nothing you can do that can't be done") and paradoxes ("There's nowhere you can be that isn't where you're meant to be") are as deep or as meaningless as you want them to be. John was not being glib: when he sings about how, with love, you can "learn how to be you in time," he wants it to be true. He sings behind the beat, insouciantly, almost speaking his lines, and chops beats from the bars, giving the song a slightly tipsy feel. The chorus, or slogan, chanted more than sung, is followed by an irresistibly sleazy run on the horns.

As on *Pepper*, the Beatles recruited the past into their vision of the future. The song is introduced with a portentous drumroll, and a martial band strikes up France's national anthem, "La Marseillaise," before dissolving, drunkenly, into the Beatles singing *love, love, love*. The extended final section runs giddy with musical quotations, from Bach to "Greensleeves" to Glenn Miller. At one point, John breaks into a rendition of "She Loves You," which already seemed to belong to another epoch (it was from four years before).*

---

* I say it was John, but this, like the question of who sang the *ahh*s on "A Day in the Life," is a subject of perennial disputation among Beatle fans. It sounds like Paul, at least at first, but on the footage of the event there is a shot of John singing it. There's also a record of John singing it in a

✆

As much as they took satisfaction in their heady achievements, the Beatles were uncertain about what to do next. There was no upcoming tour and no immediate call for a new album. George spent time in Haight-Ashbury, center of hippie culture. Ringo didn't know what to do with himself. But the Beatle most vulnerable when left to his own devices was John. Around this time—summer 1967 to early 1968—he was almost helplessly dependent on the others. He had tried acting and it was disappointing; his drawing and poetry writing weren't taking off. Only when he was working with Paul did he feel like a genius—like the kind of person who could create "A Day in the Life," now being rapturously acclaimed. John's sense of self was always fragile; under the influence of his heavy LSD intake, it had thinned to the point of dissolution, except when he was with his friends. He needed Paul to turn him on, almost literally.

For a renowned wit, John could be deeply introverted. His chauffeur in Spain told a magazine that Lennon hadn't spoken to him during the several hours it took to arrive at the film shoot. When Lennon heard about this, he was surprised, as he didn't recall not speaking. He told Hunter Davies that after the touring stopped he frequently didn't get out of bed until three in the afternoon; he joked that he was an expert at inactivity, and that his record for not talking to anyone was three days. However proud John was of his ability to do nothing, it's also true that his self-description matches that of a person who is depressed, and sometimes in a state of drug-induced psychosis. In an interview with Davies, he described episodes of what psychiatrists would call disassociation, during which he felt disconnected from his own body: "I can see my hands and realize they're moving, but it's a robot who's doing it . . . It's frightening really, when it gets too bad."

John was finding it difficult to connect with his immediate family. Paul was more likely to play with Julian, to swing him up on his shoulders and play games with him. John told Davies he found it hard to spend time with

---

rehearsal session the day before. My best guess is that, in the performance, Paul starts the phrase and John picks it up. It's hardly coincidence that both these conundrums should hail from 1967, the year when John and Paul were most in sync.

people who expect normal conversation, including, it is implied, Cynthia. Cynthia was present during John's conversation with Davies and she chips in, addressing her husband as much as Davies—you get the sense of a rare occasion in which John is actually communicating, and that she wants to seize the opportunity to be heard, with Davies unwittingly playing the role of couple's therapist. At one point Cynthia tells Davies that had it not been for her getting pregnant, she and John would not be together now, and John agrees. It isn't said with acrimony or bitterness; it is just said.

John tells Davies that the only people with whom he feels truly comfortable are Paul, George, and Ringo: "We talk in code to each other as Beatles. We always did that, when we had so many strangers around us on tours . . . We understand each other [at another point he says, 'we feel each other']." Now and again, he says, the group have to sit down and talk to one another in the conventional sense, but most of the time, they communicate in music—in songs and sounds. He says he needs to be with the other Beatles in order to remember who he is. He talks about how glad he was to see them on his return from Spain, because they made him feel normal again. "I have to see the others to see myself."

In the summer of 1967, Lennon initiated one of the strangest and most poetic of Beatle episodes: a trip to Greece to explore the possibility of buying an island where they all could live. Brian Epstein's personal assistant, Alistair Taylor, was given the task of identifying an island for sale. He found one that was available for £89,914. It had five fisherman's cottages—the idea was that one would be for communal use, plus one for each Beatle. "We're all going to live there, perhaps forever, just coming home for visits," Lennon told Davies, boyishly. His idea was that the Beatles, with partners and staff, would live in a protected compound in the middle of the island. There would be a play area in the middle, and a recording studio. From this central point, four arbors would lead off like the spokes of a wheel to the four Beatle houses. The entourage—Brian Epstein, Neil Aspinall, Mal Evans, and a few others—would live in the outer grounds.

The party set off in July: the four Beatles and their partners, and Julian, along with Mal, Neil, and Alistair, their Greek friend Alexis Mardas, and

Paula Boyd (Pattie's sister). They flew to Athens and chartered a luxury yacht with a crew of seven to sail across the Aegean, stopping off at islands, sunbathing, playing music, and taking drugs. Taylor relates a little story that gives us a glimpse of the group's bonhomie:

> My happiest memory came late one moonlit night when John, George, Mal and I sat out on deck watching a glorious Greek moon. The captain was holding the yacht steadily on a course towards the beam of light that the moon threw on to the gently rippled surface of the sea. George picked out the notes of the Hare Krishna chorus on his ukulele and John, Mal and I quietly chanted the words . . . we were totally at peace with the world as we sat there with legs crossed in the lotus position, staring together up at the shining column of marvellous moonbeams.

The group sat in silence for a long while, until Taylor said, "Just look at the moon." After a beat, John said, "Well spotted, Alistair," and everyone collapsed into giggles.

The island was just as beautiful as the Beatles hoped and a purchase was pursued. It encountered difficulties. Britain's exchange controls made it hard to transfer the funds required to renovate the cottages and build the compound. After many legal opinions, and a signed letter from the British chancellor, James Callaghan, that obstacle was overcome, but the project was abandoned anyway, partly because it was too hard to get the necessary planning permission. John had previously bought an island off the coast of Ireland for the same purpose; that came to nothing, too.* The truth is that this was a fantasy of John's which Paul merely entertained. Marianne Faithfull, recalling John's enthusiasm for the Greek project, gave an explanation for its failure that is both funny and perceptive: "The last thing Paul wanted to do was live on some fucking island."

---

* In *The Beatles Anthology* (258), Ringo mentions another scheme: "We were also going to buy a village in England—one with rows of houses on four sides and a village green in the middle. We were going to have a side each."

During the conversation with Hunter Davies, Cynthia says, "What I would like is a holiday on our own, without the Beatles. Just John, Julian, and me." Lennon, smiling, says, "You what? Not even with our Beatle buddies?" Cynthia shakes her head. "They seem to need you less than you need them."

☙

In the late summer and early autumn of 1967, a series of events in the Beatles' world converged in such a dramatic, pivotal way as to make one suspicious of the hand of an invisible narrator. In August they tried once again to shuck off the carapace of Beatledom and remake themselves, this time spiritually. They caught a train from London to Bangor, in north Wales, to take part in a retreat led by an entrepreneurial forty-nine-year-old Hindu swami known as Maharishi Mahesh Yogi. George's wife, Pattie, had begun to study his form of meditation and enthused about it to the others.

The Maharishi had already built a public profile in America and Europe (Paul remembered seeing his bearded, genial face on TV, years before). He had spotted an opportunity to package Eastern wisdom for Westerners as a form of self-improvement. He left out or disavowed aspects of Hindu philosophy that might be distasteful, such as caste or the place of women, and focused on the benefits of meditation. "Transcendental Meditation" was an easy-to-learn technique that involved the repetition of a bespoke mantra assigned to each student. The mantra didn't have a meaning; it was a sound that trained the mind. The benefits were said to be instant. You can see why this form of meditation appealed to the Beatles, especially John, to whom it promised an end to mental agitation without the side effects of drugs. It helped that the Maharishi had a sense of humor. Rather than being a forbidding authority figure, like a priest, he was a small, smiling man with an infectious giggle. Neither did he demand that his students renounce the world of social connection and sensual pleasure; the aim was not detachment, he explained, but spiritual enrichment.

On August 24, John, Paul, and George (Ringo was preoccupied by the recent arrival of his second son) attended a lecture by the Maharishi at the Hilton Hotel on Park Lane. They were introduced to him afterward and found him to be charming and witty. He invited them to attend his retreat in Bangor the next day, and in a moment of rebellious spontaneity the Beatles made the decision to go, along with their partners (except for new mother Maureen), and with minimal involvement from their management company. As a result, the journey was slightly chaotic. The Lennons arrived at the station by car minutes before departure. John leaped out and ran, without remembering that nobody from NEMS was on hand to carry his baggage. That fell to Cynthia, who had to lug the bags through a jostling crowd of reporters, photographers, and fans. John put his head out the train window and shouted, "Tell them to let you on," but it was too late. Left standing with the bags, Cynthia felt humiliated and more convinced than ever that her marriage was coming apart.

The Beatles had a few friends aboard, including Mick Jagger and Marianne Faithfull. The Maharishi and his entourage were on the same train. (Cynthia was driven to Bangor by Neil Aspinall. Jane Asher was not on the train but drove up the next afternoon.) At Bangor College, where the retreat was held, the Beatles stayed in student dormitories along with around three hundred other attendees, ate bad food from the canteen, and diligently set about learning the basics of meditation. They decided that they would soon go to visit the Maharishi in India for a more authentic experience. Then they got a phone call.

Since the Beatles had stopped touring, Brian Epstein's always fragile mental equilibrium was severely disrupted. Over the course of 1967, those who worked for him at NEMS had to cope with increasingly erratic behavior. He ignored important calls, threw tantrums, and struggled to focus. He had other artists on his roster but felt marginalized from the group he cared about most. The Beatles had been absorbed in the making of *Sgt. Pepper* and did not require much from Brian. He feared that they would replace him with someone more qualified to manage the affairs of a global corporation, and not without reason: they had already discussed with Brian a plan to consolidate Beatle affairs into a wholly owned company. In August, Epstein told *Melody Maker*, "I am certain that they would not agree to be managed by anyone else," the kind of thing you would say if you're not at all certain.

Epstein organized the press launch of *Pepper* and was cheered by the album's success, but shortly before this he had been diagnosed with severe depression and had checked into the Priory, a private psychiatric hospital.

He was being dragged down by deep psychological and social forces: the double life he was still forced to live, his intense sexual desires and intense self-loathing, and an addiction to barbiturates and amphetamines. Amid this turmoil, his father died. His beloved mother, Queenie, came to stay with him in London for a few weeks, during which he recovered a modicum of stability. But on the weekend after Queenie returned to Liverpool he died at home, his body full of a sedative called Carbrital. The coroner's verdict of death by accident was probably accurate, in a narrow sense.

In Bangor, the Beatles had to face the media just hours after getting the news (except for Paul, who had already driven home with Jane). John, George, and Ringo gave an impromptu press conference after emerging from a session with the Maharishi, who spoke to them about the ultimate irrelevance of death. Shell-shocked, they repeated similar platitudes. Privately, shock and grief mingled with nerves and uncertainty. Even in his reduced form, Brian—whom they sometimes called "Eppy," and other times, with deference that wasn't entirely a joke, "Mr. Epstein"—had been a reassuring background presence, perhaps more so than they realized: not unlike a parent, in that sense. "I knew that we were in trouble," said Lennon of this moment, later on. "I was scared."

Back in London, it was Paul who stepped into the role of the group's surrogate parent, and did what his own mother might have done: proposed work. On September 1, two days after Brian's funeral, McCartney insisted that the Beatles and their close associates meet at his house to decide what to do next. Everyone else felt a little dazed and unready, but according to Peter Brown, who was there, Paul's view was that they had to keep moving or risk losing the momentum of *Pepper*.* He suggested the Beatles delay their trip to India and make the *Magical Mystery Tour* show instead. With some trepidation, the others agreed. It was taken for granted among young creatives that filmmaking was an accessible art form not that different from music. Besides, the Beatles

---

* Brown, in shock at the loss of his former boss, recalled walking to a window during this meeting, and staring blankly at the street. He felt someone wrap their arms around him in a hug. It was Lennon. "Are you all right?" asked Lennon. "No," said Brown. "Nor am I, Peter," said John. "Nor am I." (Peter Brown and Steven Gaines, *All You Need Is Love*, 65.)

were used to everything they dreamed up going perfectly. "A record is sound and a film is visual, that's the only difference," McCartney told the press.

Going to work meant recording more songs for the soundtrack. Nine days after Epstein's death, the Beatles entered Abbey Road. Geoff Emerick remembers them being subdued, John seemingly in a state of shock, Ringo close to tears, Paul the most composed. As had become standard practice, the first song they worked on was one of John's. The other Beatles, Emerick, and George Martin gathered around to listen to John play piano and sing, to a two-note melody, "I am he as you are he / As you are me and we are all together." The group then set about laying down a backing track, although they were distracted, minds elsewhere. "I distinctly remember the look of emptiness on all their faces while they were playing 'I Am the Walrus.' It's one of the saddest memories I have of my time with the Beatles," says Emerick. When Ringo, unusually, had trouble keeping a steady beat, Paul stood in front of his friend and played tambourine, "effectively acting as both a cheerleader and a human click track." Emerick remembers Paul telling Ringo not to worry. "I'll keep you locked in."

Lennon's childhood was making an incursion into his life at this time, in an unsettling way. A few years before, Alf Lennon had resurfaced. Someone in the entertainment industry discovered Alf washing dishes in an inn in Surrey. The story made headlines—Beatle's father a lowly dishwasher—and Alf was invited to make a novelty record. "That's My Life" was a sentimental look back on a life at sea. Alf felt emboldened to visit John at Kenwood. John refused to see him. "I showed him the door. I wasn't having him in the house." He arranged for some money to be sent.

Alf did not give up hope of reestablishing a relationship with his son, however, and after Epstein's death he sent John a note of condolence. John replied in a conciliatory tone ("Dear Dad, Alf, Fred, Pater, whatever . . .") and Alf was ferried to Kenwood by John's chauffeur. John received him more warmly this time, even giving Alf one of his hugs. Come and live at Kenwood, he said, and Alf agreed. John installed him and his nineteen-year-old girlfriend, Pauline Jones, in what had been the servants' apartment at the top of the house, but then pretty much ignored him. Cynthia wasn't interested in seeing them either. Alf ended up moping around the house, alone and miserable. Eventually (at the suggestion of Cynthia's mother) he was set up, at John's expense, in his own apartment in Brighton. He found out later that John was very upset by his decision to leave. It's hard not to see this episode as John re-playing his childhood relationship with his father, but this time with himself in control—asserting mastery by reducing Alf to the status of a servant. But he only ended up replaying the pain of abandonment.

Lennon had been the Beatle closest to Epstein, and not just for tacti-cal reasons. John knew what it felt like to have a hidden monster inside. In "Walrus" he pours out his feelings about Epstein's death (and the deaths that preceded it) in an eloquent howl of rage and confusion. The lyrics to "I Am the Walrus" invoke episodes from Lewis Carroll's *Through the Looking-Glass*. In one, the Walrus and the Carpenter trick a group of docile oysters into presenting themselves for dinner. The pair of them are superior, beguil-ing, and ruthless. Alice can't decide which she likes best, concluding, "They are *both* very unpleasant characters." I'm reminded of Bob Wooler's charac-terization of Lennon and McCartney as a pair of charming psychopaths. In 1970, during his infamous *Rolling Stone* interview, Lennon said, "You have to be a bastard to make it, that's a fact, and the Beatles are the biggest bas-tards on earth." In "Walrus," John also calls himself "the Eggman": Humpty Dumpty, so adept with words that he can use them to convince himself of anything, even his own inviolability. In the story, Humpty explains to Alice that he is utterly safe on top of the wall shortly before falling off it.

Like Carroll or that other Victorian master of nonsense, Edward Lear, Lennon took too much delight in the echoes, connotations, and sheer mu-sic of words to write in neatly decipherable code. In "Walrus" he rails at "expert textperts"—those who confidently offered interpretations of Beatle lyrics. One problem for the cryptologists is that Lennon's words can't be di-vorced from his singing (his books of poetry are not on a par with his songs). His lyrics were drawn from the well of his unconscious (of "Walrus," he said, "the whole first verse was written without any knowledge"), but they were also shaped to fit the beats and sounds in his head, to flood our nervous systems as well as our brains. Just as Lennon strives to get beyond musical forms to access pure experience, he tries to break language, too: *goo-goo ga joob*. In "Walrus" he uses the nonsense to create the space for a plain and direct statement of pain: *I'm crying*.

The introductory chord sequence sounds as if it comes from somewhere outside music itself. The obsessive-compulsive tune of the verse was inspired by a distant police siren. All of the music is happening underneath, in the harmonic structure. A recursive sequence of major chords with no tonal beginning or end takes us down and around and up and down again, our disorientation enhanced by woozy strings, nightmarish brass, and chanting, cackling backing singers. The promise of repose in "Strawberry Fields Forever" is absent. In the fade-out, a radio moves randomly through different frequencies, picking up snippets of British culture, including lines from a production of *King Lear*: "sit you down, Father, rest you." "Walrus" isn't desperate or nihilistic: Lennon shows us misery and anger and, in the opening line of the song, a way out of it.

> I had "I am he as you are he as we are all together." I had just
> these two lines on the typewriter, and then about two weeks later
> I ran through and wrote another two lines, and then . . . I just
> knocked the rest of it off.

It seems odd that the song's climactic refrain should be an exultant assertion of selfhood—I *am*—at a time when Lennon was deeply uncertain about who he was. But that first line suggests that only when merged with one another are we truly ourselves. The Walrus isn't an I but an us.

23   LADY MADONNA

At the start of 1968 the Beatles prepared for a lengthy sojourn at the Maharishi's ashram in India. On Saturday, February 3, they convened at Abbey Road to begin work on a single to be released in their absence. They didn't particularly need to record one—the world would still have been waiting for them on their return—but they wanted to. They began with Paul's new song, "Lady Madonna," before moving on to one from John, called "Across the Universe." It was meant to be a contender for the single but John wasn't satisfied, even after the group tried several arrangements, and it was put aside (it would appear on the Beatles' 1970 LP, *Let It Be*). Two days later, they began recording George's song "The Inner Light," based on a raga he had recorded with Indian musicians in Bombay.

In the evening, they returned to "Lady Madonna," to which Paul decided to add a brass section. Five days later the Beatles assembled at Abbey Road on a Sunday to record a promotional film for it. The idea was to show the Beatles at work—that is, pretending to record "Lady Madonna." Once inside the studio, however, the Beatles decided there and then to record a new song—one that John had written for the *Yellow Submarine* soundtrack, called

"Hey Bulldog." "Lady Madonna" would be the A side of the new single, with "The Inner Light" as the B side.

Four songs in nine days: an incredibly productive period. The group made progress on a new business plan, too: at the end of December, they opened the Apple Boutique store on Baker Street, the first move in what would become Apple Corps (inspired by a Magritte painting that Paul owned: *Le Jeu de Mourre*). The Beatles ought to have been exhausted. They had been making records almost ceaselessly for five years. They had just experienced a crowning success with *Pepper*, followed by the shock of Brian's death, followed by their first public failure: *Magical Mystery Tour* met with critical derision in Britain and America. Yet they seemed to draw energy from adversity, and everything that happened to them consolidated their mutual bond. Paul had a geodesic dome built in his back garden at Cavendish Avenue as a kind of chapel for them to meditate in, or to smoke pot, or both. The Maharishi was firmly against drug-taking; the Beatles seem to have interpreted this by cutting out LSD but continuing to smoke marijuana. Meditation therefore replaced LSD as a means of psychic exploration for the group; even John seems to have stopped taking acid in late 1967.

The Asher-McCartney relationship endured, notwithstanding the changes in McCartney, and his continuing affairs. The couple spent ten days of December 1967 alone together in Scotland on a farm that McCartney had acquired the year before. (His choice of a getaway was influenced by John. Paul: "I was always drawn to the romantic notion of the Highlands. And John was too; he had visited relatives who had a croft in the Highlands, and he spoke romantically of it, so I had that thought in my head.") On their return at Christmas they announced their engagement. The trip, and the engagement, were an attempt to reset their passionate but troubled relationship.

If Paul and Jane had their difficulties, John and Cynthia's marriage was barely alive. John had been seeing other women, although he did not feel tied to any of them. His creative partnership with Paul was still the biggest constant in his life, and he felt insecure about it. On the tape of a private conversation from 1969 we can hear John telling Paul how comparatively weak he had felt at this time. Referring to the *Magical Mystery Tour* soundtrack, he says: "I didn't write any of that except 'Walrus' [he exaggerates here, though not by much]. I'd accept it and you'd already have five or six songs." John may also have been disconcerted by Paul's engagement to Jane. It's telling that he wrote a song around this time ("Across the Universe") that expresses a determination that his world will not be changed.

John and Paul were moving on from psychedelia. These new songs were noticeably free of studio trickery or acid-infused lyrics. "Lady Madonna" took its musical cue from a boogie-woogie jazz band hit from 1956. "Hey Bulldog," also based on a driving piano riff, is an exhilaratingly funky rock song. The spontaneity of the recording is audible; in the song's outro, Paul and John bark and howl into the same microphone, cracking each other up. If "Walrus" throbs with anger and grief, "Bulldog" is a shout of empathy—*if you're lonely you can talk to me*. McCartney's musical response to Brian's death had been even more oblique than John's. "Hello Goodbye," which became the first single from *Magical Mystery Tour*, sounds gloriously simple, but its apparent jauntiness belies musical complexity and lyrical ambiguity. The words express childlike bafflement at the way someone you love can just disappear from the world. *Why* do you say goodbye?

While his peers celebrated drugs and sexual liberation, Paul sang about the wisdom of mothers, in "Your Mother Should Know" and "Lady Madonna." Read the latter's lyrics as literal description and they don't add up to much, but as impressionistic brushstrokes they deftly portray a woman beleaguered by the ceaseless demands of others, trying to hang on to her sense of self. "Lady Madonna" evokes an idealized vision of Paul's mother: a homemaker who is also a provider, a humanly sensual Mary. That's not to say it's *about* his mother. Insofar as it's about anything, it's that two-handed piano riff, the life force itself, shaking us out of sadness, dragging us out of bed, propelling us into whatever comes next.

24   YER BLUES

In one of the most revealing scenes in *Get Back*, the Beatles are in the middle of a session when Paul, sitting with an acoustic guitar, eagerly announces to John that the night before he watched some film of the Beatles' visit to India, which had occurred just under a year previously. All four had taken Super 8 film cameras on the trip. Paul had gathered the footage and turned it into a home movie. Now he has watched it, for the first time. "It's incredible," he says, "you just sort of see us. What we're doing. It's unbelievable." This hangs in the air for a moment, until John says, "What *were* we doing?"

Like other intra-Beatle conversations captured in *Get Back*, this one is quicksilver, ambiguous, and elusive, in the rhythm of close friends who say a lot to each other without saying very much. George tends to be relatively blunt, whereas John and Paul seem always to be poised finely between seriousness and humor. Sincerity dissolves into laughter; jokes carry hidden freight. For outsiders it is all very hard to read, but what's clear is that the moment Paul starts talking about India, the hackles of John and George rise. While Paul enthuses about the footage, John mutters over or under him constantly, as if trying to deflect him from this line of

229

conversation or gently shut him up. Paul pushes on, either because he doesn't care that John is uncomfortable or because he doesn't notice.

> Paul replies to John: "I don't really know, but we totally put our own personalities under, for the sake of it. And you can really *see*, y'know, we're all sort of . . . [does an impression of someone pretending to strike a spiritual pose]."

> John (rather sharply, and while Paul is still talking): "Who's writing all them songs?"

> George, with an edge: "Do you regret having gone there?"

> Paul: "Oh no. No!"

> John, almost under his breath: "I don't regret anything, ever, not even Bob Wooler."

> Paul: "We weren't really very truthful there. Things like sneaking round the back and saying, 'It's a bit like school, isn't it?' You can see on the film that it's very *much* like school, and really, we should have said—"

> John interrupts: "We should call the film 'What we did on our holidays.'"

> Paul, to John: "There's a very long shot of you walking with him [the Maharishi]. And it's just not *you*, y'know?"

> John does an obedient-student face, which gets Paul laughing. "Yeah!"

> Paul now takes over the impression of John being a good student: "Tell me, old master . . . !"

John repeats the phrase and Paul says, chuckling: "And Linda
   [Paul's girlfriend at the time] remembered that thing you said
   the other night about when you went up in the helicopter with
   him. You just thought he might slip you the Answer."

They both laugh at this. (When the Maharishi had gone on a helicopter
trip John asked to accompany him, in the hope, he later admitted, that he
would be given the secret of everything.)

Now George speaks up: "That is the biggest joke," he says,
   witheringly, "'to be yourselves.' 'Cause that was the purpose of
   going there, to try and find who yourself really is—"

John says softly: "Yes. Well, we found out, didn't we?"

George carries on with his lecture: "—and if you were really yourself
   you wouldn't be any of who we are now." At this he stands up
   and stubs a cigarette out. There is an awkward silence. Paul
   says, "Hmm." John says, "We'll act naturally, then." He starts
   playing "Act Naturally" on the guitar.

✠

In mid-February John and George and their wives flew to New Delhi, and
proceeded, by taxi and on foot, to the Maharishi's ashram near Rishikesh in
the foothills of the Himalayas. Paul and Ringo followed four days later. They
had agreed to stay only four weeks; John and George planned to stay for two
months. Rishikesh, an ancient Hindu pilgrimage site, was now a center for
spiritual tourism. Maharishi Mahesh Yogi had the largest ashram there, a
fourteen-acre compound overlooking the Ganges, with accommodation for
seventy-five guests in six white concrete bungalows and various huts (Ringo
likened it to Butlin's holiday camp). It was a three-month course; when the
Beatles arrived, the other students, who came from twenty different countries, had already been there for a few weeks. They included Mia Farrow,
who came with her sister and brother, and was getting over her short-lived

marriage to Frank Sinatra. There was a charge for attendance, which the Maharishi waived for the Beatles, presumably because of their publicity value. In the wake of Bangor, the Maharishi had been feted by global media. *Life* had featured him, declaring 1968 "The Year of the Guru."

The four Beatles were accompanied by their partners—Jane Asher, Cynthia Lennon, Pattie Boyd, and Ringo's wife, Maureen Starkey ("Mo"). Mal Evans was there, and Neil Aspinall arrived a few weeks later. The group attended meals and lectures with the other students but largely kept themselves to themselves, with the exception of musicians they knew, like the Scottish folk singer Donovan and the Beach Boy Mike Love. The Maharishi gave twice-daily lectures to everyone, but the Beatles were granted regular private audiences, rather to the annoyance of the other disciples. All four Beatles meditated for hours during the day, interspersing sessions with sunbathing, reading, and talking.

On colder evenings they listened to records and played music in one another's rooms. John and Paul had brought their guitars. George was at first slightly miffed by this, since he viewed the retreat as an opportunity to escape from who they were at home. But that was not how John and Paul saw it. One evening the students made an excursion to Rishikesh to see a traveling cinema. Paul brought his guitar and (of course) sang to everyone, as the party made its way down an overgrown path in the fading light. The song he sang went "Ob-la-di-ob-la-da, life goes on." Everyone was slightly worried about Prudence, Mia Farrow's sister, who stayed in her room every day and hardly ever attended the communal sessions. George and John visited her bungalow in the evening, with their guitars, and sang Paul's song to cheer her up. Shortly afterward, John wrote "Dear Prudence" about her. A fellow student, Paul Saltzman, witnessed the Beatles playing happily together: "They were very tight." He said that the Beatles seemed closer to one another than to their friends or even their partners.

John and Paul had time, quiet, clear heads, and each other. The result was a quite staggering profusion of new songs, impressive not only for the profusion itself but also because it came after so many other profusions. Songs that they composed or started in Rishikesh filled the group's first double album later in the year, appeared on the Beatles albums that followed, and were also included in Beatle solo albums in the 1970s. The biggest difference was in John, who began writing at the same rate as his partner again. Some of his songs were imbued with serenity—songs like "Julia" and "Child of Nature," about a dream coming true in Rishikesh. Others, like "Yer Blues" and "I'm So Tired," were dark and troubled. It's impossible to date with precision which songs were written when, but John's notebook suggests the first two were written earlier in the stay and the latter two later on, after Paul's departure.

After ten days, Ringo decided to leave. His stomach, which had brought him such trouble as a boy, was too sensitive for the local food, Mo didn't like the bugs, and they both missed their children. Paul and Jane left as planned after four weeks, on March 23. Paul had enjoyed himself, although he did not achieve any "huge spiritual lift-off." He had trouble keeping his mind clear enough to meditate, "because the minute you clear it, a thought comes in and says, 'What are we gonna do about our next record?'" Once back in London, he worried that John and George might never return: "For a week or so, I didn't know if we'd ever see them again, or if there ever would be any Beatles again."

They did come back, but John returned a changed man. Earlier in the stay, he had seemed happy and, for someone who usually found it hard to concentrate for long periods, surprisingly focused, practicing meditation for hours a day. As the stay went on, however, Cynthia sensed him retreating into himself: "He seemed very isolated and would spend days on end with the Maharishi, emerging bleary-eyed and not wanting to communicate with me or anyone." He left their shared bungalow and moved into one by himself, ostensibly so that he could focus on meditating. There may have been another reason for his move. He was receiving regular postcards from Yoko Ono, the Japanese artist he had met nearly eighteen months before and with whom he had stayed in touch. John rose early to collect them. They contained fragments of poems and gnomic aphorisms. "I'm a cloud," said one. "Watch for me in the sky."

By the time Paul left, John was restless and unsettled. At his instigation, he and George were joined by their friend Alexis Mardas, a Greek electrician and inventor, whom John had dubbed "Magic Alex." Mardas passed on a young female American disciple's accusation that the Maharishi had made a sexual advance toward her. After long discussions through the night, with George arguing that it was just a rumor, John and George decided to leave in the morning. They began their journey home on April 10. It was a wrench for George, who was swept along by the sheer force of John's conviction, and soon regretted his decision. Even assuming the rumors of the Maharishi's indiscretions were true (several women later confirmed them with their own experiences), it is odd that it should have mattered so much to John. The Beatles were hardly puritans. McCartney was baffled. "I didn't think it was enough cause to leave the whole meditation centre," he recalled. "What's wrong with that? . . . As far as I'm concerned there's nothing wrong with someone making a pass at someone." It seems likely that by the time Mardas arrived, John was searching for an excuse to explode. Harrison said, years later, "John had wanted to leave anyway."

Why had John got himself into this state? It's impossible to say for sure, but he idealized the Maharishi with a fervency that is hard to understand without taking his formative experiences into account. Imagine: you grow up with two parents who don't seem to care about you—your father is at sea and the mother you believe will finally return to you never quite does. People who do show you love and attention are senselessly ripped away from you. The Christ you learned about at Sunday school and half believed in no longer seems real. You desperately want to be seen and acknowledged, so you seek fame, and get more of it than you ever imagined—and yet, puzzlingly, you still feel invisible and alone. You discover pot and then acid, which does wonderful things to your mind and anesthetizes your pain but which after a while leaves you feeling empty again. Then your manager and friend dies on you, too, in a state of despair owing partly to your own success, and perhaps your own rejection of him. Then at this very moment, a wise man from India arrives to tell you that your suffering has not been in vain, that death is illusory, and that if you try hard enough you can access the bliss of universal truth. So you tell everyone, not just your wife and your friends, but *everyone in the world*, that this is what you're going to do. And you try, you really, really try. But you don't get there. You discover that meditation doesn't take away all your pain—and that now that you are no longer using LSD, you have no way to numb it. You learn that the guru is, like you, a horny man on the make. You feel conned and humiliated, and your best friend doesn't even notice. He leaves you high and dry with your broken dream, having never fallen for it in the first place. You feel foolish and lost, and very, very lonely.

On the *White Album*, "Yer Blues" comes between two Paul songs, one celebratory and one tranquil: "Birthday" and "Mother Nature's Son." Despite its hint of self-parody, Lennon's song is the bleakest he ever recorded with the Beatles, from that emphasized, repeated "*lonely*" to the let-me-spell-it-out-for-you suicide wish. In his 1970 *Rolling Stone* interview, Lennon mentioned "Yer Blues" and "I'm So Tired" as songs that were deeply personal to him: "songs of such pain . . . which I meant." "I'm So Tired" describes a mind that is eating itself, which cannot find refuge or sanctuary. It's *no joke*, he says, as if to remind whoever he is addressing that while they goof around a lot, he is desperately serious about this.

John had traveled to the Maharishi's spiritual retreat full of hope, and for the first few weeks was blissfully happy. He left feeling angry and disillusioned, and the mood stuck. As George Harrison put it, later, "He went and completely reversed himself. He turned from being positive to being totally negative." The sourness of Lennon's exit is usually attributed to disillusionment with the Maharishi, but that was only part of it. Here's what John said, later in 1968: "It's just that a few things happened, or didn't happen, I don't know but *something* happened. It was sort of like [clicks fingers] and we just left and I don't know what went on, it's too near . . . I don't really know what happened."

On the way back from Rishikesh, Lennon started singing a bitter, mocking song about "Maharishi," which he later changed, at Harrison's urging, to "Sexy Sadie." On the plane, he decided to tell Cynthia about all his infidelities since they had been together. Cynthia would have known about some and not others; either way, it was a horrible experience. Lennon was pushing his wife even further away, preparing her for the worst. When John got back to London, one of the first things he did was go to see Paul at Cavendish Avenue. Later Paul recalled that John ranted about the Maharishi, while he, Paul, defended their erstwhile guru. This may well have felt quite crushing to John. Whether or not the Maharishi was a lecherous fraud was not really the point. The point was that John wanted to reconnect with his friend, to reestablish their bond, to show that they were on the same wavelength again—and Paul once again unwittingly pushed him away.

After the trip, John fell into a black hole of depression his friends said was the worst they had ever seen him in. "John was in a rage because God had forsaken him (although it was nothing to do with God, really)," George recalled. John invited Pete Shotton to stay with him at Kenwood, after arranging for Cynthia to go on holiday to Greece with friends. Shotton recalled, "He was more fucked up than I'd ever seen him." Shotton described the overriding feeling as one of humiliation. John was taking LSD again, and other pills. Sometimes Shotton would find him in torrents of tears, other times laughing maniacally. He was also drinking heavily, for the first time in years. At a music business party on April 18 he became conspicuously drunk on champagne. The drug-taking was making him delusional: at one point during this period he convened an emergency meeting of the Beatles in the Apple boardroom to declare that he was Jesus Christ. The other Beatles listened, then proposed lunch.

Lennon spent a weekend at Derek Taylor's house in the Surrey countryside, where he began to recuperate. Taylor was married, with a brood of young children, and this happy domesticity seemed to have a calming effect. John's old friends Neil Aspinall and Pete Shotton were present. After the kids had been put to bed, the men took acid and smoked pot through the night. Taylor described Lennon as a shattered man, consumed by self-doubt. He made a deliberate attempt to rebuild John's ego. Over the course of several hours, he persuaded John to retell his extraordinary life story, and emphasized how much John had achieved. Years later, Lennon recalled that night as a turning point. "He [Derek] pointed out which songs I'd written, and said, 'You wrote this, and you said this, and you are intelligent, don't be frightened.'"

Although John climbed out of the hole he fell into after India, he never recovered the equanimity of 1967. He began looking for ways to smash up the life he had and start anew, which meant distancing himself from Paul. He became a more dissonant and unpredictable character, still capable of laughter, affection, and exuberance, but more edgy, paranoid, and bitter. The Beatles' disintegration was preceded by the one inside John's mind.

25   LOOK AT ME

"Look at Me" is a song that appears on John Lennon's album with the Plastic Ono Band, released in the wake of the Beatles' breakup. But it was written in 1968, after Rishikesh. Played in the fingerpicking style John used for "Julia" and "Dear Prudence," it shares the quiet, contemplative mood of those songs though it is more melancholy than either. Lennon made a demo of it, but it never made it to a Beatles record, perhaps because he could not develop it into a fully formed song. It goes around and around without finding an exit. *Look at me,* the singer pleads. *Who am I supposed to be? What am I supposed to do?* The tone is plaintive, weary, and sad.

Despite what he went through in India, John was highly productive. "I wrote six hundred songs about how I feel," he said. "I felt like dying, crying, and committing suicide, but I felt creative." In *Get Back* we see Michael Lindsay-Hogg ask John, in early 1969, about the "wound" that had been inflicted on him, clearly quoting John himself and referring to a time around the India trip. There are no accounts of a terrible row between Paul and John in India, and Lennon never raised a specific incident, even in retrospect, yet we know that he *felt* wounded. Yoko told his biographer Philip Norman, "John said that no one ever hurt him the way Paul hurt him."

McCartney was nonplussed at John's anger toward him in the late sixties and early seventies, which seemed to go beyond the normal frustrations of co-working or the annoyances of friends. Even Yoko was baffled by John's animus toward Paul. She speculated to Norman that John might have contemplated an affair with Paul, and that Paul rejected him sexually. "I knew there was something going on here," she said, "from his point of view, not from Paul's. And he was so angry at Paul, I couldn't help wondering what it was really about." Yoko kept an audio diary in 1968. On June 4, a month after her romantic relationship with John began, she said to her tape recorder, "I'm sure that if [Paul] had been a woman or something, he would have been a *great* threat, because there's something definitely very strong between John and Paul."

There is little doubt that John was predominantly heterosexual, but as we've seen, he was also curious about same-sex desire. "I think he had a desire to [have sex with men], but I think he was too inhibited," Yoko said in 2015, before modifying herself: "No, not inhibited. He said, 'I don't mind if there's an incredibly attractive guy.' It's very difficult: they would have to be not just physically attractive, but mentally very advanced, too. And you can't find people like that." It is at least possible that in early 1968 John felt he *had* found someone like that. Perhaps John was queer, in the modern sense: fluid in his preferences, and more so than Paul. He seemed to dream of an all-consuming relationship that wrapped music and sex and love into one. Whether or not this is so, what matters is that John felt rejected and abandoned by Paul after Rishikesh. The wounding probably took place inside his head, but that, of course, doesn't make the pain any less real. In fact, knowing that it was inside his head may have made it worse.

☙

Everyone who watches *Get Back* is struck by the intensity with which Lennon and McCartney hold each other's gaze as they play through endless versions of "Two of Us." The two friends spent an unusual amount of their lives looking into each other's eyes. On tour buses, in hotel rooms, in dressing rooms, they watched the other's reaction to a new idea—a song, a phrase, a lyric, a chord. *Does it feel right? Is this shit? Am I good at this?* From 1963 onward, the rest of us get to see them looking at each other. On YouTube and Tumblr, Beatles fans have collated long strings of images of John and Paul looking at each other at press conferences, in interviews, onstage, at parties. All the Beatles make a lot of eye contact, but the frequency and intensity of Lennon and McCartney's ocular communication is striking.

McCartney, in particular, seems to believe in being able to see the soul through the eyes. When he wants to convey something meaningful to an interviewer, his eyebrows reach upward, pulling his eyes wide open. When he is listening, his eyes are trained intently on whoever he is talking to, as if trying to read what is behind the words or silently win an argument. Little Richard, recalling the days when he shared a bill with the Beatles in Germany, said, "Paul would come in and sit down and just look at me. Like he wouldn't move his eyes." Tony Barrow recalled how, whenever Paul wanted something from Brian Epstein, "Epstein's defenses would melt away as Paul looked him straight in the eye." The musician Chas Hodges, of Chas & Dave, recalled that McCartney played him a test pressing of *Revolver* in 1966; Hodges's main memory was of Paul staring at him the entire time the record was playing. In 1967, John and Paul took acid and gazed into each other's eyes until their own selves dissolved.

For John, the intimacy of the gaze was intensified by myopia. He needed to see you up close in order to truly see you; to take off his glasses in order to be seen. McCartney would recall a heated argument with Lennon, in the middle of which John took his glasses off and said, "It's only me." Yoko Ono said that early in her relationship with John, "He'd always be saying, 'What are you thinking? Why aren't you looking at me?' I always had to look at him in the right way, straight into the middle of his eyes, or he'd start to get upset."

Recall what Cynthia said: that John needed the other Beatles more than they needed him. John had known Paul planned to leave Rishikesh before him but even so, he didn't like people leaving. As 1968 went on, he began the painful process of accepting that the one person he regarded as an equal, the one he saw as his best friend and creative soulmate, didn't see him in quite the same way. When John wasn't being looked at by Paul, he didn't know who he was supposed to be.

26 HEY JUDE

On April 19, 1968, an ad appeared in British newspapers with the headline: "This man has talent." It featured a one-man band with a drum strapped to his back, a harmonica at his mouth, a guitar and sundry instruments. The copy explains that one day he made a tape and sent it to Apple Music, 94 Baker Street, London: "This man now owns a Bentley!" The ad was conceived by McCartney and embodied his intuitive belief that everybody could do what he did, if only they let themselves. Paul was now effectively the Beatles' chief creative officer, dreaming up new schemes to make the group feel as if they were always about to leave for Hamburg. Criticism of the *Magical Mystery Tour* show hardly dented his conviction that nothing the Beatles did could fail as long as they willed it. There was a frenetic quality to his entrepreneurialism. It was as if he feared that unless John was excited about what came next, he would give up.

Paul began plotting the launch of Apple almost as soon as he got back from Rishikesh. The scheme was born of necessity. The Beatles' 1962 deal with Epstein's company NEMS expired in September 1967, and the group let it lapse while they considered their options (unaware, at this stage, that NEMS was still entitled to a quarter of their earnings). They now decided to run Apple themselves, their utopian idea for it being a company run by creative people for the benefit of anyone who wished to create something. They asked Neil Aspinall, a qualified accountant, to be financial director, with Derek Taylor as the company's press officer, and quickly established a web of companies under the aegis of Apple Corps: Apple Records, Apple Electronics (under the purview of Magic Alex), Apple Music Publishing, Apple Tailoring, Apple Films. This was John and Paul's mission, mainly. Ringo was happy to go along with it. George, who had returned from his extended stay in India, was wary of the whole sprawling enterprise (though he did get involved with Apple Records). John, while enthusiastic, was only sporadically engaged with the actual business. "Paul, for the longest time, *was* Apple," recalled Peter Brown, a Beatles associate. "He was coming in every day . . . Paul oversaw everything from building the offices to designing the layouts."

In mid-May, John and Paul flew to New York to launch Apple Records to the American media, without Ringo or George. They spent two days talking to the press and appeared on *The Tonight Show*. Before the press, Paul is uncharacteristically subdued, letting John field most of the questions, perhaps aware at some level that they were biting off more than they could chew (later on, he recalled feeling nervous). John is blunt and sarcastic to the point of rudeness and doesn't pretend to have thought it through. Asked about their plans, he says, "We don't plan . . . We don't really think about it . . . Now that we haven't got a manager, there's no planning at all." Paul laughs, and says, "Just chaos." In a joint interview with the TV anchor Larry Kane, they are insouciant and extremely vague. "It's records and films and, er, what's it called, manufacturing?" says John. Paul says, "We've got a friend who's in electronics [Alexis Mardas]. He's a Greek fella, and he's invented incredible things. So, er, that'll be big."

"Chaos" was the word George Harrison used about Apple, later on. He said, "I think it was basically John and Paul's madness—their egos running away with themselves or with each other." John and Paul ran away with each other to New York to see if they could still get along. In these public appearances, the two of them are still in sync. Paul giggles at John's jokes, jabs, and riffs. Earlier in the year, Paul had been the first Beatle to admit to using LSD, which Lennon was annoyed by, but when Larry Kane asks about it, John leaps in to stick up for him, much as Paul did for John two years before. Asked about the political disruptions—Vietnam, student sit-ins, civil rights, the assassination of Martin Luther King—they respond as if they have only the faintest idea of what's going on. They still believed they were untouchable when together, even if there was now an underlying unease over where they were headed as a group, as business partners, as friends.

During a press conference at the Americana Hotel, Paul noticed a familiar face: an American photographer named Linda. They had met a year or so before, at a London club, and then a few days later, at the press launch of *Sgt. Pepper*, at Brian Epstein's house. Linda was one of the invited photographers. There are pictures of her kneeling down to talk to Paul as he reclines in an armchair by the fire, sipping champagne, dispensing wisdom.

Linda Eastman was born in 1941, nearly a year before Paul. Her mother, Louise, was a department store heiress, her father a successful copyright lawyer who specialized in arts and entertainment: Lee Epstein, the son of Russian Jewish immigrants, had changed his name to Eastman after graduating from Harvard in 1933. Linda grew up in Scarsdale, an affluent suburb in Westchester County, New York, in a household that revered the arts. The Eastman homes, in Westchester and East Hampton, were full of Matisses and Picassos and contemporary artists such as Willem de Kooning, Robert Rauschenberg, and Mark Rothko, all clients of her father's. She lost her mother suddenly, when she was twenty: Louise was killed in a plane crash.

Linda acquired an associate arts degree from Vermont College before attending the University of Arizona, where she studied art history. She married a fellow student and had a daughter with him when she was twenty-one, dropping out of college to care for Heather. The marriage did not go well (her husband suffered from mental illness, and later committed suicide). In 1965 she moved back to New York with Heather, found a job as a receptionist at *Town & Country* magazine, and started cultivating a career as a photographer. She specialized in rock stars, for whom she had an affinity.

Linda's looks and sexual promiscuity are invariably cited as the reasons for her success as a photographer. This is partly true, partly misogynist ste-reotyping. Linda *was* attractive and sexually confident (her high school year-book sobriquets included "yen for men"). But while this may have facilitated her entrée into rock photography, the reason for her success at it is that she was really, really good. The evidence is in her pictures of the Rolling Stones, Janis Joplin, Aretha Franklin, and many others. Around the time she met Paul in New York in 1968, her photo of Eric Clapton was on the cover of *Rolling Stone*, a first for a woman. It is not as if McCartney was a sexual naïf or that he believed Linda to be demure. In fact, he later said he liked knowing how sexually experienced she was ("We both played the field quite widely"). Game recognized game.

Despite being with Jane Asher, Paul kept many women on the go at this time, and it's probably fair to say that Linda was just one of them. But that weekend, in New York, something more than a fleeting attraction developed. Linda was on duty at the press conference. After the event, Paul asked for her number and she wrote it on the back of a blank check. By the time she got home, she had a message. He and John were leaving for Britain the next day, so there was no time to meet—would she like to join him on the limousine ride to the airport? So Linda sat in with Paul, John, Magic Alex, and the Beatles' lawyer, Nat Weiss. Weiss sensed that this was not just another of McCartney's girls: "Paul's whole demeanour—that cocky defensive shield he wore like armour—melted away, and, for a moment, he seemed fairly human." If Weiss could sense it, we can be certain that John did, too. For an hour or so he was stuck in a confined space with Paul and this woman whom he could probably tell was not just another conquest. A weekend that was meant to be a chance for the two of them to get back on the level was ending with Paul's attention elsewhere. But he could hardly complain, not least be-cause his attention was also being diverted by a new woman.

☮

In the 1970s, when John Lennon and Yoko Ono told the story of their re-lationship they framed it as love from the moment of their first meeting, in late 1966. Self-mythologization is natural enough for lovers, though in their case there were particular incentives. Yoko wanted to dispel the persistent rumor that she got together with John to further her career. John needed to show that it was his love for Yoko that prompted him to distance himself from McCartney, rather than the other way around.

Yoko Ono was born in 1933, seven years before John, and grew up in Tokyo. Her mother's family owned one of Japan's largest financial conglomerates; her father was a banker. The household had around thirty servants. Yoko attended exclusive schools and was educated in Western and Eastern traditions of literature, philosophy, and music. She became the first female student of philosophy at her university but dropped out after two semesters. She had a lifelong dislike of institutions and organizations: "I don't believe in collectivism," she once said. A fellow student recalled, "She never felt happy unless she was treated like a queen." Her father's bank posted him to New York, and the Onos moved to Scarsdale, the town in which Linda Eastman grew up. Ono attended the nearby Sarah Lawrence College, where she took classes in music and the arts. A teacher remembered her as very focused on work, and tightly wound: "She wasn't relaxed, ever."

Ono didn't like Sarah Lawrence: "It was like an establishment I had to argue with." She rebelled against two institutions at once, the college and the family, by dropping out of Sarah Lawrence and moving to Manhattan against her parents' wishes. She married Toshi Ichiyanagi, a Juilliard student plugged into the avant-garde music scene. Ono and Ichiyanagi became friendly with the composers John Cage and La Monte Young (the latter was influential on the Velvet Underground). Ono hosted a series of performances and concerts in a dilapidated loft in SoHo, attended by hundreds of downtown artists and musicians. She gained a reputation for her performance art. In 1961 she gave a concert at Carnegie Recital Hall, a venue attached to the main concert hall. On stage, twenty artists and musicians performed different acts—eating, breaking dishes, throwing bits of newspaper. At designated intervals, a toilet was flushed, offstage. The performance finished with Ono's amplified "sighs, breathing, gasping, retching, screaming—many tones of pain and pleasure mixed with a jibberish of foreign-sounding language." The other artists formed a collective called Fluxus. Ono was connected to it but stayed on its fringe.

In 1962 she returned to Japan and participated in the avant-garde scene. Her marriage came to an end and she married an American art promoter named Tony Cox, with whom she had a daughter, named Kyoko, in 1963. The marriage quickly fell apart, though she and Cox continued working together. In Tokyo and Kyoto and then back in New York, she performed what became her best-known work of conceptual art. For *Cut Piece* she sat onstage and invited members of the audience onstage, one at a time, to cut a piece of her clothing off, using a large pair of scissors. The performances were dramatic, unpredictable, and resonant with themes of domination, vulnerability, misogyny, and the relationship of the West to Japan (when she was a child, Ono and her family fled Tokyo to escape the Allied bombing campaign).

In 1966 Ono traveled to London to attend an art symposium and decided to stay. She and Cox released an art film known as *Bottoms*, featuring the bottoms of art-world celebrities and ordinary civilians. It was banned by the British Board of Film Censors, garnering her instant kudos among London's artists. Her meeting with John Lennon was facilitated partly by Paul McCartney, who suggested she talk to Lennon after she asked him for sheet music for a book project. She had an exhibition at Indica Gallery, the hub for avant-garde ideas run by Paul's friends. She was introduced to Lennon by the Beatles' friend John Dunbar, on the understanding that Lennon might fund her work (both John and Paul sponsored underground artists). Ono has been derided for saying she didn't know who Lennon was when they met. It does seem unlikely if taken literally, but if she meant that she had little knowledge of or interest in the Beatles, it is entirely plausible. Her art and her career were defined in part by not knowing or caring about mainstream entertainment. She was thirty-three, a mature artist, and too old for Beatlemania.

Dunbar and Ono took Lennon around the exhibition. One work consisted of an apple on a pedestal. Lennon picked up the apple and bit into it. Another was a ladder, which visitors were invited to climb up. At the top was a magnifying glass. On the ceiling above was a piece of paper with a tiny word on it: "Yes." Lennon loved it. We can imagine him climbing that ladder in a state of nervous tension, anticipating his embarrassment at not getting it; at being the klutz who can't say "Nietzsche"; at being humiliated in front of Paul's friends again. Later he said, "It's a great relief when you get up the ladder and you look through the spyglass and it doesn't say 'No' or 'Fuck you.'" "Yes" wasn't an obscure message from the avant-garde—it was a childlike affirmation of being alive. For another work, visitors were invited to hammer a nail into a board. Lennon asked Ono if he could have a go and she said yes, if he paid her five shillings. Lennon said he'd give her an imaginary five shillings, and hammer an imaginary nail in. "That's when we locked eyes," he said, "and she got it and I got it and that was it."

Well, not quite. It is hard to say how John felt about Yoko between this time and when they became partners, in 1968, seventeen months later. But they did not embark on a full-blown love affair, and there's little evidence he felt strongly about her. They were certainly friendly. She visited Kenwood for a lunch, prepared by Cynthia (the other attendees were members of a Dutch art collective called the Fool who were involved in the Beatles' psychedelic enterprises). He sponsored one of her exhibitions. After its opening he invited her to attend a recording session at Abbey Road and made a desultory attempt to seduce her. Yoko was then driven, with John, from Abbey Road to a London flat. When they got there, Neil Aspinall unfolded a bed. Ono made her excuses. Insofar as she was interested in pursuing a relationship with Lennon, she was determined it would be one of equals. Yoko said that John wrote her letters in early 1968, despite not receiving replies (he sent them to her London flat; she was temporarily in Paris). In Rishikesh he looked forward to her postcards, though on his return from India he didn't seek her out immediately. It wasn't until three weeks later that he made his move, a week before his and Paul's trip to New York.

Now he went all in. Having refused Cynthia's request to join him on the New York trip, he encouraged her to go on holiday to Greece with friends. He had virtually ceased communicating with Cynthia. She remembers saying goodbye while he lay on the bed, staring vacantly: he "barely turned his head to say goodbye." John invited Pete Shotton to stay. Shotton found him in a bad way again, swallowing pills and prone to crying jags. One night (the same day John had declared that he was Christ) they were watching TV when John asked if it was OK to invite a woman around. When he told Pete who it was, Pete was surprised. "So you fancy her, then?" "I dunno, actually," John replied. "But there's *something* about her. I'd just like to get to know her a bit better . . ."

John telephoned Yoko in London and she got a cab to Kenwood (John paid the taxi driver at the gate). They went up to his home recording studio, played around with the tape machines, and listened to some of the experimental electronic music he had made. Yoko suggested they make some music themselves, and so they did. John said later: "It was midnight when we started . . . we made love at dawn. It was very beautiful." When Cynthia returned from her trip to Greece, she found the house strangely quiet (Julian had been packed off with the housekeeper). She wandered through the house until she came into the rear living room. There she found John and Yoko sitting together, wearing identical bathrobes. "Oh, hi," said John, flatly. Upstairs, a pair of women's slippers sat outside the guest bedroom.

Cynthia fled. She came back a couple of days later and there was a brief period of reconciliation; John insisted that nothing of importance had happened. But he soon became cold and withdrawn again. Cynthia, who must have known this was the end, went to Italy with Julian and her mother. As soon as she was gone, Yoko left her daughter, Kyoko, with Cox, and moved into Kenwood. She and John immediately began collaborating on creative projects: home-made movies, experimental sculpture, conceptual art. They moved out of Kenwood so that Cynthia could stay, while John sued Cynthia for divorce. She countersued. They had an awkward meeting at Kenwood, in the company of Yoko and Cynthia's mother, who let rip at John.

Lennon's new relationship soon became public and a furor ensued—who was this strange Oriental woman, and why had John left his wife for her? Lennon and Ono moved into a series of temporary accommodations, pursued by the world's press. The first refuge they found was Paul's house on Cavendish Avenue. "Paul, in his usual way, tried to be the nice guy and was open-minded about John's weird choice," said Peter Brown (which, while ungenerous to Yoko, seems to have been typical of the reaction among John's friends and associates). "But the problem was that Yoko wasn't a very warm person—not even able to say thank you in response to anything Paul did for them." After they moved out, John and Yoko began taking a lot of drugs together, including heroin, which Paul found disturbing.

☸

Amid this professional and personal flux, the Beatles started work on a new album. Despite or because of the turmoil in his life, John was fired up again, crackling with manic, spicy energy. Everyone's eyes were on him. Once again the protagonist in the Beatles drama, he felt *seen*.

On May 30 the Beatles reconvened at Abbey Road to begin recording the group's next LP. Geoff Emerick, who played a central role in the production of what became the *White Album*, detected a new tension in the Lennon-McCartney relationship. John seemed angrier, Paul evasive. As had been the case for the previous five albums the first song the Beatles worked on was one of John's.* "Revolution" was his attempt to channel the turbulent political environment of the moment. Despite John being so vague about America's youth and civil rights movements while in New York, this would be a more directly political song than the Beatles had ever made. He was starting to see himself as an inspirational leader for the protests sweeping through Berkeley, New York, and Paris. John was characteristically equivocal about the kind of leadership he sought to provide, however, going back and forth on whether to sing that he could be counted *in* or *out* of violent protest, and eventually settling on both for the album version.

Starting in the afternoon and continuing into the night, the Beatles spent ten hours on eighteen takes of *Revolution*, with John driving them on. At the end of one of the last takes, he led them in a free-form jam riddled with distortion and feedback. Yoko was present throughout, sitting at John's side. This was a first. None of the Beatles had had partners in the studio before. She "just moved in" said George Harrison, later. "We were all trying to be cool and not mention [Yoko's presence]," said Ringo, "but inside we were all

---

* While this habit may have stemmed from Lennon's dominant personality, it's equally possible the group found his loosely formed ideas more conducive to collaboration, helping them to reconnect in the studio after a break.

feeling it and talking in corners." An engineer recalls Paul having a row with John, a couple of weeks into the sessions: "Paul was positively *livid*, accusing John of being reckless, childish, sabotaging the group."

We don't know exactly what Paul said to John. It probably wasn't as simple as a complaint about Yoko, with whom he was making an effort. "Paul has been very nice to me," Yoko confided to her tape recorder in June 1968. But there is no question that her presence in the studio was disrupting the group. If John wanted her there because he was in love and already felt dependent on her, he was also engaging in what couples therapists sometimes call "triangulation": when one member of a couple draws a third party close in order (consciously or otherwise) to make their partner feel insecure. Perhaps John wanted Paul to know that he was capable of leaving the partnership before Paul left him. For his part, I suspect Paul was ambivalent about John's change of romantic partner. On the one hand, John seemed to be using Yoko as a wedge between them, thus jeopardizing the group's work. On the other, Lennon was more creatively energized than he had been for a long time. In *Get Back*, when Paul discusses John and Yoko's behavior with a few of the others, he says, "They're going overboard about it, but John always does, and Yoko probably always does. So that's their scene." Having a moderate and sweetly cooperative John Lennon in the Beatles meant not having John Lennon in the Beatles at all. John thrived on chaos; maybe this was the chaos he needed.

Paul was also going through a big change. On June 20, about three weeks into the *White Album* sessions, he made a weeklong visit to Los Angeles to introduce Apple Records to the Beatles' American label, Capitol, which would remain their distributor. He gave a triumphant address to Capitol's sales force at their annual convention. The executives hung on his every word, pressing him for autographs and pictures. Paul then retired to a bungalow on the grounds of the Beverly Hills Hotel, where he spent the weekend pinballing between the rooms of two young women he had arranged to meet there. All of the Beatles, with the partial exception of Ringo, were promiscuous; what distinguished Paul's philandering was the scale of it, and his attention to logistical detail. He really put the work in. This particular escapade came to an end when a third woman showed up: Linda Eastman.

Paul had told Linda he would be at the Beverly Hills Hotel, and that if she fancied a trip to the West Coast (he was careful to sound casual), she could come and visit. "The moment Linda arrived that was *it*, as far as other girls were concerned," recalled the Apple associate Tony Bramwell, who accompanied Paul on the trip. "Paul was drawn to her in a completely relaxed way. It was a mood I'd never seen him in before." He and Linda spent the next two days together. As part of a small group, they sailed out to Santa Catalina Island on a yacht, sunbathing, diving off the sides into the clear blue sea, and smoking pot. The next day, the party traveled to the airport, Paul and Linda locked together "like Siamese twins." Paul flew to London, Linda to New York. Neither made or asked for promises. Paul was still officially engaged to Jane Asher, who was performing in Oxford. He had another girlfriend in London, Francie Schwartz. On returning to London and Cavendish Avenue, Jane walked in on Paul in bed with Francie. This seems to have been the last straw for Jane, who declared the end of their relationship in a TV interview. "Paul was absolutely devastated," said the Apple associate Alistair Taylor. "It was the only time I ever saw him totally distraught and lost for words. He went completely off the rails." At a time of profound uncertainty and emotional confusion, McCartney composed a song about clarity of purpose.

Shortly after his return from California, Paul drove down to Kenwood. He'd made the trip many times, but always to see John. Now John was living in Paul's house, and Paul was going to see Cynthia and Julian. Cynthia had been more or less cut off from the Beatle family. "I thought it was a bit much for [Cynthia and Julian] suddenly to be *persona non grata* and out of my life," Paul recalled later. Few people in the world had so many glorious options for how to spend their time, or so many demands on it. Yet that day he pushed everything to one side, got into his Aston Martin, and drove to Weybridge. He presented Cynthia with a single red rose. "It made me feel important and loved," she wrote in her memoir, "as opposed to feeling discarded and obsolete." McCartney had also been thinking about Julian, who was five, and how upsetting the situation must be for him. Paul had been like an uncle to Julian, who recalled, in 2002, "Paul and I used to hang out a bit— more than Dad and I did. We had a great friendship going." As Paul drove to

Kenwood, he started singing a tune whose opening two notes felt like a sigh and a hug: "Hey Jules."

We know "Hey Jude" so well that it requires an effort to hear it. "Hey Jude" begins with the base unit of sympathy: one person reaching out to another. It ends in a joyful surrender of selfhood to the collective. Today we associate it with a crude version of the latter—it has become an anthem lustily belted out at stadium gigs and football matches. But although "Hey Jude" ends with a chorale, it begins in intimacy. What makes it moving, and majestic, is the journey it takes us on from one to the other.

McCartney wrote the rest of the song in the days after his return from Kenwood. The change from "Jules" to "Jude" released the song from its immediate inspiration. "Hey Jude" is not just a song to a child. It's also that unusual thing, almost unique in the annals of pop: a song sung by a man to a close male friend. I say "almost," since there is an obvious precursor, also written, or initiated by, Paul McCartney: "She Loves You." "Hey Jude" is that song's grown-up, emotionally battle-scarred sequel. Paul played "Hey Jude" to John up in the music room at Cavendish Avenue, where Paul had his favorite piano. John and Yoko stood behind him as he sang. When Paul got to the line "the movement you need is on your shoulder," he told John he'd change that bit. "You won't, you know," said John; "that's the best line in it." John showed him these words *were* right—or rather, they were just wrong enough to be perfect.

John said, twelve years later, "If you think about it . . . Yoko's just come into the picture. He's saying 'Hey Jude'—'Hey John.' I know I'm sounding like one of those fans who reads things into it, but you can hear it as a song *to me*." We can and we do, although it's not just about John, either. It's also a song that Paul is singing to himself. That's what Paul told John when John put his theory to him, to which John replied, "Check. We're going through the same bit. So we all are. Whoever is going through a bit with us is going through it, that's the groove."

Lennon said, "'Hey Jude' is a damn good set of lyrics and I made no contribution to that." John loved "Hey Jude" and he loved it *as a Paul song*. In the 1970s, when John was asked about McCartney-led songs, he was often sniffy about them. If he admired them, he would emphasize or exaggerate his own involvement, as with "Eleanor Rigby." With "Hey Jude," he was both uncritically generous—he called it "one of Paul's masterpieces"—and eager to minimize his role. The only story John ever told about his involvement with it was the one in which he told Paul it was already finished.

He was right about the lyrics: each phrase is indelible and luminous, both personal and indeterminate enough for any of us to read ourselves into the song. "You're waiting for someone to perform with" recalls John and Paul's first meeting, but it is also about how any of us wait for the person who makes us feel more alive. The words shape and are shaped by the music: the three-step beat of "re-mem-ber," followed by the subtly different rhythm of "the minute." They are deliciously singable, dotted with McCartneyesque internal rhymes: *fool* and *cool, pain* and *refrain.* "Hey Jude" makes an argument for accepting love, and self-acceptance; I'm never not moved by that deadpan "you'll do."

Replying to a journalist who asked him, in 1966, how he felt about being known as "the cynical one," John said, "I'm cynical about society, politics, newspapers, government. But I'm not cynical about life, love, goodness, death." To be sincere and heartfelt without sounding corny or contrived was his highest aim, and it was Paul's, too. Just before recording "Hey Jude," McCartney changed his original line—"She has found you, now go and get her"—to "You have found her . . ." He was stripping out paradox and irony.

John and Paul agreed "Hey Jude" should be a single. It felt like the perfect way to end a summer of private and public strife. In the outside world, last year's Summer of Love had been succeeded by strikes, protests, and assassinations, most notably that of Martin Luther King. The Beatles, who now took their role as a kind of global shaman seriously, saw an opportunity to cheer everyone up. Their internal affairs were an uncanny microcosm of these wider ruptures and reconfigurations. The *White Album* sessions, which had been under way for a couple of months now, were not like the effortless, fluent fun of *Revolver*, and John and Paul were no longer working as closely as during *Pepper*. The group was by no means dysfunctional—they were getting a lot of songs finished—but it felt like harder work than before, and there were more arguments (Ringo walked out on the group four days before "Hey Jude" was released).

Before going into Trident Studios to record the song (they wanted to use its eight-track facility), the Beatles rehearsed it over a couple of days at Abbey Road. Some of this was captured by a camera crew for a short documentary. The footage shows that despite everything whirling around them, John and Paul were still able to climb into a song and get happily lost in it together. The basic track was recorded live at Trident. For the promotional video, shown on TV, the group played along to the record in front of an invited audience of fans. What might have been distracting only enlivened the Beatles, who were reminded of what they liked about playing to small crowds. One of the decisions made in rehearsal was to eschew an introduction and open with Paul's voice, unaccompanied. In the video, his face is framed in close-up, gazing right at us. His vocal is recorded so that he feels very close, and he sings in the richest part of his register, in a voice full of tenderness, as if channeling the memory of maternal affection. Most people who knew or encountered McCartney around this time found him charming and considerate, if cocky, but he was rarely described as *warm*—indeed he could often be cool and distant. In "Hey Jude" he radiates love. The piano is central to "Hey Jude" and to many of McCartney's songs in the later years of the Beatles. For him, it's the sound of family and friends, or a crowded pub. The first public performance of "Hey Jude" took place in the weeks after he'd written it, but before the recording, when he and Derek Taylor took a random detour from a car journey to Yorkshire to a village called Harrold, in Bedfordshire. They found a pub with a piano, and Paul played his new song to everyone.

One of the most affecting aspects of the finished track is John's backing vocal. His thinner tone adds subtle coloring to Paul's lead without competing for attention. He sounds touchingly reedy and fragile. As on "If I Fell," the two of them perform an intricate harmonic dance, John jumping from below Paul's melody to above it, sometimes in the same phrase. Instead of singing on every line, John picks his moments, so that when he comes in it really counts. Only in the last verse does the song become a full duet, as it expands into a universal thesis: that we are most ourselves when most open to each other.

There is a sense of McCartney summoning all his muses. "Hey Jude" brings together Bach (that descending bass line, counterpointing the bridge— "anytime you feel the pain . . ."), doo-wop (an echo of "Save the Last Dance for Me" by the Drifters), Broadway (it emulates classics such as "Over the Rainbow," where the title is also the beginning), Anglican church music (the opening bars resemble John Ireland's liturgical piece "Te Deum," a hymn McCartney might well have sung as a choirboy), and Black gospel (the wordless final chorus resolves in a plagal or "amen" cadence, over which McCartney testifies wildly).

The melody of "Hey Jude" takes us to unexpected places that somehow feel inevitable. In the opening lines the singer moves suddenly upward on the word "song," like he's just seen a bird. The note is not in the chord underneath: it's wrong and yet completely right. The melody lingers there before gracefully descending and then swooping up even higher for the line "Remember to let her into your heart" (in the next verse, "under your skin"). Whether it's advice to a boy who will one day be a man, or to a friend, or to himself, or all of these, "Hey Jude" invites us to risk vulnerability—to take off the armor. McCartney wasn't the best analyst of himself, but in song he could show a startling degree of insight for a twenty-six-year-old man.

If "Hey Jude" had consisted only of its first part, it would be merely beautiful. What makes it immense is its coda: a wordless chorale that at the time made it the longest pop single ever to be released. The coda isn't soldered onto the song but foreshadowed in the *na na na* phrase that ends the bridge ("by making his world a little colder"). In fact, everything builds toward it, layer by layer. The first sound we hear is just Paul, then it's Paul and piano. Then George and John come in on guitars, and John harmonizes. Ringo enters on the second verse, providing exactly the right kind of movement. A tambourine begins to thrum. Paul, John, and George sing "ahhs." The band's playing and singing aren't immaculate—there are audible flubs—but they are perfectly judged. "Hey Jude" doesn't sound like a solo performance; it sounds like a group of close friends looking out for one another. No matter how many times you've heard it, listen again to the moment when the others join in with Paul as he begins the *na na na* chorus, preceded by "better, better, better, better" (a one-word slogan for McCartneyism). It feels fragile at first, this wave, then it swells, and the audience joins in, and an orchestra, and the whole world. It's what we've been waiting for all along without realizing it—an outpouring of love, of endlessly cascading joy. What started so modestly, one human addressing another, culminates in this massed glory.

Now that we know "Hey Jude," it's hard for us to see quite how radical a decision it was to just repeat this chorus on a loop. It wouldn't have happened without India. It's a drone, and a mantra, and a very McCartneyesque form of meditation in which everyone sings. The Beatles had done something not dissimilar in Hamburg with "What'd I Say"—breaking through the terminus of a song into infinite space—and they knew how to add endless variations to endless repetition. McCartney's bluesy, gospel-tinged vamping keeps us hooked. He is a man possessed, his screams and wails musical but primal. A song that begins with Paul reaching out to help ends with him exorcising his own grief. The first three minutes of the song are lifted on to a different plane by what comes next; the two halves of "Hey Jude" make each other better.

27   JULIA

In the summer of 1968, as the Beatles began work on a new album, Lennon was intent on developing a creative partnership
with Ono. The pair of them released the electronic experiments
they made on their first night together at Kenwood as an album
on Apple Records. The cover of *Two Virgins* showed them naked,
an image shocking enough that the LP had to be packaged inside
a paper bag. It was regarded as potentially damaging to the Beatles. EMI's chairman, Sir Joseph Lockwood, was displeased and
bitchily suggested that if any of the Beatles should go naked it
should be Paul. McCartney was not keen on the cover—not for
moral or commercial reasons; he just thought it was in bad taste.
He did contribute a sleeve note, however: "When two great Saints
meet, it is a humbling experience. The long battles to prove he
was a Saint." It is a mark of how delicately balanced the relationship was at this time that Paul was invited to write the note, that
he delivered a distinctively Liverpudlian put-down, and that John
used it anyway.

Lennon seemed to have a deep need to let McCartney know
that he had someone else to focus his attention on now. Michael
Lindsay-Hogg, the young director who made the "Hey Jude"

promo, was called to a meeting in the Apple boardroom at which all four Beatles were present. After the business was discussed, Lennon announced he had something to show the group. He put a cassette in the tape machine. As everyone sat and listened, muffled whispering became murmurs of pleasure. It became apparent that this was a tape of John and Yoko having sex. "Well, that's an interesting one," said Paul, when the tape came to an end. The meeting dispersed.

There is a clue to why Lennon was acting like this in his 1980 interview with David Sheff for *Playboy*, when Sheff asks him about the *White Album* track "Why Don't We Do It in the Road." John says:

> That's Paul. He even recorded it by himself in another room. That's how it was getting in those days. We came in and he'd made the whole record. Him drumming [actually, Ringo drummed on this track]. Him playing the piano. Him singing. But he couldn't—he couldn't—maybe he couldn't make the break from the Beatles . . . I was always hurt when Paul would knock something off without involving us.

Not only was John upset by Paul's willingness to make music without him, he worried that it meant Paul—a one-man band—didn't need him anymore. If Paul might be about to leave, John had to show him he was capable of leaving first.

☮

As the sessions were going on, so were endless meetings about Apple Corps. The Beatles had invested in an expensive new head office in Savile Row and were pouring money into various projects in a chaotic fashion. In the autumn of 1968, Apple's two most senior accountants resigned, one with a letter to the Beatles that declared, "Your personal finances are in a mess. Apple is in a mess." Relationships within the group were under strain. George Harrison was upset by the way the India trip had ended, annoyed by Yoko's presence, and frustrated by the self-absorption of John and Paul. Ringo, an enormously patient man, quit the band after Paul nagged at him about a drum part. He was persuaded to return a week later (in the meantime, Paul took over on drums for "Back in the USSR"). George Martin, a civilizing presence, had been marginalized, since the Beatles were determined that the new album should have a less elaborate production than *Sgt. Pepper*, and perhaps because they wanted to be less civilized.

In *Get Back*, recorded in January 1969, we hear Harrison say glumly that the band has been "in the doldrums for at least a year." But to see only the doldrums is to miss the laughter and exuberance that still bubbled through the group, evident in recently released tapes of outtakes and studio jams from the *White Album* sessions (or what became known as the *White Album*: the album's official title, *The Beatles*, was quickly superseded by a fan-given name inspired by its plain white cover, a design that suggested a purging of psychedelia). They were also working tremendously hard. All summer, they were in the studio five nights a week, eight to twelve hours a night. The last two weeks alone of their five-month marathon yielded an extraordinary eight new tracks finished from scratch. If they were working in separate studios concurrently that was because they had so many songs to get through. There are many examples of one of them making significant contributions to the songs of other members, like Paul's circular piano figure for John's "Sexy Sadie" or John's hot jazz guitar solo on Paul's "Honey Pie." This was not a group that had forgotten how to play together, or how to enjoy themselves.

☻

Despite becoming serious about Linda, Paul was still seeing other women. In September he took a short holiday in Sardinia with Maggie McGivern. Lying on the beach one day, he asked her what she thought about marriage. Maggie was noncommittal, and later regretted it, as she felt she had pushed him away ("Paul was always slightly insecure," she said). It's hard to say for sure what or who Paul was thinking of, but in one way or another he was edging toward a new romantic commitment. This was partly in response to John's attachment to Yoko, which was partly in response to Paul drawing close to Linda. In 1986, McCartney said, "[John and Yoko] were very strong together which left me out of the picture, so then I got together with Linda and we got our own kind of strength." In both cases, enduring love emerged from mixed motivations. It's not that John and Paul split up because they found the loves of their lives so much as they found the loves of their lives in order to split up.

Shortly after Paul's return from Sardinia, Linda flew from New York to stay with him in London. On or around September 23 she arrived at Cavendish Avenue, to be informed by his housekeeper that he was at the studio, so she set off for Abbey Road, where Paul and the other Beatles were recording a John track, "Happiness Is a Warm Gun." Work on it continued the next night, until 2 a.m. When it was finished, the Beatles knew they had done a good job—it is a tour de force of ensemble playing, in three different segments. In the final section, John, Paul, and George sing crazed doo-wop backing vocals to John's lead. Paul and Linda now headed for his home, on a warm summer night. As ever, there were fans at his front gates. Paul opened an upstairs window and serenaded them with the first public performance of "Blackbird."

There are few successfully monogamous male rock stars. Different aspects of the job conspire to undermine commitment: the sexual opportunities it provides, its itinerant nature, the ego it creates or demands. Yet from late 1968 until Linda's death in 1997, Paul McCartney loved one woman only and spent no more than a handful of nights apart from her. McCartney's long marriage was later taken as evidence of his bland moderation, but it was really a manifestation of his taste for extremes. At the age of twenty-six, he flipped from being radically promiscuous to radically monogamous.

Why Linda? Shortly after her death, Paul was interviewed by Chrissie Hynde, a close friend of Linda's. He told a story, in tenderly recalled detail, from October 1968 (right after completing the *White Album*, Paul went to stay with Linda and her five-year-old daughter, Heather, in New York):

> The first year we got together, somebody had said something about
> her that wasn't amazingly complimentary. I can't remember what
> it was, but we were walking down Park Avenue in New York and
> it was late at night. We'd been to see probably her dad or something.
> We were strolling arm-in-arm, and I mentioned this thing. I said,

"Oh so-and-so said so-and-so." Well, she stopped in the middle of the street. Luckily, there was no traffic. She put her hands on her hips and she just coloured-up, not a kind of beetroot colour, more a sort of light strawberry, and she just looked me right in the eye. She said: "If you ever say that again or even suggest it," and she just tore a strip off me. I never forgot it. But you know what, I loved it.

A couple of years after this, in "Long Haired Lady," a delirious love song, Paul sang about Linda's "flashing eyes." Paul was willful but didn't want a girl he could bend to his will; he wanted a woman who would push back. He had one in Jane, of course, but that relationship foundered, at least in part, because Jane was not willing or able to offer him the other thing he was looking for: complete commitment and mutual absorption, a merging of lives and souls. ("Make it easy to be near you," he pleads in "I Will," a song from this period.) Linda had that disposition. For many men, the fact that a woman had a child by a former partner would have been off-putting; for McCartney, it sealed the deal. He was a twenty-six-year-old rock god who dreamed of having a family at home, and not because he thought it was the proper thing to do, but because he longed to be bound by one, and delighted in children. In a bootlegged jam on acoustic guitars with Donovan, from late 1968, Paul plays a song he has written for Heather. In *Get Back* we see Heather clinging to Paul like a limpet, utterly at ease with him after a few months' acquaintance.

Around this time, he ended the relationship with Francie Schwartz, who left London for home in August. She said Paul's last words to her were, "Don't cry. I'm a cunt." In her memoir Schwartz elaborates that he was "petulant, outrageous, adolescent, a little Medici prince, powdered and laid on a satin pillow at an early age." I imagine that Paul partially agreed with this. For all his formidable self-confidence, he harbored doubts about the person he was at heart, and sometimes questioned whether he had a heart at all. Iris Caldwell, his girlfriend from Liverpool, recalled that her mother had accused him of being emotionally cold. It ate at him: years later, just before the release of "Yesterday," Paul called Iris and said her mother should listen to "Yesterday" to see if it changed her mind. In an interview in the 1980s, he brought up the moment when he heard about his mother's death ("What are we going to do for money?"), and said, "I've never forgiven myself for that. Really, deep down, I never have quite forgiven myself for that." As he danced through a Beatle life in which every door seemed to open the moment he touched it, he retained, in his mind, the baleful image of himself he drew as a teenager: a face that scowled rather than smiled. He once described his public self as "pleasantly insincere." He was drawn to those who saw through his masks and loved him nonetheless. Being accepted by John confirmed to him that he was special. Being loved by Linda, and by Heather, convinced him he was good.

⊛

In October, recording sessions completed, George and Ringo headed off, Ringo on holiday, George to Los Angeles to produce an album for an Apple signing, Jackie Lomax, and then to hang out with Bob Dylan in Woodstock, New York. John and Paul worked together to finish the album, its track listing and final mixes.

On October 18, the day after a final, twenty-four-hour marathon mixing session, the flat in Montagu Square where John and Yoko were staying was raided. Police found a chunk of cannabis in a binoculars case. The couple had actually dispensed of their heavier drugs, including heroin, after a tip-off. John, who took sole responsibility, received a modest fine, but it was a nasty shock. Yoko was pregnant, and shortly after this incident was admitted to hospital with complications. The couple spent twenty days of November there. Yoko suffered a miscarriage. That period aside, they kept up a stream of public appearances, including one inside a bag on the stage of the Royal Albert Hall. Even in the hospital, they used a tape machine to make their second electronic music LP.

Two aspects of Yoko's effect on John were particularly important. One is summarized by his friend Pete Shotton, who said, "[Yoko had a] galvanising effect . . . she also enabled him to regard himself as the one thing he's always most wanted to be: an artist, with a capital A. You might almost say that Yoko brought John back to life." John's partnership with Yoko contributed to the surge in his creative energies that followed his post-India breakdown.

Yoko was a prolific generator of ideas and initiatives—art projects, stunts, manifestos—for John and she to collaborate on.

The second aspect was her force of personality. Everyone who encountered Yoko remarked on her softly spoken charisma. In meetings, she needn't say much to impose herself on the room, and she always appeared to have a firm grasp of her own purposes. Yoko was seven years older than John, and, like Linda, already a mother. She did not see herself as servile to John's needs; if anything, the opposite. "Yoko looks upon men as assistants," John half joked, in 1980. John was more than happy for Yoko to take the lead in their relationship. He admired how, despite the inequality between them in terms of wealth and fame, she seemed to need him less than he needed her, even if this triggered his insecurities. He was jealous of her ex-husband and previous boyfriends, and didn't even like it when she spoke Japanese or read Japanese newspapers. Her constant presence in the studio and elsewhere was more to do with his neediness than with her. "She enabled the child in John to resurface," said Shotton. That was true in two ways: Lennon felt playful and open to the world, and he did what he was told. Cynthia drew a parallel with Mimi: "John had grown up in the shadow of a domineering woman . . . Yoko offered the security of mother figure who always knew best." If Mimi rescued John from the instability of his early years, Yoko provided a bulwark against the instability caused, in John's mind at least, by Paul's growing independence. In more ways than one, then, Yoko was a replacement for Paul. Ono told Philip Norman that John said to her, "Do you know why I like you? It's because you look like a bloke in drag. You're like a mate."

The *White Album* shows all four Beatles lighting out for the farthest reaches of their individual musical personalities, which is perhaps why John and Paul decided to call it *The Beatles*, a title which was, like the album cover, in dialogue with *Sgt. Pepper*. It was a reassertion of identity; the Beatles becoming themselves again. In 1984, McCartney said of this time (speaking on behalf of the group, but really about himself), "We could recognize [John and Yoko's love], but that didn't diminish the hurt we were feeling by being pushed aside." Yet, as we've already seen, John and Paul remained deeply involved with each other during the making of the *White Album*. John sings that he and Paul are "as close as can be" in "Glass Onion," a densely metatexual song that cites five Beatles tracks from the previous year, three of them Paul songs.

"Julia" was the first time John had addressed the memory of his mother directly in song. He wrote it in India, where, as in Spain, his thoughts drifted toward childhood, source of all magic and pain. The melody is characteristically flat, a sign that he wants above all to communicate, to transmit thoughts directly into the heads of his audience. The song is propelled by gentle fingerpicked guitar and by John's gift for verbal rhythm ("When I cannot sing my heart / I can only speak my mind"). As he repeats "Julia" a third time, he moves to a chord which is harmonically equivalent to the one he used for "going to" Strawberry Fields—a portal to his dream world. John scribbled a lyric sheet for "Julia" in Rishikesh. By the time he recorded the demo, back in England, he added words that make a connection between his mother and his new lover (the literal meaning of Yoko in Japanese is "ocean child"). Already John had begun to weave his love affair with Yoko into a unifying autobiographical narrative; a new dream to compete with the one he and Paul had created in Liverpool.

"Julia" was the last song to be recorded for the *White Album*, on October 13. Perhaps John left it until last because he was nervous about recording something in which he was so exposed, musically and emotionally. In the rehearsal tapes, released in 2018, we can hear how nervous he is, using a jokey Scouse accent to communicate with the control room: "It's very hard to sing this, you know." George Martin reassures him: "It's a very hard song, John." Martin wasn't the only one there to give moral support. While producing that 2018 release, it became clear to Martin's son Giles that Paul had also been at the session. Clearly he wasn't there to tell John how to play "Julia." His voice appears nowhere on the tapes. But if anyone knew how vulnerable John would be feeling as he attempted to sing a song of love for his mum, it was Paul.

28   MARTHA MY DEAR

Asked to name the great loves of Paul McCartney's adult life, we might say Linda, Jane Asher, Nancy Shevell (whom he married in 2011), and John. But we would be remiss if we didn't mention Martha. She was a young puppy when he bought her, in July 1966, from a breeder in High Wycombe. He'd long wanted a dog, and now he had his own home, and a housekeeper to look after it when he wasn't around. He chose an old English sheepdog after seeing one in TV ads for Dulux paint. Martha saw Paul's partners come and go. She got to know Jane, and met Francie. She got to know Linda and Heather, and later the other McCartney children. She romped around Paul's farms in Scotland and Sussex. Paul missed her when he was away. In 1971, when he was in Los Angeles recording *Ram*, he had to borrow a dog from the engineer as a substitute.

Some of my favorite photographs of Paul and the other Beatles feature Martha, who seems to have accompanied him everywhere. As he conducts the Black Dyke Mills brass band in Bradford (they were recording tracks for an Apple Records release), Martha stands watchfully by his side. In a picture taken inside Paul's meditation dome in 1968, Martha lounges with the other Beatles (Martha is another contender for fifth Beatle). She is with Linda and Paul at their wedding, like a bridesmaid. The high-frequency tone at the end of *Sgt. Pepper*, supposedly audible only to dogs, is there because Paul thought it would be cool if there was something on the album for Martha.

It is very Paul to write a song about a dog—or rather, *to* a dog. His contemporaries, including John, were writing about revolutions and utopias and sex and drugs. But he didn't see why he couldn't write about his beloved pet. When Barry Miles asked him about the song, in 1997, Paul said it's about a dog, and that was pretty much that. But his songs are rarely about one thing, and a dog is not just a dog. "Martha My Dear" is also about the creative spark. Martha was one of Paul's muses. Hunter Davies's account of the writing of "Getting Better" starts with Martha gamboling around a park, the embodiment of McCartney's imagination running free. In the last verse of "Martha My Dear," a ragtime-meets–Noël Coward romp, Paul implores his muse to "be good to me." As a collaborator, Paul is a little like a dog himself: always wanting to play. Throw me a ball!

☥

John could be a little awkward with children and animals and envied Paul's facility with both. There's a picture of the Beatles from February 1967, the *Pepper* era, in which Paul has Martha hoisted up on his shoulder, while John holds on to her paws. And John looks so happy! Proud, almost. According to Paul, Martha helped John to open up. McCartney wrote in 2021:

> One of the unlikely side effects was that John became very sympathetic towards me. When he came round and saw me playing with Martha, I could tell that he liked her . . . Seeing me with Martha, with my guard down, all of a sudden he started warming to me. And so he let his guard down too.

There's a grainy newspaper photo of John and Paul, taken on a street near Regent's Park in London. It's dated April 13, 1967—after Paul had returned from his brief trip to the States, and during the most peaceful period of the Lennon-McCartney relationship. Paul is walking in the road, just off the pavement. John, wearing an extravagant cape, is on the pavement. He is walking Martha.

Martha died in 1981, less than a year after John.

29   GET BACK

On January 2, 1969, the Beatles are woken uncomfortably early at their respective homes and ferried by chauffeur to Twickenham Film Studios, on the outskirts of west London. George gets there at around 10:30 a.m., as does John, who arrives with Yoko and Ringo. Paul is late. The three Beatles, in their winter coats, wander into Stage One, a cold, characterless hangar. A film crew, under the eye of the director Michael Lindsay-Hogg, is setting up cameras, lighting rigs, and microphones. John and George pick up their guitars and sit down. They chat about what they got up to over Christmas. Yoko sits next to John and reads a book. When Paul turns up, he senses a certain anomie among his bandmates, and makes a mild attempt to cheer them up. "I don't dig under-estimating what's here," he says, gesturing to the vast open space, the scaffolding up against the wall. They start to run through some new songs, including one from John called "Don't Let Me Down."

What are they doing here? They are here because they know—Paul, in particular, knows—that the group has to keep moving if it is not to disintegrate. The *White Album* had sold spectacularly well. In fact, this blank-sleeved double album, crammed with weird, experimental music—including a seven-minute-long sound collage ("Revolution #9")—was their most commercially successful album to date. Despite everything, then—despite the friction between John and Paul, despite John's absorption in Yoko-related projects, despite George's resentment and Ringo's frustration, despite the draining circus of Apple—they carried on. In the week after Christmas, John and Paul (and Yoko) spent time at Paul's house, discussing what to do next and working on songs. They were still trying to make their partnership work, and still trying to make the Beatles work, even as they faced the prospect of both coming to an end.

The plan they come up with requires them to develop fourteen new songs in two weeks, and to make a TV show in which they play the songs. The nature of the show is as yet undecided. They have booked Lindsay-Hogg, a director they know and like, and told him to come up with something. The reason they have started so early in the year, and agreed to such a workmanlike schedule (the Beatles were not used to turning up before midday) is that they have the film studio and their drummer only for a short time. Ringo has a commitment: he is making a film called *The Magic Christian* with Denis O'Dell, former head of Apple Film, and O'Dell has Stage One booked. It was his suggestion that the Beatles use it as a venue for their show while he got what he needed in place. The plan is for everything—songs, show—to be completed by January 20.

Musically, the Beatles want the new work to be even more stripped back than the *White Album*. The biggest-selling artists of the last year, other than the Beatles themselves, included Aretha Franklin, Simon and Garfunkel, Bob Dylan, the Rolling Stones, Jimi Hendrix, and the Band. All of them, in different ways, are inspired by the idea of returning to musical roots. The Beatles, as ever, catch the wind but sail their own way. For them, a return to roots means a return to *their* roots: to the days of being just a band, as they were at the Star-Club and the Cavern. They want to show the world that they do not rely on tricks—that the magic emerges from four humans making songs together, beat by beat.

Perhaps we should take a step back here. The *White Album* sessions were

long, intense, and emotionally wearing. The Beatles had every right to take
a long break from recording, and from being Beatles. Yet here they are back
at work barely two months after finishing it. They could have filled the proposed show with songs from the *White Album*, but John and Paul have made
an extra commitment: to come up with *new* songs, while the cameras roll.
This isn't because they have lots ready to go—far from it. Paul has a few,
John has two or three. George, galvanized by his time with Dylan and the
Band in Woodstock, has quite a few but isn't sure which ones John and Paul
will want, or which he wants to save for a solo project. They have also given
themselves a ridiculous deadline. It's true that Ringo had a commitment,
and they have to vacate the studio. But they are the biggest group in the
world, with all the commercial and star power that implies. There are ways
to solve scheduling problems.

The Beatles know they might be about to split, and discuss the possibility
among themselves frankly, but they are not quite ready to do so. George is
increasingly frustrated by the confines of his supporting role, but he is still
keen on the Beatles and floats the idea of solo projects running alongside the
group. Ringo will play as long as the others want to. Paul believes passionately in the Beatles, and in his partnership with John, and John—well, John
is tired. He had been through a mental breakdown. The *White Album* was
exhausting; then there was his divorce, and the trauma of Yoko's miscarriage.
He is facing both ways, in and out. He tells Lindsay-Hogg that he still wants
to be a Beatle, even as he seems to be putting emotional distance between
himself and the group.

The *Get Back* project (as it became known later) is an attempt to recapture the spirit of unity the Beatles felt in Liverpool and Hamburg,
and in the van, a time when every audience needed to be won over and they
were butting up against the world's indifference. Above all, the project is
Paul's effort to fire up John. No matter how passive John is, everyone still
looks to him; if John is into it, they are all into it. Paul's theory of John—
and John's theory of John—is that he needs to feel under pressure in order
to produce. Paul has concocted this impossible set of deadlines to turn John
into a superhero again. But at Twickenham, John seems as if he might be

too deep in apathy and drugs to come flaming back to life. His principal new
song, "Don't Let Me Down," is underdeveloped. In *Get Back*, we can see
that Paul is getting anxious. At one point he approaches John to press him,
nervously but firmly, on his lack of new material. On another occasion, he
plays "Strawberry Fields" at the piano while John sits with his back to him,
fiddling on his guitar, pretending not to listen. *See, John—remember how
good you are?*

In the vast space of Stage One, the Beatles huddle together in a circle, as
if aboard a little boat, adrift in a sea of linoleum. Yoko sits and reads. John,
who pays her little attention, is glazed over, George moody, Ringo either
bored or sad or both. They play new songs, arranging them as they go, trying out backing vocals and guitar lines. They have some quietly pointed disagreements. Paul and George get into a peevish argument over how to play
a Paul song, "Two of Us." "I'll play whatever you want me to play," says
George. Paul says, "I'm only trying to help you, but I always hear myself
annoy you." George replies, with devastating indifference: "You're not annoying me. You don't annoy me anymore." McCartney clearly feels as if
he's pushing the van uphill while his bandmates sit in it, deadweight. Over
the course of the week, he cajoles and prods them into action. "We've only
got twelve more days so we've really got to do this methodically," he says.
"I really just hear myself the only one saying it. I don't get any support
or anything." He tries to break the mood of passive resistance: "I don't
see why any of you get yourself into this. What's it for? It can't be for the
money. Why are you here? I'm here because I want to do a show." He says
that they haven't been communicating well, which made the last album
hard going. "We should just have it out . . . if this one turns into that [the
previous album] it should definitely be the last for all of us because there
just isn't any point . . . All I want to see is enthusiasm!" His bandmates
do not respond accordingly, though they don't rebuke him either. They
glumly confront the possibility of a split:

George: The Beatles have been in the doldrums for at least a year.
Maybe we should have a divorce.

Paul: Well, I said that at the last meeting. But it's getting nearer, you know?

John: Who'd have the children?

Paul: Dick James.

McCartney offers a lucid diagnosis: "We've been very negative since Mr. Epstein passed away. That's why all of us in turn has been sick of the group . . . it is a bit of a drag. But the only way for it not to be a bit of a drag is for the four of us to think, should we make it positive?" John, who mostly stays quiet during these exchanges, responds positively: "I've got an incentive. I've decided . . . the whole point of it is communication. And to be on TV is communication, 'cause we've got a chance to smile at people, like 'All You Need Is Love.'" Paul agrees, adding, "There really is no one there now to say 'Do that.' Whereas there always used to be . . . But that's only growing up . . . Daddy's gone away now, and we're on our own at the holiday camp."

If McCartney is bossy it's not because he wants to be the boss. The Beatles loved being kids left to play, but somebody had to be parent. What the *Get Back* transcripts can't show us, but the film does, is the force of Lennon's presence even when silent. When the others address one another, they seem to be speaking to him. Since John stays silent during musical debates, George and Paul end up going back and forth interminably. At one point McCartney lets the group, and particularly John, know how hard it is to have the responsibility of leadership without legitimacy: "I'm scared of that, 'You be the boss.'"

After the conversation about divorce, the band rehearse "I've Got a Feeling," a true Lennon-McCartney collaboration, cooked up before Christmas. Paul had brought a riff and a refrain. John had a fragment he called "Everybody's Had a Hard Year," which became the finished song's middle eight, a reflective counterpoint to the unstoppable optimism of Paul's refrain. Paul and John also run through ragged versions of old songs—a *lot* of old songs. They play older Beatles numbers like "Love Me Do," and many rock and roll standards from their performing repertoire: Carl Perkins, Elvis, Little Richard. This was partly because the idea of the show was to include some older songs, but also because they needed a reminder of what they loved about playing together in the first place.

The bickering is recognizable to anyone who has been shut indoors with their siblings for too long. So much of it is familial and familiar: the pained inarticulacy, the weight of the unsaid, frustration mingled with love. But while later accounts of the Twickenham sessions emphasized the animosity, Peter Jackson's film reveals flashes of joy and gusts of laughter. The Beatles can be direct (as when Paul tells John, about one of John's songs, "That's a weak bit"), but for the most part they are gentle with one another, almost to a fault. We see old songs roar into life with blistering force, and new ones gain authority. While Paul has firm musical opinions, he mostly persuades rather than insists. John isn't bitter or caustic so much as quiet and wan, but he often breaks into a wide grin, especially when the group is making music.

In the middle of this uneasy stalemate, Paul created a song that was to give its name to the project and, much later, to Jackson's documentary. It instantly became the most famous sequence in *Get Back*: McCartney, in his canary-yellow jumper, hunched over his bass, diving into himself and dredging up a pearl. He and the others are waiting for John, who is late. Paul plays chords on the bass (a bass guitar has only four strings, rather than six, and is not usually used this way) simply because that's what he has on his lap. He sings what seems to be an aimless oral doodle, using gibberish syllables. But as he keeps going, a tune emerges, and words, and a refrain: "Get back . . . get back . . ." Consciously or otherwise, and probably otherwise, McCartney has landed on an idea that captures the spirit of the project.

The sequence has become legendary as a live demonstration of McCartney's genius, although as Adam Gopnik points out, it does not present us with a solitary endeavor: "Paul does it, but he does it *for the group*." McCartney has an audience to play for, before he has a song. Sitting in front of him, as he hacks away, are George and Ringo, who are openly bored. Ringo yawns. But they are listening. After a while, George mutters, to himself more than to anyone,

"It's good. It's . . . you know. Musically and that, it's great." He picks up his guitar and adds a choppy riff after every refrain. Ringo starts clapping out a rhythm. John arrives, straps on his guitar, and immediately finds the right chord. Over the days and weeks to come, the group painstakingly re-fine, rewrite, and rehearse "Get Back," running through many different versions of it, some jokey, some more serious, including one about immigrants, designed as a rebuke to a recent, inflammatory speech by the right-wing politician Enoch Powell ("Ob-La-Di, Ob-La-Da" was also written in this spirit).* They work on the transitions, on the rhythms, on every aspect of the arrangement. John helps Paul with the words. After a long, arduous, circuitous process, they eventually settle on the version we know, which feels as effortless as breathing.

---

* It now seems entirely unremarkable that artists should be welcoming toward immigrants, but as with so much else about the Beatles that's partly because they shaped the norms we take for granted. In the spring of 1968, Mick Jagger warned that immigration would "break up" British society, "Because they are different and they do act differently and they don't live the same, not even if they were born here they don't." (Quoted in Dominic Sandbrook, *White Heat*, 675.)

ABOVE: **The Quarry Men play at the Woolton parish church garden fete, July 6, 1957. The day Paul met John.** © Geoff Rhind

AT RIGHT: **First picture of John and Paul together: with the Quarry Men at New Clubmoor Hall, Liverpool, November 23, 1957.** Lesley Kearney, by permission of the Quarry Men

BELOW: **At George's brother Harry's wedding, Childwall Abbey Hotel, December 20, 1958.** Mark Lewisohn

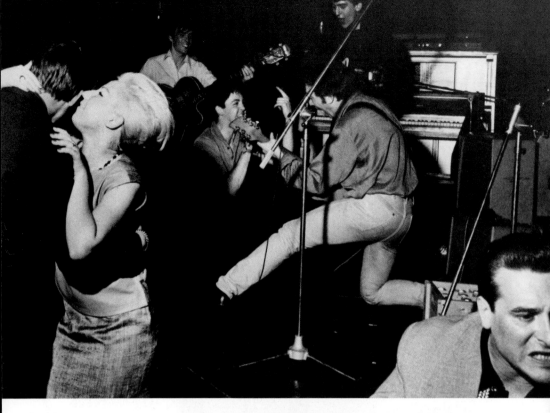

ABOVE: **The Beatles
at the Top Ten Club,
Hamburg, April–June
1961. John and Paul:
each other's favorite
audience.** Gerd Mingram
/ Gürt Zinter Archive

AT RIGHT: **A Cavern
lunchtime gig,
December 8, 1961.**
Keystone Press / Alamy

BELOW: **Backstage at the
Finsbury Park Astoria,
London, December 30,
1963.** Val Wilmer /
Redferns / Getty Images

Filming the "If I Fell" sequence for *A Hard Day's Night*, March 24, 1964. © David Hurn / Magnum Photos

During a break from recording *The Music of Lennon & McCartney*, Granada TV special, November 2, 1965. Robert Whitaker / Getty Images

ABOVE: **The press launch party for** *Sgt. Pepper* **at Brian Epstein's house in Belgravia, London, May 19, 1967. John was making everyone laugh by introducing himself to Paul in a plummy voice.** John Downing / Getty Images

AT RIGHT: **Linda Eastman, photographer, talks to Paul at the** *Sgt. Pepper* **launch party.** John Pratt / Getty Images

BELOW: **John in his music room at Kenwood, June 29, 1967. (The photo of John and Paul on his cabinet was taken by David Bailey in 1965.)** Beatles Book Photo Library

ABOVE: **After spending time with the Maharishi in Bangor, the Beatles met with him again at a private house in Kensington, August 31, 1967.** ANL / Shutterstock

AT LEFT: **Rishikesh, India, late February 1968.** © Paul Saltzman / Contact Images

BELOW: **John and Paul at London Heathrow airport after their trip to New York to promote Apple Records, May 16, 1968.** Stroud / Express / Getty Images

ABOVE: **John and Yoko at Kenwood, November 26, 1968.** Susan Wood / Getty Images

BELOW: **Paul and Linda following their marriage at Marylebone Register Office, London, March 12, 1969.** Getty Images

ABOVE: **John and Yoko on their wedding day in Gibraltar. John is holding the marriage certificate. March 20, 1969.** Mirrorpix / Alamy

AT LEFT: **Paul and Linda (and Martha) on their farm in Scotland, near Campbeltown, around the time that Paul started High Court proceedings to seal the breakup of the Beatles, December 31, 1971.** Evening Standard / Getty Images

BELOW: **John and May Pang at the Troubadour, West Hollywood, March 12, 1974. Harry Nilsson is in the foreground.** Michael Ochs Archives / Getty Images

ABOVE: **Paul and Linda with *(left to right)* Heather, Stella, and Mary in the back garden of Cavendish Avenue, London, April 4, 1976.** David Montgomery / Getty Images

BELOW: **John and Sean at home in the Dakota building, probably 1979.** Everett Collection Inc / Alamy

30   TWO OF US

Beatles fans have long known about the moment George Harrison quit the band during the Twickenham sessions, which is captured on audiotape. "I think I'll be . . . I'm leaving the band," George says, quietly, just before a Friday lunch break. "When?" asks John, sounding notably unsympathetic. "Now." George's departure seems to energize John, who suddenly starts talking like the group's leader: "I think if George doesn't come back by Monday or Tuesday we ask Eric Clapton to play . . . the point is if George leaves, do we want to carry on with the Beatles? I do." Peter Jackson's *Get Back* provided more context for George's departure. We see how, whenever George presents his songs to the group, Paul and John appear indifferent at best. About one, John says, "Is this a Harrissong?" That was the name of the publishing company George set up in 1966, to separate the royalties to his songs from Northern Songs, the company set up to publish Lennon-McCartney songs; Lennon's remark is a reminder of the divided economic structure of the group.

When George joined the Quarry Men, eleven years before, he was "little George," a kid allowed to play with the older boys. He proved to be the best guitarist in the group and its most nerveless performer. After John and Paul's agreement to write only with each other, he began to write his own songs. They were not very good at first. More fragile characters would have been fatally intimidated by the prospect of showing their efforts to the most successful songwriters in the world, but George persisted, and improved. Songwriting aside, he made many vital, uncredited contributions to Lennon-McCartney songs, such as the melodic, jazz-style solo on Paul's cover of "Till There Was You," the guitar figure on "And I Love Her," the guitar fills on "She Loves You" and "I Want to Hold Your Hand," and the backwards solo on "I'm Only Sleeping." Above all, George's introduction of Indian music and philosophy to the Beatles was pivotal to the group's evolution. Rather than dabble, he went deep, learning sitar at the feet of a master (if Ravi Shankar hadn't thought the English kid was serious, he wouldn't have bothered), assimilating the modes and construction of ragas. The effort was made because of, rather than despite, John and Paul's dominance. In large families, younger siblings often have to go out of their way to define themselves. George carved out a speciality in Indian music because he loved it but also as a triumphantly creative response to his marginal status. By early 1969, Harrison was writing more and better songs—songs that any other group would have leaped on. He'd just been to see his friend Bob Dylan, who treated him like a peer. Now he was in a freezing warehouse in Twickenham with two friends who persisted in treating him like the kid who tags along. We see all of this history in George's glowering face.

It didn't help that his bandmates spent hours working on a song that seemed to be about each other. In *Get Back* we watch George watching John and Paul play "Two of Us" again and again, gazing at each other over their acoustic guitars, working out harmonies, finding the right phrasing, doing silly voices, breaking off to giggle at each other's jokes.

Paul came up with the idea for "Two of Us" while on a car trip in the countryside with Linda. "One of the great things about Linda was that while I was driving and going, 'Oh my God, I think I'm lost,' she'd simply say, 'Great!'" Paul always felt he had to be going somewhere; Linda showed him that sometimes it was OK to go nowhere. But in truth, "Two of Us" doesn't feel like a song about new lovers bursting with excitement for their future together (by the time of the Twickenham sessions, Linda was pregnant). It feels elegiac, wistful. If it was inspired by Linda, it is also about the journey Paul had been on with John. McCartney has hinted as much: "Lying behind the phrase 'We're on our way home' is less the literal sense of going back to London, but more about trying to get in touch with the people we once were." He doesn't say who "we" is here, but the words of "Two of Us" suggest who was on his mind. Paul and Linda did not have memories longer than the road that stretches out ahead. They were not chasing paper (in a song from later that year, McCartney used "funny paper" to refer to the business disputes the Beatles were now subject to). The music conjures up the people he and John once were—teenagers with guitars singing in Everly-style harmony. In rehearsals of "Two of Us" at Twickenham they sing into the same microphone.

From late 1968 to early 1969 McCartney wrote many songs that ache with yearning for home: songs for the end of a journey—"Two of Us," "The Long and Winding Road," "Let It Be," "Get Back," "Golden Slumbers." These songs seem to emerge from an intimation that the dream he and John created in Liverpool was coming to an end. He was not ready to give up on the Beatles, however. In the wake of George's departure, he keeps returning to the need for a plan, a method, a program of work:

Paul: To wander aimlessly is very unswinging. Unhip.

John: And when I touch you, I feel happy inside. I can't hide, I can't hide. [pause] Ask me why, I'll say I love you.

Paul: What we need is a *schedule*.

John: A garden schedule.*

---

* American readers may need reminding that British people pronounce schedule "shed-dule."

John's contributions here are jokey, gnomic, and riddling. He talks in Beatle, dropping in lyrics from the early years of the band. John is playing to the gallery—there were others around, and cameras—but he is also attempting to communicate with Paul in their shared code. Does Paul know what John is getting at? It's hard to say, but John *expects* Paul to understand him because he has such faith in what Paul calls, in another conversation from these sessions, their "heightened awareness" of each other's mind.

McCartney once recalled a dream he had when he and John were teenagers, about digging up gold coins in the garden. When he told John, John said he'd had the same dream. That their minds were merged had been an article of faith.* But by 1969 Paul, at least, had realized that their reluctance to talk directly about what was going on between them was a problem. At Twickenham, when John and Yoko weren't around, he spoke to Neil Aspinall about John's uncommunicativeness: "With our heightened awareness, the answer is not to say anything, you know. But it isn't. Cause I mean, we screw each other up totally if we don't do that . . . Like, we don't know what the *fuck* each other's talking about."

On the Sunday after George quit, the group met at Ringo's house for a peace summit. It didn't go well, partly because Yoko did more talking than John. George walked out in anger, and left for Liverpool. The next week, the rest of the group reconvened at Twickenham. Lindsay-Hogg had planted a few hidden microphones around the studio, including one in a flowerpot in the canteen (he did warn the Beatles he was doing this, even if they didn't know the specific locations). We hear John and Paul discuss the future of the band (Yoko, Linda, and Ringo were also involved, though they are edited out of Jackson's version). It is a densely allusive exchange and not easy to interpret, but there are moments of clarity. "It's a festering wound," says John, about their relationship with George, "and yesterday we let it go even deeper. But we didn't give him any bandages." John acknowledges that he

---

* In footage from January 26, 1969, we hear John arriving at the session. He sounds energized. "Hey!" he says. "Did you dream about me last night?" Paul says, "I can't remember." John continues, "Very strong dream . . . I thought you must have been there. I spent about three hours touching you." Paul, clearly not in the mood for it, barely responds.

has treated George roughly and says he's always been like that with people, ever since school. "We all feel guilty about our relationship to each other," he adds. John sounds ambivalent about George's departure, however, and what it means for the Beatles: "Do I want him back, Paul? I'm just asking, do I want it back, whatever it is, enough?"

They talk more about each other than they do about George. John says that when he plays new songs to Paul, he has to pretend to himself that he's drunk because he's so nervous about what his partner will say. He says he doesn't have Paul's ability to instantly "hear" the whole arrangement of a song in his head: "I don't see any further than the guitar, and the drums . . . I don't hear any of the flutes playing, you know?" He says he was sometimes so frightened that he let Paul take his songs in directions he later regretted. "And then, my only chance was to let George take over, or interest George in it, because I knew he'd . . ." Paul interrupts: "'She Said She Said.'"

John's song "She Said She Said," one of the tracks on *Revolver*, started off as a fragment, inspired by a weird conversation John and George had while on LSD at the LA pool party the Beatles hosted in 1965. John wasn't sure how to develop it until George visited him at Kenwood and suggested putting the "she said" fragment together with another one John had lying around, which began "When I was a boy . . ." Later, during the recording of "She Said She Said" at Abbey Road, an argument ensued, possibly over McCartney's attempt to run the session. McCartney stormed out, leaving the others to finish the track. The incident suggests that Paul was not immune to jealousy when it came to his songwriting partner. If he was on edge during that session, it was because they were recording a song he knew that John and George had worked on together—a song about an experience they had shared without him. But by 1969 he had learned to reinterpret the episode as evidence of how hard it had become for John to handle his (Paul's) opinions in the studio. In the flowerpot conversation he tacitly accepts most of what John says, only pushing back to point out that sometimes *he* is the one who feels that the others are not listening to him.

Yoko tries to steer the conversation toward its ostensible topic: "Go back to . . . talking about George." But the two of them understand that the malaise begins with them. Paul reassures John that he is still the leader: "You have always been the boss. I've been sort of secondary boss. George has been the third boss." He suggests that John is stymieing himself: "You're not sure whether to go left or right on an issue." He encourages John to be as crazy or as dramatic as he wants to be: to "kick the telephone box in," by which he seems to mean just doing something decisive, even if that means breaking up the band. In effect, he invites John to do anything other than nothing.

⊛

The *Get Back* documentary is a study in many things but one of them is miscommunication. Long relationships often run into problems because a couple know each other *too* well—or think they do. In the first few years, partners build a mental model of the other person that is so accurate, so sensitive, it can feel as if they're one mind in two bodies. But over the years, as those individuals change and develop, the model doesn't get updated. The partners start to misread each other, generating puzzlement, frustration, and resentment, until before they know it they are estranged. John and Paul built their models of each other in Liverpool and Hamburg, and came to read each other about as well as any two people can. But by late 1968 they had both changed in a way that neither had fully accounted for. They were like kids who have been listening avidly to Radio Luxembourg all night and now find the signal drowning amid waves of static. John thought Paul understood how insecure he felt, specifically about their relationship, and sought emotional reassurance. Paul thought John needed to feel he was the most important person in the group: hence his insistence, in the canteen, that John is the boss. But John didn't want power, not anymore. He wanted love.

At one point during one of the many eyeball-to-eyeball run-throughs of "Two of Us," McCartney stops and says to John that their songs seem to be telling a bigger story: "Get Back" and "Two of Us"; "Don't Let Me Down" and "Oh! Darling." John says it out loud: "It's like you and me are lovers." McCartney, suddenly inarticulate, grunts assent, and they both flick their hair. They rehearse "Two of Us" while doing Elvis impressions. They do it in Scottish accents. They do it through clenched teeth, like ventriloquists— they do it any way but straight. Only after endless jokey variations do they settle on the song's final form: acoustic, gentle, entirely heartfelt. Music was still a place where John and Paul could let each other in.

31   DON'T LET ME DOWN

George was persuaded to rejoin the group on the condition they get out of Twickenham. The Beatles relocated to their own newly built studio, in the basement of the Apple building. In this smaller, more intimate space, they found their groove. Lennon was revitalized, and everyone cheered up, assisted by the arrival of Billy Preston. Preston, a singer and keyboardist, had first met the Beatles in Hamburg, aged sixteen, when he was part of Little Richard's touring band. He happened to be in London, where he bumped into Harrison, who invited him to jam with them at Apple. Preston was an abundantly talented musician and a delightful presence. His keyboard contributions ignited songs that the Beatles had been hacking away at for weeks. There is a moment captured on film when Preston finds the right riff to play on his first run-through of "I've Got a Feeling" and Paul breaks into an amazed and grateful grin. Preston made them smile, and he raised their game. He became an auxiliary member of the band for the next four months.

The Beatles spent weeks vacillating over what they wanted to do for a finale to the TV show. Lindsay-Hogg proposed ideas he felt befitted their fame and cultural status: an amphitheater in

Libya, a cruise ship. John and Paul were open to some kind of spectacular, but Ringo didn't want to go abroad and George was not keen on any large-scale live show. Eventually, someone suggested playing a gig on the roof of the Apple building. It seemed like a good compromise, but even this was hard to agree on, since Harrison remained reluctant and Lennon would not throw his weight behind it. Paul, too, resisted the rooftop idea, worrying that it would be an anticlimax. Fundamentally, the Beatles were nervous about embarrassing themselves, and unsure if they still had it in them. Lindsay-Hogg recalls that having spent days getting everything set up for the shoot, he had to wait while the Beatles debated whether or not to do it, even as they were literally about to step out onto the roof. But step out they did.

They played five songs on the rooftop ("Get Back," "Don't Let Me Down," "I've Got a Feeling," "One After 909," "Dig a Pony"), running through three of them twice. During the band's first performance of "Get Back" there is a shot of them taken from a camera mounted on the neighboring roof. In the documentary, we got overhead shots of them at Twickenham, marooned in an island in Studio One. Here we look down on them as the beat kicks in and Billy Preston hits his riff, and we see them dancing—dancing like they danced at the Cavern and the Kaiserkeller. It's the precise moment that John receives the enormous *yes* for which he was always searching. During the performance, all four seem amazed by how *good* they sound. Paul keeps glancing across at John and grinning. He can see that John is happy, and because John is happy, Paul is euphoric.

☻

"Don't Let Me Down" was one of only two new songs John brought to these sessions. It had two parts and he wasn't sure how they should fit together. The lyrics are deliberately simple: the Beatles refer to them as "corny." "There's no clever words in it," said John, who had a vision of a song that eschewed sophistication and lunged straight for the heart. It didn't seem like it would amount to much. Throughout January, the Beatles kept running at it, taking it to pieces, arguing over vocal arrangements, honing each transition, absorbing it into their fingers and their bodies. By the time they played it on the roof, it was immense: a rush of pure feeling.

Insofar as Beatles songs are ever about one thing, "Don't Let Me Down" is about John's leap into a new life with Yoko. In 1970, he said (about another song), "When it gets down to it, when you're drowning, you don't say, 'I would be incredibly pleased if someone would have the foresight to notice me drowning and come and help me,' you just *scream*." "Don't Let Me Down" is an unusual kind of love song, in that the verse isn't addressed to the lover. The singer is telling someone about how he's in love for the first time. Then he screams. "Don't Let Me Down" is about John's experience of falling in love; about being terrified of the fall and wanting a friend to hold his hand as he leaps. To express something so personal he leaned on his beloved 1950s-style rock and roll: the Drifters, Arthur Alexander, Sam Cooke. Paul, who intuitively understood the sound and sentiment John was aiming for, suggested the appropriate drum parts for Ringo.

From Paul's perspective, in one way "Don't Let Me Down" is just a track for the new album, a block of wood he has to help chisel into a sculpture. In another, it's about his best friend choosing someone else over him—and in doing so, threatening to break apart the group that has been at the center of both of their lives ever since they met. In the *Get Back* documentary we see him trying to rationalize John's sudden and complete dependence on Yoko. You can tell he's baffled by the way his once irrepressible, domineering friend has become quiescent and submissive. He seems annoyed by John's dalliances with avant-garde art. (When Lindsay-Hogg asks, "Where's John?" Paul replies, "Probably in a bag in his dressing room with Yoko. I think they brought their own bag with them today.") After all, it was he, Paul, who had spent years trawling London's underground scene. He knew what was bullshit and what wasn't. Paul's little speech about India can be seen as an attempt to remind John that while every guru can teach you something, it's unwise to surrender your personality to any.

But Paul is trying hard to adapt to, rather than resist, the change in his relationship with John: to accept that there are no longer just two of us. In conversation with Ringo and others, he admits, sheepishly, to trying to impress Yoko by coming up with ideas she might like—songs about white walls. He acknowledges that if John is forced to choose between the Beatles and Yoko, he'll choose Yoko, and he chuckles about how absurd it would be if in fifty years' time people said the Beatles split up because Yoko sat on an amp. The energy that McCartney pours into "Don't Let Me Down," in rehearsal and in performance, is generated by something more than creative perfectionism. He knows how much his friend has staked on this new love affair, and he wants to be the friend he promised to be in "Hey Jude."

You can hear all of this in the rooftop performance. John's searing lead vocal is counterpointed by Paul's passionate bass playing; the song becomes almost a duet between singer and bass. George Martin once remarked that whenever Paul had something to say, he said it most eloquently on the bass: "He wanted to make that bass sing." Paul's vocal harmonies are eloquent, too: he matches John's fierce commitment to the four words of the chorus. Toward the end of the song, as John improvises around the title phrase, Paul soars high up above him and floats on a wordless falsetto, hovering like a thing with feathers.

32   THE BALLAD OF JOHN AND YOKO

The resignations of Apple's accountants shocked Lennon and McCartney into a realization that something drastic needed to be done. During the Twickenham sessions, John had told a reporter, "Apple is losing money every week because it needs closely running by a big businessman . . . if it carries on like this, all of us will be broke in the next six months." Meanwhile the problems multiplied. In December 1968, Brian Epstein's brother, Clive, told the Beatles he was putting NEMS up for sale. NEMS had the rights to a quarter of the Beatles' royalties. Epstein had been made an offer for NEMS by a firm of merchant bankers and he was interested in taking it, but went to the Beatles first, out of loyalty.

Paul was annoyed by John's frankness, partly because he was working on a plan. Linda's father, Lee Eastman, was an eminent lawyer who represented many clients in music and entertainment. When Paul heard about Epstein's sale, he asked his father-in-law to help him out. Eastman didn't come to London himself at first, but sent his son, closer to the Beatles in age and sensibility. John Eastman, suave and brash, made Epstein a competitive offer for NEMS and Epstein accepted. Eastman returned to New York, his first mission accomplished. This apparent success was actually the start of a business rift between Lennon and McCartney, the first to appear since they had agreed to share the proceeds of their songwriting. Although John (and the others) at first agreed to having the Eastmans represent them as legal advisers, he soon changed his mind. This probably shouldn't have come as a surprise to Paul. By virtue of his relationship with Linda, the Eastmans were personally close to him, but not to John, George, or Ringo. Yoko had no particular reason to trust Paul or Paul's girlfriend's family with her partner's finances. And, crucially, John and Yoko now had their own man.

Allen Klein, like the Eastmans, was a New Yorker, but from an altogether different background. Born in Newark, the son of a butcher, he was proud of coming from the wrong side of the tracks. His mother died when he was a baby; he spent part of his childhood in an orphanage. After gaining an accountancy degree, he found work in the record business in 1957 and made a name for himself as someone who would go into battle on behalf of musicians against the suits and win. Klein was short, plump, and scruffy, and he spoke like a gangster, fast and profane. He formed a quick rapport with his clients. Smooth-talking executives routinely used every trick in the accounting book to rip off naive and hapless artists, and Klein was expert at calling them on it. By the late 1960s he had represented Bobby Darin, Sam Cooke, and British bands, including the Animals, the Kinks, and the Rolling Stones. Like many who start at the bottom of society and gate-crash its upper echelons, Klein had an eye for human weakness and a strong grasp of power dynamics. He was also self-interested and unscrupulous, something of a shark himself.

Klein had openly courted the Beatles for years but didn't get to meet one of them until January 27, 1969, when John and Yoko took a meeting with him after work, at the Dorchester Hotel. Klein came prepared. He had read the new biography of the Beatles by Hunter Davies. He made sure to let John know about his hardscrabble background. He was careful to woo Yoko, too, implying that he might get her a film deal. John was smitten by Klein, impressed by how much Klein knew about his work and enamored of his us-against-them bravado. That very evening, John dictated letters to EMI,

NEMS, and the Beatles' music publisher, Dick James, authorizing Klein to act on his behalf. In *Get Back* we see him say to George and Ringo (Paul had stepped out for a meeting): "I want to tell you all at once [about Klein]. I just think he's fantastic." John knew that Paul would be wary of Klein, which meant he couldn't rely on the group's usual power bloc, and needed the other two to take his side. We also see Glyn Johns, the producer for the *Get Back* sessions, tactfully try to warn Lennon off Klein, and Lennon ignoring him.

Conversely, John was wary of the Eastmans from the start, contemptuous of their privilege. His animosity was connected to his feelings toward Linda. John had been relatively relaxed about Paul's relationship to Jane, at least as long as he knew it was noncommittal on Paul's part, but he never got on well with Linda. He thought she was "tweedy," a straight, and a tool of her father. He found Paul's attachment to her baffling, as he admitted in a September 1971 interview: "I was very surprised with Linda. I wouldn't have been surprised if he'd married Jane Asher, because it had been going on for a long time and they went through a whole ordinary love scene. But with Linda it was just like, boom! She was in and that was the end of it." Asked if the suddenness of Linda's arrival was disruptive, he gave an answer not unlike that of a cuckolded partner: "Paul had met her before, you see. I mean, there were quite a few women he'd obviously had that I never knew about. God knows when he was doing it, but he must have been doing it." The idea of letting Linda's family take control of his money at the same time as Linda took over Paul was bound to disturb him. For her part, Yoko saw in the Eastmans exactly the kind of establishment figures that she and other avant-garde artists in New York hated: the kind who hung Matisses and Picassos in their homes but blanched at truly subversive art.

To Paul, it was clear that Klein could not be trusted, and that he, Paul, should be. He found Lennon's recalcitrance baffling and distressing. It soon became apparent, however, that he was isolated. At Lennon's suggestion, Paul, George, and Ringo met with Klein the evening after Lennon's meeting (two days before the rooftop concert). Klein told them the price that John Eastman had agreed for NEMS was too high. Paul, who felt there was little point discussing it without the Eastmans, left the meeting earlier than the rest. Ringo and George stayed longer and agreed, informally, to be represented by Klein.

When the Eastmans found out about this, John Eastman flew back to London and confronted Klein testily at a meeting with the Beatles. It was agreed that both parties should represent the Beatles for now, the Eastmans in legal matters, Klein in financial affairs. Klein was empowered to delay the deal with Clive Epstein while he carried out an audit of the Beatles' accounts. Exasperated by this delay, and by a clumsily worded letter from the Eastmans, Epstein called the deal off and, on February 17, sold 70 percent of NEMS to Triumph Investment Trust, the merchant bankers who made the original offer. The Eastmans were left looking clumsy and impotent. Klein returned to London and called a meeting with EMI to redirect royalties to Apple, and with Triumph, to try, unsuccessfully, to win back NEMS. The upshot was that the Beatles' income from EMI was frozen until a deal could be settled. Klein flew back to New York in mid-March to resume his audit.

Paul and Linda were married at Marylebone Registry Office in London, on March 12. It was a small ceremony, attended by none of the other Beatles, although the streets around the venue were thronged by fans and press. The night before, it did not seem certain that it would go ahead. Paul and Linda had a furious row. Even though Linda was four months pregnant, and even though he was in love, McCartney was nervous about this final commitment, and stressed by the dispute between him and his friends in which his prospective wife's family was now embroiled. Mal Evans recalled him saying, in early March, "What do you think, Mal, should I get married?" Maggie McGivern remembered getting a call from a distressed McCartney around the same time. It was a difficult period for Linda, who later said: "Paul was really upset; there was a whole business and legal thing happening which took everyone's energy; and I hated it. I thought it was going to be all peace and love and music, and it was wartime." Still, the couple went through with it. After the wedding the McCartneys traveled to Liverpool and spent a few days with Paul's family before flying to New York.

Just over a week later John and Yoko got married. Yoko's divorce from

Tony Cox had been finalized in January (there is a touching moment in *Get Back* when Lennon receives the divorce papers and the others celebrate with him). They could have wed in Britain, once Yoko's immigration status was negotiated, but having seen Paul get married, John wanted to do it right away. The couple went to Paris first but could not find a way to get legally betrothed until the Apple executive Peter Brown discovered that they could do so in the British colony of Gibraltar. They wore all white, Yoko in a mini-dress, John in a jacket and rollneck, both in sneakers (John had the beginnings of a thick beard, sprouted since the rooftop concert). Lennon told the press, "Everything we do we shall be doing together. I don't mean I shall break up the Beatles or anything, but I want to share everything."

From Gibraltar the couple returned to Paris, traveled on to Amsterdam, spent a week in a suite at the Hilton Hotel and declared a "Bed-In for Peace." Lounging in bed in white pajamas, surrounded by flowers and hand-lettered signs reading "Hair Peace" and "Bed Peace," they received the world's press. They then went to Vienna to be interviewed inside a white sack. They gave hundreds of interviews over the next year, repeating and elaborating on the same messages. Unlike Paul and Linda, John and Yoko did not yearn for time alone. They wanted to be on display.

☮

Three weeks after the *Get Back* sessions came to an end, the Beatles were back in the studio. Nobody was forcing them back in. The *White Album*, just six months old, was generating plentiful revenues for EMI. But they wanted to work. In fact, the group might have restarted sooner had it not been for George having to have his tonsils out (illness may have been another factor in his frustration at Twickenham). At Trident Studios, where "Hey Jude" had been recorded, the Beatles and Billy Preston started on a new Lennon song: "I Want You (She's So Heavy)." It ended up on *Abbey Road*, though at the time the Beatles thought they were adding material for the *Get Back* album, for which they didn't yet have, by their lights, a full quotient of songs. There is something almost compulsive about the Beatles' recording schedule around this time. As they came apart, they increased their rate of production, making a double album in 1968 and enough material for *two* albums in 1969, as well as creating songs that would be used on solo albums. Making music together was their way of processing emotional turmoil, and the greater the turmoil, the harder they had to work to process it.

At the end of March, a new problem arose: Dick James decided to sell his share of Northern Songs, the Lennon-McCartney publishing company, to ATV, a TV company run by the cigar-smoking show business impresario Lew Grade. John and Paul now risked losing all control of the rights to their own songs, and to an establishment figure they didn't like. Lennon, asked about it while in Amsterdam, said, "I don't have to ring Paul. I know damn well he feels the same as I do." When he was back, he and Paul summoned James to a meeting at Paul's house and berated him for selling them out. Lennon and McCartney were now fighting battles on two fronts: for control of both NEMS (management) and Northern Songs (publishing). This would have been fraught enough had they been united. An uneasy détente prevailed. McCartney, as well as Lennon, called Klein to ask him to fight the ATV deal. McCartney also consented to Klein representing them legally and effectively taking over the Apple business. Still the business meetings and lawsuits grew like bindweed.

It was in this context that, a couple of weeks after Lennon's return from his honeymoon, John and Paul went into Abbey Road to record a defiantly ebullient pop song.

☮

John had become interested in the idea of songs as reportage: instant dispatches from his travels. "The Ballad of John and Yoko" details the couple's transit from Southampton to Paris, Amsterdam, and Vienna, verse by verse, right down to Peter Brown telling them they could get married in Gibraltar. "It's a piece of journalism," John said later, but his apparently plain reporting is executed with tremendous wit and skill. In the middle section he drops in a reflection on death and the soul, and gives us a glimpse of an intimate conversation with Yoko, before bouncing us back to the narrative. Lennon's overt reference to Jesus Christ in the chorus was deliberately provocative (it also suggests that the meeting at which John had declared he was Christ was not entirely an aberration). It was as if he had now decided, looking back on the 1966 tour, that he had been too defensive and would now go on the offense. John was no longer the droopy figure of January: his manic quality had returned.

On April 14 Lennon went to Cavendish Avenue and played McCartney the unfinished song. George was away for the weekend, Ringo was on his film set, but John was impatient—he wanted it done there and then. Paul, whatever his feelings about Yoko, leaped at the chance. The two of them went from Paul's house to Abbey Road, where, with the help of George Martin, they made the record. Paul played drums and bass and piano, John guitars. According to those present, the mood was high-spirited. The tape captures John addressing Paul, on drums, as "Ringo"; Paul laughs and responds, "OK, George." The "Ballad" is the only Beatles song that features just John and Paul. It was quickly released as a single. "It has always surprised me how with just the two of us on it, it ended up sounding like the Beatles," said Paul, years later.

Musically, it is an affectionate callback to the romantic, 1950s-style Latin-esque pop songs they used to play at the Cavern, like "The Honeymoon Song" and "Besame Mucho," both sung by Paul and dancing to his bass line. The "Ballad" is a reminder of what masterful arrangers the two of them were. Lennon's lead guitar licks add a subversive, almost satirical commentary on his words. McCartney's piano chords are used very sparingly at first—just a bar to add color at the end of the chorus. They come in full-time on the last verse, so that the song gains momentum in its final section. Best of all is the vocal harmonizing. Here again, the restraint is impressive. Paul does not join in until the penultimate verse, when he uses his voice like a marker pen to highlight single words (*head*, *said*, *drag*). On the last verse he sings every word, helping John bring the song home. The lyrics are about John and Yoko but the music is all John and Paul.

33   OH! DARLING

In April and May of 1969, John and Paul found themselves dragged deeper into an interconnected series of escalating disputes. Klein, now in charge at Apple headquarters, was swinging an axe at its budgets and firing staff, including longtime Beatles associates, while the Beatles themselves looked the other way. It was a miserable time for everyone who worked there, though, as Derek Taylor put it, "There was no alternative that could deal with this writhing thing that was Apple, that could put it in a container and hold the lid down." Lee Eastman, concerned that he was losing any grip he had over the Beatles' affairs, flew over to London for meetings. Eastman was fifty-nine, more than twice the age of Lennon or McCartney, twenty-one years older than Klein, and rather pompous. Over the course of two meetings, he let his personal antipathy toward Klein get the better of him. At one point, he yelled, "You are a rodent, the lowest scum on earth!" This only allowed Klein to play the grown-up in the room. Lennon addressed Eastman as "Mr. Epstein," having discovered that this was his original name. This was intended to needle him and it worked—Eastman got mad at him, too. McCartney said relatively little during these meetings, presumably angry at Lennon and Klein, and mortified by his father-in-law.

In April, less than a week after the recording of "The Ballad of John and Yoko," Lennon and McCartney had a furious row. During a meeting at Apple over the battle for control of Northern Songs, Lennon learned that McCartney had bought some additional shares in the company, on the advice of the Eastmans, without telling the other Beatles. McCartney regarded it as a mere business matter. To John it was a breach of the band's democratic protocol, and of friendship. Peter Brown, the Apple executive, said: "At one point I thought he was really going to hit Paul." Paul left the meeting after lunch, while John stayed on until that evening's recording session. John, George, and Ringo now moved to sever ties with Eastman altogether. They signed a letter informing him that he could not represent the Beatles. It marked the beginning of a legal rift between Paul and the other three Beatles, and a poisoning of their relationship.

Apple scruffs, the female fans who gathered every day outside Savile Row, Abbey Road, and Paul's house on Cavendish Avenue, could tell when something was up. One of them, Gill Pritchard, recalled Paul emerging from Abbey Road in tears one night. He didn't return the next day. Another scruff, speaking in 1996, continued the story:

> John was really angry because they were all waiting and he came storming out of the studio and made off towards Paul's house . . . when he got there he stood outside and just banged on the door again and again, calling for Paul to open up. Paul didn't answer so John climbed the gate and hammered on his door. Then they had a screaming match. He was shouting that George and Ringo had both come in from the country and Paul didn't even bother to let anyone know he couldn't make the session.

In late April, Klein proposed a formal agreement to manage the Beatles. On May 7 the Beatles, along with their lawyers, convened to review Klein's proposal. They all agreed to it in principle, with minor changes discussed.

After much toing and froing over the next couple of days, Apple's lawyer managed to obtain signatures from George, John, and Ringo. Paul did not sign. Now the agreement just needed to be ratified by Apple's board, which included the four Beatles. On the afternoon of May 9 the Beatles assembled at Olympic Studios in Barnes, southwest London, to meet with Glyn Johns, who had been trying to turn the tracks recorded in January into an album. The day turned into a long series of debates between McCartney and the others over the Klein contract. Klein insisted that the agreement had to be signed that day so that he could inform his board. McCartney didn't directly object to having Klein as manager but wanted the group to push back on his proposed 20 percent commission. He also believed they didn't need to make a decision right away. In the 1990s, McCartney recalled it like this:

> The other three said, "You've got to sign a contract—he's got to take it to his board." I said, "It's Friday night. He doesn't work on a Saturday, and anyway Allen Klein is a law unto himself. He hasn't got a board he has to report to. Don't worry—we could easily do this on Monday. Let's do our session instead. You're not going to push me into this."

McCartney disliked—hated—the feeling of being pushed around.

> They said: "You're stalling." I replied, "No, I'm working for us; we're a big act." I remember the exact words: "We're a big act—The Beatles. He'll take 15%." But for some strange reason (I think they were so intoxicated with him) they said, "No, he's got to have 20%, and . . . You've got to sign now or never." So I said, "Right, that's it. I'm not signing now."

McCartney's objections, both to the fee and to Klein's artificial deadline, seem sensible enough: the Beatles were by far the most powerful party in this negotiation. But Lennon had become determined to impose his leadership over the group's affairs. McCartney had been in this position before, in Liverpool: the odd one out, refusing to submit to Lennon's force field. But this was dire. Later, Paul described the events of May 9, 1969, as the day that the unity of the group fractured irreparably. The others wanted this over with and decided to go ahead, without Paul's signature. John, George, and Neil Aspinall, acting as directors of Apple, ratified the deal at about 8 p.m. that evening, and after a final acrimonious exchange of words with Paul, they left the building. Paul wandered alone through Olympic Studios, angry and miserable, until he happened upon someone he knew: the American rock musician Steve Miller. Paul saw an opportunity to do what he always did when he felt things falling apart: throw himself into music. He played the drums, hard, on a song of Miller's called "My Dark Hour."

⊛

In April and May, as the group's conflicts intensified, its music-making became if anything more focused. One of the quirkiest examples of John and Paul's double life during this period was a session that took place at Abbey Road on April 30, for "You Know My Name (Look Up the Number)." The track has the quality of a private joke, a mash-up of Goons-style radio comedy and avant-garde happenings. John and Paul had started work on it in 1967 but it went into dormancy, only for the pair of them to return to it now (George and Ringo did not participate). The two sides of the duo's dealings at this time, business and music, converge most spectacularly in Paul's song "You Never Give Me Your Money," which the group recorded at Olympic Studios, three days before the May 9 showdown, over the course of a long evening session that ended at around 4 a.m. the next morning, imparting a small-hours feel to the recording.

From its title to its tripartite structure, the song is as strange and multi-layered as anything the Beatles ever did. The opening section somehow makes financial and legal conflicts feel very personal and full of emotion, conveyed by McCartney's pure, tender vocal, his sensitive piano-playing, and Harrison's sympathetic guitar. The first verse ends with the singer breaking down, the second with whoever he is singing to breaking down. The barrelling honky-tonk section that comes next is the sound of freedom. The lyrics verge on nonsensical but in an abstract manner they capture the giddy liberation of throwing over school and career for rock and roll. Then the music moves into slow motion as McCartney sings about the magic feeling of having nowhere to go. There's immense depth of emotion in that moment: defiant, optimistic, and elegiac all at once. The third section—"one sweet dream"—is unavoidably the dream of the Beatles themselves, as well as a dream of escape from the Beatles. Over dueling guitars, the song ends with a chant that evokes the world to which John and Paul's songs so often return, childhood, before dissolving into an avant-garde sound collage. They did get to heaven, even if they had to leave it now.

Ⓞ

More funny paper flew over the first part of the summer as Klein attempted to extricate the Beatles from NEMS. He put the *Get Back* album and film on hold. John and Yoko traveled to Montreal to be near the North American youth protest movement (they couldn't enter the US due to Lennon's drugs conviction), and once again staged a bed-in for the world's press. They made a single called "Give Peace a Chance," released under the name the Plastic Ono Band—another example of Lennon's knack for slogans. Toward the end of June they paused their campaign to go on holiday. Lennon took Yoko and Kyoko (still under the care of her father but visiting John and Yoko periodically) and Julian on a tour of his childhood: a seaside resort in Wales, then Liverpool, then Scotland, all by car. In Scotland they stayed in the remote village of Durness, in the Highlands, the area where John had spent his happiest childhood holidays.

The McCartneys holidayed in France and Greece. Upon their return, McCartney called George Martin to ask him if he'd produce a whole new album. The impetus was partly commercial: Klein had told the Beatles that in order to strengthen his hand in negotiations with EMI, they needed to show they were still a going concern. All of them were individually capable of refusing to play along, but the appetite to make music together remained. Martin gladly agreed on condition the sessions were at Abbey Road. Some of the tracks the Beatles had recorded in the spring were retrospectively recruited for this new album, which became *Abbey Road*, but there was still a lot to do.

On July 1 Paul went into the studio without any of the others to record his vocal for "You Never Give Me Your Money," as if he needed to be alone in order to express his pained ambivalence about what was happening to the group. As he did so, John Lennon crashed his car into a Highlands ditch. He was driving on narrow, winding country roads in bad weather, with Yoko beside him, and Julian and Kyoko in the back. Panicked by an oncoming car, he drove off the road. They were taken by ambulance to hospital in nearby Golspie; luckily, the children were unharmed. Lennon suffered a head injury requiring stitches. Ono, who was pregnant, suffered mild injuries to her back and forehead. After a week in hospital, they flew by helicopter back to London. The accident meant that Lennon did not join the others for the first three weeks of recording at Abbey Road. When he finally did, he insisted on a bed being wheeled into the studio so that Yoko, still recuperating, could be with him while he worked.

The other Beatles had made good progress on the album, including on a new George song called "Here Comes the Sun." When John arrived, he brought in a song called "Come Together." Its lyrics were in the vein of "I Am the Walrus," a stream of quasi-nonsense crafted into richly suggestive, rhythmically compulsive lines. He wrote them by taking the words of a Chuck Berry song called "You Can't Catch Me" and getting them wrong, just as he had done with "Come Go with Me" all those years ago.

George Martin said that "Come Together" was "virtually built around John's ad lib vocal sounds." Lennon chose words for their physical feel—for how they make the mouth move—as well as for meaning: *ju-ju*, *mojo*, *toe-jam* all push the tongue toward the top of the mouth so that it can make a funky little explosion (like *juba juba juba* in "Walrus"). Lennon was a master at mixing up cryptic lyrics with lines of startling clarity. In "Come Together," the key lines come just before the chorus. "One thing I can tell you is you got to be free" might be banal in another context; here it sounds like it's written in the sky. Another of these lines sounds like it's directed at Paul: "Got to be good-looking 'cause he's so hard to see."

Even if John was semi-detached from the group during these sessions, he was still capable of galvanizing them. When he brought "Come Together" to Paul it was a Bo Diddley–style rock and roller. McCartney reinvented it as a swampy, funky, bass-heavy track that sounds unlike anything else the band did. Everything about the performance, especially Ringo's drumming, is superb. Their collective mastery is evident in the way they use silence and space to generate power, as when the band drops out on those pre-chorus lines. John's dream of being a figure around whom people came together may have been vain in the context of global politics, but in the studio, it still worked.

The last new Beatles song on which all four Beatles worked together in the studio was another of John's: "Because." On August 1, John, Paul, and George spent hours creating and rehearsing its complex three-part harmony, and then hours more recording it, sitting around a microphone, watching one another's faces. Outside the studio, John and Paul continued to maneuver. Tony Bramwell wrote, "One week Paul would be in the office, the next it would be John and Yoko ruling the roost. It was difficult for those of us who'd grown up being faithful to them, and who suddenly found ourselves having to play them off against each other, behind each other's backs."

The basic tracks for the new album were all laid down now. What remained were overdubs (additional vocal and instrumental tracks). The Beatles had begun recording "Oh! Darling" on April 20, six days after John and Paul had made "The Ballad of John and Yoko," and two days after they nearly came to blows at Apple. In July, Paul recorded his lead vocal. "Oh! Darling" was one of the many McCartney songs that had floated around the sessions at Twickenham and Apple in January. Musically it evokes the kind of 1950s ballad beloved of John in particular. It's based on a doo-wop chord progression played on the piano to a steady, rolling 12/8 beat.

Paul took a long run-up at his vocal. He didn't want to sound smooth or controlled; he wanted to sound desperate, a man on the edge, racked by emotions that threaten to overwhelm him. He came into Abbey Road four times over the course of a week to roughen his vocal cords in preparation. His final take is magnificently unhinged and makes "Oh! Darling" much more than rock and roll pastiche.

Lennon adored "Oh! Darling." He considered it "more my style than his" and said that if Paul "had any sense, he should have let me sing it." He even claimed, eccentrically, that Paul "didn't sing it too well." Perhaps John was unsure what to do with his feelings about this song. Did he believe that it was about him, or for him? That would hardly have been unreasonable: it is, after all, a song about a partnership on the verge of splitting up, and the fear of living without it. *I'll never make it alone!* John would surely have noticed that Paul was singing "I'll never let you down" at the same time as he, John, was singing, "Don't let me down" (indeed, he connected the two songs in the "like you and me are lovers" conversation). During the *Get Back* rehearsals of "Oh! Darling," Lennon liked to call back to McCartney:

> Paul: Believe me when I tell you—
>
> John: Oh, I do!

The Beatles recorded backing vocals for "Oh! Darling" on August 11. It was the last day John and Paul sang together as Beatles.

34 THE END

It is fitting that the Beatles' final album is named after the place where they created most of their records, and that it concludes with a symphonic medley of songs that sounds very much like a grand finale. At the time, however, they didn't know for sure that it would be their final album. McCartney has always maintained that even when he wrote its last track, "The End," he wasn't thinking about the end. But this just shows how much of John and Paul's music came from a level deep beneath conscious awareness. Paul wanted not to believe that his partnership with John and the other Beatles was ending, even as he sought the most graceful cadence to close this twelve-year song.

☙

The Beatles approved a final mix of *Abbey Road* on August 20.* On Tuesday, September 9, John, Paul, and George met at Apple to discuss the *next* album. They even discussed a Christmas single, a tradition they had stuck to, with the exception of 1966, since 1963. Ringo was in hospital for an intestinal ailment, so

---

* A few more adjustments were made in the following days; the actual master was cut on August 25, 1969.

the others asked Anthony Fawcett, an Apple aide, for a tape recorder to be brought to the room. The tape opens with John's voice: "Ringo—you can't be here, but this is so you can hear what we're discussing." Lennon suggests that each of the three of them have four songs on the next album, with two spaces for Ringo. He adopts a brutally unsentimental tone, referring to "the Lennon and McCartney myth." He proposes that Paul give songs like "Maxwell's Silver Hammer" and "Ob-La-Di, Ob-La-Da" to other Apple artists, rather than take them to the Beatles. Paul stays fairly quiet. He may simply have been wearied by the whole saga. He had good reason to be tired: Linda had given birth to Mary twelve days before. John seems keen to bolster George's position in the group (and perhaps to strengthen his alliance with him against Paul). He says that "we" (John and Paul) have "always carved up the singles between us." The subtext here is economic as well as artistic—John is suggesting that George be allowed to make more money. "Well, the thing is," says Paul, flatly, "I think that until now, until this year, our songs have been better than George's. Now this year his songs are at least as good as ours." The first part might sound rough, but the second sentence is remarkable.

George says that he doesn't want a greater share of songs for ego reasons but to get his songs "out there," and to make more money, "seeing as I'm spending as much as the rest of you, and I don't earn as much as the rest of you." He goes on to complain that John and Paul have never spent much time on his songs. Raising his voice, John hotly disputes this. Referring to the *White Album*, George says, "I don't think you appeared on any of my songs. I don't mind." John says, "Well, you had Eric [Clapton] or someone like that." At this point, there is a long pause, as the three men who played at birthday parties in the houses of aunties and slept on top of one another in freezing vans, who have seen one another fuck and wank and vomit and cry, who discovered drugs together, and who played to sixty thousand screaming fans, wonder what on earth is happening to them. Slowly, very quietly, Paul says, "When we get in a studio, even on the worst day, I'm still playing bass, Ringo's still drumming, and we're still there, you know."

✦

A few days after this meeting, John and Yoko gave an interview in which Lennon said, "The Beatles are always discussing, 'Should we go on or shouldn't we? Why are we together for now?' And when it gets down to it, I like playing rock and roll and I like making rock and roll records." It's true—the Beatles had been debating whether or not to go on since their first return from Hamburg. John then reflected that while he could easily get other musicians to play with, he wouldn't have the rapport, the nonverbal communication, that he had with his friends. "I try not to use anybody but the Beatles," he concluded, before making what is almost a cheerleading chant: "Where's our biggest market? It's Beatles! Who are our closest friends? Beatles! Who do we have the most arguments with? Beatles. So Beatles is it!" The constant stream of activity John had kept up since getting together with Yoko was reaching a febrile pitch, and his decision-making was even more mercurial than usual. On the evening of that interview, he took a call from a Canadian promoter inviting him to join the Toronto Rock and Roll Festival, alongside Little Richard and the Doors, the next day. Lennon said yes, then decided against it in the morning, then was persuaded to go through with it, and got on a plane.

The following Friday, McCartney was asked for his favorite tracks from the new album. He named "Come Together" (John), "Something" (George), and "Because" (John). He said that he wanted the Beatles to play live again but only on a small scale. "I personally—if we're going to do anything— prefer to just go right back to a small club. Just have fifty people in and sing to them, have a bit of a singsong." It was a typically McCartneyesque fantasy and a slightly forlorn one. Paul said, "[John] did this Toronto thing and had a really great time . . . I don't particularly like the idea of performing to all those people, but I'd hate to stop *him* doing that. He loves it!"

The next day, September 20, Klein convened John, Paul, and Ringo (George was visiting his mother) at Apple, to sign the deals he had negotiated with EMI and Capitol.* They guaranteed the band an increased royalty rate,

---

* The date of this meeting is a little uncertain. It could have been September 16: McCartney's diary entry for that day reads "THE END." (Diary entry reproduced in McCartney, *The Lyrics*, 111.)

while committing them to make two albums and three singles a year until 1976. It is unclear how realistic each of the Beatles themselves regarded this commitment as being. After the signing, the three Beatles discussed the future of the group. Paul floated his idea of playing small venues, and John— well, Paul has described the moment vividly enough: "John looked at me in the eye and said: 'Well, I think you're daft. I wasn't going to tell you 'till we signed the Capitol deal but I'm leaving the group!'" A year later, Lennon recalled it like this: "Paul just kept mithering on about what we were going to do, so in the end I just said, 'I think you're daft. I want a divorce.'" In 1995, McCartney said, "We had to react to [John] doing it; he had control of the situation. I remember him saying, 'It's weird this, telling you I'm leaving the group, but in a way it's very exciting.' It was like when he told Cynthia he was getting a divorce. He was quite buoyed up by it." In 2021 Paul described John's behavior as "wildly hurtful. Talk about a knockout blow. You're lying on the canvas, and he's giggling and telling you how good it feels to have just knocked you out." Perhaps John just wanted to see the look on Paul's face—to see his power reflected in Paul's eyes. After a childhood scarred by betrayal, he organized his adult life around making sure it couldn't happen again. If he couldn't get Paul to unconditionally commit to him, he could make himself safe by acting first. McCartney's word, "buoyed," is apt; it means "to keep afloat."

In 1975 Mal Evans recalled the meeting and its immediate aftermath: "That was really, truly, a heartbreaking experience. I drove Paul home. And we got to Paul's house, and he spent the next hour in the house crying his eyes out." If Paul was blindsided by John's declaration, it was because he still didn't want to believe his partnership with him, and therefore the Beatles, was breaking up. After a few weeks in London, bruised and disoriented, he retreated to his farm in Scotland with his family. His low profile when *Abbey Road* was released fanned a bizarre rumor that he was dead, and had been since 1966, when he was secretly replaced by a look-alike. A forerunner of today's viral conspiracy theories, it was absurd and yet obscurely related to McCartney's state of mind: unsure if he existed as an artist or whether he was just a shadow, the outline of a Beatle. A reporter and photographer from

Life tracked him down in Scotland, to show the world McCartney was alive. After initially trying to repel them, McCartney gave an interview. He said, "The Beatle thing is over. It has been exploded, partly by what we have done and partly by other people. We are individuals, all different. John married Yoko, I married Linda. We didn't marry the same girl."

John was more expansive. He gave an interview right after the "divorce" meeting in which he told McCartney's friend Barry Miles, "I don't write for the Beatles. I write for myself." He spoke about how his life had changed since 1968: "I'm more myself than I was then, because I have the security of Yoko. That's what's done it. It's like having a 'mother' and everything." In an interview with the *NME* he referred to "differences of opinion on how things should be run" between him and Paul. In November he told *Melody Maker*, "The Beatles can go on appealing to a wide audience as long as they make nice albums like *Abbey Road*, which have nice little folk songs like 'Maxwell's Silver Hammer' for the grannies to dig." He was constructing a public narrative in which McCartney was the cute populist, Lennon the fearless artist.

What John did not do was publicly declare that he had left the Beatles. In the same *NME* interview, he said, "The Beatles split up? It just depends . . . I don't know if I want to record together again. I go off and on it, I really do." This may have been because Klein didn't want him to declare his hand, but more likely it was the truth: John wasn't sure what he wanted. When George was asked about the divorce meeting (from which he was absent) years later, he made little of it: "Everybody had tried to leave, so it was nothing new." All the other Beatles had walked out on the group in the past and reversed their decisions; it was quite possible John would, too. McCartney recalled that he, George, and Ringo weren't sure if "it was one of John's little flings . . . I think John did kind of leave the door open."

Now the Beatles entered a period of limbo. In January 1970, Paul, George, and Ringo returned to Abbey Road to put the final touches to tracks for the long-delayed *Get Back* album (it would be released, later that year, as *Let It Be*). John and Yoko kept up their frenetic program of avant-garde projects and political statements. They released a single, "Cold Turkey," a song that

Paul and the other Beatles had declined. In the first weeks of 1970 they went to Denmark, where they spent time with Kyoko, who was with her father, Tony Cox. Lennon shaved his beard and cut his hair short, in a symbolic break with his former self. In Denmark, John told the press, "We're not breaking up the band, but we're breaking its image." He and Yoko sent a postcard from Denmark to Paul on January 15, which read, "WE LOVE YOU AND WILL SEE YOU SOON."

John was vacillating. For the last year and a half, he had alternated between wanting to reassure Paul they were still friends and trying to provoke him. It's doubtful that John knew how upset Paul was by his behavior: he would probably have assumed that Paul was fine. Paul was *always* fine. Everything worked out for him. When Paul got a girl pregnant, before they were famous, the problem went away. When Paul wanted a child with Linda he got one (Yoko miscarried again in October 1969). Paul had joked about how, with Heather and now Mary, he had acquired an "instant family." You can imagine the phrase lodging in Lennon's brain and turning septic. Paul's flight to Scotland felt to John like a deliberate withdrawing of attention from him. He couldn't have that.

A few days after his return to England, Lennon woke up with a phrase in his head and turned it into a song. "Instant Karma" was of a piece with Lennon's fascination with mass marketing, which often turns on oxymorons. What if karma, the ancient notion that the consequences of our actions flow through generations, was repackaged into something that might help or hurt you in the moment? "The idea of instant karma was like the idea of instant coffee," John said later. The song flew out of him. He recruited George Harrison and the producer Phil Spector to record it. Ten days after he thought of the phrase, "Instant Karma" was in the shops. In an interview to accompany its release, Lennon said that the Beatles' current hiatus might either be "a rebirth or a death."

To open "Instant Karma," Lennon borrowed the chord change that opens "Some Other Guy." Over a thumping bass-drum beat, he addresses someone very particular, in a fierce, rasping vocal. The karma he's singing about does not sound like the good kind. It's going to get you and knock you on the head (like Maxwell's silver hammer). If you don't want to be dead, you'd better stop laughing in the face of love. Instant karma is going to look you "right in the face," eyeball-to-eyeball. You need to get yourself together, *darling*, he says, and *join the human race.* In effect, John tells Paul to descend from his superhuman realm, return from splendid isolation in Scotland, and be part of the dirty, compromised world of business. Come and join your brothers, he says, and get your share. Who in the *hell* do you think you are? We're all superstars. We *all* shine on.

"Instant Karma" became Lennon's first big post-Beatles hit and the first that any of the Beatles would have as solo artists. At Cavendish Avenue, McCartney had been making experimental recordings on a four-track recorder. He now decided to pull this material together into a solo album. He might have called it *Paul McCartney*, he might have called it anything, but he called it *McCartney*—a surname that was no longer a suffix. He had been content for the album to sound homemade and makeshift, but on hearing that Lennon had released a highly commercial single, he returned to Abbey Road to make two tracks to a much higher level of finish: "Maybe I'm Amazed," a heart-wringing song of gratitude to Linda for helping him survive the toughest time of his adult life, and "Every Night," also about being rescued from depression by love. McCartney may have been keeping these strong songs for the next Beatles album. But not anymore.

☮

The Beatles' house did not collapse all at once, but in stages: a chimney here, a ceiling there. Now and then it seemed as if the structure might be saved. A Beatle would give an interview indicating they might record together again, then cast doubt on the prospect days later. For several months, none of them seemed sure what was going on. When George threw a party for his wife, Pattie, at their new home, on March 17, 1970, all of the Beatles turned up with their partners. Reports suggested that everyone got along. It would be the last time all four were present in the same location.

Within the next few weeks, two events served to push Paul decisively away from John and the others. The first stemmed from a row over release dates. Paul's first solo album, *McCartney*, was scheduled for release, on Apple, on

April 17, which clashed with the proposed release of *Let It Be*, the Beatles album that had been salvaged from the *Get Back* sessions. In McCartney's absence, Apple and the other three Beatles felt the group effort should take precedence, and decided to postpone *McCartney*'s release to June. John wrote Paul a handwritten note, dated March 31, explaining the decision. It finished, "We're sorry it turned out like this—it's nothing personal. Love John and George." Less than heroically, they sent Ringo to deliver the note (placed in an envelope, addressed "From us to you") to Paul, at Cavendish Avenue. In 1971, Ringo recalled what happened next: "He told me to get out of his house. He was crazy; he went crazy, I thought. I got brought down because I couldn't believe it was happening to me. I'd just brought the letter."

McCartney won this battle; *McCartney*'s release went ahead as originally planned. To promote it, he spoke to Jann Wenner, the founder of *Rolling Stone*, on April 9. When the conversation touched on Apple and the Beatles, McCartney reiterated his hostility to Klein. Asked about John, his tone softened. "I will see him when I see him," he said. "And I love him just the same." Just after this, Paul telephoned John, and they had something of a heart-to-heart. A couple of weeks later, Paul said, "I told him on the phone the other day that at the beginning of last year I was annoyed with him. I was jealous because of Yoko, and afraid about the breakup of a great musical partnership. And it's taken me a year to realise they were in love. Just like Linda and me."

Now came an event that blasted any comity away. Paul asked the Apple press office for help putting together a Q&A as part of the promotional materials for *McCartney*, since he wasn't in the mood for doing interviews. Apple sent him a list of questions the press might ask. McCartney answered them and introduced a few questions himself. This is an extract:

Q: *Are you planning a new album or single with the Beatles?*

A: No.

Q: *Is this album a rest away from the Beatles or the start of a solo career?*

A: Time will tell. Being a solo album means it's "the start of a solo career . . ." and not being done with the Beatles means it's just a rest. So it's both.

Q: *Is your break with the Beatles temporary or permanent, due to personal differences or musical ones?*

A: Personal differences, business differences, musical differences, but most of all because I have a better time with my family. Temporary or permanent? I don't really know.

Q: *Do you foresee a time when Lennon-McCartney becomes an active songwriting partnership again?*

A: No.

McCartney's answers were just blunt enough that the press leaped upon the Q&A as a definitive declaration that the Beatles were splitting up—and that they were splitting up because Paul was leaving. On April 10 the *Daily Mirror* front page read: "PAUL IS QUITTING THE BEATLES." The afternoon before, Paul had called John on the phone, perhaps to prepare the ground. John was at a private clinic, undergoing therapy. We only have John's account of the conversation: "Paul said to me, 'I'm now doing what you and Yoko were doing last year. I understand what you were doing,' all that shit. So I said to him, 'Good luck to yer.'"

John was blindsided by Paul's Q&A and enraged by it. If anyone was going to end the Beatles, John felt it ought to be him. He'd started them, after all. He said: "We were all hurt that he didn't tell us what he was going to do. I think he claims that he didn't mean that to happen, but that's bullshit." John described Paul as "a good PR man . . . he really does a job." He berated himself: "I was a fool not to do it, not to do what Paul did, which was to use it to sell a record." John was probably right about this; in 1986 McCartney conceded that he had publicity in mind. But in truth, Paul's move was terrible PR. It landed him with the reputation as the man who split up the world's most beloved band. He realized after the fact how bad it looked: "When it was printed as news it looked very cold, yes, even crazy . . . And yes, John was hurt by that."

John offered a brisk public response, telling a journalist: "I was happy to hear from Paul. It was nice to find that he was still alive. Anyway you can say I said jokingly, 'He didn't quit, I sacked him!'" Klein refused to recognize that the Beatles were no more, telling the press that McCartney's position represented a "permanent maybe." In the months that followed, McCartney suffered anxiety and depression.

> I was going through a bad time, what I suspect was almost a nervous breakdown. I remember lying awake at nights shaking, which has not happened to me since. One night I'd been asleep and awoke and I couldn't lift my head off the pillow . . . I thought, Jesus, if I don't do this I'll suffocate. I remember hardly having the energy to pull myself up . . . I just couldn't do anything.

Later in April, McCartney spoke to the journalist Ray Connolly and said:

> I didn't leave the Beatles. The Beatles have left the Beatles—but no one wants to be the one to say the party's over. John said last year he wanted a divorce. All right, so do I. I want to give him that divorce. I hate this trial separation because it's just not working . . . John's in love with Yoko, and he's no longer in love with the other three of us.

☿

If Paul now recognized it was over, he was only catching up with himself. Deep down, he had known it back in 1969, and it came out in music. In just over two minutes, "The End" moves from raw rock and roll to orchestral sweep, encompassing the Beatles' career. It's like the curtain call of the musical that John and Paul never wrote, constructed from the base elements of rock and roll. The song begins with two exclamations, followed by a question: "Are you going to be in my dreams, tonight?" Guitars climb up in counterpoint to the vocal line, before falling silent in honor of the drums (Ringo's solo, a duty reluctantly accepted). As Ringo settles into his backbeat, rock guitars clang out a two-chord pattern: I to IV and back again, the most basic rock progression of all. The chords are played with a bluesy flattened seventh, the trick Tony Sheridan taught them at the Top Ten Club. Then voices are added: "Love you! Love you!" (McCartney, overdubbing himself). "The End" thus starts at the beginning, when John and Paul first fell in love with rock and roll, with each other, and began to dream.

Next comes a conversation of three guitars: Paul, George, and John, the original trio, given a total of just six bars each to say their last words (the Beatles always understayed their welcome). The rock and roll stops and a solo piano emerges, busy and precise. McCartney, echoed by little curlicues of guitar, sings a rhyming couplet that somehow says everything that needs to be said.

On his last line, the orchestra comes in, accompanying us down the steps at first, then moving up through a series of ethereal chords as if we're being lifted to the heavens on a cloud. George's eloquent, yearning guitar draws "The End" to an end.*

---

* Of course, "The End" does not actually end *Abbey Road*. Twenty seconds of silence later arrives "Her Majesty," a stocking filler unlisted on the album sleeve. Why did John and Paul (who both agreed to this addition) choose to subvert the grandeur of "The End" with a joke song about the Queen? Well, for one thing, they had always been wary of grandeur; for another, they couldn't bear the thought of ending.

35   GOD

After the split, the business of the Beatles kept grinding on. May 1970 saw the release of *Let It Be*, the album of the *Get Back* sessions, which Phil Spector had cobbled together and overdubbed with strings (it was Klein's idea to name it after Paul's song, which did nothing to mitigate Paul's contempt for the finished product). Around the same time, Michael Lindsay-Hogg's film of the same name was released. Its downbeat mood reinforced the misleading perception that by 1969 the Beatles could hardly stand one another's company.

McCartney was now almost powerless at Apple and yet could not release his music under any other label. For him, this was a nightmare scenario. He pressed the group to agree to a formal separation, using an interview, in April, to make his case: "Give us our freedom, which we so richly deserve." He was addressing John and the other Beatles, as well as Klein. His tone was conciliatory: "There's no one who's to blame. We were fools to get ourselves into this situation in the first place."

Klein and the other Beatles were worried about tax liabilities that would be incurred when the Beatles ceased as a financial entity. They believed McCartney to be in thrall to the Eastmans.

George Harrison put it starkly: "The reality is that he's outvoted, and we're a partnership . . . we're trying to do what's best for the Beatles as a group, or best for Apple as a company. We're not trying to do what's best for Paul and his in-laws."

In March 1970—before McCartney's Q&A—John and Yoko put their peace campaign on hold and retreated to their new mansion, Tittenhurst Park, in an attempt to kick heroin. (The journalist Ray Connolly accompanied them to a Harley Street clinic, where Yoko had a pregnancy examination. "She's a junkie," Lennon informed the nurse.) Also in March, Lennon was given an advance copy of a new self-help book called *The Primal Scream* and became immediately convinced it was the Answer for which he was always searching. The book's beguiling premise was that people could be freed of their psychological pain by reliving repressed childhood traumas while screaming. Its author, a psychotherapist named Arthur Janov, claimed his method cured "80 percent of all ailments." John got in touch with Janov, who lived in California, and persuaded him to fly to England to treat him. The sessions began at Tittenhurst but were interrupted by building work and moved to a London hotel. After four weeks Janov had to return home to his family, so John and Yoko followed him, renting a house in Bel Air. John spent four more months in Janov's clinic. Janov made his patients talk about their childhood traumas, pressing them at the rawest points and encouraging them to scream when they felt upset. Lennon had several sessions a week, during which he cried and screamed to release his pain.

In his book, Janov described his approach as "psychophysical." He claimed that his female patients had discovered that it enlarged their breasts, and that men who hadn't been able to grow beards sprouted facial hair and exuded a manly odor. Janov clearly liked women to be women and men to be men. He believed that homosexuality was a mental illness, resulting from childhood trauma: not an uncommon belief among psychiatrists at the time, but one held by Janov with unusual fervor. We don't know to what extent Lennon explored his sexuality with Janov, although they did discuss his relationship with Epstein, including the Spanish holiday.

"Primal therapy" was regarded as highly dubious by most psychiatrists at the time, and there is still no convincing evidence for its efficacy. In 2022, a neuroscientist who studies the vocal expression of emotion said of primal therapy: "We know that such consistent expressions of anger as a therapeutic method have no or even negative effects on the therapeutic outcome. Our own research shows that positive screams—joy and pleasure—are much more relevant for humans, and they induce social bonding as a positive effect." In other words, the kinds of screams that burst out of Paul in music are beneficial, while John's screams in therapy probably served to thicken his misery. Janov observed of Lennon: "The level of his pain was enormous . . . He was almost completely nonfunctional. He couldn't leave the house, he could hardly leave his room." Janov did not claim to have alleviated John's misery but blamed this on the fact that his patient had to leave his care before completing the course.

In September the Lennons returned to England. Yoko had suffered a third miscarriage. Shortly afterward John heard from his father, whom he hadn't seen for more than a year. Alf had decided to write his autobiography and wanted John's consent. John invited him to Tittenhurst, on John's thirtieth birthday, October 9. At fifty-seven, Alf had become a father again. He arrived with his young wife, Pauline, and their baby son. It was not a happy occasion. Pauline remembered John as pale, haggard, and distracted. He embarked on a long, unhinged rant that included threats to his father. Alf felt compelled to memorialize the conversation in a four-page handwritten statement, deposited with his solicitor, to be made public if he should "disappear or die an unnatural death." (His account was later corroborated by Pauline.) According to Alf, John "reviled his dead Mother in unspeakable terms, referring, also, to the Aunt who had brought him up, in similar derogatory terms, as well as one or two of his closest friends." Alf said that John threatened to have him "done in," carried out to sea, and dumped "twenty—Fifty—or perhaps you would prefer a hundred fathoms deep." This was all delivered with "malignant glee." Alf and John never met again.

It was around this time—as Lennon came out of the Janov therapy, dealt with the news of Yoko's miscarriage, and threatened to kill his father—that he started work on his first solo album, *John Lennon/Plastic Ono Band*. He booked time at Abbey Road and recruited Ringo and Klaus Voormann (bass) as his primary collaborators. Billy Preston contributed piano parts; Phil Spector dropped in and out. Yoko recorded tracks for her own album (*Yoko Ono/Plastic Ono Band*) separately. The two albums were made in just over a month. John wrote his songs during the Janov treatment. Just as he reported on his honeymoon trip with Yoko in song, he was now reporting on the emotions and thoughts that had flooded through him over the previous months.

On December 8, three days before the album's release, John and Yoko sat down with Jann Wenner of *Rolling Stone* for a wide-ranging interview. When it came out, it exploded any lingering public hopes of an imminent Beatles reunion. Lennon set about attacking the Beatles "myth." Being a Beatle was "awful, it was fucking humiliation." He said that the Beatles' image was a lie—that they had never been the nice people they were portrayed as. He painted a picture of himself as a tortured genius at odds with the forces of commercialism: "It's no fun being an artist . . . I read about Van Gogh or Beethoven, any of the fuckers . . . These bastards [the public] are just sucking us to death." He dismissed George Martin as a mere arranger. Of George Harrison's new solo work, which was getting rave reviews, he said: "Personally, at home, I wouldn't play that kind of music . . . he was working with two fucking brilliant songwriters and he learned a lot from us . . . Maybe it was hard for him sometimes because Paul and I are such egomaniacs, but that's the game." He was unpleasant about Glyn Johns, Neil Aspinall, and Derek Taylor, and almost everyone except Ringo and Yoko.

John accorded Paul a certain degree of respect—one of two brilliant songwriters. But he also portrayed him as superficial, glib, and PR-focused, a commercially minded foil to his own unruly artistic genius. He consistently downplayed the importance of their collaboration. He ignored McCartney's contributions to his songs, and overplayed his own contributions to Paul's. He described what he called the "Paul and Linda" album, *McCartney*, as "rubbish" and said, tellingly, "I expected just a little more because if Paul and I are sort of disagreeing and I feel weak, I think he must feel strong." When asked why he had hired Klein against McCartney's wishes, he said, "That's what leaders do . . . Maneuvering is what it is, let's not be coy about it . . .

That's how life's about, isn't it, is it not?" When John was feeling wounded he tended to reduce everything to a power play. Still, it was clear John continued to think of himself as in some kind of partnership with Paul, albeit a remote one. He said he hoped *John Lennon/Plastic Ono Band* would "scare him into doing something decent [laughs], and then he'll scare me into doing something decent, like that."

Lennon later apologized to most of those he insulted or offended in the interview. He confessed to George Martin that he had been "stoned out of my fucking mind" on heroin when he gave the interview. Years later, he casually admitted to lying about his collaboration with McCartney: "It was when I felt resentful, so I felt that we did everything apart. But actually, a lot of the songs we did eyeball-to-eyeball." In print, the interview appears more vicious than it does on the tape, now publicly available. John's spoken words make richer sense when you can hear all the harmonics: the ambivalence and humor as well as the anger and contempt. When I listen to it, I hear, most of all, someone who is depressed.

John and Yoko had first met Wenner in San Francisco earlier in the year. Wenner and his wife took them for a drive around town, and when they passed a movie house showing the newly released *Let It Be* documentary, they agreed to go in—John hadn't seen it. When John saw an image of Paul singing on the rooftop at Apple, he broke down crying. Outside the theater, the four of them shared a hug.

☙

Lennon/Plastic Ono Band opens with the tolling of a funeral bell. Then comes "Mother," the first of several songs on the album that confront Lennon's childhood traumas directly, shorn of metaphor and wordplay. Perhaps Lennon hoped that *Lennon/Plastic Ono Band* would exorcise his demons. But there is no sense of catharsis, just exhaustion and disillusionment, typified by "I Found Out," in which Lennon sings, in a snarling voice, about what he has learned—that there is no Jesus about to come from the sky, no guru who can "see through your eyes." Jesus gets two mentions, the second time paired with a punning allusion to his erstwhile partner: "I seen religion from Jesus to Paul." In "Isolation," John sings about how "we" are trying to change the world while everybody tries to "pull us down." He then slips into the first person and adopts a harsh, accusatory tone that seems to arrive from a different song altogether, as he addresses someone in particular—*you.* "I don't expect *you* to understand," he sings, "after *you've* caused so much pain."

The album's penultimate and defining song is "God." It's a vocal tour de force. Lennon displays his extraordinary ability to almost literally sing his heart out; to make emotion tangible. "God" has three sections. The first begins, "God is a concept by which we measure our pain," a phrase that came to Lennon in conversation with Janov. Then comes a long litany of ideas and idols in which John does not believe. The first is magic, then I-Ching, Bible, Hitler, Jesus, Kennedy, mantra, and others. Lennon generates much drama from the repetition of "I don't believe in—," helped by Preston's fire-and-brimstone piano and Ringo's sensitive drumming. For the last phrase, he sings, in a voice that sounds ancient: *I don't believe in Beatles*—at which point, the music stops. After a short pause, Lennon re-enters, unaccompanied, suddenly vulnerable, to sing "I just believe in"—the band returns—"me." Then "Yoko and me." That's reality, he says. In the last section, his tone becomes wistful and tender. "The dream is over," he sings, repeating it twice, in order to work in a mention of "Yesterday," the song that was almost a synonym for McCartney in Lennon's mind. It is not the only John-and-Paul key word in the song. John had used "walrus" to refer to both himself and Paul in Beatles songs; it seems to have come to mean the two of them together. When he sings, "I was the walrus but now I'm John," it is a declaration of independence. "Dear friends," he concludes, addressing his former bandmates and the world at large, "you'll just have to carry on. The dream is over."

In some ways, *Plastic Ono Band* is similar to *McCartney*. Both have a half-cooked quality to them, and both mention spouses by name. In other ways, they're very different. *McCartney* is defiantly light in mood, full of sweetly eccentric fragments and quirky instrumentals. Even songs about depression, like "Maybe I'm Amazed" and "Every Night," have a redemptive arc. *Plastic Ono Band* takes aim at big themes, evident in its titles alone—Mother,

Love, God—and paints a bleak, grandiose canvas. *McCartney* opens with "Lovely Linda," an expression of joy in new love. John sings about "Yoko and me" like they're the last survivors of a shipwreck, clinging to each other for safety.

☙

McCartney spent the spring and summer of 1970 at his Scottish getaway, fixing up the property, working on new songs, trying not to let the business complications and bitterness overwhelm him. In August, he wrote a letter to Lennon suggesting that they "let each other out of the trap." Lennon replied with a photograph of him and Yoko and a speech bubble that read "How and why?" McCartney replied: "'How' by signing a paper which says we hereby dissolve our partnership. 'Why' because there is no partnership." John replied with a card that read, "Get well soon. Get the other signatures and I will think about it."

As the year went on, McCartney became persuaded by John Eastman that the only way to free himself was to sue. To do this, he would have to do open battle with his three best friends. He would also become even more firmly identified in the public's mind as the man who split up the Beatles. Speaking in 1971, he said, "All summer long in Scotland I was fighting with myself as to whether I should do anything like that. It was murderous." On a hike with John Eastman in the Scottish countryside, he decided to go ahead. A London legal team was instructed to prepare the case. At the end of August, Paul wrote to *Melody Maker*, "In order to put out of its misery the limping dog of a news story . . . my answer to the question, 'will the Beatles get together again . . .' is no."

36   HOW DO YOU SLEEP?

On December 31, 1970, McCartney's lawyers filed writs at the High Court to Lennon, Harrison, Starkey, and Apple Corps Ltd, for the dissolution of "The Beatles and Co." In an accompanying personal affidavit, McCartney explained why he'd been "driven to make this application." He argued that the Beatles had long since ceased being a group, that the other Beatles were imposing on him a manager he found unacceptable, and that his artistic freedom was being unfairly restricted. McCartney was now deep into the process of making his second solo album. *McCartney* sold decently but was disdained by critics as well as Lennon. The reviews stung him, not least because George Harrison's first solo album, *All Things Must Pass*, had been rapturously received. Reviewers were puzzled by *McCartney*'s homespun, fragmentary feel. Paul resolved to make an album with impeccable production values and fully developed songs: an album that would blow everyone away. John Eastman suggested he go to the US to make it, and McCartney liked the idea. He didn't want to go back to Abbey Road.

In New York, Paul auditioned session musicians and put together a small group to help him make the album. One of the tracks on which he worked with them was a song he can be seen playing at the piano in *Get Back*, called "The Back Seat of My Car." It's a dream of escape in a Californian idiom: the car, an open road, a girl. He had developed it into a three-part medley that includes an anthemic coda with a defiant message: "We believe that we can't be wrong." The coda is launched with one of the most atavistic screams McCartney ever committed to tape.

Over the summer of 1970 McCartney wrote at least thirty songs, enough for three albums, and recorded twenty-nine demos. The musicians and engineers who worked on *Ram* in New York talk with wonder about the awesome intensity of his commitment to the work. He asked Eirik Wangberg, his chief engineer, to build a studio next to the one he was working in; the first was for making *Ram* and the other was for ideas he had while making it. In the middle of recording a *Ram* track, he would tear off his headphones, go to the other studio, and start playing something different. It's as if McCartney was metabolizing all the tumult, the Sturm und Drang of the last eighteen months, in music. Several of the songs that made it on to *Ram* have a kind of edge-of-sanity feel; the crazed lyrics of "Monkberry Moon Delight" are delivered in a monstrously hoarse voice that anticipates Tom Waits. On "Too Many People," the album's opener, Paul made a thinly veiled attack on John and Yoko. "You took your lucky break and broke it in two," he sings, putting the blame for the breakup on Lennon, and reminding him that he was just as lucky to have found Paul as the other way around.

Ram does not feel like a dark album overall. It has too many moments of antic comedy and blissed-out pastoral. In "Long Haired Lady," Paul sings "bees are buzzing about my sweet delectable baby" in a voice blooming with love. Linda challenges his sweet talk in her untutored singing voice, derided at the time, but which now sounds touchingly true. Linda was Paul's creative partner now. Overcoming her reservations, he had persuaded her to sing, play piano, and be part of what he was making. Their voices blended well. Wangberg recalled the first studio playback of the finished version of "Long Haired Lady." As McCartney listened, tears rolled down his cheeks.

On December 1 John and Yoko arrived in New York to promote the Plastic Ono Band album. This is when John gave his interview to Jann Wenner. A couple of days later, though before it was published, John telephoned Paul, who was still in the city. They had a civil chat and arranged to meet for dinner, but the meeting fell through. McCartney returned to the UK and headed to his Scottish farm. Shortly after he got there, the new edition of *Rolling Stone* was sent up from London. He opened it on his farmhouse table and scanned Lennon's interview for mentions of his name. He saw John call *McCartney* "rubbish." Then he read the rest. Asked about the interview in 1971, Paul put on a brave face. "This open hostility, that didn't hurt me. That's cool. That's John." It wasn't true. "I hated it," he admitted in 1974. "I sat down and pored over every little paragraph, every little sentence . . . And at the time I thought, 'It's me. I am. That's just what I'm like. He's captured me so well; I'm really a turd, you know.'"

Linda took it upon herself to write a letter to John, protesting the interview and defending her husband. We know about it only because John sent a two-page reply to her and Paul, which found its way into the public realm in 2001. A sample:

> I hope you realize what shit you and the rest of my "kind and unself-ish" friends laid on Yoko and me, since we've been together . . . We both "rose above it" quite a few times—and forgave you two—so it's the least you can do for us—you noble people. Linda—if you don't care what I say—shut up!—let Paul write . . .

Lennon is notably more hostile to Linda than to Paul. He tells Linda to "get that into your petty little perversion of a mind." Addressing Paul, he implies that his marriage won't last more than two years ("I reckon you'll be out then"). He ends the typed letter by sending love to both of them but scribbles a postscript expressing annoyance at Linda's failure to address the letter to Yoko as well as him.

In January, after the issuing of McCartney's High Court writ, he and Linda returned to New York to resume work on *Ram*. McCartney released his first solo single, "Another Day," a deceptively chirpy song about a woman suffering from low-level depression, to coincide with the first court hearing in London, on February 19. Paul was the only Beatle to attend in person. The others were heard only via statements read out in court. John defended Klein's management of Apple and painted a benign picture of the group's internal disagreements (his side had to walk a fine line between portraying McCartney as unreasonable and persuading the judge that they could still be a functioning group). It included some outrageous narrative-shaping:

> From our earliest days in Liverpool, George and I on the one hand and Paul on the other had different musical tastes. Paul preferred "pop type" music and we preferred what is now called "underground." This may have led to arguments, particularly between Paul and George, but the contrasts in our tastes, I am sure, did more good than harm musically speaking and contributed to our success.

In fact, musical differences played very little role in the disintegration of the Beatles. McCartney's statement cited the recently released solo albums from Lennon and Harrison as evidence that the partnership was no longer viable: "One has only to look at recent recordings by John or George to see that neither thinks of himself as a Beatle." He quoted from "God": "I don't believe in Beatles." Once the statements were given, the McCartneys returned to America to work on *Ram*, in New York and Los Angeles. On March 12, Mr. Justice Stamp delivered his verdict. He found in favor of McCartney on every count. A receiver was appointed to Apple; the judgment included a withering assessment of Klein's integrity. The other Beatles lodged an appeal, but on April 26 it was withdrawn. Their barrister said that his clients had concluded "it is in the common interest to explore . . . a means whereby the plaintiff may disengage himself from the partnership by agreement." Paul was free to go.

☿

Ram was released in May and sold very well, reaching number one in the UK and number two in the US, despite poor reviews. When John played it, he immediately picked up on the digs at him in "Too Many People." Indeed, he heard messages across the album, including the refrain from "Back Seat of

My Car." Five days later he went into his home studio at Tittenhurst Park and recorded "How Do You Sleep?"

John was making his second album, *Imagine*, released in September 1971. He accepted that his first album was hard to listen to, and, like McCartney, set out to make his next one more commercial. He used strings and hired the pianist Nicky Hopkins to create a softer musical world for meditative, searching ballads like "How?" and "Jealous Guy." He included a song called "Oh Yoko!," as sentimental as anything McCartney ever wrote. There was a rip-roaring political song, "Gimme Some Truth," a vessel for John's almost rap-like feel for verbal beats (it was kicking around in January 1969; in *Get Back* we see McCartney helping him with it; it is clear they have worked on it before). John composed the title track on his grand piano at Tittenhurst. His friend the DJ Howard Smith remembers Lennon coming to visit him and being very excited. "I think I finally wrote a song with as good a melody as 'Yesterday,'" John said. He played "Imagine" through and asked Smith what he thought. "It's beautiful," said Smith. "But is it as good as 'Yesterday'?" asked John.

On the LP's second side, between two ballads, came the musical nail bomb of "How Do You Sleep?," a deliberately disproportionate response to Paul's passive-aggressive barbs on *Ram*. Lennon sings it in a harsh whine, using a fake American argot. Referring to the "Paul is dead" conspiracy rumor, he accuses McCartney of dying a creative death: "Those freaks was right when they said you was dead." He says, "You live with straights who tell you, you was king," and that Paul "jump(s) when your momma tell you anything." Of course, he works in a mention of his bugbear: "The only thing you done was yesterday." His next line referred to the new McCartney single: "Since you're gone you're just another day." The third and final verse turns on that feminizing, damning word "pretty." Lennon says that McCartney is just "a pretty face" who makes "muzak" and suggests that his solo career won't last more than "a year or two." The last line of the verse is an imperious dismissal: "You must have learned something in all those years." The needling refrain, *how do you sleep at night?*, ends on a sinister hiss.

It's a creepy song, and still a shocking one. It's also preposterous.

"Yesterday" is the only good song Paul wrote? McCartney is just a pretty face, whose career is going nowhere? (Let's recall that *Ram* was about to hit number one.) Lennon completed the lyrics at Tittenhurst in the presence of Yoko, Klein, Klaus Voormann, George Harrison, and, for some of the time, Ringo. There was lots of giggling as Yoko and others threw in lines. The underground journalist Felix Dennis, who was around, said, "Some of it was absolutely puerile . . . It's quite obvious that Paul must have been some sort of figure of authority in Lennon's life, because you don't take the piss out of somebody that isn't a figure of authority. The mood there wasn't totally vindictive. As I felt it, they were taking the piss out of the headmaster." According to Dennis, Ringo was the only one to say, "That's enough, John."

Even *Rolling Stone*, Lennon's most reliable media champion, found "How Do You Sleep?" distasteful. It described the track as a "horrifying and indefensible . . . character assassination." In his promotional interviews for *Imagine*, John spent a lot of time rowing back from it. In one, he said, "It's not serious. Like, if Paul was really, really hurt by it . . . I'll explain it to him . . . If he really thinks it's serious." In another, he said the song was "an outburst. Things are still the same between us. He was and is my closest friend, except for Yoko." The questions continued for years, and John's rationalizations varied. In 1972 he said he'd written the song "to encourage Paul by writing and saying things that I thought would spur him on." In 1975 he said, "It's not about Paul. It's about me."

How could John have made such a vicious attack on an old friend, and why did the others enable him? To answer that, recall John's words in the Wenner interview: "If Paul and I are sort of disagreeing and I feel weak, I think he must feel strong." McCartney had just won the court case. "Another Day" was number two in the UK. *McCartney* had been number one in the US. Paul *seemed* strong to John, who hadn't enjoyed commercial success with his first album, and who was struggling with a drug addiction, while trying to help Yoko track down her daughter and nursing her through the agony of miscarriages. It wasn't just that John didn't know that Paul was experiencing intense anguish over the breakup; it's that he could barely conceive of it.

To John and George, Paul must have always seemed the invulnerable one.

Paul was the one who always got the girl, who won at cards, who could put up shelves, who could sing anything and play anything, who always brought new songs, who never seemed to tire. Ken Mansfield, the American executive recruited by the Beatles to help run Apple, conveys a vivid impression of McCartney, from 1968: "Paul was the energetic one, the one that seemed like the popular kid in high school . . . He was always presenting the next project or place to go . . . To me, Paul was the unabashed leader of the group, the hard-charging one with the ideas . . . he was like a hyper-kinetic kid that never slowed down . . . In all honesty, he wore me out. It was fun, the times I got to hang out with him or work with him, but his tempo was maddening and his energy pool bottomless." Imagine working with someone like that, not just for a few days or nights at a time, but almost every day for over a decade, and you can see why the other Beatles resented Paul sometimes, and also why they assumed that nothing they said or did could ever hurt him.

Perhaps "How Do You Sleep?" was performative—a display of viciousness by which John sought to convince Yoko, and himself, that he had moved on from Paul. This is how McCartney came to see it. In 1980 he told Hunter Davies (in what he thought was an off-the-record conversation): "I understood what happened when he first met Yoko. He had to clear the decks of his old emotions . . . You prove how much you love someone by confessing all the old stuff. John's method was to slag me off." Whatever the reason, if someone makes a furious attack on a friend or lover, it's not necessarily a sign that the relationship is exhausted. In another of John's defensive answers to a question about "How Do You Sleep?" he said, almost indignantly, "If I cannot have a fight with my best friend, I don't know who I can fight with."

In October, Yoko and John celebrated John's thirty-first birthday with friends, including Ringo, in a hotel room in Syracuse, New York, where Yoko had an exhibition. There is a tape of a rowdy sing-along, led by John on an out-of-tune guitar. It includes a slightly drunk and maudlin rendition of "Yesterday." John gets the words wrong ("now it looks as though I've lost my way"), and replaces "she" with "he": *why he had to go, I don't know, he wouldn't say . . .*

37   DEAR FRIEND

In 1970 and 1971 both John and Paul must sometimes have felt that they were up against a foe who knew all their weaknesses and would not stop at anything to exploit them. John thought of Paul as perennially successful, snug and smug inside his happy family. Paul saw John taking delight in trashing his ability as a songwriter. John would not have imagined that Paul was scared of him, but for McCartney, fighting Lennon was painful. He later explained, "I didn't want to get into a slanging match." McCartney understood the dynamics of escalation: "You start off with a perfectly innocent little contest and suddenly you find yourself doing duel to the death with the Lennon figure." By "the Lennon figure" he meant the implacable enemy that his friend presented as, from a distance. Paul knew that getting into a verbal battle with *that* Lennon was a terrible idea: "Part of it was cowardice. John was a great wit."

"Dear Friend" is, at least on the face of it, a call for a truce. It came out at the end of 1971, two months after the release of "How Do You Sleep?" on *Imagine*, in September, though it had been recorded in July. Later on, Paul said:

"Dear Friend" was written about John, yes . . . after John had slagged me off in public, I had to think of a response, and it was either going to be to slag him off in public—and some instinct stopped me, which I'm really glad about—or do something else. So I worked on my attitude and wrote "Dear Friend," saying, in effect, let's lay the guns down, let's hang up our boxing gloves.

The song takes the form of a letter in which the singer asks his friend to pause and consider whether their friendship is over ("Is this really the borderline?"). It consists of two four-line verses, repeated in sequence. In the second, the singer asks his friend to share in his joy: "I'm in love with a friend of mine," he sings, "young and newly wed," on that last word swooping up to hold a high falsetto note.*

Looked at another way, "Dear Friend" has a tougher message. "Are you afraid or is it true?" it asks, at the end of each verse, as if zeroing in on the insecurity behind John's aggressive bluster. The absence of a middle section or development gives that recurring question a stark and insistent quality, like the tolling of a bell.

"Dear Friend" appeared on *Wild Life*, McCartney's first album with his new group, Wings. Most of the songs on *Wild Life* were loosely played and produced, but McCartney took care over the arrangement of this one: his simple piano part is joined, in the second half of the song, by strings, flutes, brass, and an oboe (most lonesome of wind instruments). McCartney sings high in his register, sounding fragile and, in the first half of the song, tentative. For a few bars he slips into wordless keening. Then the orchestral instruments enter, conveying a sense of raised stakes, and McCartney makes a subtle change to his vocal coloring. In the first two verses he sounds sad and regretful; when he repeats these verses, he sings them with a little more

---

* Note that Paul uses the same word for John and for Linda in this song. In 1968 John was asked by an interviewer, Jonathan Cott, about the use of the word "friend" in Beatles songs. John replied, "Yeah, I don't know why. It's Paul's bit that—'Buy you a diamond ring, my friend'—it's an alternative to 'baby'" (*Rolling Stone*, November 23, 1968). The elision of friend and lover, which the Beatles, and in particular Paul, made repeatedly, was unusual in pop. Other examples are found in "I'll Follow the Sun," "I'll Get You," and "We Can Work It Out."

edge. There is a trace of impatience, almost a taunt in that probing question "Are you afraid?" which becomes, in the very last verse, "Are you a fool?" The lyrics lend themselves to both readings: soft and tough; truce and ultimatum. "Dear Friend" contains the mixed-up emotions of a breakup with someone you still care about deeply.

38   JEALOUS GUY

Ram was intended as a definitive statement of who Paul McCartney was after the Beatles. Now it was done, he wanted to perform for live audiences again, as part of a group. But with who? He asked Linda, who was reluctant at first, not being an experienced musician. Paul persuaded her it would be OK, and she was assigned backing vocals and keyboards. He recruited Denny Seiwell, the drummer on *Ram*, and Denny Laine, former guitarist in the Moody Blues. Laine could sing, and McCartney wanted another male voice in the vocal lineup. The idea was for this to be a group of equals, even if in reality it never could be. After rehearsing new material in Scotland, the group entered Abbey Road at the end of July and recorded most of *Wild Life* in a week (the band name came later, in September).

Ram was painstakingly made and lavishly produced; *Wild Life* was almost aggressively loose and improvised. McCartney was switching wildly between modes of music-making, partly because he was, for the first time in his career, low on confidence and uncertain of his own instincts. *McCartney* had been criticized for being lazily made and so Paul had locked himself in a studio for months to make *Ram*. He was deeply proud of it but critics—and in the 1970s, music critics were more influential than they ever had been or would ever be again—hated it. In this, they were heavily influenced by John Lennon.

John's failure to come out for violent revolution in 1968 had damaged his reputation among leftists. He and Yoko now sought to regain credibility by funding radical causes, adopting revolutionary rhetoric, and acting as leaders of the avant-garde world. "I've always been politically minded, you know, and against the status quo," he told *Red Mole* magazine, in Britain. "It's pretty basic when you're brought up, like I was, to hate and fear the police as a natural enemy and to despise the army . . . I mean, it's just a basic working class thing." When it came to the Beatles, John contrasted Paul's predilection for melodies with his passion for authentic rock and roll ("The thing that made the Beatles what they were was the fact that I could do my rock 'n roll, and Paul could do the pretty stuff"). In his telling of the Beatles story, he had to fight for his artistic vision in the teeth of opposition from the music industry and Paul McCartney. The rock press was utterly seduced by this talk and turned Lennon and McCartney into identity markers for a culture war. You were either for John or for Paul; for working-class rebels (John, Yoko, and Klein) or for middle-class straights (McCartney and the Eastmans)—a narrative so compelling that it still shapes the Beatles' story today.

John's label for Paul, a "good PR man," stuck, even though, as the Beatles historiographer Erin Torkelson Weber notes, "the title rightfully belonged to Lennon." From 1969 until the end of 1971, John and Yoko gave more than a dozen major interviews and over fifty-five radio interviews, and appeared on Dick Cavett's TV show multiple times. They gave countless smaller interviews, too, sometimes as many as ten a day. Allen Klein also put their case to the media. Meanwhile, McCartney retreated to Scotland or worked in the recording studio, and refused most interview requests. Rather than attempt a counternarrative, he offered only silence punctuated by legal statements and brief self-justifications.

John's interviews were riveting: startlingly indiscreet and emotionally vivid. He seemed to be a truth-teller who divulged everything, no matter how uncomfortable. His compelling performances obscured factual inaccuracies, wild exaggerations, and self-contradictions. When Paul did speak to the press, he was the polar opposite: terse, casual, blandly reasonable—dull. He revealed very little of how he was feeling. He didn't speak about his depression or how much Lennon's public remarks stung him. His guardedness increased the suspicion with which the music press viewed him. Much of the scorn he faced was displaced anger at the end of childhood dreams. For all that rock critics liked to present themselves as clear-eyed radicals, they were also young men (nearly all of them were men) who had fallen in love with the Beatles in the sixties and were very upset about the breakup. Even though reviewers found "How Do You Sleep?" shocking, they made sense of it through Lennon's narrative. *Rolling Stone* argued that its vituperation embodied "the traditional bohemian contempt for the bourgeoisie." It was taken as indisputable evidence that John despised Paul.

☿

In an interview to promote *Wild Life*, McCartney responded mildly to a question about "How Do You Sleep?" "I think it's silly. So what if I live with straights?" he said. "I like straights. I have straight babies." The interview took place in the control room in Studio Two at Abbey Road. Paul gestured to the studio below: "I used to sit down there and play and John would watch me from up here and he'd really dig some of the stuff I played to him. He can't say all I did was 'Yesterday' because he knows, and I know, it's not true." He dispensed faint praise: "John's whole image now is very honest and open. He's alright is John. I like his *Imagine* album, but I didn't like the others . . . *Imagine* is what John is really like, but there was too much political stuff on the other albums." McCartney discussed the Beatles' legal wranglings in a defensive, peeved tone: "Everyone thinks I'm the aggressor but I'm not, you know." Despite his victory in the lawsuit, there was still a lot of unwinding of Beatles business to do, and the parties and their representatives remained at loggerheads. "I just want the four of us to get together somewhere and sign a piece of paper saying it's all over, and we want to divide the money four ways," McCartney said. "No one else would be there, not even Linda or Yoko, or Allen Klein. We'd just sign the paper and hand it to the business people and let them sort it all out. That's all I want now. But John won't do it.'"

When Lennon read McCartney's interview, he bashed out a three-page letter on a typewriter and sent it to *Melody Maker*. It was a diatribe. "If *you're not* the aggressor (as you claim) who the hell took us to court and shat all over us in public? As I've said before—have you ever thought that you might *possibly* be wrong about something?" Lennon picks up almost every one of McCartney's remarks and hurls them back at him. "So *you* think 'Imagine' ain't political? It's 'Working Class Hero' with sugar on it for conservatives like yourself!!" There is a sudden switch of tone toward the end (with a reference to a Beatles song, "Any Time at All," thrown in): "No hard feelings to you either. I know basically we want the same, and as I said on the phone and in this letter, whenever you want to meet, all you have to do is call." He reverted to adolescent vituperation in a postscript: "The bit that really puzzled us was asking to meet WITHOUT LINDA AND YOKO. I know you're camp! But let's not go too far!" John's queasy joke about sexuality might have reflected insecurity, brought to the surface in Janov's therapy, over his affection for Paul.*

Just over a year since their last album had been released, the world's favorite group had been reduced to this unseemly public bickering, the contemporary equivalent of a social media feud. John and Paul, perhaps recognizing that their fighting had become a grisly spectacle, now quietly reestablished relations. John was the first to reach out. He currently felt strong, relative to Paul. His album had been well reviewed and "Imagine," the single, had been a big hit. He was living with Yoko in a Greenwich Village apartment. On a trip to New York in mid-August, the couple had decided, almost on impulse, to stay for good (John never returned to Britain). Before the *Melody*

---

* A few years later, Lennon wrote a "self-interview" for *Interview* magazine, in the course of which he asked himself questions on a random selection of topics, including this one: "Q. Have you ever fucked a guy?" His answer: "Not yet . . ." His next question: "There was talk about you and PAUL . . ." A: "Oh I thought it was about me and Brian Epstein . . ." (*Interview*, November 1974, 11–12.)

Maker exchange, John sent Ray Connolly, a friendly journalist also trusted by McCartney, on a peace mission. He gave Connolly a letter to deliver to Paul in London. "He wanted to tell Paul something without going through the lawyers," said Connolly. Connolly dropped the letter into McCartney's mailbox and later called Jim McCartney to check that Paul had received it.

In December, Paul called John on the telephone, and they had a friendly chat. A few days later, John sent Paul a postcard that read, "Happy Xmas! (War is over if you want it)," along with what he thought was a bootlegged copy of the Beatles' failed audition for Decca in 1962 (actually a collection of their early BBC performances). John wrote: "Dear Paul, Linda et al. This is THE DECCA AUDITION!!! . . . They were a good group fancy turning THIS down! Love John + Yoko."

In December 1971, the McCartneys met with Lennon and Ono and agreed to an informal truce in their public war. John and Paul stopped sniping at each other in the press and in songs and restored amicable personal relations, albeit on a tentative basis. It seems to have been at this meeting that John talked to Paul about a track on his new album, "Jealous Guy." In an interview given a few years after John's death, McCartney recalled the aftermath of the breakup:

> It was a weird time. The people who were managing us were whispering in our ears and trying to turn us against each other and it became like a feuding family. In the end, I think John had some tough breaks. He used to say, "Everyone is on the McCartney bandwagon." He wrote "I'm Just a Jealous Guy" and he said that the song was about me.

"Jealous Guy" does something unusual in rock—it makes an apology, and not a showy or dramatic one, but one that sounds like the singer means it. Like "If I Fell," it expresses male vulnerability. But it's also about having the humility to acknowledge one's flaws without aggrandizing them. I'm *just* a jealous guy—the truth is as simple, and as pathetic, as that. Here's what John said about it:

The lyrics explain themselves clearly: I was a very jealous, possessive guy. Toward everything. A very insecure male. A guy who wants to put his woman in a little box, lock her up and just bring her out when he feels like playing with her. She's not allowed to communicate with the outside world—outside of me—because it makes me feel insecure.

In 1971, he spoke about his problem with jealousy: "I love Yoko, I want to possess her completely . . . That's the danger, it's that you want to possess them to death. But . . . that's a personal problem." Early in their relationship, he made Yoko tell him about all her past boyfriends. Cynthia said that John was controlling and jealous toward her, too. May Pang, with whom he went out later in the 1970s, describes John's occasional but intense and frightening bouts of jealousy in her memoir. If jealousy was a problem for John, it was also a muse: one that made him feel alive. Some of his earlier songs were electrified by it: "No Reply," "I'll Get You." The literary critic Parul Sehgal observes that jealousy can be creative. When we feel jealous, "We tell ourselves a story about other people's lives, and these stories make us feel terrible. " At its heart, jealousy is "a quest for truth, painful truth."

The person who was the object of John's jealousy perhaps more often, and for longer, than any other was Paul McCartney. John was insecure about Paul's charisma, his way with women, and his musical abilities. It wasn't just that John envied Paul's success, though. He was also possessive of him. In the Beatles, John got upset when Paul worked with others on songs and was wary of Paul's romantic partners (or worse, like the night in Hamburg, in 1962, when he found Paul in bed with a girl—and cut up her clothes). Now, nine years later, John came across a promotional booklet called *The Beatles from Apple*, and scrawled bitter notes all over it (the book was discovered after his death). Over an entry on Paul's marriage to Linda, he scribbled out "wedding" and wrote in "funeral." To a photo of Paul from 1962, he added a speech bubble that stated: "I'm always perfect." Amid the vitriol was a hint of tenderness and regret. Under a photo of him and Paul together, he wrote, "The minutes are crumbling away."

If, in 1961, John feared that Paul would choose his family over the Beatles, in 1971, he knew the battle was lost. That stoked his anger, and it made him sad. We hear the anger in "How Do You Sleep?"; we hear the sadness in "Jealous Guy." There is one particular aspect of the "Jealous Guy" arrangement that evokes John and Paul's mutual history: the whistling. It's a lovely, intimate, wistful way to fill an instrumental break that might otherwise have been taken by piano or guitar. John didn't whistle on many songs. He whistles on "Two of Us." In a 1964 interview, Paul talked about their songwriting partnership: "The way we work, it is like, we just whistle. John will whistle at me and I'll whistle back at him."

39   LET ME ROLL IT

In 1973, John and Yoko decided it was time to leave their bohemian West Village pad for somewhere grander. They secured an apartment in the Dakota building on the Upper West Side, overlooking Central Park. It had a vast living room and kitchen, and multiple bedrooms and bathrooms. As well as a home, it would be the headquarters for John and Yoko's business affairs, and their assistant, May Pang, was assigned to work there full-time. Right after moving in, Yoko showed her around. "It's a beautiful apartment," Pang said. "I know you'll be happy here." Yoko didn't respond right away, but stared out the window to the park. "Our life here is doomed," she said quietly. Then she lit a cigarette and told Pang a story.

The previous November, Ono and Lennon had attended a party at the Prince Street apartment of the prominent antiwar activist Jerry Rubin, along with other left-wing cognoscenti, including Allen Ginsberg. John and Yoko were not in a good way. Their joint 1972 album, *Some Time in New York City*, was savaged by reviewers and did poorly in the charts. Lennon, hurt by its reception, felt creatively aimless and paranoid (he was worried that the Nixon administration was tapping his phone in an effort to gather evidence to get him thrown out of the country; it turned out he was right). He stressed about money: the long legal aftermath of the Beatles' breakup meant that it was hard for either him or the other Beatles to access funds. Meanwhile, Yoko was more prolific than ever, recording enough new songs for a double album. ("I began to think that if George Harrison can put out a triple album, then *I* should be able to put out a triple album," she said. "But I decided to stop at 22 songs.")

The couple were no longer as close as they had been. Lennon confided in a friend that the "JohnandYoko" days were over. Later on, Yoko told the biographer Philip Norman that she and John did not have a sexual relationship at this time: "Physically I was starting to feel like I didn't really want to get into it with him." John was binge drinking. At Rubin's party he had a meltdown, spitting insults at the guests. Yoko was not able to calm him, but Rubin's female roommate did. After talking to her, John took her into a bedroom, where they loudly made love, while all the guests pretended not to hear. According to Ono, she just felt sorry for John, although it's hard to believe that she didn't feel humiliated.

According to May Pang, Yoko told her about this incident as a way of laying the groundwork for the proposition she made a few months later: that Pang have an affair with Lennon. Yoko wanted a period of separation from John, but knew that John needed to be looked after or else he was liable to spin out of control. Pang had been working for Ono and Lennon since 1970, after she met them while working for Allen Klein's company, ABKCO. Pang was diligent and organized. In her early twenties, and a rock fan, she was thrilled by her proximity to the Beatles, and to John and Yoko in particular. She was entranced by her bosses. John was friendly, voluble, funny; Yoko was charismatic, eccentric, and willful. May saw how Yoko exerted an implacable force on those around her. If Yoko wanted to get something done, no matter how outlandish or unlikely, she would find a way to wear down the resistance of anyone who refused her. John and Yoko did a lot of their business from their bedroom at the Dakota. Pang was fascinated by their relationship:

I believe they did love each other, but their love was unlike any concept of love that I have known or read about. They spent enormous amounts of time in bed together, but they rarely kissed or touched . . . They behaved more like children snuggling against each other to ward off any demons that might be loose in the night.

One August morning, Yoko came into Pang's office and carefully but clearly explained her idea. John has already agreed, she said. Lennon had recently started recording a new album, and Pang had been accompanying him to the studio. Yoko suggested she take him home after this evening's session. Pang was shocked. She said very little. When the meeting was over, she felt sick. She considered quitting, but worried that Ono, "always an extremist," would get her ostracized from the music business. When John tried to kiss May in the elevator that afternoon, she pulled away. When he suggested they go home together that night, she refused. But over the following days he kept asking, and eventually she agreed. Before long, John moved out of the Dakota and into Pang's apartment and they began a full-fledged love affair that lasted for eighteen months but which was always tangled up in the force field between John and Yoko.

The album Lennon was making was called *Mind Games*, appropriately enough. Ono wanted Lennon out of her way (she was having an affair with a young guitarist in Lennon's band), but she didn't want him out of her orbit. She called him frequently. She often spoke to Pang, too, advising her on how to handle Lennon's moods. In September 1973 John and May moved to Los Angeles, partly to distance themselves from Ono, and John started work on a new album of rock and roll standards. Ono called them fifteen times a day or more, and to Pang's frustration, John seemed to welcome her remote monitoring. Yoko would even make insinuations about Pang's motives to him, causing John to fly into rages at Pang when drunk.

We might conclude that John was scared of Yoko. Certainly, as Pang discovered, he was very worried about upsetting or angering her. But perhaps it would be more accurate to say that John was *enthralled* by Yoko:

held captive by a fascination with her mind that endured throughout the 1970s, no matter how sexually or romantically estranged the two of them became. If Yoko had theories about people, he wanted to hear them; if she made predictions, he believed them; if she made decisions, he submitted to them. Pang's memoir sheds light on John's animosity and suspicion toward McCartney at the start of the decade and (to a lesser extent) later on. Whispering to each other in bed or on the phone, John and Yoko reinforced each other's suspicions and insecurities about anyone outside of the cocoon they had spun together: a paranoid folie à deux.

In many ways, May was good for John. She was calm and loving, and she didn't do drugs or alcohol. During the time they were together, Lennon changed his behavior in three significant ways. First, he loosened up, socially. Yoko had particular ideas of who she did and didn't want to be around John. May was more relaxed, encouraging John to spend time with old friends, such as Paul, Ringo, and Mick Jagger, and new ones, including Elton John and David Bowie. Yoko wasn't keen on him seeing either Julian or Cynthia, and John, full of guilt and nerves, had gone along with her. May coaxed him into spending time with Julian for the first time in over two years, and in reestablishing friendly relations with his ex-wife. Secondly, John became creatively productive again. He made *Mind Games* and started on his album of rock and roll standards. (May shared John's love of rock and roll, in contrast to Yoko, who would ask for it to be switched off if John was playing it at home.) He produced a new album by the singer Harry Nilsson. He made the *Walls and Bridges* album, a commercial success that included his first solo number one, "Whatever Gets You thru the Night," featuring Elton John. He collaborated with Bowie and helped out on Ringo's solo projects.

The third change in behavior was less positive. Between periods of sobriety and hard work, Lennon went on drunken benders, aided and abetted by the gang of friends and collaborators he assembled in LA, among them Phil Spector, Nilsson, and the Who's drummer, Keith Moon, all of whom had voracious appetites for booze and drugs. The chief engineer on the *Rock 'n' Roll* sessions recalled, "There was a lot of speed, cocaine, everything going on. Everybody was obnoxious." Over a couple of nights out at the Troubadour club, with Pang and Nilsson, Lennon was so insufferable—heckling the acts, abusing staff—that one night the manager had him physically removed from the premises. Lennon swung wild punches at the bouncers as they threw him out onto the street, where photographers captured him in disarray. This public behavior, though undignified, was hardly the worst of it. Pang describes in horrific detail what John was like during one of his drunken meltdowns: weepy, angry, verbally and physically abusive, dangerous to Pang and anyone in his vicinity. The next day, he would genuinely have no memory of it. It was awful for Pang, but by now she was desperately in love, and when John wasn't drunk, he was kind and loving.

ⓒ

In February 1972 McCartney did what he had proposed the Beatles do, back in 1969: he shucked off the accoutrements of superstardom and went back on the road. One morning the members of Wings, along with Paul's children and Martha, met outside Paul's house in London, got into a van, and drove around the country looking for places to play. They would drive to a university town, check into cheap accommodation, find the university's social secretary, and suggest that they play a gig that evening, for a nominal fee. Flabbergasted students found themselves watching a Beatle and his new group run through a ropey but energetically delivered set of rock and roll standards and post-Beatles material (they didn't play any Beatles songs). Paul didn't feel ready for the public spotlight, even if the press quickly caught on. He said, "I'm starting all over again and working my way upward." He was trying to rediscover the musician inside the public persona: "A year ago, I used to wake up in the morning and think, I'm Paul McCartney. I'm a myth. And it scared the hell out of me."

He had also been goaded by John. In Lennon's vituperative November 1971 letter, John cited Paul's proposal that the Beatles play small venues, and listed, competitively, some of the relatively modest live gigs he had performed at: "In fact we've been *doing* what you've been *talking* about doing for three years . . . So go on and do it! Do it! Do it!" We can imagine Paul reading that and determining that he *would* do it—that he would in fact do something more radical than John would ever dare. So it was that this huge global rock star traveled haphazardly around England, staying in B&Bs, performing in a group with an amateur keyboardist to a few hundred people at a time for fifty pence a head. It was completely nuts, but then so much of what McCartney did during these years was nuts. For a singer who had somehow acquired a reputation for being a businessman rather than an artist, he was making some very strange moves. He commissioned a jazz band to make an instrumental album of *Ram* and later marketed it under the pseudonym Percy Thrillington. He decided that his new group's first two singles would be a protest song and a kids' song ("Give Ireland Back to the Irish," "Mary Had a Little Lamb"). Yes, he was smoking a lot of pot, but McCartney was always a deeply eccentric artist, a fact obscured by John Lennon's more flamboyant idiosyncrasies. Henry McCullough, a member of Wings from this era, remarked that while McCartney had a reputation as being down to earth, he was actually rather spacey: "He does what he does. We were put in his bubble, basically."

John's social glasnost included more openness to Paul, although their relationship had already been thawing. Early in 1972, John sent Paul (and Linda) a friendly note suggesting that Wings and the Plastic Ono Band play a charity concert in New York, in aid of Irish civil rights.* That didn't come to anything, but they talked on the phone throughout the year, mostly about nothing in particular—what they were up to, what they were listening to (McCartney recalls playing songs to each other down the phone). Gary van Syoc, who played in Elephant's Memory, John's backing group for much of 1972, recalled his surprise at Lennon's apparently friendly relationship with his former partner:

> The media would be reporting on this huge Lennon and McCartney feud . . . Then as we recorded *Some Time in New York City*, Paul called two or three times, and everything would just come to a halt.

---

* It was a cause both of them cared about. Paul's song "Give Ireland Back to the Irish," written right after their conciliatory meeting in New York, seems to have been inspired in part by John's protest song "The Luck of the Irish." The immediate trigger for Paul's song was the event that became known as "Bloody Sunday," January 30, 1972.

They would be yukking it up, and laughing for over an hour at a time . . . you would swear they were best friends.

In August, John invited Paul to appear onstage with him at a charity concert. Paul declined because Allen Klein was involved. Lennon played the gig with Elephant's Memory. He said of it, "The weird thing was turning left and right and seeing different faces . . . Oh it isn't one of them . . ." McCartney wrote a song he played live—intended for his next album but left off—called "Best Friend." Over a playful rock and roll boogie, he asked his best friend, "Why do you treat me so bad?"

By March 1973, all four Beatles were on good terms. John, George, and Ringo collaborated happily on a track for Ringo's new album while they were in Los Angeles. "Paul would most probably have joined in if he was around, but he wasn't," John told a journalist. A key reason for this spirit of reconciliation is that Lennon and the others had fallen out with Klein. John had argued with Klein over his right to take political stances, and he and Harrison were suspicious that Klein had misused the proceeds of the Concert for Bangladesh—a pair of benefit concerts that Harrison had organized. By April 1973, John, George, and Ringo had formally parted ways with Klein. "Let's say possibly Paul's suspicions were right," said Lennon.

By the time that Lennon left Yoko and got together with Pang, this is where John and Paul were—edging toward each other, but both too scarred by the events of the last few years, and too uncertain about what they wanted, to make a more definitive move. In the summer of 1973 each of them recorded songs that said more about how they were feeling than anything they said in public, and probably anything they said in private, too.

☾

When John was asked, in his 1980 *Playboy* interview, about a track on *Mind Games* called "I Know (I Know)," he dismissed it as "just a piece of nothing"—an odd way to talk about a track that is so obviously heartfelt. Lennon sings in the feathery voice he used on his most tender love songs. "I Know (I Know)" is another song of apology. The first hint that he has Paul on his mind is the opening guitar riff, which bears an unmistakable resemblance to "I've Got a Feeling," the last fifty-fifty Lennon-McCartney collaboration. Then there are the words. The singer says that he's sorry, and declares his guilt. He says he realizes what he has done and that he "never could read your mind." Now, he says, "my eyes can see," and "today, I love you more than yesterday." It's not the only reference to a Beatles song: he also sings, "I know it's getting better all the time." It's unlikely it was addressed to Yoko: there's no evidence he was seeking to restore his relationship with her at this time. Then there is the title, and its curious repetition. Paul described their locking eyes on that first LSD trip with John: "Like, just *staring* and then saying, 'I *know*, man,' and then laughing . . ."

⊛

By late 1973 Paul had successfully broken himself down and built himself up again. Early in the year he released *Red Rose Speedway*, an intriguing but rather sketchy collection of songs (Linda described it as "non-confident"). He almost immediately went back into the studio, with a stripped-down group composed mainly of him and Linda and Denny Laine, to make what would become the most successful album of his post-Beatles career. *Band on the Run* was recorded mainly in Lagos, Nigeria, under stressful conditions: Linda and Paul were mugged, they lost the master tapes, they were confronted by a hostile Fela Kuti concerned about cultural appropriation (Paul quickly befriended him). The jeopardy brought out the best in McCartney. *Band on the Run* is purposeful, confident, and full of big, tuneful songs. Its title track exudes a sense of liberation from the tangled mess of the Beatles' breakup. Separately, Paul's Bond theme tune, for *Live and Let Die*, was a massive hit. After three years, McCartney was in full flight again.

John would have responded viscerally to everything about the sound of "Let Me Roll It": its rolling bass-and-organ intro, which harks back to classic rock and roll, and the jagged, distorted snarl of a guitar riff that enters and takes over the track, and which resembles the one John used for "Cold Turkey." Then there is Paul's vocal. It uses tape echo, an effect that John liked to use. These apparent musical call-outs were so striking that contemporary reviewers called "Let Me Roll It" a Lennon pastiche. Asked about this in 1979, McCartney said, "I still don't think it sounds like him but that's your opinion." But with the passing of years McCartney admitted to the connection. In 2021 he said, "I remember first singing 'Let Me Roll It' and thinking, 'Yeah, this is very like a John song.'"

In the same interview he said, "Anyone can understand how exposed you feel when you offer your heart to, or reveal your affections for, another person. It's very difficult. The hesitation we feel in that situation—of wanting to reach out but being reluctant to be completely open—is made physical in the abrupt starting and stopping of the riff." McCartney doesn't declare that "Let Me Roll It" is "about" Lennon. To do so would diminish it. But it is almost certainly *inspired* by his feelings about John—feelings he drew on to create something we can all relate to. The guitar riff smolders; the chorus blazes, unembarrassed by love. Right before the fade-out, McCartney emits a scream that is so weirdly piercing, so unearthly, that it sounds like a fusion of synth and voice. But it's Paul, making the sound of pain leaving the body.

40   I SAW HER STANDING THERE

In March 1974 Paul and Linda McCartney traveled to Los Angeles to attend the Academy Awards, where "Live and Let Die" was nominated for Best Original Song. Shortly before they went, they received a visit from Yoko Ono in London. Ono, clad in black, seemed diminished and haunted. She discussed John's sojourn with Pang and wondered aloud if her marriage was over. McCartney had heard about his friend's misadventures in LA, and recognized the symptoms. He asked Ono, "Do you still love him? Would you think it was an intrusion if I said to him, 'Look, man, she loves you and there's a way to get back'?" Ono said yes, she did love him, but that if she took him back it would be with conditions. John would have to move back to New York, and he couldn't expect to move in with her right away; he would need to court her all over again.

In LA, on March 28, Paul took part in a very loose jam session with John and a crowd of musicians, including Stevie Wonder, at the Record Plant recording studio. Quite a lot of substance abuse was going on. John and Paul duetted, briefly, on the old R&B song "Stand by Me," but neither they nor anyone else were on top form. Paul arranged to meet John at his rented home the following day. Lennon and Pang's Santa Monica beachside home had become something of a frat house for dissolute rock stars and their hangers-on. Ringo Starr and Keith Moon had moved in. They partied by the pool, slept all morning, rose, and passed around the drugs. When McCartney arrived, John was still in bed. Harry Nilsson offered Paul a snort of something. "What is it?" asked Paul. "Elephant tranquilizer," said Nilsson. "Is it fun?" asked Paul. Nilsson reflected. "No." Paul declined.

There was a piano in the house, and if there is a piano near Paul, he must play it. He played Beatles songs, with Starr and Moon singing along. Eventually John turned up. Meeting in the courtyard, John and Paul were unsure of how to be with each other, until John, perhaps quoting Arthur Janov, said, "Touching is good!" and they hugged. The two chatted lightly for a while before Paul indicated that he wanted a private word. In another room, he delivered Yoko's message.

It's a remarkable episode, a real-life "She Loves You." It's hard to say how much difference it made to John's relationship with Yoko—they didn't reunite until nearly a year later. Still, why did Paul do it? Maybe he was still hoping to revive his partnership with John, and knew that could happen only when John felt secure and stable. Things in Los Angeles were out of control, despite May's best efforts, and Yoko, for all of her difficulty, did seem to provide order. If Paul could be the one who helped her get John back, perhaps Yoko would cease to see him as a threat and give her blessing to them working together. The man who wrote "Hey Jude" still wanted to make his friend happy, or at least less unhappy.

It would be wrong to suggest that Lennon was always out of his head during this time. He was more productive than he had been in his last year with Yoko, and between spasms of misery, he was in a good mood, evident in the way he talked in public around this time. In his songs, too, bitterness and cynicism were replaced by warmth and nostalgia, the most significant expression of which is a song on *Walls and Bridges* called "#9 Dream." When Lennon was interviewed in 1980, while sitting with Yoko, he dismissed it: "I just churned that out . . . I just sat down and wrote it, you know, with no real inspiration, based on a dream I had." This is belied by everything about the song. Around its nonsense-syllable chorus, Lennon built an intricately, lovingly constructed song that *feels* like a floating, gauzy dream of the past. The title echoes "Revolution #9," the experimental sound collage he made for the *White Album*. Lennon oversaw the woozy, psychedelic string arrangement that makes this track the most Beatlesque of anything he made after the breakup. If "God" and the *Plastic Ono Band* album represented Lennon's Reformation period—an iconoclastic and unsentimental rejection of the Beatles and the sixties—then "#9 Dream" represents the Counter-Reformation. The Beatles, it seems to say, really were magical. John believed again.

The original title of "#9 Dream" was "Walls and Bridges," which John eventually decided to use as the title of the album. For him, the phrase described the way we can separate ourselves from others or find connections to them ("Walls keep you in either protectively or otherwise. Bridges get you somewhere else"). He went to work on the track a matter of days after catching up with Paul in person. John and May moved back to New York, into a new apartment, in the summer of 1974, and one of their first visits was from Paul, Linda, and the children. John and Paul spent the evening telling tales of Liverpool and Hamburg.

In September, John appeared as a guest on the Saturday afternoon show of the New York disc jockey Dennis Elsas. Asked whether he'd seen the other Beatles, John said he'd recently spent "a couple of Beaujolais evenings" with Paul, "reminiscing about when we were only . . . thirty-eight." Elsas surmised that "relationships [with the other Beatles] are cordial," to which John said, "Oh, very warm! *Very* warm, my dear." The bile that was so evident in 1971 (and which would return, to a lesser degree, in 1980) is absent, as is the political posturing. John sounds optimistic, playful, at ease with himself. Around this time, he asked May Pang, "What would you think if I started writing with Paul again?"

In a sign of Lennon's newfound comfort with the legacy of the Beatles, he played on Elton John's cover of "Lucy in the Sky with Diamonds." Elton was finishing his US tour with a show at Madison Square Garden in New York, on Thanksgiving night, November 28, 1974. After he played

keyboards on "Whatever Gets You thru the Night" he made Lennon promise to appear onstage with him if it got to number one. Lennon agreed because he didn't think it would happen, but it did, and Elton held him to the
promise. At a rehearsal, they agreed to do "Whatever Gets You thru the
Night," "Lucy in the Sky with Diamonds," and a third song. Elton suggested "Imagine." John demurred. He said he wanted to do another Beatles
song, and specifically one of Paul's: "I Saw Her Standing There." The idea
of it seemed to excite him.

John hadn't performed live for two years. On the day of the show, he vom-
ited with fear. But he made it to the side of the stage that night, and when
Elton announced him, he walked out to the most incredible ovation, a tsu-
nami of love that went on and on. John turned around to Elton's band as if to
say, *What's this about?* "It's for you, John," they mouthed. After ripping
through two songs, John introduced "I Saw Her Standing There": "We tried to
think of a number to finish off with, so I can get out of here and be sick. And
we thought we'd do a number of an old estranged fiancé of mine, called Paul."

☮

Tony King, Apple's general manager in the US, was close to both John and
Elton, and instrumental in organizing Lennon's Madison Square Garden appearance. He arranged seats for Yoko and a friend. Yoko sent two gardenias
backstage, one for John and one for Elton. John was wearing his when he
walked out onstage. Yoko also turned up at the after-show party. Later, John
and Yoko memorialized this night as the beginning of their reunion. That
was an exaggeration—they didn't reunite for another several months. But
King's sense is that John was already heading in her direction, whether he
consciously realized it or not. John loved May, but she did not hold the same
fascination for him as Yoko. Only Yoko made him feel as if he were in the
hands of an omniscient intelligence. He was also tired of living like a bohemian. He liked the grandeur of the Dakota, and felt like a king there. Yoko
liked being famous, and perhaps realized that her status was ultimately tied
to and dependent on John, whom she still loved. She had made her decision.
"You know, May," she told Pang, coolly, "I'm thinking of taking him back,"

as if discussing the return of a painting that had been on loan. Pang was up-set, but resigned herself to the inevitable. Yoko always got what she wanted.

It wasn't just a game to Yoko, however. Not long after Yoko and John separated, Tony King met Yoko for coffee near the Dakota, at Lennon's sug-gestion. He was expecting an imperious, aloof figure, but as soon as they started talking about John, Yoko broke into a sobbing fit.

☺

In November, Paul and Wings went into Abbey Road to start on a new al-bum (*Venus and Mars*). He and Linda wanted to make some of it overseas, and planned a trip to New Orleans, a city that moved to the rhythms and sounds of Black R&B. In one of his conversations with John, Paul floated the idea of John coming to visit him there in the new year. May Pang re-called Paul phoning their apartment in January to firm up the invitation, as the McCartneys were about to set off. When John got off the phone, he was enthusiastic about the chance to hang out in New Orleans and see Paul. Pang was pretty sure that Paul would persuade him to record with him, and that, deep down, was what John wanted. In a note to Derek Taylor, Lennon wrote, in characteristic pidgin, that he was going to attend a recording session with David Bowie in January, "Then possibley down to New Orleons to see the McCartknees."

Before Christmas, the Beatles had arranged a meeting to agree on the final dissolution of the group's partnership. After nearly four years of legal wrangling, the papers were ready. Since John, Paul, and George were all in New York, it was agreed they would meet at the Plaza Hotel to sign the doc-ument. But John, who was at the Dakota, didn't show up, even after George harangued him over the phone. Instead, he delivered a balloon with a sign that read, "Listen to this balloon." John said he couldn't come because his astrologer said it wasn't the right day: Yoko had become a devotee of astrol-ogy and numerology. John did sign the papers shortly afterward, on a trip to Disney World in Florida, with May, Cynthia, and Julian: part of Pang's semi-successful campaign to reconnect John with his son. (In an interview given three months afterward, Lennon made a jokey but heartbreaking remark: "I think [Julian] likes Paul better than me . . . I have the funny feeling he wishes Paul was his dad. But unfortunately he got me.")

In January, then, John was at a crossroads. The legal battle over the Beatles was behind him. He had never been more successful or acclaimed as a solo artist. He had a number one single and album (the success of "Whatever Gets You thru the Night" had propelled *Walls and Bridges* to number one). He'd collaborated with two of the hottest young pop stars in the world. Madison Square Garden had reminded him of how much he was loved. He was on the verge of working with his closest friend and creative partner again. A world of possibilities lay before him, and now he turned away from all of them.

Yoko called Lennon and Pang's apartment to tell John she had found a cure for smoking: hypnotism. She wanted John to try it but it would require him staying at the Dakota for a few days. John agreed. Yoko made appointments and then canceled them at the last minute because the stars were not right. Pang could see that she was playing games with John; worse, she could see that John liked it. She could feel him slipping away. At the start of February, Yoko said the stars were aligned. John went to the Dakota to be hypnotized. He never did make it to New Orleans.

On the stage of Madison Square Garden, John chose to share the moment—*his* moment—with Paul, rather as he'd chosen to share his group with him, all those years ago. Why did John choose a Paul song, when he had so many of his own? And why did he mention Paul, when to everyone in the crowd, it was just a Beatles song?

"I Saw Her Standing There" didn't just hark back to the beginnings of the Beatles; it is a song about the beginning of a relationship—one that is fated and exclusive: *How could I dance with another?* I think John drew Paul toward him in that moment because he didn't want to face what was in front of him alone. He was thrilled by the crowd and terrified by its hunger. He was delighted by his solo success and anxious about whether he could repeat it. Everything that was exciting was also overwhelming. If he couldn't look across the stage and see his friend, he could at least summon his presence.

41   COMING UP

John went back to his apartment with May only briefly. "Yoko has allowed me to come home," he told her, shamefaced, and began to pack. Pang and Lennon continued to see each other and make love, surreptitiously now, for months, and stayed friendly for years. But, at least according to her account, a light had gone out inside John. "His spirit, his wit, his insight, seemed to have disappeared and he appeared to have no energy at all." Lennon stopped recording, and withdrew from social life. He told May that Yoko insisted he needn't worry about not making music—that he had nothing to prove anymore. Those days were behind him.

Typically, John was launching himself into a new era by renouncing the one before. In public, he referred to his life with May as a "previous incarnation." The pivotal event was Yoko's pregnancy (John dated the conception to February 6, 1975, around the time he left May's apartment for good). Yoko was forty-two, and after several miscarriages, this was unexpected and glorious news, especially for John; Yoko suggested that he was more pleased than she was. She made it clear that John would have to take on the lion's share of parenting duties, and John agreed. Under Yoko's direction, he gave up alcohol, swore off sugar, and returned to a macrobiotic diet. After doing promotional duties for his *Rock 'n' Roll* album, he stopped talking to the press (he gave hardly any interviews for four years). On October 9, the day of John's thirty-fifth birthday, Sean Ono Lennon was born, by cesarean section. "I was just all eyes for the baby," John recalled. "I just sat all night looking at it saying, 'Wow, it's incredible, wow!' You know, just all night."

From then on, John spent his days looking after Sean (a task he shared with staff) or hanging out in his bedroom at the Dakota. He watched TV and wrote letters and postcards to relatives, or to people he'd come across in the news. He kept a diary in which he wrote down whatever he was ruminating on. He took walks in Central Park with Sean, or went to his favorite local café. He baked bread enthusiastically for a while, until he got bored. He sent assistants to buy books and records, and expensive liver for his three cats. He was a dutiful and doting father, though he still had a terrible temper—at one point Sean was taken to hospital to check for damage to his eardrum. Yoko saw much less of Sean, though she was affectionate and loving when she did. John didn't forsake songwriting altogether: he jotted down lyrics when they came to him and made demos of songs, or fragments of songs, at the piano.

Yoko ran the couple's business affairs with invincible confidence. She was John's interface with the outside world, deciding whom, if anyone, he should see or talk to on the phone. She would direct him on occasional trips abroad, too, under instruction from tarot cards. The couple took a three-month trip to Japan with Sean, and met Yoko's extended family. When it was time to go home, Yoko's cards instructed her to fly home separately from John and Sean and their staff. John later talked about this period as one of blissful domesticity, but there is a sense of anomie to it, of squandered time and talent. Yoko's will had substituted for his own sense of purpose. May Pang saw John at the end of 1978 and asked him if he ever wanted to record again. "Of course I do," he said, "I never stopped wanting to make music." But he didn't, as the years slipped by. Meanwhile, he watched his best friend reconquer the world.

⊛

Since its release at the end of 1973 *Band on the Run* had grown steadily into a huge success. It reached number one in America in 1974, propelled by the hit single "Jet," and became the bestselling album of the year in the UK. McCartney's new group, which had started with amateurish gigs in small venues, and which had already undergone changes of personnel, now achieved global liftoff. Wings spent four months rehearsing for and planning a mammoth, yearlong world tour to coincide with the release of *Venus and Mars*, the album they made in New Orleans. In the autumn of 1975 they toured Britain, playing sold-out shows, before heading to Australia, where their reception at the airport resembled the days of Beatlemania. This time, as Paul shook hands with screaming fans, he was carrying his four-year-old daughter, Stella. The Beatles, first to everything, always had to invent models for themselves as they progressed, and in the 1970s, they had to be the first solo artists famous for being ex-members of a group. They were also the first aging rock stars. On tour, McCartney kept being asked whether he was too old for rock and roll and whether he was "past it." He was thirty-three. "I suppose I am from another age," he conceded.

After taking the winter off, and a short tour of Europe, the longest leg of the tour began. Starting in Fort Worth, Texas, Wings played thirty-one concerts in twenty-one major venues across the US and Canada. It was on the scale of a Beatles tour—in fact, it was much bigger. Wings put on a spectacular show, complete with lasers and dry ice. A convoy of five thirty-two-ton trucks carried the band's entourage and equipment. The McCartneys were ferried in a private jet. The tour was a sellout and a critical success. In a sign of McCartney's growing ease with his own past, the set included Beatles numbers, including "Yesterday" and "Lady Madonna." They played to sixty-seven thousand people at the Seattle Kingdome, breaking the record for the largest ever rock gig, which had been set by the Beatles at Shea Stadium. McCartney said, "We were right back up to the level where I'd left off." In March 1976, Wings released a fifth studio album, *Wings at the Speed of Sound*. It went to number one in the US, as did the single, "Silly Love Songs," in which Paul teased critics, perhaps including John, who accused him of being vapidly sentimental. The McCartneys threw a lavish wrap party at a rented house in Benedict Canyon, attended by Bob Dylan, the Eagles, Warren Beatty, and Steve McQueen. Linda said of Paul, "He's very much back to his old self again"—a telling remark. McCartney was once again the cocky, cheerful, endlessly creative showman with whom she had fallen in love in 1968. It had taken him the best part of a decade to recover from the breakup.

✥

Just before Christmas 1975, John and Yoko were in their bedroom at the Dakota, hanging out with their friend the photographer Bob Gruen, when they heard voices outside their apartment door. Nobody was supposed to get that far without having been announced by the building's concierge, and so Gruen was dispatched to see who it was. As he approached the outer door of the apartment, he could hear singing. When he opened the door, he discovered the McCartneys, singing "We Wish You a Merry Christmas." Gruen invited them in, and when they met John and Yoko, "It was like old friends meeting by surprise and really glad to see each other." They drank tea and chatted. McCartney told them about the tour and griped about having to cancel planned concerts in Japan—the McCartneys had been busted for dope by the British authorities in 1972, and the Japanese had refused them entry.

In the following months, the Beatles were asked to consider a reunion. A US promoter publicly offered them $50 million for a one-off gig. None of the former Beatles ruled it out, but neither did they pursue it. John and Paul talked on the phone quite a bit during this time. Coincidentally, their fathers died within two weeks of each other, at the end of March 1976. John had never reconciled with Alf. Paul, who had been close to Jim, did not take a break from his tour to attend his father's funeral. His brother, Mike, said, "Paul would never face that sort of thing." Denny Laine said he didn't even mention his father's death to the other members of Wings—it was like it hadn't happened.

At the end of April, just before McCartney's triumphant tour of North America, Paul and Linda paid another visit to the Dakota. They laughed about an offer that the *Saturday Night Live* producer Lorne Michaels made on his show: to pay the Beatles $3,000 for a guest appearance: "All you have to do is sing three Beatles tunes. 'She loves you, yeah, yeah, yeah'—that's a thousand dollars right there." John and Paul briefly considered getting a car down to the *Saturday Night Live* studio, twenty-two blocks south at Rockefeller Plaza, and surprising everyone. But it was late, and they were tired. The McCartneys went home and John and Yoko settled down to watch a film. On Sunday evening, the next day, McCartney returned to the Dakota alone. This time he brought his guitar. He didn't warn John he was coming. John, who had been looking after Sean all day, wasn't in the mood. "It's not 1956," he snapped. "Turning up at the door isn't the same anymore." Perhaps he was sick of Paul's face. *Wings at the Speed of Sound* had hit the top of the charts, and John had been reading about how many millions of dollars the McCartneys were making. Perhaps he was just tired; babies can be hard work. Either way, McCartney took his guitar and left, and the next day flew to Texas to start his tour.

They continued to speak on the phone, but the conversations were strained, and sometimes John got angry or upset. "I used actually to have some very frightening phone calls with him," said Paul, years later. In 1977, a year after their last face-to-face encounter, Paul and Linda happened to be staying in a hotel across the park from the Dakota. Paul nervously picked up the phone, called John, and told him he'd like to see him. "What for?" said Lennon. "What the fuck d'you want, man?" When Paul told John what he'd been up to that evening—eating pizza with the kids, reading fairy tales—John said, "You're all pizza and fairy tales." The call ended with Paul slamming down the phone.

McCartney's tour became the triple album *Wings over America*, another number one on the *Billboard* chart. *Wings over America* proved to be the group's commercial peak. Subsequent albums sold respectably but not as well. Wings still had hits—"Mull of Kintyre" was one of the biggest-selling singles of all time in Britain. But they underwent more changes of lineup, and lost momentum as the music scene turned from rock toward disco, punk, and new wave. In July 1979, McCartney had recently released a Wings album with which he wasn't very satisfied: *Back to the Egg*, which turned out to be the group's last. A little bored and frustrated, he returned to the mode he had been in early in the decade: breaking down what he had built up to start something new. He decided to make some music by himself, without collaborators, and set up a makeshift studio at home, with synthesizers, drum machines, and sequencers. The music he made was completely different to the music he'd been making with Wings. It was minimalist, discordant, weird. He wasn't sure if he would release it.

In January 1980, Wings set off for Japan to play a sold-out tour of eleven concerts over thirteen days. Five years after first refusing them entry, the Japanese authorities had relented. Yet no sooner had the group landed at Tokyo airport than a search of McCartney's luggage revealed a huge bag of marijuana. He was arrested and thrown in jail and the tour was canceled. McCartney's humiliation became front-page news around the world. He was in jail for nine days. While recuperating in Scotland, he decided to release his musical experiments as an album, called *McCartney II*. Discussing how it came about, he said, in a revealing slip of the tongue, "I was just doing this for my own insanity." *McCartney II* was released in May and preceded by a single, the album's opening track. "Coming Up" is based on a repeating pattern of quick guitar licks layered over drums and bass, everything slotting together like interlocking cogs. McCartney sings short, question-and-answer musical phrases, using a vocal that's been sped up so it sounds a little cartoonish. As he sings the title phrase and the bass starts climbing the scale, it is impossible not to feel your mood lift a little. "Coming Up" is an optimism machine.

⚛

In jail, Paul received a good-luck card from John, who was very amused by the news. The last time they had seen each other in person, Paul had been complaining that the Japanese wouldn't let him into the country. So what did he do when they finally said he could? He whacked a bag of dope into his suitcase. John's theory was that the Beatles had spent so much time traveling the world without ever having their bags checked at customs that Paul had been complacent. His other theory—one shared by Paul—was that it was an act of self-sabotage.

John had been spending time at a recently acquired beach house in the hamlet of Cold Spring Harbor, once a whaling town, now a commuter suburb on Long Island. He'd been sent there by Yoko on the advice of the tarot cards. Yoko was a true believer in the occult, but she also used tarot cards and stars to move John around, with his tacit collusion, for various reasons.* On this occasion, she'd fallen back into heroin addiction and wanted time alone to get clean; supposedly, John didn't know about her habit. As it happened, John loved his time by the ocean. His father had been a sailor, his grandfather, too, and ever since he was a kid he'd been captivated by the romance of seafaring. Inside the Dakota, he'd been reading books about navigation and maritime adventure. With him in Cold Spring Harbor was his assistant, Fred Seaman (John was amused by his name), and he asked Fred to find a small boat he could learn to sail in.

John was in good spirits. Fred used to drive him around the neighborhood in Lennon's Mercedes, with the car radio on. On one of these aimless trips, the radio played a propulsive electronic track with a weird vocal. "Fuck a pig," said John, sitting up straight. "It's Paul!" The next morning, the tune was still in his head. "It's driving me crackers," he told Seaman. John asked Seaman to get hold of McCartney's latest album. He found out there were two versions of the song—the original, electronic version, and a live performance recorded with Wings, which was more like a conventional pop song. Naturally, John preferred the first one: "I thought that 'Coming Up' was great," he told a reporter later that year, "and I like the freak version that he made in his barn . . . if I'd have been with him, I would have said, 'Yes, *that's* the one.'"

"Coming Up" galvanized John more than anything had in years. He was suddenly eager to know what was going on in music, to feel part of it all again. He had Seaman pull together cassettes they could listen to in the car. John liked the new wave stuff: the Pretenders, the B-52's, Madness. A few days later, John did something he'd wanted to do forever: he bought a sailboat—a single-mast fourteen-footer. Its young owner, Tyler Coneys, piloted it to the little dock below the house. When John boarded, he was beside himself. "All my life I've been dreaming of having my own boat!" he said to

---

* Ringo proposed one: "She used to send him away on his own so he'd grow up." (Ringo Starr, *Postcards from the Boys*, 81.)

Coneys. "I can't wait to learn how to sail!" He shaved, for the first time in months.

John never talked about the lyrics of "Coming Up," but of course he would have listened to them, perhaps more closely than anyone else would or could. The words could not be more typically Paul. The singer is addressing someone he wants to make better. "I wanna help you with your problem," he says. At first you think he's addressing a lover, but then he says, "You want a *friend* to rely on, one who'll never fade away." "Stick around," he sings, and soon you'll be coming up "like a flower." What can we glean from the lyrics about the person Paul is offering to help? It's someone who wants "peace and understanding," someone who is always "searching for an answer." "We're nearly there," says the singer. "It's coming up."

42   (JUST LIKE) STARTING OVER

John took lessons in sailing from Tyler Coneys, and after mastering the basics, he decided he wanted to go on a sea voyage. Yoko consulted with her "directional man," a Japanese astrologer who advised on the karmic ramifications of travel. It was agreed that John should travel to Bermuda, a 635-mile voyage from Newport, Rhode Island. A forty-three-foot schooner, the *Megan Jaye*, was chartered. Before John went, Yoko's directional man recommended that he reset his psychic alignment with a trip to South Africa. John flew to Cape Town on May 23. He visited Table Mountain a couple of times, and a massage parlor. A couple of days into his trip, he called May Pang for a chat. He told her that he was starting to write again, and hinted that he would return to the recording studio soon. After only five days, John cut his trip short, against instructions, and flew back to New York.

Just before sunset on June 4 the *Megan Jaye* set sail from Newport, heading southeasterly for Bermuda. A crew of five was on board: John, Tyler Coneys and his two cousins, also experienced sailors, and a captain, recruited for the trip: Hank Halsted. John got along well with Captain Hank, a grizzled thirty-year-old. As the other crewmates fell victim to seasickness, the two of them spent a lot of time together at the wheel, swapping stories. Halsted started to understand how much the voyage meant to Lennon, and how eager he was to learn. "The guy made himself so wide open to experience and growth. It would have been like standing in the middle of a six-lane highway saying 'Come and get me . . .' That's really the way he approached it."

On Saturday, June 7, the *Megan Jaye* sailed into a storm. "It was brutal," said Coneys. "The massive waves were coming up behind like buildings. We'd be surfing down these liquid mountains. I was like, 'Oh, my God. I hope we live.'" But Lennon was not afraid. "He did not wish he was home. He was in all his glory." The storm refused to abate all day, and with the other crewmates sick, Halsted had now been at the wheel for thirty hours straight. "I got to the point where I knew I was going to be dangerous." He called on John to steer the ship, so that he could sleep. John was nervous— "All I've got are these skinny little guitar-playing muscles"—but there was no other option. "Focus on the horizon, not the compass," Halsted told him, and went to his bunk. John took the wheel, and became the man he had once been for the Beatles: the one who could be relied on in a crisis; who always found a way to go further than anyone else; who faced down every terror; who sought the outer reaches of experience. He said later:

> I was there, driving the boat, for six hours, keeping it on course. I was buried under water. I was smashed in the face by waves for six solid hours. It won't go away. You can't change your mind. It's like being on stage; once you're on, there's no getting off. A couple of the waves had me on my knees. I was just hanging on with my hands on the wheel—it's very powerful weather—and I was having the time of my life! I was screaming sea shanties and shouting at the gods. I felt like the Viking, you know, Jason and the Golden Fleece.

When Halsted returned, he was amazed at the change in his shipmate. "I met a different guy. He was totally washed, exuberant, ecstatic." John seemed to have gone through "a full-on catharsis."

The *Megan Jaye* docked in Bermuda after seven days at sea. A couple of days later John was reunited with Sean, who arrived with his nanny and Fred Seaman. Fred brought John's guitar and a bag of cassette tapes: song fragments John had recorded at the Dakota over the past decade. They moved into a rented cottage, along with the Coneys cousins. John was in high spirits, performing sea shanties and his own songs for everyone. But he was restless, and keen to work. He instructed Fred to find them a more isolated property so that he could leave the Coneys behind. Fred went into town to buy a boom box, some bongos, and a tambourine. The new place already had a piano. On June 18, Paul's birthday, John moved into the house and started to make music.

Although there was no official split, the Japan debacle effectively broke Wings apart. The other members, who lost out on large sums of money when the tour was canceled, were upset with McCartney for failing to apologize. Meanwhile, Paul invited George Martin to work with him on some new material. It's as if Paul was calling on Martin to help him rediscover his sense of direction. Indeed, the latter half of 1980 saw a reversal of a pattern that had held through most of the previous decade: John now had a clearer sense of creative purpose than Paul.

John stayed in Bermuda until the end of July. He and Sean would play on the beach in the mornings before John went to work on new songs. Yoko was enthusiastic about his plan to record again, partly because she saw an opportunity to record her own songs, too. In New York, she spoke to a producer they had worked with before, Jack Douglas, and told him that John wanted to make an album. She added, "I'm going to have a few songs on it, and John doesn't know yet." Douglas began putting together a group of musicians under a veil of secrecy. John did not want the press to find out. As Douglas puts it, "You know, he was very, very insecure about this stuff. He didn't think he had it anymore, you know. He thought he was too old, he just couldn't write, he couldn't sing, he couldn't play, nothing."

Lennon returned to New York at the end of July and began recording just over a week later. The idea was now that it would be a shared album, with one John song followed by one Yoko song. John was happy to share the pressure, and the burden, of making a whole album. It would be called *Double Fantasy*, the name of a flower that John came across in the Bermuda Botanical Gardens: "I just thought, 'Double Fantasy'—that's a great title! 'Cause it has so many meanings . . . it means anything you can think of. It means double-couple."

John's new songs were strong. They included "Watching the Wheels," the latest in a line of his songs going back to "I'm Only Sleeping" and "Nowhere Man" in which John defended idleness and passivity against ambition and busyness, this time with reference to his life at the Dakota. "Beautiful Boy (Darling Boy)," a rapturous song about parental love, is as soppy as anything Paul McCartney ever wrote, and utterly irresistible. It includes the words "getting better," which, in conversation with Douglas, John explicitly connected to Beatles days. In fact, having started the 1970s with "God," John had reached the other end of the decade sounding more "Paul" than Paul. "Woman," a delicate, flowing ballad, reminded Earl Slick, one of the guitarists Lennon recruited to play on it, of "Here, There and Everywhere." John himself said it reminded him of a Beatles track. "(Just Like) Starting Over," a slight but touching love song, harked back even further, to the music that both John and Paul fell in love with as teenagers: doo-wop and rock and roll.

By all reports, the *Double Fantasy* sessions were fun. John worked with energy, good humor, and focus. Between takes he would happily tell Beatles stories to rapt musicians and engineers. To Douglas's surprise, John was eager to take direction: "He'd say, 'If you think that's better, I'll do it.'" Yoko's more experimental songs sound more of the moment than John's; they have some of the spirit of Talking Heads and other new wave groups, while being utterly idiosyncratic.*

When word of Lennon's return to music-making got out, he received good wishes from around the world. McCartney sent a bouquet of flowers to the studio. In September, while still working on the album, Lennon embarked on a media round, his first in five years. He threw himself into it

---

* At one point, John made a suggestion from the control room—"Mother dear, why don't you . . ."—to which she replied, "Fuck you very much, John," causing the studio to explode with laughter. (Quoted in Tim Riley, *Lennon: The Man, the Myth, the Music,* 632.)

with his old alacrity, spending hours at a time with interviewers, giving long, seemingly candid answers, while once again consciously fashioning a narrative and a persona. In 1971 he had cast himself as a revolutionary at war with the establishment. Now he was a contented house-husband—though he argued, with justification, that this *was* radical, in its way. He presented an idealized version of his marriage to Yoko, leaving out the drugs and infidelities. In her memoir, May Pang describes being appalled at what she regarded as his dishonest account of their affair, which got reduced to a "lost weekend."

Lennon's longest interview was with David Sheff for *Playboy*, to whom he spoke about the Beatles in depth. When the conversation turned to McCartney, he sounded nostalgic. He described their "eyeball-to-eyeball" writing sessions, although he claimed that by the mid-sixties, "The creativity of songwriting had left Paul and me . . . it had become a *craft*." This was so self-evidently at odds with the development of the Beatles' music that Sheff suggested it was "a little hard to believe." Lennon framed his reply in terms of a marriage: "Well, it was fertile in the way a relationship between a man and a woman becomes more fertile after eight or ten years . . . We were different. We were older. We knew each other on all kinds of levels that we didn't when we were teenagers." This sounds like something more intimate and complex than a question of craft. John continued on this theme, as if carried along by the momentum of his metaphor:

> The early stuff—the "Hard Day's Night period," I call it—was the sexual equivalent of the beginning hysteria of a relationship. And the "Sgt. Pepper–Abbey Road" period was the mature part of the relationship. And maybe, had we gone on together, maybe something interesting would have come of it. It wouldn't have been the same. But maybe it was a marriage that *had* to end.

Overall, John was much warmer about Paul and the Beatles than he had been in the early 1970s. Back then Lennon accused them of being so hostile to Yoko that she was driven to take heroin. Now he told David Sheff that they had treated her well, and Yoko agreed: "They were very civilized and kind to me." He told another interviewer, Jonathan Cott, "I love those guys, I love the Beatles, I'm proud of the music." The journalist Robert Hilburn interviewed Lennon at the recording studio, in a break between *Double Fantasy* sessions. He was surprised at how affectionately Lennon spoke about his former bandmates. When Hilburn mentioned McCartney, John said, "Paul? My dear one." Hilburn asked him if, in the Beatles days, he was ever surprised by Paul's songs. John said, "No, he never surprised me because, like, can you be surprised by your *brother*? From age 15 on?"

In late November and early December, with the album released, John and Yoko gave several more interviews. On December 8 John spoke to the DJs Dave Sholin and Laurie Kay. He emphasized that he wasn't competing with anyone anymore, wasn't trying to be hip, but simply wanted to enjoy himself, like he had as a teenager. Then he said, "I was saying to someone the other day, there's only two artists I've ever worked with for more than a one-night stand, as it were. That's Paul McCartney and Yoko Ono. And I think that's a pretty damned good choice." Instead of leaving the thought there, he kept talking about Paul. He gave an account of how they first met, and of how he invited Paul to join the Quarry Men, and how Paul played hard to get. "George came through Paul, and Ringo came through George . . . But the only—The person I actually picked as my *partner* . . . was Paul. Now, twelve or however many years later, I met Yoko, I had the same feeling. It was a different *feel*, but I had the same feeling."

When the interview was finished, Sholin gave John and Yoko a lift to the Record Plant recording studio, where they were recording a new Yoko track ("Walking on Thin Ice"). In the car, Lennon was ebullient, doing impressions of Roy Orbison and Little Richard. Sholin asked him how he was getting along with Paul. John said, "I love him. Families—we certainly have our ups and downs and our quarrels. But when all's said and done, I would do anything for him, and I think he would do anything for me."

That night, John and Yoko left the recording studio at about 10:30 p.m., and got into a waiting limousine. When they arrived back at the Dakota, Yoko left the car first and walked toward the entrance. John was a few paces behind, clutching a stack of cassettes. As he approached the entrance, four bullets tore into his chest. He staggered on toward the safety of the Dakota, dropped the cassettes, and fell. Blood poured across the pavement. Police officers carried him to their car and rushed to a nearby hospital. John was pronounced dead on arrival.

The author Robert Rosen is one of the few people to have read the journal that Lennon kept at the Dakota (after John's death, the diaries were stolen by Fred Seaman, who showed them to Rosen in 1981). Rosen says that Lennon wrote about Paul a lot—almost every day. When he was asked, in 2010, what the most disturbing elements of the diaries were, Rosen cited John's jealousy of Paul ("pretty shocking"), his love of money, and his obsession with the occult. The first two went together, of course. John and Paul had got rich together, so for John to see Paul's earnings soar far above his own, in the mid-1970s, was hard. The peak of McCartney's earning power came in 1978 when he signed a recording deal with Columbia that made him the highest-paid recording artist in the world. But by 1980 McCartney's imperial phase was over, and the relative decline in his fortunes allowed Lennon's jealousy to recede. Insofar as Lennon could still be dismissive toward McCartney in public it was because he was nervous about coming back and being seen as a competitor. "Paul" was a concept by which he measured his own anxiety.

"(Just Like) Starting Over" is one of the first songs Lennon recorded for *Double Fantasy*. It became the opening track on the album, and the first single. It fitted perfectly with the story of Lennon's return. It begins—and thus the album begins—with the chiming of a bell, intended as an allusion to the ominous bell that opened "Mother," showing the emotional distance Lennon had traveled in the past ten years.

Although John never discussed its lyrics in detail, he did say that "(Just Like) Starting Over" was for the co-creator of *Double Fantasy*, Yoko. It is a mature love song: a man appealing to his partner to rediscover the joy they felt in each other's company when they first met. But it also seems to be about a double couple. It's a doo-wop song, and it wasn't Yoko who shared John's love of doo-wop. It turns on the word "darling," pivotal in the pre-chorus and the bridge. Both John and Paul loved to sing that word—oh, "darling." The singer dreams of going away with his partner, together, all alone, like they used to in the early days. That's not something John and Yoko did (quite the opposite); John and Paul were the ones who liked to get away, to Caversham, to Paris, to the lounge of the Marietta Hotel, to an empty house on Forthlin Road. Then there are what seem to be coded messages to McCartney, not much subtler than those in "How Do You Sleep?" In two lines, John makes three possible references to Wings: "spread our wings," "my love" ("My Love" was a big hit for Wings), and "another day" (also mentioned in "How Do You Sleep?"). An earlier version of the song included a line about "the walrus." It was cut; too overt, perhaps. "(Just Like) Starting Over" is two love songs, one inside the other.

There are two photographs of John and Paul posing with fans in the street, both from the summer of 1980, which are often paired together on-line. John is in New York, Paul is in London. They have strikingly similar outfits: sports jacket, open-necked shirt. They're wearing their hair the same way, too—in a way that resembles the early Beatles, clean-shaven and moptopped. Of course, they didn't coordinate this look. They don't appear to have seen each other in person that year, although they spoke on the phone. But then, they never did coordinate except symbiotically, in an organic interaction that thrived when they were physically close. During the 1970s they were like what quantum physicists call "entangled particles," a pair of electrons that somehow remain connected over vast distances: sometimes one spins up while the other spins down, at other times they both spin up or both spin down, but they are always correlated. John's friend Harry Nilsson recalled, "Someone told me they saw John walking down the street wearing a button saying I LOVE PAUL. And this girl who told me that said she asked him, 'Why are you wearing the button that says I LOVE PAUL?' He said, 'Because I love Paul.'"

43   HERE TODAY

Paul was at home in Sussex, alone, when the phone rang. Linda had taken the kids to school. Ahead of him was a day of work on a new song, under the supervision of George Martin, at Martin's recording studio in central London. It was Paul's manager who broke the news. As Linda parked the car, she saw her husband coming out to meet her, and she could tell something was badly wrong. He looked desperate.

George Martin phoned, and after sharing in the shock with Paul, he asked if he wanted to cancel the day's work. Paul didn't want to cancel. Of course he didn't. The answer was always to make music. It must have been reassuring to be with Martin, too. "He was just very, very quiet, and upset," said Denny Laine, who was also at the session, which was to record McCartney's song "Rainclouds." Laine recalled Paul saying, "I'm never going to fall out with anybody again in my life." An assistant came in to say that Yoko Ono was on the phone (she had got the studio's number from Linda). Paul came to the office to take the call. The assistant cleared the room and closed the door as McCartney began to sob.

A crowd of reporters and photographers had gathered outside the entrance to the studio, on Oxford Street, and waited. It was dark by the time McCartney emerged. Journalists swarmed around him. White lights snapped on. Shoppers stopped and stared. What would have happened these days? McCartney would have been hustled to his car without taking questions. Publicists would have already drafted a statement for his approval and issued it within hours of the news. A TV interview would have been arranged, for when he was composed enough to know what to say. His team would have drafted an Instagram post. Once again, McCartney was having to go to places nobody had been. In the living room at his aunt and uncle's house, his reaction to his mother's death had been stilted and oddly practical. So it was now at the death of his best friend—except this time the world was watching. As he stepped out into the street, Paul automatically switched to his public persona—the friendly star who will always stop and talk to the press. But because he was churning away inside, the persona malfunctioned. Usually he holds the gaze of his interviewers. Now his head swivels around as if he desperately wants to avoid being looked at, as if he wants to disappear. At first glance he seems offhand, brusque, businesslike. Look again and you see a bereaved child: furious, lost, scared.

☙

John Lennon's murder elicited an outpouring of public grief. Vigils were held in multiple countries. Beatles music and Lennon solo albums were played nonstop on the radio. *Double Fantasy*, which had sold creditably before his death, went to number one. Jann Wenner published a special edition of *Rolling Stone* devoted to Lennon. On its cover he used a photograph taken by Annie Leibovitz on the day of the murder, showing Lennon, naked, curled up like a baby next to a fully clothed Yoko. The image was used across the world. People mourned Lennon partly because he represented the optimism and liberation of the 1960s. His peace campaigns and political activism (in reality pursued only for a brief period of his life) fused with the love people felt for his music, and the pain they felt at his passing, to create a mythical figure. As the journalist Ray Connolly—who knew and liked John—put it, "You could already smell the dubious whiff of incense at the public canonization of a newly martyred saint." Lennon became revered as the towering genius behind the Beatles, the visionary who imagined a better world, the gentle proselytizer for peace and loving partner of Yoko Ono. His flaws, frailties, and contradictions were erased or smoothed away. And for Lennon to be raised in status, McCartney had to be lowered. Robert Christgau, then America's most influential rock critic, sympathetically quoted his own wife: "Why is it always Bobby Kennedy or John Lennon? Why isn't it Richard Nixon or Paul McCartney?"

The sanctification of Lennon (which McCartney would have imbibed on the day that the news broke, no doubt contributing to his discombobulation) might not have endured for so long had it not been for the publication of Philip Norman's book *Shout! The True Story of the Beatles*, which came to market just three months after Lennon's death. It was the most comprehensive and well-told history of the band to date. *Shout!* was a runaway bestseller and set a template for the Beatles story that lasted for decades. Its author was, as he later admitted, a Lennon partisan who did not like McCartney, and the story he told in *Shout!* hewed to the one Lennon sketched out in his early 1970s interviews. Promoting the book on TV, Norman declared, "John Lennon was three-quarters of the Beatles."

☙

In January, McCartney returned to the studio to work on what he now decided would be a solo album (the end of Wings was announced later that year). He asked George Martin to produce it. The bulk of the sessions took place at a studio complex Martin had built on the Caribbean island of Montserrat. Paul drew other people from the Beatles' world toward him: Ringo played drums on some of the tracks. George Harrison was down to play guitar on one song, although they never got around to it. Geoff Emerick, now a producer in his own right, helped out. McCartney also invited artists he admired but hadn't worked with before to join him. Stevie Wonder collaborated on a couple of tracks. Eric Stewart, from 10cc, sang backing vocals. Another guest was Carl Perkins. Perkins was a rock and roll pioneer who began his career at Sun Studio with Elvis Presley, and made country-influenced rockabilly records that all the Beatles adored. They covered several of his songs, including "Matchbox," "Honey Don't," and "Everybody's Trying to Be My Baby." Perkins was only ten years older than McCartney, but seemed from a different era altogether. His genial, avuncular presence in Montserrat was another steadying influence.

Perkins spent eight days on the island, writing and recording a song called "Get It" with McCartney. He got to know Linda and the whole family, sharing dinners and stories and jokes. On the night before he was due to leave, he sat out on the patio by himself with his guitar, reflecting on what a beautiful time he'd had, and wondering how to convey his gratitude. "I'm kind of sentimental, and I can't say certain things out loud, but sometimes I can sing it," he said later. There on the patio he wrote a song called "My Old Friend." The next morning, he met the McCartneys for breakfast, as he had done every day. He brought his guitar and told them he'd written a song to say thank you for their hospitality. The McCartneys were delighted. Perkins sang his song, full of the direct, guileless sentiment of country music. Somehow it seems to be about more than a week of fun with new friends. In the middle of it, Perkins promises that should he and his friend never meet again in this life, they will meet "over yonder," and asks, "Won't you think about me every now and then?" As Perkins sang this line, McCartney stood up from the table and left the room in tears. Perkins stopped, alarmed. Had he done something wrong? Linda got up and gave him a hug. "He needed that," she told Perkins, thanking him for helping Paul connect with his grief. What was it about the song that triggered his crying jag? Linda explained that John's last words to Paul were "Think about me every now and then, old friend."

※

After Montserrat, McCartney did more work on the album in England. Eric Stewart recalled him saying, "I've just realised that John has gone. John's gone. He's dead and he's not coming back." He looked completely dismayed, said Stewart, as if it had just hit him. Stewart got the impression that McCartney was dwelling on all the things he wanted to tell Lennon and now couldn't.

Paul wrote "Here Today" in Sussex. It must have felt like the scariest commission anyone had ever received. The whole world expected a musical elegy for John, though even the public's expectation may not have been as intimidating as the spectral presence of his former collaborator. A lyricist who didn't like to overthink had to think hard about every word. Nonetheless, the result is a graceful and moving reflection on living with a ghost. "Here Today" does not try to capture everything about John Lennon, or John and Paul, or the Beatles. It merely asks, over open, questioning chords, what *if*? What if you could hear me sing this song? There is anxiety in the way Paul double guesses what his subject would think about his tribute to him. But there is also wry humor and a sense of solace.

"Here Today" is played on the guitar, the instrument that Paul hugged tightly in the wake of his mother's death. Its title evokes "Yesterday," as does the string quartet, arranged by Martin (it also evokes "Here, There and Everywhere"). The song has an unusual structure: two verses followed by two bridge sections. In the first bridge, the singer, overcoming the nervousness of the verse and growing in confidence, speaks "for me." He says he still remembers how it was "before," and that he's no longer holding back the tears. Three words—"tears no more"—are drawn out, with the next three slipped in unobtrusively behind them: "I love you." Then comes a second bridge section, longer and more complex, in which he recalls their first encounter: how they were both playing hard to get. He plays a discordant minor chord under that thought, as if there's something a little painful about it. We "didn't understand a thing," he says, "but we could always sing." He moves on, swimming toward something, trying to get deeper. He sings about "the night we cried." McCartney later explained that this was about a night during the Beatles' second 1964 American tour in Key West, Florida, where they were rerouted due to a hurricane. He and John got drunk together and ended up "crying about, you know, how wonderful we were, and how much we loved each other, even though we'd never said anything." *Never understood a word*, he sings, *but you were always there with a smile.*

It's not much to say someone was always there with a smile, is it? Yet at a time when Lennon was being memorialized by everyone else as a visionary there is something touching and truthful about the slightness of this. You always made me laugh—well, there are few things more cherishable in a friend than that.* In the final verse, that tentative "if" is still there, though McCartney sounds more confident when he declares his love now. He concludes, "You are here today, for you are in my song"—a declaration that John lives inside this little artifact, this crystal ball, that Paul has crafted. "Here Today" resolves beautifully.

Five months after Lennon's death, McCartney phoned Hunter Davies, author of the 1968 Beatles biography, and a friendly journalist, at home. He began complaining about all the people who had been talking about Lennon in public and getting it wrong, including Davies. What had really upset him, he said, was an interview with Yoko in which she was quoted as saying that Paul had hurt John more than any other person. He said these were some of the cruelest words he had ever read. "I can't understand why Yoko is saying this." Nobody had ever talked about the times when John hurt *him*. "People keep on saying I hurt him, but where's the examples, when did I do it?" He had been racking his brain and the only incident he could think of was when he recorded "Why Don't We Do It in the Road" without John (only Paul and Ringo play on the track). "I did hear [John] some time later singing it. He liked the song and I supposed he'd wanted to do it with me. It's a very John sort of song anyway . . . I wrote it as a ricochet off John."

McCartney went on like this for over an hour, wrestling with what Lennon thought about him. "He was always thinking I was cunning and devious . . . I never set out to screw him, never. He could be a manoeuvring swine . . . Now, since his death, he's become Martin Luther Lennon." He said they were only ever in *creative* competition: "I wrote 'Penny Lane,' so he wrote 'Strawberry Fields.' [Note: he gets the order wrong.] That was how it was. But that was in compositions." He said they had arguments about the supposed slights in Paul's songs throughout the seventies. "We

---

* It's difficult to convey how important shared laughter was to both of them except by pointing to the recorded incidents where we see or hear it overflowing: the outtake of "And Your Bird Can Sing," on which we hear them giggling at something uncontrollably; the promotional film for "We Can Work It Out," in which John keeps making Paul laugh when he should be miming; John's riff about Scouts and masturbation, in *Get Back*, which leaves Paul, who had been trying to be stern, completely helpless.

had great screaming sessions . . . he got really crazy with jealousy at times."
He told a story from the Beatles years that he often returned to. "We were
once having a right slagging session and I remember how he took off his
granny glasses. I can still see him. He put them down and said, 'It's only me,
Paul . . .' That phrase keeps coming back to me all the time. 'It's only me.'
It's become a mantra in my mind."

In 1982, McCartney appeared on BBC Radio's *Desert Island Discs*, for its
fortieth anniversary edition (he turned forty the same year). Guests are invited
to imagine themselves as castaways and to choose eight records to take with
them. Since this was a special edition, McCartney's appearance was filmed
for a documentary. The show was presented by its original host, Roy Plomley, a gentle man and attentive listener, in some ways reminiscent of George
Martin. McCartney picks records by Chuck Berry, Elvis, and Gene Vincent.
When "Searching" by the Coasters plays, his face lights up as he sings along
and remembers performing it at the Cavern. When the time comes for Mc-
Cartney to choose his eighth and final record, he says, "To sort of sum up the
whole thing, I've chosen one off John Lennon's record *Double Fantasy.*" The
song is "Beautiful Boy." Although he is trying to sound chirpy he can barely
look at Plomley while introducing it. "It's very moving, to me." Then the
record plays and John's voice fills the room, full of tender love for a boy who
has now lost his father. McCartney bites his lip. His eyes dart around and he
moves his face away from the camera, almost turning his back on Plomley.
He hums the tune, clearly trying very hard not to cry.

The solo album that McCartney made with George Martin was released
in 1982. It was called *Tug of War*, after its opening track and single: a song
about the futility of fighting. McCartney was prolific in 1981, producing
enough music for two albums; the next one was *Pipes of Peace*. He had taken
up the theme with which John was most strongly associated. But it's hard to
listen to the first song he released after Lennon's death and not hear, in his
weary, regretful tone, something more personal. Losing John so suddenly
was always going to be hard, but the fact that they never fully reconciled
gnawed at him for years. Perhaps surprisingly, the person who helped him
the most was Yoko Ono. From that first phone call at AIR Studios, Ono was

quick to tell him that John spoke of him fondly. She said that not long before
he was shot, John had put on one of Paul's records and wept. In 1984, Mc-
Cartney talked about how he clung to the memory of his last phone call with
John, which was friendly. "You find yourself holding on to little bits of the
wreckage to keep yourself afloat." In 1986, he gave a raw, honest interview to
Chris Salewicz, for *Q* magazine. Salewicz later put the tape of the interview
online. The contrast with McCartney's cheerful public persona is striking:
this is someone obsessive, anguished, self-questioning. At one point McCartney says, of himself and the other Beatles, "We're coming to." They were
still, sixteen years later, in the process of waking from the dream.

Over the following decades, which saw George Harrison pass away, and
Linda, Paul grew gradually more at peace with the memory of John. He
spoke affectionately of John's contradictions and unpredictability, and about
how he still thought of him as a collaborator: "I still check my songs with
him." In a 1995 interview he used a striking phrase—he called John "a delicious broth of a boy." I had to look it up. "Broth of a boy" is an old Irish
term for an irrepressible, hotly bubbling young man. Byron uses it in *Don
Juan*: Juan was a broth of a boy, "a thing of impulse and a child of song."

By the 2020s, any rawness or torment in McCartney's interviews had almost gone. The 2021 *Get Back* documentary reminded him and millions of
others that he and John and all the Beatles still liked one another, even in
1969. In 2023 McCartney masterminded the release of a new Beatles song,
"Now and Then," based on a demo that John had made at the Dakota during
his years of seclusion, the title echoing what were, according to Carl Perkins,
John's last words to Paul. It was a project that McCartney had doggedly pursued over the course of nearly thirty years. We can imagine what he heard in
its lyrics, which are about missing someone, and wanting them to be there.

Paul has told and retold the story of his relationship with John so many
times that it has lost its rough edges, like a stone smoothed by running water.
He emphasizes how well the two of them were getting along toward the end
of the 1970s. To me it always sounds like he is trying a little too hard to convince us, or himself. Just a few weeks prior to Lennon's death, he described

John and Yoko as "very suspicious people," in a semiprivate interview with Peter Brown, and expressed frustration at not being able to get John to trust him. I'm not sure the bafflement and hurt ever entirely disappeared, or the sense that he is missing a part of himself.

In 2022, the year of McCartney's eightieth birthday, I watched him play to sixty thousand fans at a stadium in New Jersey. He delivered a blockbuster show lasting three hours, full of Beatles songs, Wings songs, solo songs. Its emotional climax was a performance of "I've Got a Feeling," sung as a virtual duet with Lennon. McCartney asked Peter Jackson to adapt footage from the rooftop concert to fit his live performance. It was moving to watch McCartney, his back turned to the audience, gazing up at a giant moving image of his friend as he was in 1969. At the same time, perhaps it was a little neat. After all, what did Paul love about John, if not that you couldn't play him like a tape?

☙

There are several reasons why we get Lennon and McCartney so wrong, but one is that we have trouble thinking about intimate male friendships. We're used to the idea of men being good friends, or fierce competitors, or sometimes both. We're used to the idea, these days, of homosexual love. We're thrown by a relationship that isn't sexual but is romantic: a friendship that may have an erotic or physical component to it, but doesn't involve sex. Our ancestors had a better grasp of this. In Plato's *Symposium*, Aristophanes describes how a pair of friends can be "lost in an amazement of love and friendship and intimacy" yet unable to "explain what they desire of one another. For the intense yearning which each of them has towards the other does not appear to be the desire of sexual intercourse, but of something else, which the soul of either evidently desires but cannot identify." As Aristophanes suggests, the anomalous nature of these relationships can make them hard for the *participants* to understand, let alone onlookers.

When the French philosopher Michel de Montaigne was young he had one such friendship, with the writer and jurist Étienne de La Boétie. They were friends for six years before La Boétie died at the age of thirty-two, in 1563. They were in love: rejoicing in each other's company, minds and souls deeply connected. This is how Montaigne described the start of their friendship:

> We sought each other before we met . . . from reports we had each heard of the other . . . And at our first meeting, which happened by chance at a great feast and town gathering, we found ourselves so taken with each other, so well acquainted, so bound together, that from that moment on nothing could be as close as we were to one another.

When La Boétie died, Montaigne was brokenhearted. He never stopped grieving for him, and his pain only increased with age. In an essay called "On Friendship" he wrote about his feelings for La Boétie, without naming him, transmuting the deeply personal into the universal. He struggled to articulate *why* he loved his friend so much, what it was that made them soulmates. In the end, after multiple scratchings out, he settled on a simple formulation: "Because it was him; because it was me."

At one point in his 1981 conversation with Hunter Davies, McCartney said rather miserably, "I realise now we never got to the bottom of each other's souls." In the end, McCartney had to settle for not knowing, and not understanding. So do we all. What we can say for sure is that they loved each other, that through music they found a way to share this love with everyone in the world, and that in doing so they made the world an immeasurably better place. Because it was John; because it was Paul.

ACKNOWLEDGMENTS

This book germinated during the lockdowns of 2020, when I wrote and published, via my newsletter, a ten-thousand-word essay called "64 Reasons to Celebrate Paul McCartney." I didn't expect many people to read it—it was just something I needed to write. But they did, in great number. Surprised by the scale and intensity of the response, I started to wonder if I could write a whole book about the group I have loved since childhood, and when I asked myself which aspect of the story I was most interested in, the answer quickly became obvious. I'd like to thank all previous Beatles authors for not getting there before me.

Having said that, *John & Paul* is indebted to countless Beatles books. I have space to mention only a small handful of them here. *Can't Buy Me Love* by Jonathan Gould is the best one-volume group biography available, highly perceptive about the context of the band's success and about their music. Mark Lewisohn's *Tune In* is the most comprehensive guide to the Beatles' childhoods and the group's pre-fame career. I am, like all Beatles authors, indebted to Lewisohn's in-depth primary research. Steve Turner's acutely observed *Beatles '66* was my guide through that pivotal year in the group's history. Hunter Davies's *The Beatles*, first published in 1968, remains perhaps the most essential source for Beatles authors, valuable in particular for its contemporaneous interviews with the Beatles and their families. Philip Norman's *Lennon* was

389

very useful, particularly for its interviews with Yoko Ono. Peter Doggett's *You Never Give Me Your Money* is a lucid guide to the group's breakup and its aftermath. James Campion's *Take a Sad Song* is a great compendium of stories and insights about "Hey Jude." Rob Sheffield's *Dreaming the Beatles* helped alert me to the possibilities of discussing the Beatles' emotional lives in conjunction with their music; I'm indebted in particular to Sheffield's account of Lennon's appearance with Elton John at Madison Square Garden. Louis Menand's account, for *The New Yorker*, of Yoko Ono's early artistic career gave me a new and important perspective on her. Ken Womack's *John Lennon 1980* was a helpful reference for the last year of John's life.

The flourishing of Beatles podcasts in recent years did much to revitalize my fascination with and love for the group. Again, I have space to mention only a few, but I'd like to give thanks for *Screw It We're Just Going to Talk About the Beatles*, *Something About the Beatles*, *My Favourite Beatles Song*, *Your Own Personal Beatles*, *I Am the Eggpod*, *Beatles Books*, and *Gimme Some Truth* (presented by Obadiah Jones, my fact-checker). The *Weird Studies* podcast is not specifically about the Beatles but its discussion of *Sgt. Pepper* colored my thinking about the album.

Perhaps the most important aspect of the podcast subculture is that it has introduced many more female voices into the Beatles conversation, raising its level of insight and emotional intelligence. It was through podcasts that I discovered two Beatles experts who have been reshaping a narrative formed mostly by men: Erin Torkelson Weber, the historiographer and author of *The Beatles and the Historians*, and Christine Feldman-Barrett, author of *A Women's History of the Beatles*. I am grateful to the all-female *Another Kind of Mind* for its penetrating exploration of the group's relationships. I owe a special debt to Diana Erickson, creator and presenter of *One Sweet Dream*. Diana's deeply insightful podcast, and her generosity as a conversation partner, have been vital to *John & Paul*.

Thank you to my agent, Toby Mundy, for his sage advice and his enthusiasm throughout. Thank you to Laura Hassan at Faber and Jamie Raab at Celadon for seeing the potential of this idea and for helping to realize its final form. *John & Paul* was worked on by crack team of editors, including and especially Laura. Thanks to Fred Baty for his helpful notes and to Robert Davies, Ian Bahrami, and John McGhee for their assiduous and skillful copyediting and proofreading. Thanks to the highly professional production teams at Faber and Celadon. Thanks to Lorin Stein for helping to get my draft into shape, and to Luke Meddings for generously reading a draft and making important points. Special thanks to Obadiah Jones, my indefatigable, indispensable fact-checker. All remaining errors are most certainly mine alone. Thanks to my endlessly resourceful picture researcher, Amanda Russell. Thanks to the publicity and marketing teams at Faber and Celadon for bringing such enthusiasm and creativity to the task.

Along the way, many people have helped me either by answering queries and making suggestions or just by providing encouragement and support when I most needed it. Thanks to Stephen Brown, Rhona Mercer, P. B. Conte, Tyler Cowen, Adrian Dannatt, Ed Docx, Dr. Christine Feldman-Barrett, Adam Gopnik, Verity Harding, Stephen Leslie, Katie Martin, Sasha Neal, Tim Riley, Juliet Rosenfeld, Adrian Sinclair, Bob Spitz, Jesse Tedesci, and Joe Wisbey. For services beyond the call of duty, thanks to Robin Allender, Duncan Driver, Michael Lindsay-Hogg, Tom Holland, and Stewart Wood. Thanks to all those I've inadvertently left off this list. Thank you, first and last, to Alice.

NOTES

While writing the book I was often asked if I had sought an interview with Paul McCartney. I did not. Since I could have interviewed only one of the principals, I felt that to do so would have unbalanced the book. In fact, although I drew on countless published interviews with the principals and others, I didn't carry out any myself (except one with Michael Lindsay-Hogg). Since the Beatles lived so much of their lives in the public eye and since so many people have been fascinated by them for so long, there is a vast amount of available information about Lennon and McCartney, without a corresponding depth of insight. The gaps in the literature are perhaps now less about what happened than why, and it was here that I felt I might contribute something new. One unfortunate but unavoidable consequence of focusing on John and Paul is that George and Ringo have been pushed to the side of the story. I know that I've done them a disservice; I hope it isn't an egregious one. I've tried, at points, to convey what indispensable contributions they made to the Beatles.

PROLOGUE

1   **"Er, very shocked, you know":** https://www.youtube.com/watch?v
       =s6_62zKxOr0.

3   **"The Beatles are mutants":** quoted in Philip Norman, *Shout!: The
       Beatles in Their Generation* (1981; repr., New York: Fireside, 2005),
       331–32.

3   **"There is no doubt in my mind"**: George Martin, *All You Need Is Ears* (1979; repr., New York: St. Martin's Griffin, 1994), 259.

4   **"Talking is the slowest"**: Hunter Davies, *The Beatles* (1968; repr., London: Ebury, 2009), 412.

4   **"'A drag' isn't how the world will see it"**: https://www.youtube.com/watch?v=s6_62zKxOr0.

1: COME GO WITH ME

11   **"How are we going to get by"**: interview in Ray Coleman, *McCartney: Yesterday—and Today* (London: Boxtree, 1995), 28.

11   **"I learned to put a shell around me"**: The Beatles, *The Beatles Anthology* (London: Cassell, 2000), 19.

11   **"We had no idea what my mum had died of"**: McCartney interview with Ricky Ross for BBC Radio Scotland, broadcast July 4, 2019.

12   **"Listen, loves"**: "Portrait of Paul," *Woman* magazine, August 21, 1965.

12   **"Daft prayers"**: Davies, *The Beatles*, 105.

14   **"He was only five"**: Mark Lewisohn, *The Beatles: All These Years: Tune In, Extended Special Edition* (London: Little, Brown, 2013), 108.

14   **Julia, in tears**: described in Julia Baird, *Imagine This: Growing Up with My Brother, John Lennon* (2006; repr., London: Hodder & Stoughton, 2017), 31.

15   **"I wanted everybody to do"**: Davies, *The Beatles*, 89.

16   **"I noticed this quality he had"**: Lester quoted in Philip Norman, *John Lennon: The Life* (London: HarperCollins, 2008), 353.

17   **she did not act like a mother**: Lennon, "Mother": "Mother, you had me but I never had you."

17   **"Mimi said to me that day"**: Davies, *The Beatles*, 98.

18   **"It was *amazing*"**: Davies, *The Beatles*, 110.

20   **"He looked like Elvis"**: Davies, *The Beatles*, 113.

20   **"I'd been kingpin"**: Davies, *The Beatles*, 113.

21   **"That was the day"**: Davies, *The Beatles*, 98.

2: I LOST MY LITTLE GIRL

25   **"The minute he got the guitar"**: Davies, *The Beatles*, 110.

25   **"Well that takes care of that problem"**: quoted in Pete Shotton and Nicholas Schaffner, *John Lennon: In My Life* (New York: Stein & Day, 1983), 58.

27 **beautiful hands:** Barry Miles, *Paul McCartney: Many Years from Now* (London: Secker & Warburg, 1997), 46.

27 **"Your little friend's here":** from an interview with Mike Read for BBC Radio 1, October 13, 1987, quoted in Lewisohn, *Tune In*, 9.

28 **"a very beautiful woman":** McCartney, interviewed by Julia Baird, 1988, quoted in *Imagine This*, 145.

28 **a tinge of sadness:** Miles, *Paul McCartney*, 48.

28 **"We never argue":** interview with Hunter Davies, *Sunday Times*, September 18, 1966.

29 **"We decided on that":** interview with Mark Lewisohn and Kevin Howlett, June 6, 1990, quoted in Lewisohn, *Tune In*, 7.

29 **"Who writes the words?":** Brian Epstein, *A Cellarful of Noise: The Autobiography of the Man Who Made the Beatles* (1964; repr., London: Souvenir, 1984), 98.

30 **"Little George":** McCartney interview with Anthony Cherry, BBC Radio 2, June 28, 1992.

31 **"I never took it that seriously":** quoted in Lewisohn, *Tune In*, 178.

31 **"I was such a bully":** interview with Paul Drew, April 1975, quoted in Lewisohn, *Tune In*, 445.

32 **"carried away":** Helen Anderson, quoted in Lewisohn, *Tune In*, 282.

32 **"Oh Nigel":** quoted in Lewisohn, *Tune In*, 182.

32 **"fuck it, fuck it":** Davies, *The Beatles*, 131.

33 **"Each of us knew":** Lewisohn, *Tune In*, 188.

3: WHAT'D I SAY

40 **"You couldn't talk to the Beatles":** Koschmider, quoted in Lewisohn, *Tune In*, 701.

40 **"We did 'mach schauing' all the time":** Lennon, quoted in Davies, *The Beatles*, 162.

41 **"All the other bands said":** Reinhard "Dicky" Terrach, quoted in Lewisohn, *Tune In*, 1199.

41 **"The audience saw them sideways":** Hans-Walther "Icke" Braun, in Braun and Volker Neumann, *Icke, Evelyn Hamann und die Beatles: Eine Art Biografie* (self-published, 2018). Translation courtesy of Jesse Tedesci.

41 **"I had been reading Shakespeare":** *The Beatles Anthology*, 46.

42 **"No heat, no wallpaper":** *The Beatles Anthology*, 46.

42   **"phoney"**: letter to Arthur Kelly, October 18, 1960. https://entertainment.ha.com
/itm/music-memorabilia/autographs-and-signed-items/1960-george-harrison
-letter-from-hamburg-incredible-content-this-three-page-letter-on-lined-paper
-is-not-dated-but-almost-c/a/612–23505.s.

43   **the characters in his drawings**: Shotton and Schaffner, *John Lennon: In My Life*, 34.

43   **"Go on you fucking Krauts"**: as recalled by Johnny Byrne, guitarist for Rory
Storm and the Hurricanes, quoted in Bob Spitz, *The Beatles: The Biography*
(London: Aurum, 2007), 217.

43   **"The whole place just shook"**: Johnny Byrne, quoted in Spitz, *The Beatles*, 216.

43   **leapfrogging contest**: Craig Brown, *One Two Three Four: The Beatles in Time*
(London: 4th Estate, 2020), 46.

43   **strawberry fight**: Braun and Neumann, *Icke*, 67.

44   **"the artist in the band"**: Thorsten Knublauch, *The Beatles: Mach Schau in
Hamburg* (Doorwerth, 2021), 105.

44   **"They looked absolutely astonishing"**: quoted in David Pritchard and Alan
Lysaght, *The Beatles: An Oral History* (New York, 1998), 48.

4: WILL YOU LOVE ME TOMORROW

48   **"I just trusted my instinct"**: Spitz, *The Beatles*, 9.

48   **"Get your knickers down"**: Chris Salewicz, *McCartney: The Biography* (London:
Queen Anne), 105; Spitz, *The Beatles*, 864.

48   **"Hamburg didn't change anyone else"**: Lewisohn, *Tune In*, 411.

49   **"a polite, orderly way"**: Dave Foreshaw, quoted in Spitz, *The Beatles*, 11.

49   **"pussyfooting around"**: Spitz, *The Beatles*, 234.

49   **"Everybody who was anywhere"**: Neil Aspinall, quoted in Lewisohn, *Tune In*, 413.

49   **"no one . . . was aware"**: Lewisohn, *Tune In*, 418.

50   **"very polite young man"**: Lewisohn, *Tune In*, 410.

50   **"The group had got going again"**: Davies, *The Beatles*, 178.

50   **"Paul would always give in"**: Lennon interviewed by Peter McCabe and
Robert D. Schonfeld, September 5, 1971, at the St. Regis Hotel. http://www
.beatlesinterviews.org/db1971.0905.beatles.html.

50   **"I never liked the bosses"**: McCartney, interviewed by Janice Long for *Listen to
What the Man Says*, BBC Radio 1, December 22, 1985.

51   **"John started"**: Lewisohn, *Tune In*, 429.

51   **"John said to Paul"**: Neil Aspinall, quoted in Lewisohn, *Tune In*, 429.

51 **"So he had to make a decision"**: Lennon, interviewed by Peter McCabe and Robert D. Schonfeld, September 5, 1971, at the St. Regis Hotel.

53 **"Despite all his mucking around"**: Lindy Ness, quoted in Lewisohn, *Tune In*, 539.

5: BESAME MUCHO

56 **"beat the shit"**: anonymous source in Spitz, *The Beatles*, 247.

56 **"Let me ask you this"**: Astrid Kirchherr, quoted in *Beatles Book Monthly*, May 1994.

57 **"the power the bass player had"**: McCartney, interviewed in *Bass Player* magazine, July/August 1995.

57 **"The record label asked"**: documents quoted in Lewisohn, *Tune In*, 466.

57 **"At nights"**: Peter Mackey, quoted in Lewisohn, *Tune In*, 496.

58 **"a succession of climaxes"**: *Mersey Beat*, August 31–September 14, 1961, 22.

58 **"ageless children"**: Muggeridge's diaries, quoted in Brown, *One Two Three Four*, 38–39.

59 **"The group was in debate"**: Lennon, interviewed by Elliot Mintz, January 1, 1976, quoted in Lewisohn, *Tune In*, 965.

59 **"*definitely* going to collapse"**: Bob Wooler, quoted in Lewisohn, *Tune In*, 988.

59 **"I thought this was disastrous"**: Wooler, interviewed by Johnny Beerling, BBC Radio 1, January 13, 1972.

59 **When Stuart heard**: The Beatles, *The Beatles Anthology*, 64.

59 **"They were so tight"**: quoted in Lewisohn, *Tune In*, 500.

60 **"After trauma"**: Bessel van der Kolk, *The Body Keeps the Score* (London, 2014), 20.

60 **"At times, they reminded me"**: quoted in Spencer Leigh, *The Best of Fellas: The Story of Bob Wooler, Liverpool's First DJ* (Liverpool, 2002), 67.

60 **"They both had bowler hats on"**: quoted in Lewisohn, *Tune In*, 500.

61 **"All the kissing"**: Lennon interviewed by David Sheff, September 1980, published in *Playboy*, January 1981.

61 **"They were strong willed"**: quoted in Lewisohn, *Tune In*, 486.

61 **"Throughout my schooldays"**: Epstein, *A Cellarful of Noise*, 20.

62 **"a sort of wistfulness"**: quoted in Debbie Geller, *The Brian Epstein Story* (London, 2000), 13.

62 **"I fancy Rome"**: Epstein's journal, 1960, quoted in Geller, *The Brian Epstein Story*, 35.

63 **"I had never seen anything"**: Epstein, *A Cellarful of Noise*, 39.

63   **"Everything about the Beatles"**: Brian Epstein, interviewed by Kenneth Harris, *Observer*, May 17, 1964.

64   **an "expert"**: Lennon, interviewed by Peter McCabe and Robert D. Schonfeld, September 5, 1971 at the St. Regis Hotel.

64   **"queer"**: McCartney: "We'd heard that Brian was queer, as we would have called him, nobody used the word 'gay' then." Miles, *Paul McCartney*, 88.

64   **"He may be late"**: Harrison, quoted by Epstein in an interview with Bill Grundy for the BBC's *Frankly Speaking*, broadcast March 23, 1964.

64   **"You're going to be bigger than Elvis"**: Epstein, quoted by Harrison in *I Me Mine: The Extended Edition* (Guildford, 2017), 33.

64   **"I make a lot of mistakes"**: Lennon, quoted in *Rolling Stone*, February 4, 1971.

65   **"Brian was in love with John"**: McCartney, quoted in *The Beatles Anthology*, 266.

65   **"I was pretty close"**: Lennon, quoted in *Rolling Stone*, January 21, 1971.

65   **Alistair Taylor claimed**: Alistair Taylor, *A Secret History* (London, 2001), 29.

66   **"on the way out"**: Epstein, *A Cellarful of Noise*, 46.

66   **"British Elvis Presleys"**: Lennon, quoted in Lewisohn, *Tune In*, 1053.

66   **"I didn't *change* them"**: Epstein, quoted in Davies, *The Beatles*, 220.

66   **"selling out"**: Lennon, quoted in *Rolling Stone*, January 21, 1970.

68   **"Paul tried to be comforting"**: Astrid Kirchherr, *Hamburg Days* (Guildford, 1999), 140.

6: TILL THERE WAS YOU

69   **"Girls used to say"**: quoted in Lewisohn, *Tune In*, 432.

70   **"I could never see the difference"**: quoted in *The Beatles Anthology*, 68.

70   **"to the left and right"**: quoted in *The Beatles Anthology*, 68.

70   **"We went on from 'Love Me Do'"**: quoted in *The Beatles Anthology*, 68.

71   **"[John] liked women"**: Cilla Black, *What's It All About?* (London, 2003), 250.

7: PLEASE PLEASE ME

75   **"the greatest thing"**: Epstein, *A Cellarful of Noise*, 12.

76   **"They pulled into the car park"**: quoted in Lewisohn, *Tune In*, 666.

77   **"great big white sight-screens"**: quoted in Mark Lewisohn, *The Complete Beatles Recording Sessions* (London, 1988), 6.

77   **"all of a sudden"**: Chris Neal, quoted in Lewisohn, *Tune In*, 669.

79 **"It was their charisma"**: quoted in Lewisohn, *Tune In*, 671.

79 **"*Still* I was thinking"**: quoted in Lewisohn, *Tune In*, 672.

79 **"a lot of joking"**: Lindy Ness quoted in Lewisohn, *Tune In*, 675.

80 **"I thought he was rather loud"**: quoted in Lewisohn, *Tune In*, 678.

80 **"Being unable to deal"**: Lewisohn, *Tune In*, 677. His source for Harrison's quote is evidence given at the Royal Courts of Justice, May 6, 1998.

81 **"I watched his face drain"**: Cynthia Lennon, *A Twist of Lennon* (London: Star, 1978), 73.

81 **"Liverpool? You're joking"**: quoted in Lewisohn, *Tune In*, 698.

81 **"What do you mean, *group*?"**: quoted in Lewisohn, *Tune In*, 698.

81 **"We hated it . . . run of the mill"**: McCartney interviewed by Nicky Campbell, BBC Radio 1, November 19, 1991.

82 **"'We'd sooner have no contract'"**: Lennon, interviewed by Paul Drew, US radio, 1975 (via Lewisohn, *Tune In*, 727).

83 **"It was an option"**: quoted in *The Beatles Anthology*, 96.

83 **"An attitude came over John and Paul"**: Harrison, interviewed by Alan Freeman, BBC Radio 1, December 6, 1974.

84 **"Gentlemen, you've just made"**: George Martin, *All You Need Is Ears*, 130.

86 **"Everyone was stunned"**: Pat Dawson (née Hodgetts) quoted by Mike Evans, "Polythene Pat Remembers" (1974), http://www.meetthebeatlesforreal.com/2022/06/polythene-pat-remembers.html.

8: SHE LOVES YOU

89 **She recalls him working out lyrics**: quoted in Lewisohn, *Tune In*, 781.

89 **"you *don't* know what I mean"**: McCartney, quoted in *The Beatles Anthology*, 23.

89 **"a frantic guy"**: Lennon, quoted in *The Beatles Anthology*, 93.

90 **"They are a vocal-instrumental group"**: Maureen Cleave, "Why the Beatles Create All That Frenzy," *Evening Standard*, February 2, 1963, 6.

90 **"PAUL: Cliff and the Shadows"**: Michael Braun, *Love Me Do: The Beatles' Progress* (London: Graymalkin Media, 1964), 38.

91 **"I mean, we don't believe"**: McCartney, quoted in Cleave, "All That Frenzy," 8.

91 **"We're kidding everyone"**: Lennon, quoted in *Life*, February 21, 1964, 34B.

91 **"This is going wrong"**: interview with Dibbs Mather, *Dateline London*, BBC, December 10, 1963.

91   **"I'm not going to change into a tap-dancing musical"**: Braun, *Love Me Do*, 63.

92   **"consumed with happiness and awe"**: Lennon, *A Twist of Lennon*, 94.

95   **"It was the assumption"**: Miles, *Paul McCartney*, 121.

96   **singled out on a BBC radio show**: McCartney, interview in Mark Lewisohn, *Complete Recording Sessions* (London: Little, Brown, 2013), 10.

9: IF I FELL

100   **"It's nice to know"**: *Jack Paar Show*, January 3, 1964.

100   **"They've got their own groups"**: Geoffrey Giuliano, *Blackbird: The Life and Times of Paul McCartney* (New York, 1991), 82.

101   **cheerfully insouciant selves**: https://www.youtube.com/watch?v=hgU6foVr-wY.

101   **There is footage**: *The Beatles: The First U.S. Visit*, directed by Albert and David Maysles.

103   **"prisoners of success"**: Jonathan Gould, *Can't Buy Me Love* (London: Piatkus, 2007), 231.

105   **John's and Paul's vocal lines do not move in parallel**: Gould, *Can't Buy Me Love*, 235.

106   **"One gets the impression"**: William Mann, "What Songs the Beatles Sing," *The Times*, December 23, 1963.

106   **"Sometimes the harmony"**: Miles, *Paul McCartney*, 175.

10: I DON'T WANT TO SPOIL THE PARTY

107   **"Material's becoming a hell of a problem"**: Lennon, quoted in *Melody Maker*, October 17, 1964.

107   **"They were doing things"**: Bob Dylan, quoted in *Rolling Stone*, March 16, 1972.

109   **"very personal"**: Lennon in 1974, quoted in Keith Badman, *The Beatles: Off the Record* (2000; repr., London: Omnibus, 2007), 135.

109   **"what a bastard"**: Lennon, interviewed by Jann Wenner, *Rolling Stone*, January 21, 1971.

110   **"a smart cookie"**: McCartney, quoted in *The Beatles Anthology*, 98.

110   **"We used to sit in a cafe"**: Lennon, interviewed by David Sheff, September 1980, published in *Playboy*, January 1981.

110   **"I'd really just like to touch you"**: quoted in Shotton and Schaffner, *John Lennon: In My Life*, 73.

110   **"It was terrible"**: Lennon, interviewed by Jann Wenner, *Rolling Stone*, January 21, 1971.

111 **According to Billy J. Kramer:** quoted in Spitz, *The Beatles*, 416.

111 **REALLY SORRY BOB:** Norman, *John Lennon*, 310.

111 **"I must have been frightened":** Lennon, interviewed by Peter McCabe and Robert D. Schonfeld, September 5, 1971, at the St. Regis Hotel.

11: TICKET TO RIDE

117 **"I *meant* it":** Lennon, quoted in Jann Wenner, *Lennon Remembers* (London: Talmy, Franklyn, 1972), 115.

117 **"It was me singing 'help'":** Lennon, interviewed by David Sheff, September 1980, published in *Playboy*, January 1981.

117 **"Lennon needs the others":** Phyllis Battelle, "Can't Judge Beatles by Their Reputations," *Lebanon Daily News* (Lebanon, PA), April 28, 1965.

118 **"I really wanted to live in London":** Lennon interview with Brian Matthews, BBC, "November 30, 1965.

119 **"it would be silly for me to buy a house in Weybridge":** McCartney interview with "Ken Douglas, WKLO Philadelphia, August 16, 1966.

12: YESTERDAY

121 **"I just fell out of bed":** quoted in Coleman, *Yesterday—and Today*, 6.

122 **"He was playing this 'Scrambled Eggs'":** quoted in Coleman, *Yesterday—and Today*, 16.

122 **"slow hunch":** Steven Johnson, *Where Good Ideas Come From: The Natural History of Innovation* (London, 2010).

122 **"And if we don't like a number":** quoted in *Liverpool Echo*, April 28, 1964, 4.

123 **"Are you *kidding*?":** quoted in Coleman, *Yesterday—and Today*, 43.

123 **"I wish it had been me":** quoted in Coleman, *Yesterday—and Today*, 46.

126 **"small miracle":** Wilfrid Mellers, *Twilight of the Gods: The Music of the Beatles* (New York, 1973), 57.

126 **"frail bewilderment":** Mellers, *Twilight of the Gods*, 57.

127 **"Sid, at Shea Stadium":** Sid Bernstein, quoted in *New York Times*, August 15, 2000.

127 **"we all regarded it as a filler":** quoted in Coleman, *Yesterday—and Today*, 60.

128 **"The old bugbear":** quoted in Coleman, *Yesterday—and Today*, 61.

128 **"I got up to his level":** quoted in Davies, *The Beatles*, 512.

128 **"Beautiful—and I never wished":** interview with David Sheff, *Playboy*, January 1981.

129 **"One of his favourite songs":** Coleman, *Yesterday—and Today*, 98.

13: WE CAN WORK IT OUT

132   **"So she doesn't like the Beatle":** *The Celebrity Game,* originally aired June 19, 1964, in the UK. Quoted in *Miami News,* June 21, 1964, 10.

133   **"You've got Paul":** interview with David Sheff, *Playboy,* January 1981.

134   **"In ten minutes":** quoted in *The Beatles Anthology,* 179.

134   **"John and I had decided":** quoted in *The Beatles Anthology,* 190.

134   **"It alters your life":** quoted in *The Beatles Anthology,* 255.

134   **"a very organised life":** Barrow, interviewed for the *Daily Telegraph,* quoted in Salewicz, *Paul McCartney,* 166.

135   **"The time they spent working together":** Cynthia Lennon, *John* (London: Hodder & Stoughton, 2005), 154.

135   **"the clash between John and Paul":** Smith, quoted in Salewicz, *Paul McCartney,* 175.

138   **"altogether a good album":** *New Musical Express,* December 3, 1965, 8.

139   **"I could hardly make out":** interview with Howard Smith, WABC FM New York, September 9, 1971. https://www.youtube.com/watch?v=3TFpZE98OAM.

14: IN MY LIFE

141   **the song's primary author is Lennon:** Mark Glickman, Jason Brown, and Ryan Song, "(A) Data in the Life: Authorship Attribution in Lennon-McCartney Songs," *Harvard Data Science Review,* July 2, 2019.

142   **"My recollection . . . is at variance with John's":** quoted in Miles, *Paul McCartney,* 277–78.

143   **"I write poems":** quoted in Steve Turner, *Beatles '66: The Revolutionary Year* (London: HarperCollins, 2016), 47.

143   **"Mine are normally a bit soppier":** *London Life,* December 4–10, 1965, 26.

143   **"John doesn't like to show":** McCartney, quoted in an unpublished *Newsweek* article by Michael Lydon (intended for March 1966 publication). Interview *circa* December 1965. https://shrout.co.uk/L&MSongwriters%201966 .htm.

144   **"There are only about 100 people":** *New Musical Express,* November 12, 1965, 10.

145   **"We try to give people a feeling":** *Flip* magazine, May 1966.

145   **"to transmit that feeling":** Leo Tolstoy, "What Is Art?" (1897).

146   **"The thing about John":** quoted in Coleman, *Yesterday—and Today,* 98–99.

146   **"He is the best person I've met"**: quoted in Tom Doyle, *Man on the Run: Paul McCartney in the 1970s* (Edinburgh: Polygon, 2013), 289.

15: TOMORROW NEVER KNOWS

149   **"something left-field"**: quoted in Turner, *Beatles '66*, 41.

149   **"Everyone gets our records and says"**: interview with Alan Walsh, *Melody Maker*, September 9, 1967, 13.

150   **"John, Ringo and I played it"**: quoted in Turner, *Beatles '66*, 41.

150   **"half Beatle and half not"**: *Evening Standard*, March 25, 1966, 8.

150   **"It got false"**: interview with Barry Miles, September 23–24, 1969, partially published later in *Fusion*, *Oz*, and *Mojo* (November 1995) magazines.

150   **"We lived together when we played together"**: from transcript of *Get Back* sessions, January 1969, in John Harris et al., *The Beatles: Get Back* (London: Callaway Arts & Entertainment, 2021).

151   **"You don't have to like something"**: quoted in Miles, *Paul McCartney*, 236–37.

152   **"Nice-looking young man"**: quoted in Miles, *Paul McCartney*, 241.

152   **"I like it to be comfortable"**: quoted in *New Musical Express*, June 24, 1966.

153   **"We've got interested in things"**: interview conducted in February 1966; published in *Rave*, April 1966.

153   **"With any kind of thing"**: interview with Barry Miles, published in *International Times*, January 16–29, 1967, 8.

153   **"a whole song in one chord"**: interview with Hunter Davies, *Sunday Times*, September 18, 1966.

154   **"I just sort of stand there"**: *New Musical Express*, March 11, 1966.

154   **"I'm dying to move into town"**: *New Musical Express*, March 11, 1966.

154   **"I can get away from everyone"**: *Rave* magazine, February 1964.

154   **"One must surrender consciously"**: Dr. Marie-Louise von Franz in Carl Jung (ed.), *Man and His Symbols* (New York, 1964), 163.

154   **"We've never had time before"**: interview with Maureen Cleave, *Evening Standard*, March 4, 1966, 10.

155   **"they were the most important part"**: https://youtu.be/Io_AYbcsntE?si=2A3iy4eNzvT2SvhM&t=20.

155   **"Paul and I are very keen"**: *New Musical Express*, March 11, 1966.

155   **"extremes of frivolity and shyness"**: Robert Freeman, *Yesterday: The Beatles 1963–1965* (New York, 1983), 10.

155   **"I did some drawings at the time"**: interview with Jann Wenner, *Rolling Stone*, January 21, 1971.

155   **"You see, there's something else"**: interview with Maureen Cleave, *Evening Standard*, March 4, 1966, 10.

156   **"ought to get down to writing"**: *New Musical Express*, March 11, 1966.

157   **"the void"**: Timothy Leary, Ralph Metzner and Richard Alpert, *The Psychedelic Experience* (1964; repr., New York, 2007), 116.

157   **Walter Everett points out**: here and in the subsequent chapter I'm drawing on Walter Everett's analysis of "Tomorrow Never Knows" and "Eleanor Rigby," as given in the *Something About the Beatles* podcast, episode 251: "*Revolver*: Art and Music."

158   **"The light is the life energy"**: Leary, Metzner, and Alpert, *The Psychedelic Experience*, 116.

159   **"like an orange"**: quoted in Lewisohn, *Complete Recording Sessions*, 99.

160   **too "heavy"**: David Sheff, *All We Are Saying: The Last Interview with John Lennon & Yoko Ono* (London: Pan, 2020), 181.

160   **During a televised press conference**: London Airport press conference, February 22, 1964.

16: ELEANOR RIGBY

164   **"Americans seem to believe"**: *David Frost at the Phonograph*, interview recorded August 1, 1966

164   **"There they were in America"**: McCartney interviewed by Maureen Cleave, *Evening Standar*d, March 25, 1966, 8.

164   **"When I meet intelligent and hip people"**: *Melody Maker*, April 10, 1965.

165   **"temperamental and moody"**: Epstein, *A Cellarful of Noise*, 95.

165   **"shrivelling wit"**: Maureen Cleave in *Evening Standard*, March 25, 1966, 8.

165   **"I knew perfectly well"**: Tony Barrow, *John, Paul, George, Ringo and Me: The Real Beatles Story* (London: SevenOaks, 2005), 49.

166   **"Why don't you have Eleanor Rigby dying"**: Shotton and Schaffner, *John Lennon: In My Life*, 124.

166   **"By that time"**: Lennon, interviewed by David Sheff, September 1980, published in *Playboy*, January 1981.

17: HERE, THERE AND EVERYWHERE

169   **"I remember one of my special memories"**: Coleman, *Yesterday—and Today*, 98–99.

171   **"It's so neat"**: McCartney interview with Terry Gross, *Fresh Air*, NPR, November 3, 2021.

18: STRAWBERRY FIELDS FOREVER

173   **"We have been Beatles"**: quoted in "Old Beatles: A Study in Paradox," *New York Times Magazine*, July 3, 1966.

174   **"We'll take a couple of weeks to recuperate"**: Harrison interviewed in the *Daily Mirror*, July 9, 1966, 5.

175   **"Christianity will go"**: Lennon interview with Maureen Cleave, *Evening Standard*, March 4, 1966, 10.

176   **"He was terrified"**: quoted in Turner, *Beatles '66*, 283.

176   **"I couldn't stand"**: Starr interview with Art Unger for *Datebook*, August 1966, quoted in Turner, *Beatles '66*, 300.

176   **"I've reached the point in my life"**: Lennon interview with Art Unger, 1965, quoted in Turner, *Beatles '66*, 283.

176   **"I didn't mean what everybody thinks"**: Astor Towers press conference, Chicago, August 11, 1966. https://youtu.be/5ZaI7m1xpAg?si=KizdUDzngF6wq-cN.

178   **"A lot of it was just insincere"**: McCartney quoted in *Detroit Free Press*, August 19, 1966, 26.

178   **"By the time I was nineteen"**: second press conference, Chicago, August 11, 1966.

179   **"When we started at the Cavern"**: McCartney quoted in *Daily Express*, August 27, 1966.

179   **"That's it. I'm not a Beatle anymore"**: Barrow, *John, Paul, George, Ringo and Me*, 208.

179   **"There is so much I would like to do"**: quoted in Turner, *Beatles '66*, 312.

180   **"I couldn't hardly speak"**: Lennon interview with Leonard Gross, *Look*, December 13, 1966, 59.

180   **"life without the Beatles"**: Lennon, quoted in *The Beatles Anthology*, 231.

180   **"psychoanalysis set to music"**: Lennon, quoted in *The Beatles Anthology*, 231.

181   **"the sense you have"**: Brian Eno interview with David Marchese, *New York Times*, November 20, 2022.

184   **"microtonal borderland"**: Ian MacDonald, *Revolution in the Head: The Beatles' Records and the Sixties* (1998; rev. ed., London: Vintage, 2008), 219.

185   **"Let everything happen to you"**: Rainer Maria Rilke, "Go to the Limits of Your Longing," in *Rilke's Book of Hours: Love Poems to God*, trans. Joanna Macy and Anita Barrows (New York, 1997).

19: PENNY LANE

187 **"He went off to make a film":** McCartney quoted in Coleman, *Yesterday—and Today*, 102.

189 **"Paul and I want to write a stage musical":** Lennon quoted in *Rave*, February 1964, 10.

189 **"we are resigned to the fact":** McCartney interview with Keith Altham, *New Musical Express*, November 12, 1965, 10.

190 **"one of the most competitive":** quoted in Thomas Kitts, *Ray Davies: Not Like Everybody Else* (New York, 2008), 104.

192 **Adam Gopnik has proposed this single:** Adam Gopnik, "Strawberry Fields Forever/Penny Lane," in Andrew Blaumer (ed.), *In Their Lives: Great Writers on Beatles Songs* (New York: Blue Rider, 2017).

20: A DAY IN THE LIFE

195 **"Paul had changed so much":** Jane Asher, quoted in Davies, *The Beatles*, 434.

196 **"Make it so I don't sound like me":** McCartney, quoted in Geoff Emerick, *Here, There, and Everywhere: My Life Recording the Music of the Beatles* (New York, 2006), 147.

197 **"You get a wonderful sound":** George Martin, *Summer of Love: The Making of Sgt Pepper* (London: Pan, 1995), 61.

200 **"that was something. I dug it":** Lennon, quoted in *Rolling Stone*, November 23, 1968.

200 **"Paul's contribution":** Lennon, interviewed by David Sheff, September 1980, published in *Playboy*, January 1981.

21: GETTING BETTER

203 **"George, I'm not feeling too good":** quoted in Martin, *Summer of Love*, 109.

204 **"get with John":** quoted in Martin, *Summer of Love*, 110.

204 **"maybe this is the moment":** quoted in Miles, *Paul McCartney*, 382.

204 **"something disturbing":** quoted in Miles, *Paul McCartney*, 383.

204 **"this fantastic *thing*":** quoted in Derek Taylor, *It Was Twenty Years Ago Today* (London and New York, 1987), 21.

204 **"The last four songs":** quoted in Davies, *The Beatles*, 391.

205 **"pluck it out of a mass of noises":** Davies, *The Beatles*, 380.

205 **"singing it very loudly":** Davies, *The Beatles*, 381.

205   **Davies was also around to see how "Getting Better" came into being:** this
       passage draws on Davies, *The Beatles*, esp. 384.

206   **"Once more":** Davies, *The Beatles*, 385.

206   **"they'd got it at least":** Davies, *The Beatles*, 388.

207   **"This is the new thing":** Lennon, quoted in Derek Taylor, *Fifty Years Adrift*
       (Guildford, 1984), 296.

207   **"They'd wander round":** Cynthia Lennon, *John*, 183.

207   **McCartney remembers being at John's house:** interview in *Rolling Stone*, July
       25, 2013.

22: I AM THE WALRUS

209   **"I thought it would be nice to lose our identities":** McCartney, quoted in
       Playboy, December 1984.

209   **"we weren't the Beatles anymore":** McCartney, quoted in Joe Smith, *Off the
       Record: An Oral History of Popular Music* (New York, 1988), 201.

211   **"We realised for the first time":** interview with Alan Aldridge, *Observer*
       magazine, November 26, 1967.

213   **"You would hear it from cars":** Ellen Sander, *Trips: Rock Life in the Sixties* (1973;
       repr., Mineola, NY, 2019), 95.

213   **"In every city":** Langdon Winner, quoted in *The Rolling Stone Illustrated History
       of Rock & Roll* (New York, 1976), 183.

214   **"[We] don't really want to be spanked anymore":** recording made July 12, 1967,
       by fans Leslie Samuels, Donna Stark, and Beverly Sayers. https://www.youtube
       .com/watch?v=2p-JGoORkx0.

216   **He told Hunter Davies:** quotations in this section are from Davies, *The Beatles*,
       290, 418, 422.

218   **"My happiest memory":** Alistair Taylor, *With the Beatles* (2003; repr., London,
       2012), 177.

218   **"The last thing Paul wanted":** Marianne Faithfull, quoted in Miles, *Paul
       McCartney*, 377.

219   **"What I would like":** Cynthia Lennon, quoted in Davies, *The Beatles*, 298.

220   **"Tell them to let you on":** quoted in Cynthia Lennon, *John*, 197.

220   **"I am certain":** *Melody Maker*, August 19, 1967, 14.

221   **"I knew that we were in trouble":** Lennon interview with Jann Wenner, *Rolling
       Stone*, January 21, 1971.

222   **"A record is sound":** quoted in Barry Miles, *Beatles in Their Own Words* (London, 1978), 111.

222   **"the look of emptiness":** Emerick, *Here, There and Everywhere*, 214.

222   **"I showed him the door":** Lennon, quoted in *Evening Standard*, March 4, 1966, 10.

222   **"Dear Dad":** letter from John Lennon to Alfred Lennon, September 1, 1967, reproduced in Hunter Davies (ed.), *The John Lennon Letters* (London: Weidenfeld & Nicolson, 2016), 102.

223   **"You have to be a bastard":** Lennon interview with Jann Wenner, *Rolling Stone*, January 21, 1971.

223   **"the whole first verse":** Lennon, quoted in *Rolling Stone*, November 23, 1968.

224   **"I had 'I am he'":** Lennon, quoted in *Rolling Stone*, November 23, 1968.

23: LADY MADONNA

226   **"I was always drawn":** McCartney quoted on paulmccartney.com, "You Gave Me the Answer: Life on the Farm in Scotland," November 30, 2021.

227   **"I didn't write any of that":** comment at a private September 9, 1969, meeting, taped because Ringo could not attend. Quoted in Anthony Fawcett, *John Lennon: One Day at a Time* (New York: Grove, 1981), 92.

24: YER BLUES

232   **"They were very tight":** Paul Saltzman, interviewed by Nikhila Natarajan, *Firstpost*, December 18, 2015.

233   **John's notebook suggests:** Lennon's notebook is reproduced in the booklet from the fiftieth anniversary deluxe reissue of the *White Album*, 42, 44, 58.

233   **"huge spiritual lift-off . . . if there ever would be any Beatles again":** McCartney, quoted in Miles, *Paul McCartney*, 409, 414, 428.

233   **"He seemed very isolated":** Cynthia Lennon, quoted in Ray Coleman, *John Lennon* (London: Pan, 1984), 341.

233   **fragments of poems and gnomic aphorisms:** interview with Lennon in *Look* magazine, March 18, 1969.

234   **"I didn't think it was enough":** McCartney, quoted in Miles, *Paul McCartney*, 429.

234   **"John had wanted to leave":** Harrison, quoted in *The Beatles Anthology*, 286.

235   **"songs of such pain":** Lennon, interviewed by Jann Wenner, *Rolling Stone*, January 21, 1971.

235   **"completely reversed himself":** Harrison, quoted in Taylor, *Fifty Years Adrift*, 330.

235   **"a few things happened":** interview with Jonathan Cott, *Rolling Stone*, November 23, 1968.

236   **John ranted about the Maharishi:** Miles, *Paul McCartney*, 428–29.

236   **"John was in a rage":** Harrison, quoted in Taylor, *Fifty Years Adrift*, 330.

236   **"He was more fucked up":** Pete Shotton, quoted in Spitz, *The Beatles*, 760.

236   **"pointed out which songs I'd written":** Lennon, interviewed by Jann Wenner, *Rolling Stone*, January 21, 1971.

25: LOOK AT ME

239   **"I wrote six hundred songs":** unreleased home recording of "Maharishi Song," c. 1969. https://youtu.be/IF76fXSpdSI?si=L9tKKIt4LC26jHWQ.

240   **"no one ever hurt him":** Yoko Ono interview with Philip Norman, *New York* magazine, May 25, 1981, 40.

240   **"there was something going on here":** Yoko Ono, quoted in Norman, *John Lennon*, 669.

240   **"if [Paul] had been a woman or something":** audio and transcript of Yoko Ono audio diary at https://amoralto.tumblr.com/post/40350502633/june-4th-1968-emi -studios-while-the-beatles#40350502633.

240   **"I think he had a desire":** Yoko Ono interview with Tim Teeman, *Daily Beast*, October 13, 2015.

241   **"Paul would come in":** Little Richard, quoted in Norman, *Paul McCartney: The Life*, 231.

241   **"Epstein's defenses would melt away":** Barrow, *John, Paul, George, Ringo and Me*, 49.

241   **Hodges's main memory:** as told to Pete Paphides, "Listen to What the Man Said: The Tao of Paul McCartney in Ten Songs," *Medium*, June 17, 2022.

241   **"It's only me":** Miles, *Paul McCartney*, 588.

241   **"'What are you thinking?'":** Yoko Ono, quoted in Norman, *John Lennon*, 549.

26: HEY JUDE

244   **"Paul, for the longest time":** Peter Brown, quoted in Spitz, *The Beatles*, 759.

244   **"We don't plan":** press conference at the Americana Hotel, New York, May 14, 1968. https://www.youtube.com/watch?v=lC5bUE2d_c0&t=605s.

244   **"It's records and films":** interview with Larry Kane, May 13, 1968. https://www .youtube.com/watch?v=rkegOnIj_rU.

244   **"John and Paul's madness":** Harrison, quoted in *The Beatles Anthology*, 287.

246   **"We both played the field"**: McCartney interview with Chrissie Hynde, *USA Weekend*, October 30, 1998.

246   **"Paul's whole demeanour"**: Nat Weiss, quoted in Spitz, *The Beatles*, 761.

247   **"I don't believe in collectivism"**: Yoko Ono, "To the Wesleyan People," January 23, 1966, reproduced in *Yoko Ono: One Woman Show, 1960–1971* (New York, 2015), 147.

247   **"She never felt happy"**: quoted in Louis Menand, "Yoko Ono's Art of Defiance," *New Yorker*, June 13, 2022.

247   **"She wasn't relaxed, ever"**: quoted in Menand, "Yoko Ono's Art of Defiance."

247   **"It was like an establishment"**: quoted in Menand, "Yoko Ono's Art of Defiance."

247   **"sighs, breathing, gasping"**: Jill Johnston, "Life and Art," *Village Voice*, December 7, 1961, reproduced in *Yoko Ono: One Woman Show*, 77.

249   **"It's a great relief"**: Lennon, interviewed by Jann Wenner, *Rolling Stone*, January 21, 1971.

249   **"That's when we locked eyes"**: Lennon, interviewed by David Sheff, September 1980, published in *Playboy*, January 1981.

249   **"barely turned his head"**: Cynthia Lennon, *John*, 212.

250   **"So you fancy her, then?"**: quoted in Shotton and Schaffner, *John Lennon: In My Life*, 168.

250   **"It was midnight when we started"**: Lennon, interviewed by Jann Wenner, *Rolling Stone*, January 21, 1971.

250   **"Oh, hi"**: quoted in Cynthia Lennon, *A Twist of Lennon*, 183.

250   **"Paul, in his usual way"**: Peter Brown, quoted in Spitz, *The Beatles*, 774.

251   **"just moved in . . . talking in corners"**: Harrison and Starr, quoted in *The Beatles Anthology*, 308.

252   **"Paul was positively *livid*"**: Alan Brown quoted in Spitz, *The Beatles*, 779.

252   **"Paul has been very nice to me"**: audio and transcript of Yoko Ono audio diary at https://amoralto.tumblr.com/post/40350502633/june-4th-1968-emi-studios-while-the-beatles#40350502633.

253   **"The moment Linda arrived"**: Tony Bramwell, quoted in Spitz, *The Beatles*, 781.

253   **"like Siamese twins"**: Tony Bramwell with Rosemary Kingsland, *Magical Mystery Tours: My Life with the Beatles* (London: Robson, 2005), Kindle edition.

253   **"Paul was absolutely devastated"**: Alistair Taylor, *With the Beatles*, 217.

253   **"I thought it was a bit much"**: McCartney, quoted in Miles, *Paul McCartney*, 465.

253   **"It made me feel important"**: Cynthia Lennon, *A Twist of Lennon*, 189.

253   **"Paul and I used to hang out"**: Julian Lennon, quoted in *Mojo*, February 2002.

254   **"You won't, you know"**: quoted in Miles, *Paul McCartney*, 465.

254   **"Yoko's just come into the picture"**: Lennon, interviewed by David Sheff, September 1980, published in *Playboy*, January 1981.

254   **"Check. We're going through the same bit"**: interview with Jonathan Cott, *Rolling Stone*, November 23, 1968.

255   **"one of Paul's masterpieces"**: Lennon, interviewed by David Sheff, September 1980, published in *Playboy*, January 1981.

255   **"I'm cynical about society"**: Lennon, quoted in *Look* magazine, December 13, 1966.

27: JULIA

260   **"Well, that's an interesting one"**: McCartney, quoted in Michael Lindsay-Hogg, *Luck and Circumstance: A Coming of Age in Hollywood, New York, and Points Beyond* (New York: Knopf, 2011), Kindle edition.

260   **"That's Paul"**: Lennon, interviewed by David Sheff, September 1980, published in *Playboy*, January 1981.

260   **"Your personal finances are in a mess"**: Stephen Maltz, *The Beatles Apple and Me* (Kindle e-book, 2015).

261   **"Paul was always slightly insecure"**: Maggie McGivern, interviewed in 1997, quoted at https://sentstarr.tripod.com/beatgirls/mcgiv.html.

261   **"very strong together"**: McCartney interview with Chris Salewicz, *Q*, October 1986.

262   **"The first year we got together"**: McCartney interview with Chrissie Hynde, *USA Weekend*, October 30, 1998.

263   **"Don't cry"**: quoted in Francie Schwartz, *Body Count* (San Francisco, 1972), 89.

263   **Iris Caldwell . . . recalled**: Norman, *Paul McCartney*, 213.

264   **"I've never forgiven myself"**: McCartney interview with Joan Goodman, *Playboy*, December 1984.

264   **"pleasantly insincere"**: *New Musical Express*, August 17, 1968.

264   **"galvanising effect"**: Shotton and Schaffner, *John Lennon: In My Life*, 171.

265   **"Yoko looks upon men"**: Lennon, interviewed by David Sheff, September 1980, published in *Playboy*, January 1981.

265   **"She enabled the child in John to resurface":** Shotton and Schaffner, *John Lennon: In My Life*, 171.

265   **"John had grown up":** Cynthia Lennon, *John*, 256.

265   **Ono told Philip Norman:** Norman, *John Lennon*, 552.

265   **"We could recognize":** McCartney, quoted in *Playboy*, December 1984.

266   **Paul had also been at the session:** Giles Martin, interviewed in *Rock Cellar*, November 6, 2018.

28: MARTHA MY DEAR

268   **Paul said it's about a dog:** Miles, *Paul McCartney*, 498.

268   **Hunter Davies's account:** Davies, *The Beatles*, 383.

268   **"One of the unlikely side effects":** Paul McCartney, *The Lyrics: 1956 to the Present*, ed. Paul Muldoon (London: Allen Lane, 2021).

29: GET BACK

271   **"I don't dig under-estimating":** McCartney, quoted in Peter Doggett, *You Never Give Me Your Money: The Battle for the Soul of the Beatles* (London: Vintage, 2009), 58.

276   **"Paul does it":** Adam Gopnik, "A Close Read of the Beatles in *Get Back*," *New Yorker*, December 16, 2021.

30: TWO OF US

279   **"I think I'll be . . . leaving the band":** *The Beatles: Get Back*, 91.

280   **"One of the great things about Linda":** McCartney, *The Lyrics*, 737.

281   **"Lying behind the phrase":** McCartney, *The Lyrics*, 737.

282   **digging up gold coins:** McCartney interview with Jane Graham in *The Big Issue*, February 16, 2012.

282   **"With our heightened awareness":** audio of recording session, January 13, 1969, https://amoralto.tumblr.com/post/50727836802/january-13th-1969-as-everyone -waits-for-john-and.

282   **a densely allusive exchange:** a full transcript of the flowerpot conversation by Dan Rivkin is available at theymaybeparted.com.

31: DON'T LET ME DOWN

288   **"There's no clever words in it":** *Get Back* documentary, January 6, 1969.

289 **"When it gets down to it"**: Lennon, interviewed by Jann Wenner, *Rolling Stone*, January 21, 1971.

289 **"Probably in a bag in his dressing room"**: audio of recording session, January 10, 1969. https://theymaybeparted.com/2021/03/15/jan-10-et-cetera.

290 **"make that bass sing"**: George Martin, *Summer of Love*, 85.

32: THE BALLAD OF JOHN AND YOKO

291 **"Apple is losing money"**: Lennon interview with Ray Coleman, *Disc*, January 18, 1969, 8.

293 **"I was very surprised with Linda"**: Lennon interview with McCabe and Schonfeld at St. Regis Hotel, August–September 1971.

294 **"What do you think, Mal"**: unpublished memoir by Mal Evans quoted in Kenneth Womack, *Living the Beatles Legend: The Untold Story of Mal Evans* (New York, 2023), Kindle edition.

294 **"Paul was really upset"**: Linda McCartney, as told to Danny Fields, quoted in Doggett, *You Never Give Me Your Money*, 73.

295 **"Everything we do"**: Lennon, quoted in *Liverpool Daily Post*, March 22, 1969, 1.

296 **"I don't have to ring Paul"**: Lennon, quoted in *Daily Telegraph*, March 31, 1969, 2.

296 **"It's a piece of journalism"**: Lennon, interviewed by David Sheff, September 1980, published in *Playboy*, January 1981.

297 **"It has always surprised me"**: McCartney, quoted in Miles, *Paul McCartney*, 551.

33: OH! DARLING

299 **"There was no alternative"**: Derek Taylor, quoted in Doggett, *You Never Give Me Your Money*, 81.

299 **"You are a rodent"**: court testimony from 1971, quoted in Doggett, *You Never Give Me Your Money*, 78.

300 **"At one point I thought"**: Peter Brown, quoted in Doggett, *You Never Give Me Your Money*, 78.

300 **"John was really angry"**: Wendy Sutcliffe, interviewed for *Mojo*, 1996, quoted in Doggett, *You Never Give Me Your Money*, 80.

301 **"The other three said . . . I'm not signing now"**: McCartney, quoted in *The Beatles Anthology*, 326.

304 **"virtually built around"**: Martin, *Summer of Love*, 97.

305   **"One week Paul would be in the office"**: Tony Bramwell, quoted in Doggett, *You Never Give Me Your Money*, 97.

305   **"more my style than his"**: Lennon, interviewed by David Sheff, September 1980, published in *Playboy*, January 1981.

34: THE END

308   **"Ringo—you can't be here"**: Quotations from this conversation are from Fawcett, *One Day at a Time*, 96–97, and Richard Williams, "This Tape Rewrites Everything We Knew About the Beatles," *Guardian*, September 11, 2019.

309   **"The Beatles are always discussing"**: recording of interview from September 12, 1969. https://thecoleopterawithana.tumblr.com/post/667147033648447488/john-lennon-and-yoko-ono-give-a-series-of.

309   **McCartney was asked for his favorite tracks**: interview with David Wigg for BBC Radio 1, *Scene and Heard*, taped September 19, 1969, broadcast September 21 and 28, 1969.

310   **"John looked at me in the eye"**: McCartney, quoted in *The Beatles Anthology*, 347.

310   **"Paul just kept mithering on"**: Ray Connolly, "John Lennon: The Lost Interviews," *Sunday Times*, July 25, 2014.

310   **"We had to react to [John]"**: McCartney, quoted in *The Beatles Anthology*, 347.

310   **"wildly hurtful"**: McCartney, *The Lyrics*, 193.

310   **"heartbreaking experience"**: Mal Evans interview with Laura Gross, KCSN, November 29, 1975. https://thecoleopterawithana.tumblr.com/post/180256532730/amoralto-november-29th-1975-beatles-roadie.

311   **"The Beatle thing is over"**: McCartney, quoted in *Life*, November 7, 1969.

311   **"I don't write for the Beatles"**: Lennon interview with Barry Miles, September 23–24, 1969, quoted in Doggett, *You Never Give Me Your Money*, 104.

311   **"differences of opinion"**: Lennon interview in *New Musical Express*, December 13, 1969, 3.

311   **"go on appealing"**: Lennon interview in *Melody Maker*, December 6, 1969, 21. Interview conducted on November 25, 1969.

311   **"Everybody had tried to leave"**: Harrison, quoted in *The Beatles Anthology*, 348.

311   **"one of John's little flings"**: McCartney, quoted in *The Beatles Anthology*, 349.

312   **"We're not breaking up the band"**: New Experimental College press conference, January 5, 1970. https://www.hs.fi/paivanlehti/09012020/art-2000006366438.html.

312   **"instant family"**: interview with David Wigg for BBC Radio 1, *Scene and Heard*, taped September 19, 1969, broadcast September 21 and 28, 1969.

312   **"The idea of instant karma"**: Lennon, interviewed by David Sheff, September 1980, published in *Playboy*, January 1981.

312   **"a rebirth or a death"**: interview with David Wigg for BBC Radio 1, *Scene and Heard*, February 5, 1970, broadcast February 15, 1970.

314   **"We're sorry it turned out like this"**: letter dated March 31, 1970, reproduced in *The Beatles Anthology*, 351.

314   **"He told me to get out of his house"**: Starr, quoted in *Melody Maker*, July 31, 1971, 15.

314   **"I will see him"**: McCartney interview with Jann Wenner, *Rolling Stone*, April 30, 1970.

314   **"I told him on the phone"**: McCartney interview with Ray Connolly, *Evening Standard*, April 21, 1970, 24.

314   **"*Are you planning a new album*"**: Apple press release for *McCartney*, April 10, 1970.

315   **"Paul said to me"**: Lennon, quoted in Keith Badman, *The Beatles Diary*, vol. 2: *After the Break-Up, 1970–2001* (1999; new ed., London, 2009), Kindle location 201.

315   **"We were all hurt"**: quoted in Badman, *Off the Record*, 494.

315   **"a good PR man"**: Lennon, interviewed by Jann Wenner, *Rolling Stone*, January 21, 1971.

315   **in 1986 McCartney conceded**: McCartney, interview in *Rolling Stone*, September 11, 1986.

315   **"When it was printed"**: McCartney, interview in *Playboy*, April 1984.

316   **"I was happy to hear from Paul"**: Lennon, quoted in *Disc and Music Echo*, April 18, 1970.

316   **"permanent maybe"**: Allen Klein, quoted in *Disc and Music Echo*, April 18, 1970.

316   **"I was going through a bad time"**: McCartney, quoted in Miles, *Paul McCartney*, 570.

316   **"I didn't leave the Beatles"**: McCartney interview with Ray Connolly, *Evening Standard*, April 21, 1970, 24.

35: GOD

319   **"Give us our freedom"**: McCartney interview with Ray Connolly, *Evening Standard*, April 21, 1970, 24.

320   **"The reality is that he's outvoted"**: Harrison, quoted in Doggett, *You Never Give Me Your Money*, 135.

320   **"She's a junkie"**: quoted in Ray Connolly, *Being John Lennon: A Restless Life* (London: Weidenfeld & Nicolson, 2018), 322.

320   **"80 percent of all ailments"**: Arthur Janov, *The Primal Scream* (New York, 1970).

320   **"psychophysical"**: Janov, *The Primal Scream*, 154.

321   **"such consistent expressions of anger"**: Sascha Frühholz, quoted in Nicola Davis, "Little Evidence Screaming Helps Mental Health, Say Psychologists," *Guardian*, September 23, 2022.

321   **"The level of his pain was enormous"**: Arthur Janov, quoted in Norman, *John Lennon*, 639–40.

321   **"reviled his dead Mother"**: quoted in Norman, *John Lennon*, 654.

322   **"awful, it was fucking humiliation"**: Lennon, interviewed by Jann Wenner, *Rolling Stone*, January 21, 1971.

323   **"stoned out of my fucking mind"**: Martin, quoted in *Goldmine*, November 12, 1993.

323   **"It was when I felt resentful"**: Lennon, quoted in Sheff, *All We Are Saying*, 137.

323   **took them for a drive:** This story is related in Joe Hagan, *Sticky Fingers: The Life and Times of Jann Wenner* (Edinburgh: Canongate, 2017), 6.

325   **In August, he wrote a letter:** letters from McCartney and Lennon quoted in Doggett, *You Never Give Me Your Money*, 136–37.

325   **"All summer long"**: McCartney, interviewed in *Life*, April 16, 1971.

325   **"to put out of its misery"**: McCartney, quoted in *Melody Maker*, August 29, 1970.

36: HOW DO YOU SLEEP?

327   **"driven to make this application"**: quoted in Doggett, *You Never Give Me Your Money*, 154.

328   **He asked Eirik Wangberg:** related in an interview with Wangberg for the *One Sweet Dream* podcast, hosted by Diane Erickson, May 3, 2023.

329   **"rubbish"**: *Rolling Stone*, January 21, 1971, 35.

329   **"This open hostility"**: McCartney, interviewed in *Life*, April 16, 1971.

329   **"I hated it"**: McCartney, interviewed in *Rolling Stone*, January 31, 1974.

329   **"I hope you realize what shit"**: https://www.rrauction.com/auctions/lot-detail /348280907074043-john-lennon-typed-and-hand-annotated-letter-to-paul-and

-linda-mccartney-an-intense-letter-discussing-yoko-art-the-media-and-his-exit
-from-the-beatles.

330 **"From our earliest days"**: quoted in Doggett, *You Never Give Me Your Money*, 158.

330 **"One has only to look at recent recordings"**: quoted in Doggett, *You Never Give Me Your Money*, 161.

330 **"it is in the common interest"**: quoted in *Birmingham Post*, April 27, 1971, 7.

331 **"I think I finally wrote a song"**: Lennon, quoted by Howard Smith, interviewed for *Mojo*, July 6, 2013.

332 **"Some of it was absolutely puerile"**: quoted in Miles, *Paul McCartney*, 585.

332 **"horrifying and indefensible"**: *Rolling Stone*, October 28, 1971.

332 **"It's not serious"**: interview with Howard Smith, September 9, 1971. https://youtu.be/HEWEDhHthzA?si=ixJBCdOyXFflpky1.

332 **"an outburst"**: Lennon, interviewed in *Washington Post*, October 9, 1971.

332 **"to encourage Paul"**: Lennon, interview with Ray Connolly, *Radio Times*, May 1972.

332 **"It's not about Paul"**: interview with Bob Harris for *The Old Grey Whistle Test*, BBC2, April 18, 1975.

333 **"the unabashed leader"**: Ken Mansfield, interviewed in *Daytrippin' Beatles Magazine*, February 2, 2013.

333 **"I understood what happened"**: McCartney, quoted in Davies, *The Beatles*, 512.

333 **"If I cannot have a fight"**: Lennon, interviewed on the *Mike Douglas Show*, February 1972.

37: DEAR FRIEND

335 **"I didn't want to get into a slanging match"**: McCartney, quoted in Miles, *Paul McCartney*, 586–87.

335 **"Part of it was cowardice"**: McCartney, quoted in Miles, *Paul McCartney*, 586.

336 **"'Dear Friend' was written about John"**: McCartney, interviewed for *Club Sandwich*, 1994.

38: JEALOUS GUY

340 **"I've always been politically minded"**: Lennon, interviewed in *Red Mole*, February "12, 1971.

340 **"The thing that made the Beatles"**: Lennon, interviewed in *Cash Box*, December 11, 1971, 25.

340   **"the title rightfully belonged"**: Erin Torkelson Weber, *The Beatles and the Historians: An Analysis of Writings About the Fab Four* (Jefferson, NC, 2016), Kindle location 1797.

341   **"traditional bohemian contempt"**: *Rolling Stone*, October 28, 1971.

341   **"I think it's silly"**: McCartney interview with Chris Charlesworth, *Melody Maker*, November 20, 1971.

342   **"If *you're not* the aggressor"**: Lennon's letter published in *Melody Maker*, December 4, 1971.

343   **"He wanted to tell Paul something"**: Ray Connolly, quoted in Doggett, *You Never Give Me Your Money*, 184.

343   **"Happy Xmas!"**: postcard reproduced in Davies, ed., *The John Lennon Letters*, 233.

343   **"It was a weird time"**: McCartney interview with Diane de Dubovay, *Playgirl*, February 1985.

344   **"The lyrics explain themselves"**: Lennon, interviewed by David Sheff, September 1980, published in *Playboy*, January 1981.

344   **"I love Yoko"**: Lennon, interviewed on *Woman's Hour*, BBC Radio, May 28, 1971.

344   **"We tell ourselves a story"**: Parul Sehgal, "An Ode to Envy," TED Talk, 2013.

344   **scrawled bitter notes**: Excerpts from the annotations were quoted in the *Observer*, July 20, 1986, 1.

345   **"The way we work"**: McCartney, quoted in Alfred G. Aronowitz, "Yeah! Yeah! Yeah! Music's Gold Bugs: The Beatles," *Saturday Evening Post*, March 21, 1964, 33.

39: LET ME ROLL IT

347   **"It's a beautiful apartment"**: May Pang and Henry Edwards, *Loving John* (New York: Warner, 1983), 56.

348   **"if George Harrison can put out a triple album"**: Yoko Ono, interviewed in *Rolling Stone*, March 1, 1973.

348   **"Physically I was starting to feel"**: Yoko Ono, quoted in Norman, *Lennon: The Life*, 705.

349   **"I believe they did love each other"**: Pang and Edwards, *Loving John*, 49.

349   **"always an extremist"**: Pang and Edwards, *Loving John*, 62.

350   **"There was a lot of speed"**: Roy Cicala, quoted in Doyle, *Man on the Run*, 138.

351   **"I'm starting all over again"**: McCartney, quoted in David Bennahaum, *The*

Beatles . . . After the Break-Up: In Their Own Words (London and New York, 1991), 28.

351 **"In fact we've been *doing*":** Lennon's letter, published in *Melody Maker*, December 4, 1971.

352 **"He does what he does":** Henry McCullough, quoted in Doyle, *Man on the Run*, 87.

352 **"The media would be reporting":** Gary van Syoc interview with Bob Wilson for *Live for Live Music*, December 18, 2015.

353 **"The weird thing was turning left and right":** Lennon, quoted in Doggett, *You Never Give Me Your Money*, 196.

353 **"Paul would most probably have joined in":** Lennon interview with Chris Charlesworth, *Melody Maker*, November 3, 1973.

353 **"possibly Paul's suspicions":** Lennon, quoted in Badman, *The Beatles Diary*, vol. 2, 95.

353 **"just a piece of nothing":** Lennon, interviewed by David Sheff, September 1980, published in *Playboy*, January 1981.

354 **"Like, just *staring*":** McCartney, quoted in Taylor, *It Was Twenty Years Ago Today*, 21.

354 **"non-confident":** Linda McCartney, quoted in *Sounds*, April 3, 1976.

354 **"I still don't think it sounds like him":** McCartney, quoted in Paul Gambaccini, *Paul McCartney in His Own Words* (London and New York, 1976), 83.

355 **"I remember first singing":** McCartney, *The Lyrics*, 421.

40: I SAW HER STANDING THERE

357 **"Do you still love him?":** McCartney's recollections, from an interview with Chris Salewicz, *Q*, October 1986.

358 **"What is it?":** quoted in Hagan, *Sticky Fingers*, 372.

358 **"Touching is good!":** story told by Hagan on the Beatles Books podcast, November 2021, based on his interview with McCartney. In 2016, McCartney, interviewed by *Rolling Stone*, used a slightly different version of the phrase: "[John] hugged me. It was great, because we didn't normally do that. He said, 'It's good to touch.' I always remembered that—it's good to touch." David Frick, "Paul McCartney Looks Back," *Rolling Stone*, August 10, 2016.

358 **"I just churned that out":** Lennon, interview with Andy Peebles for BBC Radio 1, December 6, 1980.

359 **"Walls keep you in":** Lennon, quoted in Nicholas Schaffner, *The Beatles Forever* (New York, 1992), 174.

359   **"a couple of Beaujolais evenings"**: Lennon interview with Dennis Elsas, WNEW-FM, September 28, 1974, https://www.youtube.com/watch?v=hfU _b5nsvrU.

359   **"What would you think"**: Pang, quoted in Danny Fields, *Linda McCartney* (Los Angeles, 2000), 209.

360   **Elton suggested "Imagine"**: Tony King, *The Tastemaker: My Life with the Legends and Geniuses of Rock Music* (London: Faber and Faber, 2023), 7.

360   **"You know, May"**: Yoko Ono, quoted in Pang and Edwards, *Loving John*, 267.

361   **Yoko broke into a sobbing fit**: King, *The Tastemaker*, 106.

361   **Pang was pretty sure**: Pang and Edwards, *Loving John*, 286.

361   **"Then possibley"**: reproduced in Davies, ed., *The John Lennon Letters*, 324.

361   **"Listen to this balloon"**: Chip Madinger and Scott Raile, *Lennonology*, e-book via lennonology.com, 435.

362   **"I think [Julian] likes Paul"**: Lennon interview with Francis Schoenberger for *Bravo*, March 28, 1975.

41: COMING UP

363   **"Yoko has allowed me to come home"**: Lennon, quoted in Pang and Edwards, *Loving John*, 291.

363   **"His spirit, his wit"**: Pang and Edwards, *Loving John*, 318.

363   **"previous incarnation"**: John Lennon, *Skywriting by Word of Mouth, and Other Writings* (New York, 1986), 14.

364   **"all eyes for the baby"**: interview with Eliot Mintz, Earth News Radio, January 1976. https://youtu.be/o4tAmScwAQ4?si=CUILKZSe_XWelf0M.

364   **"I never stopped wanting"**: Lennon, quoted in Pang and Edwards, *Loving John*, 325.

365   **"I suppose I am from another age"**: McCartney interview with Chris Welch, *Melody Maker*, September 20, 1975.

365   **"right back up to the level"**: McCartney, quoted in Doyle, *Man on the Run*, 201.

365   **"very much back to his old self"**: Linda McCartney, quoted in Doyle, *Man on the Run*, 204.

366   **"It was like old friends"**: Doyle, *Man on the Run*, 183.

366   **"Paul would never face"**: Mike McCartney, *Thank U Very Much: Mike McCartney's Photo Album* (London: Arthur Barker, 1981), 186.

366   **"All you have to do"**: https://www.youtube.com/watch?v=ZHA3W416zSc.

367 **"It's not 1956":** Sheff, *All We Are Saying*, 82.

367 **"some very frightening phone calls":** Miles, *Paul McCartney*, 588.

367 **"What for?":** Lennon, quoted in Doggett, *You Never Give Me Your Money*, 247.

368 **"I was just doing this for my own insanity":** interview with Tim Rice, 1980. https://www.youtube.com/watch?v=xm5Hs2MhzOk&t=680s.

369 **"Fuck a pig":** Lennon, quoted in Fred Seaman, *The Last Days of John Lennon: A Personal Memoir* (New York, 1991), 122.

369 **"I thought that 'Coming Up' was great":** Lennon interview with Robert Hilburn, *Los Angeles Times*, October 10, 1980.

369 **"All my life I've been dreaming":** Lennon quoted in Seaman, *The Last Days*, 130.

42: (JUST LIKE) STARTING OVER

372 **"The guy made himself so wide open":** Hank Halsted, quoted in Womack, *John Lennon 1980*, 117.

372 **"It was brutal":** Tyler Coneys, quoted in Womack, *John Lennon 1980*, 117.

372 **"I was there, driving the boat":** Lennon, quoted in Sheff, *All We Are Saying*, 78.

373 **"I'm going to have a few songs on it":** Jack Douglas's recollections of Yoko Ono, quoted in *Beatlefan*, 1999.

374 **"I just thought 'Double Fantasy'":** Lennon interview with Laurie Kaye and Dave Sholin, December 8, 1980.

374 **"reminded him of a Beatles track":** Jonathan Cott, *Days That I'll Remember: Spending Time with John Lennon and Yoko Ono* (New York: Doubleday, 2013), 204.

374 **"He'd say, 'If you think that's better'":** Jack Douglas, quoted in *Beatlefan*, 1999.

375 **"lost weekend":** Pang and Edwards, *Loving John*, 315.

375 **"The creativity of songwriting":** Lennon, interviewed by David Sheff, September 1980, published in *Playboy*, January 1981.

376 **"I love those guys":** Lennon, quoted in Cott, *Days That I'll Remember*, 198.

376 **"Paul? My dear one":** Lennon interview with Robert Hilburn, *Los Angeles Times*, October 10, 1980.

376 **"more than a one-night stand":** http://www.beatlesarchive.net/john-lennons-last -interview-december-8-1980.html.

376 **"I love him":** Lennon, quoted by Dave Sholin, *Daily Express*, December 8, 2021.

378 **"they saw John walking down the street":** Harry Nilsson to Geoffrey Giuliano, 1984. https://www.youtube.com/watch?v=NqQ21dMsfys.

43: HERE TODAY

379   **"He was just very, very quiet"**: Denny Laine, quoted in Howard Sounes, *Fab: An Intimate Life of Paul McCartney* (London: Harper, 2010), 367.

380   **"the dubious whiff of incense"**: Ray Connolly, *Daily Mail*, December 3, 2005.

381   **"Why is it always Bobby Kennedy"**: Robert Christgau, "John Lennon 1940–80," *Village Voice*, December 22, 1980.

381   **"John Lennon was three-quarters"**: Philip Norman, *Shout!*, xxviii.

382   **"I'm kind of sentimental"**: Carl Perkins interview for *Goldmine*, 1995, and TV, 1997. https://youtu.be/oDcpnle0HnY?si=0TkciAfNDXnkFV0m.

382   **"John has gone"**: McCartney, quoted by Eric Stewart, in Sounes, *Fab*, 373.

383   **"crying about . . . how wonderful we were"**: McCartney, quoted in John Harris, "I'm Still Standing," *Guardian*, June 11, 2004.

384   **"I can't understand why Yoko is saying this"**: McCartney, quoted in Davies, *The Beatles*, 508–9.

386   **"You find yourself holding on"**: McCartney interview for *CBS Morning News*, October 15, 1984.

386   **"I still check my songs"**: McCartney interview with Sarah Ferguson for *ABC News 7:30*, August 2023.

386   **"delicious broth"**: McCartney interview in *Mojo*, November 1995.

387   **"very suspicious people"**: McCartney, quoted in Peter Brown and Steven Gaines, *All You Need Is Love: The End of the Beatles* (London, 2024), 30.

387   **"intense yearning"**: translation from the *Symposium* based on that by Benjamin Jowett.

388   **"We sought each other"**: Montaigne translation from Saul Frampton, *When I Am Playing with My Cat, How Do I Know She Is Not Playing with Me?: Montaigne and Being In Touch with Life* (London, 2011).

388   **"we never got to the bottom"**: McCartney, quoted in Davies, *The Beatles*, 513.

BIBLIOGRAPHY

Badman, Keith. *The Beatles Off the Record*. London: Omnibus, 2000; repr. 2007.

Baird, Julia. *Imagine This: Growing Up with My Brother, John Lennon*. London: Hodder & Stoughton, 2006; repr. 2017.

Barrow, Tony. *John, Paul, George, Ringo and Me: The Real Beatles Story*. London: André Deutsch, 2005.

The Beatles. *The Beatles Anthology*. London: Cassell, 2000.

Blaumer, Andrew (ed.). *In Their Lives: Great Writers on Great Beatles Songs*. New York: Blue Rider, 2017.

Bose, Ajoy. *Across the Universe: The Beatles in India*. London: Penguin, 2021.

Bramwell, Tony. *Magical Mystery Tours: My Life with the Beatles*. London: Robson, 2005.

Braun, Michael. *Love Me Do!: The Beatles' Progress*. London: Graymalkin Media, 1964; repr. 2019.

Brown, Craig. *One Two Three Four*. London: 4th Estate, 2020.

Brown, Peter. *The Love You Make: An Insider's Story of the Beatles*. New York: New American Library, 1983; repr. 2002.

Campion, James. *Take a Sad Song*. Guilford, CT: Backbeat, 2022.

Coleman, Ray. Lennon. London: Pan, 1984; repr. 2000.

———. McCartney: *Yesterday—and Today*. London: Boxtree, 1995.

Connolly, Ray. *Being John Lennon*. London: Weidenfeld & Nicolson, 2018.

Cott, Jonathan. *Days That I'll Remember: Spending Time with John Lennon and Yoko Ono*. New York: Doubleday, 2013.

Davies, Hunter. *The Beatles*. London: Ebury, 1968; repr. 2009.

Davies, Hunter (ed.). *The John Lennon Letters*. London: Weidenfeld & Nicolson, 2016.

Doggett, Peter. *You Never Give Me Your Money: The Battle for the Soul of the Beatles*. London: Vintage, 2009.

Doyle, Tom. *Man on the Run: Paul McCartney in the 1970s*. London: Polygon, 2014.

Elson, Howard. *McCartney—Songwriter*. London: Comet, 1986.

Epstein, Brian. *A Cellarful of Noise: The Man Who Made the Beatles*. London: Souvenir, 1964; repr. 2021.

Evans, Mike. *The Beatles: Paperback Writer*. London: Plexus, 2012.

Fawcett, Anthony. *John Lennon: One Day at a Time*. New York: Grove, 1981.

Feldman-Barrett, Christine. *A Women's History of the Beatles*. New York: Bloomsbury Academic, 2022.

Garry, Len. John, Paul & Me *Before the Beatles*. Peterborough: FastPrint Publishing, 2014.

Gooden, Joe. *Riding So High: The Beatles and Drugs*. London: Pepper & Pearl, 2017.

Gould, Jonathan. *Can't Buy Me Love*. London: Piatkus, 2007.

Hagan, Joe. *Sticky Fingers: The Life and Times of Jann Wenner*. Edinburgh: Canongate, 2017.

Harris, John, et al. *The Beatles: Get Back: By the Beatles*. London: Callaway Arts & Entertainment, 2021.

Inglis, Ian. *The Beatles in Hamburg*. London: Reaktion, 2012.

King, Tony. *The Tastemaker: My Life with the Legends and Geniuses of Rock Music*. London: Faber and Faber, 2023.

Kozinn, Alan, and Adrian Sinclair. *The McCartney Legacy Volume 1: 1969–73*. London: Dey Street, 2022.

———. *The McCartney Legacy Volume 2: 1974–80*. London: Dey Street, 2024.

Lennon, Cynthia. John. London: Hodder & Stoughton, 2005.

———. *A Twist of Lennon*. London: Star, 1978.

Lewisohn, Mark. *The Beatles—All These Years—Extended Special Edition—Volume 1: Tune In*. London: Little, Brown, 2013.

———. *The Beatles—All These Years—Volume 1: Tune In*. London: Little, Brown, 2013.

———. *The Complete Beatles Recording Sessions*. London: Bounty, 2013.

Lindsay-Hogg, Michael. *Luck and Circumstance: A Coming of Age in Hollywood, New York, and Points Beyond*. New York: Knopf, 2011.

Macdonald, Ian. *Revolution in the Head: The Beatles' Records and the Sixties*. London: Vintage, 1998; rev. ed. 2008.

Madinger, Chip, and Scott Raile. *Lennonology*. e-book via lennonology.com.

Mansfield, Ken. *The White Book*. Nashville, TN: Thomas Nelson, 2007.

Martin, George. *All You Need Is Ears*. New York: St. Martin's Griffin, 1979; repr. 2021.

———. *Summer of Love: The Making of "Sgt. Pepper."* London: Pan, 1995.

McCartney, Mike. *Thank U Very Much: Mike McCartney's Family Album*. London: Arthur Barker, 1981.

McCartney, Paul. *The Lyrics: 1956 to the Present*. ed. Paul Muldoon. London: Allen Lane, 2021.

Meddings, Luke. *What They Heard: How the Beatles, the Beach Boys and Bob Dylan Listened to Each Other and Changed Music Forever*. London: Weatherglass, 2021.

Miles, Barry. Paul McCartney: *Many Years From Now*. London: Secker & Warburg, 1998.

Norman, Philip. *John Lennon: The Life*. London: HarperCollins, 2008.

———. Paul McCartney: *The Life*. London: Weidenfeld & Nicolson, 2016.

———. Shout!: *The Beatles in Their Generation*. New York: Fireside, 1981; repr. 2005.

Pang, May, and Henry Edwards. *Loving John: The Untold Story*. New York: Warner, 1983.

Pedder, Dominic. *The Songwriting Secrets of the Beatles*. London: Omnibus, 2010.

Riley, Tim. Lennon: *The Man, The Myth, The Music—The Definitive Life*. London: Virgin, 2011.

———. *Tell Me Why: The Beatles, Song by Song, Album by Album, the Sixties and After*. Cambridge, MA: Da Capo, 2002.

Rosen, Robert. *Nowhere Man: The Final Days of John Lennon*. New York: South Village, 2000; repr. 2015.

Salewicz, Chris. *McCartney: The Biography*. London: Queen Anne, 1986.

Sheff, David. *All We Are Saying: The Last Interview with John Lennon & Yoko Ono*. London: Pan, 2020.

Sheffield, Rob. *Dreaming the Beatles*. New York: Dey Street, 2018.

Shotton, Pete, and Nicolas Schaffner. *John Lennon: In My Life*. New York: Stein & Day, 1983.

Sounes, Howard. Fab: *An Intimate Life of Paul McCartney*. London: Harper, 2011.

Southall, Brian, and Rupert Perry. *Northern Songs: The True Story of the Beatles' Song Publishing Empire*. London: Omnibus, 2006.

Spitz, Bob. *The Beatles: The Biography*. London: Aurum, 2007.

Stanley, Bob. *Yeah Yeah Yeah: The Story of Modern Pop*. London: Faber & Faber, 2013.

Taylor, Derek. *As Time Goes By: Living in the Sixties*. London: Faber & Faber, 2018.

Turner, Steve. *Beatles '66*. London: HarperCollins, 2016.

————. *A Hard Day's Write: The Stories Behind Every Beatles Song.* London: Little Brown/Carlton, 1995.

Wenner, Jann. *Lennon Remembers.* London: Talmy, Franklyn, 1972.

Womack, Kenneth. *John Lennon 1980.* London: Omnibus, 2020.

INDEX

Abbey Road, 295–96, 303–7, 310–11, 317n, 375
"Across the Universe," 214, 225
"Act Naturally," 231
"Ain't She Sweet," 57
Alexander, Arthur, 289
"All My Loving," 96, 116
All Things Must Pass, 327
"All Together Now," 212
"All You Need Is Love," 214–15, 275
All You Need Is Love (Brown and Gaines), 221n
Altham, Keith, 144, 189
"And I Love Her," 132, 145, 280
"And Your Bird Can Sing," 147, 384n
Animals, 292
"Another Day," 329–30, 332
"Another Girl," 124
"Any Time at All," 78, 342
Apple Corps, 33, 226, 236, 243–44, 252–53, 259–60, 264, 267, 272, 287–91, 294–96, 299–302, 305–10, 313–15, 319–20, 327, 333, 360, 387
dissolution of, 330
Ardmore and Beechwood (A&B), 75, 77, 82–83, 86
Aristophanes, 387
Asher, Claire, 95
Asher, Jane, 94–96, 110, 118–22, 132, 136, 143, 151–52, 167, 171, 187, 195, 209, 220–21, 226–27, 232–33, 246, 253, 267, 293

Asher, Margaret, 95, 96
Asher, Peter, 95, 151
Asher, Richard, 95
"Ask Me Why," 77, 86
Aspinall, Neil, 51, 76, 166, 180, 187, 217, 220, 232, 236, 244, 249, 282, 302, 322

B-52's, 369
"Baby's in Black," 109
"Baby You're a Rich Man," 212
Bach, Johann Sebastian, 162, 215, 257
    second Brandenburg Concerto, 192
"Back in the USSR," 163, 261
"Back Seat of My Car, The," 328, 330–31
Back to the Egg, 367
Bacon, Francis, 143
Baird, Julia (John's half-sister), 59
"Ballad of John and Yoko, The," 296–97, 300, 305
Band, 272–73
Band on the Run, 354, 364–65
Barrow, Tony, 65n, 111, 134–35, 165, 175–76, 179, 241
BBC, 67, 74, 87, 91, 94, 96, 111, 126, 162, 215, 343, 385
Beach Boys, 101, 138, 171, 176, 189–90, 232
Beatles. *See also specific individuals; albums; and songs*
    Abbey Road multitrack recording and, 131–32

Apple crisis, and Paul/Eastmans vs. John/Klein, 291–96, 299–303, 309–10, 314, 319–20, 330, 340
Apple founded by, 244–45
breakup of, 309–17, 332–33
Decca audition and, 66–67, 73
dissolution papers signed, 361–62
early recording backing Sheridan, 57
Ed Sullivan Show and, 69, 100–101
EMI/Parlophone deal, and first single, 73–82
Epstein as manager and, 61–67
Epstein as manager of Lennon-McCartney songwriting, 83
film *Hard Day's Night* and, 101–5, 107
film *Help!* and, 117–18, 122, 124–25, 169–70
first American singles, 99–100
first American tour, 100–101, 107–8
first hit single "Please Please Me," 79–80, 82, 84–86
first national TV appearance, 85–86
George quits and rejoins, 279–84, 287
Get Back project and, 33–34, 229, 239, 271–85, 295, 319
Hamburg gigs and, 23, 38–45, 47, 54–57, 67–69, 71, 73, 84

Beatles (*continued*)
John and Paul share songwriting rights, 27–30, 31n
John and Paul split song income, excluding George and Ringo, 82–83
last day Paul sings with, 306
Liverpool gigs and, 23, 38, 47–54, 57–59, 69, 71, 86
London Paladium and, 92–93
Music of Lennon & McCartney TV tribute and, 144
name "Beatles" coined, 37
near breakup after Hamburg, 50–51
Olympia, Paris, concert, 100
Paul learns bass for, 56–57
Paul's lawsuit for formal separation, 319–20, 325, 327–30, 332
Quarry Men as precursor of, 7–8, 16, 18–19, 25–26, 30–31, 35–37
record final album *Abbey Road*, 303–8
record first album *Please Please Me*, 88–90
Ringo joins, 80–83
Ringo quits and rejoins, 260–61
rooftop concert on Apple building, 287–90, 387
Royal Variety gig and, 69
second American tour and Shea stadium triumph, 127–28
Sutcliffe and, 36–37, 53, 56
third American tour, 164, 174–79
tour of Australia and New Zealand, 102–3
tour of Germany, Japan, and Indonesia, 173–75
tours of 1963 in Britain, 87
Wooler as press officer, 58–59
Beatles Anthology, The, 218n
Beatles for Sale, 108–9, 112
Beatles from Apple, The (booklet), 344
Beatty, Warren, 365
"Beautiful Boy (Darling Boy)," 374, 385
"Be-Bop-a-Lula," 17
"Because," 305, 309
Bed-in for Peace, 295

Beethoven, Ludwig van, 101, 322
Fifth Symphony, 199n
"Being for the Benefit of Mr. Kite!," 207–8
Berio, Luciano, 152
Berlin, Irving, 171
Bernstein, Sid, 127
Berry, Chuck, 24, 37, 40, 49, 58, 108, 139, 304, 385
"Besame Mucho," 57–58, 297
Best, Mona, 35–36, 38
Best, Pete, 38, 42, 44, 47, 54, 56, 59, 64, 68, 80–81
"Best Friend," 353
Billboard, 127–28, 367
"Birthday," 235
Black, Cilla, 71, 123n
"Blackbird," 262
Bloody Sunday, 352n
Bloom, Harold, 2
Bottoms (film), 248
Bowie, David, 350, 361
Boyd, Pattie (George's wife), 134, 150, 218–19, 232, 313
Boyd, Paula, 218
Boyle, Bernie, 59
Bramwell, Tony, 253, 305
Braun, Icke, 41
Bron, Eleanor, 167
Brown, Dan, 175
Brown, Peter, 221, 244, 250, 295–96, 300, 387
Browne, Nicky, 188
Browne, Tara, 143, 188
Burroughs, William, 152
Byron, George Gordon, Lord, 386

Cage, John, 151–52, 197, 247
Caldwell, Irish, 263
Callaghan, James, 218
"Can't Buy Me Love," 100, 103, 205
Capitol Records, 99, 127, 135, 252, 309–10
Cardew, Cornelius, 151
Carroll, Lewis, 223
Cass and the Cassanovas, 35
"Cathy's Clown," 84, 115
Cavett, Dick, 340
Chantels, 53
Charles, Ray, 41, 112, 128
Chas & Dave, 241
Chaucer, Geoffrey, 36, 94–95
"Cheek to Cheek," 171

"Child of Nature," 233
Christgau, Robert, 381
Churchill, Winston, 159
Clapton, Eric, 246, 279, 308
Cleave, Maureen, 90–91, 150, 154–55, 164–65, 173, 175
Coasters, 57, 385
Cochran, Eddie, 20
Cocteau, Jean, 44
Cogan, Alma, 121–22, 193
"Cold Turkey," 311–12, 354
Cole, Nat King, 149
Coleman, Ornette, 152
Coleman, Ray, 146, 164–65
"Come Go with Me," 17–19, 21, 304
"Come Together," 304–5, 309
"Coming Up," 368–70
Como, Perry, 128–29
Concert for Bangladesh, 353
Coneys, Tyler, 369–73
Connolly, Ray, 167, 316, 343, 380
Cooke, Sam, 289, 292
Cookies, 52
Cott, Jonathan, 200, 336n, 376
Courtenay, Tom, 143
Coward, Noël, 268
Cox, Kyoko (Yoko's daughter), 248, 250, 303–4, 312, 332
Cox, Tony (Yoko's second husband), 248, 295, 312
Crickets, 25, 37
Crosby, Bing, 27, 79–80, 86, 129
Crowley, Aleister, 210
"Cry for a Shadow," 57
Cut Piece (Ono), 248

Daily Mirror newspaper, 111, 315
Dalí, Salvador, 189
Darin, Bobby, 292
Datebook magazine, 175
Davies, Hunter, 204–5, 207, 216–17, 219, 268, 292, 333, 384, 388
Davies, Peter Maxwell, 126
Davies, Ray, 190
Davis, Rod, 35
Day, Doris, 16
"Day in the Life, A," 78, 195–202, 204, 207, 209, 211–12, 215n, 216
"Day Tripper," 136, 139, 144, 147
Dean, James, 31

"Dear Friend," 335–37
"Dear Prudence," 232, 239
Decca, 64, 66, 73, 343
Del-Vikings, 18
Dennis, Felix, 332
Derry and the Seniors, 35, 38–40
Desert Island Discs (radio show),
    126, 385
Diddley, Bo, 305
Dietrich, Marlene, 69
"Dig a Pony," 288
Dodd, Ken, 138
Don Juan (Byron), 386
Donovan, 232, 263
"Don't Let Me Down," 271, 274,
    284, 288–90, 306
Doors, 309
Doran, Terry, 205
Double Fantasy, 374, 376–77,
    380, 385
Douglas, Jack, 373–74
Dowland, John, 126
Drifters, 257, 289
"Drive My Car," 135
Dunbar, John, 143, 151–52, 187, 248
Durband, Alan, 36, 122
Dykins, Bobby, 13–14, 16, 32, 59
Dylan, Bob, 100, 107–8, 109, 115,
    123, 135–38, 143, 176, 264,
    272–73, 280, 365

Eagles, 365
Eastman, John, 291–94, 325, 327
Eastman, Lee, 245, 291–94,
    299–300, 319
Eastman, Louise, 245
Eckhorn, Peter, 47, 54–55
Ed Sullivan Show (TV show), 69,
    99–101, 160
"Eleanor Rigby," 70, 146, 152,
    161–68, 176–77, 187, 204, 255
Elephant's Memory, 352–53
Elsas, Dennis, 359
Emerick, Geoff, 184, 196, 222,
    251, 381
EMI, 64, 73–80, 82, 84, 92, 96,
    99, 127, 131, 259, 292–95,
    303, 309
"End, The," 307, 316–17
Eno, Brian, 181
Epstein, Brian, 26, 29, 61–67,
    73–77, 80–81, 83, 86, 92, 99,
    109–11, 126–27, 149, 158,

164–65, 173–76, 188, 217,
    241, 245, 320, 342n
    suicide of, 220–23, 227
Epstein, Clive, 61–62, 291, 294
Epstein, Harry, 61–62
Epstein, Minnie "Queenie," 61, 221
European Broadcasting Union, 215
Evans, Mal, 166, 188, 196–97, 199,
    217–18, 232, 294, 310
Evening Standard newspaper,
    90, 175
Everett, Walter, 157, 162–63
Everly Brothers, 53, 84, 86, 109, 115
"Everybody's Had a Hard Year," 275
"Everybody's Trying to Be My
    Baby," 381
"Every Night," 313, 324

Faithfull, Marianne, 123, 143, 152,
    187, 218, 220
"Falling in Love Again," 69
Family Way, The (film), 187
Farrell, Bernadette, 69–70
Farrow, Mia, 231–32
Farrow, Prudence, 232
Fawcett, Anthony, 308
Fellini Satyricon (film), 102
Finney, Albert, 143
"Fixing a Hole," 211
Fluxus, 247
"Fool on the Hill," 190n, 213
"For No One," 151, 163, 171
Franklin, Aretha, 246, 272
Fraser, Robert, 143, 189
Freeman, Alan, 152
Freeman, Robert, 108, 155
Freewheelin' Bob Dylan, The, 100
Freud, Sigmund, 184, 201
"From Me to You," 88–90, 97, 99
Frost, David, 75, 164
Fury, Billy (Ronald Wycherley), 37

Gabor, Zsa Zsa, 91, 132
Gaines, Steven, 221n
Garland, Judy, 69, 71
Garry, Len, 35
Gaye, Marvin, 128
Gentle, Johnny, 37
Gershwin, George, 29
Gershwin, Ira, 29
"Get Back," 271–77, 281, 284, 288
Get Back (album, *later* Let It Be),
    295, 303, 311, 314, 319

Get Back (documentary), 2, 4, 23,
    33, 205, 229, 239–41, 252,
    261, 263, 273–80, 284–85,
    289, 293, 295, 303, 306, 314,
    319, 328, 331, 384n, 386
"Getting Better," 203–8, 211, 268
Gilvey, Jim, 50
"Gimme Some Truth," 331
Ginsberg, Allen, 347
"Girl," 137–38, 147
"Give Ireland Back to the Irish,"
    352
"Give Peace a Chance," 303
"Glass Onion," 266
"God," 324–25, 330, 359, 374
"God Only Knows," 171
"Golden Slumbers," 281
"Good Morning Good Morning,"
    207, 211
"Goodnight," 129
"Good Vibrations," 190
Goons, 74
Gopnik, Adam, 192, 276
Gordy, Berry, 52
Gould, Jonathan, 105
Grade, Lew, 296
Granada Television, 144–45
Graves, Robert, 143
Greenberg, Clement, 211
Griffiths, Eric, 35
Gruen, Bob, 366
Gustafson, Johnny, 60
Guy, Buddy, 152

Hall, Billy, 14
Halsted, Hank, 371–72
Hammerstein, Oscar, II, 29
Hamp, Johnnie, 144
Handel, George Frideric, 143
Hanton, Colin, 35
"Happiness Is a Warm Gun,"
    19, 262
"Hard Day's Night, A," 78, 102,
    113, 117, 198, 375
Hard Day's Night, A (album),
    100–101, 104–6
Hard Day's Night, A (film), 15–16,
    101–7, 117, 164
Harrison, George, 2–3, 24, 39,
    42, 44, 47, 51–54, 56, 59, 64,
    67–68, 78–81, 83, 85, 89, 91,
    96, 104, 110, 112, 117–18,
    123–26, 134–35, 137, 139, 142,

Harrison, George (*continued*)
144, 149–50, 155, 162, 164–65,
169, 172–79, 190, 195–96, 203,
206, 210n, 217–19, 221, 225,
229–36, 244, 251, 257, 260–62,
264, 271–84, 287–88, 292–97,
300–302, 304–5, 307–9,
311–13, 317, 320, 322, 327,
330, 332, 348, 353, 361, 376,
381, 386
joins Quarry Men, 30–36
marries Pattie Boyd, 150
quits and rejoins Beatles,
279–84, 287
songwriting and, 83, 280, 283
Harry, Bill, 63
Hart, Lorenz, 145
Haworth, Jann, 210
"Hello Goodbye," 227
"Hello Little Girl," 25–26
"Help!," 117–18, 125, 137, 157,
181
Help! (album), 117, 120–27, 135,
138
Help! (film), 117–18, 122, 167,
169–70
Hemingway, Ernest, 60
Hendrix, Jimi, 210, 272
"Here, There and Everywhere,"
170–72, 374, 383
"Here Comes the Sun," 304
"Here Today," 382–84
"Her Majesty," 317n
"Hey Bulldog," 226, 227
"Hey Jude," 146, 254–60, 290,
295, 358
Hicks, Tommy (Tommy Steele), 37
Highsmith, Patricia, 62
Hilburn, Robert, 376
Hodges Chas, 241
Holly, Buddy, 24–26, 28, 31, 37,
77, 108, 198
"Honey Don't," 381
"Honeymoon Song, The," 162,
297
"Honey Pie," 261
Hopkins, Nicky, 331
"How?," 331
"How Do You Do It," 81–82
"How Do You Sleep?," 331–33,
335, 341, 345, 378
How I Won the War (film), 180
Hurricanes, 35, 38, 42–44, 48, 80

Huston, Chris, 48
Huxley, Aldous, 117, 156
Hynde, Chrissie, 262

"I Am the Walrus," 222–24, 227,
304
Ichiyanagi Toshi, 247
"I Don't Want to Spoil the Party,"
78, 109, 113
"I Feel Fine," 112–13, 115
"If I Fell," 104–6, 143, 147, 172,
256, 343
"I Found Out," 323
"I Know (I Know)," 353–54
"I'll Cry Instead," 104
"I'll Follow the Sun," 336n
"I'll Get You," 336n, 344
"I Lost My Little Girl," 23–24, 26,
28, 33–34
Imagine, 331–32, 335, 341
"Imagine," 331, 342, 360
"I'm a Loser," 109, 112–13
"I'm Down," 125, 127, 135
"I'm Happy Just to Dance with
You," 104
"I'm Looking Through You,"
136, 143
"I'm Only Sleeping," 280, 374
"I'm So Tired," 233, 235
In His Own Write (Lennon), 101–2
"In My Life," 19, 137–38, 141–47,
182, 188
"Inner Light, The," 225–26
"In Spite of All the Danger,"
31
"Instant Karma," 312–13
Interview magazine, 342n
"I Put a Spell on You," 136
"I Saw Her Standing There," 89,
360, 362
Isley Brothers, 89
"Isolation," 323–24
"It's All Too Much," 212
"I've Got a Feeling," 275, 287–88,
354, 387
"I've Just Seen a Face," 124–25,
132
"I Wanna Be Your Man," 145
"I Want to Hold Your Hand"
96–100, 110, 280
"I Want You (She's So Heavy),"
295
"I Will," 19, 263

Jackson, Peter, 2, 4, 23, 33, 276,
279, 282, 387
Jacky and the Strangers, 169
Jagger, Mick, 103, 220, 277n, 350
James, Dick, 81, 86, 275, 293, 296
Janov, Arthur, 16n, 320–22, 342,
358
"Jealous Guy," 331, 343–45
"Jet," 365
John, Elton, 350, 359–60
John, Paul, George, Ringo and Me
(Barrow), 65n
John Lennon (Norman), 16n
John Lennon/Plastic Ono Band,
321–25, 359
Johnny and the Moondogs, 36
Johns, Glyn, 293, 301, 322
Johnson, Betty, 129
Johnson, Steven, 122
Jones, Pauline, 222
Joplin, Janis, 246
Juke Box Jury (TV show), 94
"Julia," 145, 233, 239, 266
Jung, Carl, 154, 156
"(Just Like) Starting Over," 19,
374, 377–78

Kane, Larry, 244–45
Kay, Laurie, 376
Kennedy, John F., 99, 254
Kennedy, Robert F., 381
Kesey, Ken, 212
King, B.B., 152
King, Martin Luther, Jr., 245, 255
King, Tony, 360–61
King James Bible, 158
King Lear (Shakespeare), 224
Kinks, 112, 190, 292
Kirchherr, Astrid, 44–45, 47, 53,
56, 67–68
Klein, Allen, 292–94, 296,
299–303, 309–11, 314, 316,
319–20, 322–23, 330, 332,
340, 342, 348, 353
Kolk, Bessel van der, 60
Koschmider, Bruno, 38–40, 42–43,
47, 55
Kramer, Billy J., 110–11
Ku Klux Klan, 179
Kuti, Fela, 354

La Boétie, Étienne de, 387–88
Laborintus 2 (Berio), 152

"Lady Madonna," 225–27, 365

Laine, Denny, 146, 339, 354, 366, 379

Lear, Edward, 101, 223

Leary, Timothy, 3, 156–59

Lee, Peggy, 69

Leiber, Jerry, 29

Leibovitz, Annie, 380

Lennon, Alf (John's father), 12–14, 32, 222–23, 321, 366

Lennon, Cynthia Powell (John's first wife), 54, 59, 92, 96, 104, 109–11, 118, 134–35, 154, 166, 176, 180, 193, 205, 207, 217, 219–23, 226–27, 232–36, 241, 344, 350, 361

divorces John, 249–51, 253, 265, 310

marries John, 81

Lennon, John. *See also* Beatles; *and specific albums; and songs*

Apple crisis, and battle vs. Paul and Eastman, 291–94, 296, 299–303, 314–15, 319–20, 325, 341–42

aunt Mimi and, 14–17, 26–27, 182, 265

Beatles final tour and, 180

birth of, 13

breakup of Beatles and, 309–17, 332–33, 328–29, 332

break with Klein and, 353

break with Yoko and affair with May Pang, 344, 347–51, 357–61

charisma of, 8, 181

childhood of, 12–15

Cold Spring Harbor sailing and, 368–72

death of, 1–2, 4–5, 146–47, 376–88

death of Alma Cogan and, 193

death of Epstein and, 220–23

death of mother Julia and, 32–33, 68

death of Sutcliffe and, 67–68

death of uncle George and, 16, 68

decides to split songwriting rights fifty-fifty with Paul, 82–83, 86

divorces Cynthia, 250, 253–54, 361

drinking and, 72–73, 109–11, 135, 363

drugs and, 207–8, 320, 332, 350–51

Dylan and, 109, 123, 135–36

early musical interests of, 16, 18–19, 129, 139

education of, 14–15, 26, 36

Epstein and, 63–65, 109–12

father Alf and, 13–14, 32, 222–23, 321, 366

films *How I Won the War*, 180–82

final dissolution of Beatles partnership signed, 361–62

first meets Paul at Woolton church and adds to Quarry Men, 7–9, 17–21, 24–31, 35–36, 83, 167–68

first solo hit "Instant Karma" and, 312–13

friendship and tensions with Paul, 128–29, 134–36, 187, 239–42, 260, 343–45, 352–55, 362, 366–68, 377, 382, 386–88

friendship with Sutcliffe, 31–32, 36–37

George added to Quarry Men, 30–31

goads Paul to tour with Wings, 351–52

guitar playing, 8, 25

harmonica playing, 77

impact of, on modern culture, 2–3

insecurity of, 128–29, 187, 224, 343–45, 377

interviews, 90–92, 141–46, 200, 260, 322–23, 328–29, 332, 340–41, 353–54, 358, 374–76

Kenwood home, 118–19, 135, 153–54, 166, 195, 207, 214, 222

last phone call with Paul, 386

Liverpool musical idea and, 188–89

LSD and, 134–36, 156–61, 163, 181–83, 188, 192–93, 200, 203–8, 215, 236, 245

LSD trip with Paul, 203–4, 207–8

Madison Square Garden concert with Elton John, 359–60, 362–63

Mann on songwriting with Paul, 105–6

mental instability of, 112, 216, 236–37

mother Julia and, 12–17, 193, 266

moves to Dakota with Yoko, 347

moves to LA and records with Spector, 350–51, 348

musical tastes of, vs. Paul's, 70–71

new sources on collaboration with Paul, 2–4

Paul as go-between for Yoko and, 94, 357–61

Paul's "Coming Up" renews interest in music, 369–70

Paul's dog Martha and, 268–69

Paul's interviews on, 146–47, 341–44

Paul's *McCartney* and, 313–14

Paul's romance with Jane Asher and, 94–96, 227

Paul's romance with Linda Eastman and, 246, 261–62, 294–95, 311, 344

Paul writes "Dear Friend" for truce with, 335–36

personality of, 15–17, 164–66, 206–7, 216–17

photo of, mirroring Paul's, 378

politics and, 34, 164, 215, 245, 255, 303, 340, 353

pot and, 135, 206–7, 264

primal therapy and, 320–21

reconciles with Yoko, 360–64

records "Ballad of John and Yoko" with Paul, 296–97

records *Double Fantasy*, 373–78

records first solo album *Lennon/Plastic Ono Band*, 321–25, 328–29

records musical nail bomb vs. Paul "How Do You Sleep?," 331–32, 335, 341–42

records second solo album *Imagine*, 331–32

religion and, 70, 175–77, 188–89, 236, 296–97, 323–24

Lennon, John (*continued*)
romance and marriage to
Cynthia Powell, 54, 59, 81,
92, 109, 118, 193, 207–8, 217,
219, 222–23, 226–27, 235–36,
249–50, 344
romance and marriage to Yoko
Ono, 34, 193, 240–41, 246–52,
259–61, 264–66, 271–72,
282–84, 289–90, 294–97, 303,
309, 311–12, 320–21, 332–33,
344, 363–65, 369, 373–78
Shotton kicked out of Quarry
Men by, 25
singing influences lyrics of, 223–24
son Julian and, 92, 109, 193,
216–17, 253–54, 303, 361–62
son Sean and, 363–65, 373
trips to Paris with Paul, 59–61,
66, 187
trip to Barcelona with Epstein,
109–12
trip to Bermuda by sailboat,
371–73
trip to Denmark with Yoko, 312
trip to Greece to find island for
Beatles, 217–18
trip to India with Maharishi,
225, 229–36, 239–42, 266
trip to Scotland with Yoko and
auto accident, 303–4
trip to south of England to visit
Paul's cousin Bett and, 36
trip to Wales with Maharishi,
219–21
uncle George and, 14–16
women and, vs. Paul, 71
Wooler assaulted by, 110–12
writes first song, inspired by
Holly, 25–26
Lennon, Julian (son of John and
Cynthia), 92, 104, 109, 118,
154, 180, 193, 207, 216–17,
219, 250, 253, 254, 303, 304,
350, 361, 362
Lennon, Julia Stanley (John's
mother), 12–13, 15–17, 28,
59, 80, 92, 104, 266, 321
death of, 32, 68
Lennon, Pauline, 321
Lennon, Sean Ono (John and
Yoko's son), 363–64, 373
Lennon (Riley), 374n

Lenoir, J. B., 152
Leopold and Loeb, 60
Lerner, Alan Jay, 29
Lester, Richard, 15–16, 103, 117,
122, 180
"Let It Be," 10, 146, 281
Let It Be (album, formerly *Get
Back*), 225, 311, 314, 319
Let It Be (documentary), 4, 323.
See also *Get Back*
"Let Me Roll It," 354–55
Lewisohn, Mark, 48–49
Life magazine, 232, 311
"Like Dreamers Do," 75
Limpensel, Willi, 40
Lindsay, Helen, 62
Lindsay-Hogg, Michael, 4, 219,
239, 259, 271–73, 282,
287–89, 319
Little Richard, 7, 20, 24, 26, 37,
49, 58, 84, 86, 108, 125, 139,
241, 287, 309, 376
"Live and Let Die," 354, 357
Live and Let Die (film), 354
Lockhart-Smith, Judy, 74
Lockwood, Sir Joseph, 259
Loewe, Frederick, 29
Lomax, Jackie, 264
London Life magazine, 143
"Long and Winding Road, The,"
281
"Long Haired Lady," 263, 328
"Long Tall Sally," 20, 48, 58,
125, 153
"Look at Me," 239
Love, Mike, 232
"Lovely Linda," 325
"Lovely Rita," 163
"Love Me Do," 70, 76–79, 82–85,
276
"Love of the Loved," 123n
Lowe, John "Duff," 31, 35
"Luck of the Irish, The," 352n
"Lucy in the Sky with Diamonds,"
207–8, 210, 213, 359–60, 360
Lyrics, The (McCartney), 309

Madness, 369
"Magical Mystery Tour," 212
Magical Mystery Tour (album),
212, 226–27
Magical Mystery Tour (show),
221–22, 243

Magic Christian, The (film), 272
Magritte, René, 189, 226
Le Jeu de Mourre, 226
Maharishi Mahesh Yogi, 219–21,
225–26, 230–36
Man and His Symbols (Jung), 154
Mann, William, 105–6
Mansfield, Ken, 333
Marcos, Ferdinand, 174
Marcos, Imelda, 174
Mardas, Alexis, 217–18, 234,
244, 246
Martha and the Vandellas, 115
"Martha My Dear," 268
Martin, George, 3, 26, 73–82,
84, 86, 88–89, 93, 95, 123,
126, 139, 158–59, 161, 166,
183–84, 187, 195, 197, 199n,
201, 203–4, 206, 222, 261,
266, 290, 297, 303–4, 322–23,
373, 379, 381, 383, 385
Martin, Giles, 266
Marvelettes, 96
Marx, Karl, 210
"Mary Had a Little Lamb," 352
Massey & Coggins, 50–51
"Matchbox," 381
Matisse, Henri, 245, 293
"Maxwell's Silver Hammer," 308,
311, 313
Mayall, John, 152
"Maybe I'm Amazed," 313, 324
McCartney, 313–15, 322, 324–25,
327, 329, 332, 339
McCartney, Ginny (Paul's aunt), 9,
12, 110, 124
McCartney, Heather (Paul and
Linda's daughter), 245,
262–64, 267, 312
McCartney, Jim (Paul's father),
9–12, 15, 24, 26, 29, 50–51,
54, 64, 65, 110, 343
death of, 366
McCartney, Linda Eastman (Paul's
first wife), 231, 245–47,
252–53, 261–68, 280–82,
292–95, 308, 311–14, 322,
328–29, 336, 339–44, 352,
354, 357, 359, 361, 365–67,
379, 382, 386
marries Paul, 294–95, 344
McCartney, Mary Mohin (Paul's
mother), 9–12, 70, 110

McCartney, Mary (Paul and
    Linda's daughter), 312
McCartney, Paul. *See also* Beatles;
    *and specific albums; and
    songs*
adopted daughter Heather and,
    262, 264
affairs and, 187, 226, 246, 252,
    261, 263
ambition of, 65–66, 165, 243
Apple Corps and, 243–45, 252,
    260–61
Apple crisis, and battle vs.
    John and Klein, 291–94, 296,
    299–303, 314–15, 319–20,
    325, 341–42
attempts to reconcile with John,
    343, 352–54, 359–60, 366–68
auntie Gin and, 12
bass playing, 56–57, 290
birth of, 9
breakup of Beatles and, 307–17,
    341–42
Cavendish Avenue home of, 152
childhood of, 9–12
Christmas mixtape by, 149–50
Cynthia Lennon and, 253
death of Epstein and, 220–22, 227
death of John and, 1–2, 4–5,
    376–87
death of John's mother Julia and,
    32–33
death of mother Mary and, 9,
    11–12, 33, 264
death of Sutliffe and, 68
decides to split songwriting
    rights fifty-fifty with John,
    82–83, 86
Desert Island Discs appearance,
    126
drugs and, 108
Dylan and, 107–8, 136
early musical tastes of, 10,
    24–25, 70–71
early songwriting, 24–30
education of, 26, 36
Epstein as manager and, 64–67, 83
experiments in sound, 152,
    159–60, 268
fans and, 69–70, 214
father Jim and, 50–51, 54
final dissolution of Beatles
    partnership signed, 361–62

first meets John, and joins
    Quarry Men, 7–9, 17–21,
    24–31, 35–36, 83, 167–68
first solo single "Another Day,"
    329–30
friendship and tensions with
    John, 70–71, 143–44, 147,
    150–51, 208, 239–43, 260–61,
    322–23, 329, 331–33, 340–41,
    345, 375–76, 387–88
George asked to join Quarry
    Men by, 30–31
guitar playing, 24–25, 27, 30
Hendrix and, 210
impact of, on modern culture,
    2–4
interviews, 90–92, 143–47,
    152–53, 165, 176–78, 189,
    244–45, 262–64, 314–15,
    333–36, 341–42, 345, 384–87
Ivor Novello award and, 187
job as electrical apprentice,
    50–51
John's Madison Square Garden
    performance and, 362
John's relationship with Yoko
    and, 252, 254–55, 259–62,
    289–90, 333, 335–36
John's return to music with
    Double Fantasy and, 374–75
John's son Julian and, 253–54,
    362
John's trip with Epstein to
    Barcelona and, 109–11
last phone call with John,
    386
lawsuit to dissolve Beatles, 325,
    327–30, 341–42
Liverpool musical idea and,
    188–89
London social scene and, 94–96,
    118–19, 121, 134–35, 143–44,
    150–53, 156
LSD and, 134, 156–57, 188, 193,
    195–96, 200, 245
LSD trip with John, 203–4, 208
as lyricist, 162–63
Magritte paintings and, 189
Mann on songwriting with John,
    105–6
Martha, sheepdog, and, 205–6,
    267–69
Martin and, 158–59

musical versatility of, 131–32
Music of Lennon & McCartney
    TV tribute, 144
new sources on relationship with
    John, 3–4
performs with image of John on
    screen, in 2022, 387
personality of, 146–47, 164–67,
    229, 263–64
politics and, 164, 175–77
records *Band on the Run*, 354,
    364–65
records "Coming Up" and
    praised by John, 369–70
records first Wings album *Wild
    Life*, 336–37, 339–40
records last Wings album *Back to
    the Egg*, 367
records *Red Rose Speedway*, 354
records solo album *McCartney*,
    313–14, 322–25, 329
records solo album *Ram*,
    327–31, 339
records *Wings over America*, 367
records with Martin after
    breakup of Wings, 373, 381–83
releases Beatles song "Now and
    Then" in 2023, 386
religion and, 164
romance and marriage to Linda
    Eastman, 245–46, 252–53,
    261–64, 267, 280–81, 294,
    329, 339
romance and marriage to Nancy
    Shevell, 267
romance with Dot Rhone and, 54
romance with Jane Asher and,
    94–96, 132–33, 151, 171–72,
    195, 209, 226, 267
sees souls through eyes, 240–41
tour of Japan and arrest of,
    368, 373
tours with Wings, 339, 351–52,
    365–66
trips to Paris with John, 59–61,
    66, 187–88
trip to Bordeaux and Spain,
    188
trip to Greece to find island for
    Beatles, 217–18
trip to India with Maharishi,
    225–26, 229–33, 236, 239–42
trip to Kenya, 188

McCartney, Paul (*continued*)
    trip to Obertauern, Austria, to
        film *Help!*, 169–70
    trip to Paris with Fraser to buy
        art, 189
    trip to Wales with Maharishi,
        219–21
    twenty-first birthday party
        and John's attack on Wooler,
        110–11
    vocals and, 69–71, 124, 290
    writes "Dear Friend" about
        John, 335–37
    writes *Family Way* soundtrack,
        187
    writes "Let Me Roll It" about
        John, 354–55
    writes *Live and Let Die* theme
        song, 354, 357
    Yoko aids, after loss of John,
        385–86
    Yoko's reconciliation with John,
        94, 357–61
McCartney, Peter Michael "Mike"
    (Paul's brother), 9, 11–12, 25,
    110, 366
McCartney, Stella (Paul and
    Linda's daughter), 365
McCartney II, 368
McCullough, Henry, 352
McDonald, Ian, 184
McFall, Ray, 50–51
McGivern, Maggie, 187, 261, 294
McQueen, Steve, 365
Megan Jaye (schooner), 371–72
Mellers, Wilfrid, 126
Melody Maker magazine, 167, 220,
    311, 325, 342–43
Merry Pranksters, 212
Mersey Beat, 58, 62–63
Michaels, Lorne, 366
"Michelle," 136, 138, 143, 146
Miles, Barry, 16n, 143, 151, 153,
    156, 204, 268, 311
Miller, Glenn, 215
Miller, Max, 90
Miller, Roger, 138
Miller, Steve, 302
Milligan, Spike, 101
Milton, John, 158
Mind Games, 349–50, 353
Miracles, 52, 142, 172
"Monkberry Moon Delight," 328

Monroe, Marilyn, 210
Montaigne, Michel de, 387–88
Moody Blues, 339
Moon, Keith, 350, 358
Moore, Tommy, 37–38
Mortimer, Celia, 89
"Mother," 323, 377
"Mother Nature's Son," 162, 235
Motown, 52, 86, 135, 151
Muggeridge, Malcolm, 58
"Mull of Kintyre," 367
Munro, Matt, 127
Murray, Mitch, 81–82
*Music of Lennon & McCartney,
    The* (TV show), 144–45
"My Bonnie," 62
"My Dark Hour," 302
"My Funny Valentine," 70, 145
"My Love," 378

NEMS (North End Music Stores),
    49, 59, 62, 64, 134, 220,
    243–44, 291, 293–94, 296, 303
Nerk Twins, 36, 169
Ness, Lindy, 53
New Musical Express (NME)
    magazine, 88, 138, 311
Nicol, Jimmie, 206
Nietzsche, Friedrich, 156, 249
"Night Before, The," 124
Nilsson, Harry, 350–41, 358, 378
"#9 Dream," 358–59
Nixon, Richard, 347–48, 381
"No Reply," 109, 113, 344
Norman, Philip, 16n, 240, 265,
    348, 381
Northern Songs, 279, 296, 300
"Norwegian Wood," 136–38,
    147, 158
Novello, Ivor, award, 187
"Now and Then," 386
"Nowhere Man," 137, 143–44, 374

"Ob-La-Di, Ob-La-Da," 232,
    277, 308
"Octopus's Garden," 190n
O'Dell, Denis, 272
"Oh! Darling," 19, 284, 305–6
"Oh Yoko!," 331
Oliver! (musical), 122
"One After 909," 50, 288
O'Neill, Eugene, 143
"On Friendship" (Montaigne), 388

Ono, Yoko (John's second wife),
    16n, 34, 94, 187, 193, 233,
    239–41, 246–54, 259–66,
    271–74, 282–84, 289–97,
    303–5, 309–16, 320–25,
    328–29, 332–33, 340–44,
    347–50, 353–54, 357–81,
    387
    birth of Sean, 363–64
    death of John and, 379, 381,
        384–86
    marries John, 294–96
    miscarriages, 264, 273, 312,
        321, 332
"On Safairy with Whide Hunter"
    (Lennon-McCartney story),
    30n
Orbison, Roy, 79, 84, 376
Osborne, John, 143
Our World (TV special), 215
"Over the Rainbow," 69, 71, 257
Owen, Alun, 103

Paar, Jack, 100
Pang, May, 344, 347–53, 357–64,
    371, 375
Paolozzi, Eduardo, 56
Paramor, Norrie, 79
Parker, Bobby, 112
Parlophone Records, 73–75, 79, 81
Parnes, Larry, 37
Passover Plot, The (Schonfield),
    175
Paul McCartney (Miles), 16n
"Penny Lane," 141, 162, 189–93,
    195, 197, 201–2, 384
Perkins, Carl, 381–82, 386
Pet Sounds, 189
Phillips, Esther, 145
Picasso, Pablo, 245, 293
Pipes of Peace, 385
Plastic Ono Band, 239, 303, 328,
    352
Plato, 387
Playboy magazine, 260, 375
"Please Mr. Postman," 96
"Please Please Me," 79–88, 97,
    99, 117
Please Please Me, 89, 96
Plomley, Roy, 385
Poole, Brian, and the Tremeloes, 66
Portable Nietzsche, The, 156
Porter, Cole, 144

Postcards from the Boys (Starr), 369n
Powell, Enoch, 277
Presley, Elvis, 7, 16, 18, 20, 24, 26–27, 37, 64, 66, 70, 103, 137, 139, 145, 189, 285, 381, 385
Preston, Billy, 287–88, 295, 322, 324
Pretenders, 369
Primal Scream, The (Janov), 320–21
Pritchard, Gill, 300
"P.S. I Love You," 76–77, 82–83
Psychedelic Experience, The (Leary), 156–57, 160
Psycho (film), 166

Q magazine, 386
Quarry Men, 7, 18–21, 24–26, 30–31, 35–36, 165, 190, 279–80, 376

Ra, Sun, 152
"Rainclouds," 379
Ram, 267, 328–32, 339–40
Ram (instrumental jazz version), 352
"Raunchy," 30
Red Mole magazine, 340
Red Rose Speedway, 354
"Revolution," 19, 251
"Revolution #9," 272, 359
Revolver, 150, 160, 170–73, 198, 241, 255, 283
Rhone, Dot, 54
Richard, Cliff, 37, 49, 66, 79, 90–91, 138, 151
Rikki and the Redstreaks, 49
Riley, Tim, 374n
Rilke, Rainer Maria, 184–85
Robbins, Bett (Paul's cousin), 36, 69
Robbins, Mike (Bett's husband), 36
Robinson, William "Smokey," 19, 52–53, 142, 172
Rock 'n' Roll, 350, 364
Rodgers, Richard, 29, 145
Rolling Stone magazine, 33n, 110, 200, 223, 235, 246, 314, 322, 329, 332, 336n, 341, 380
Rolling Stones, 103, 138–39, 145, 176, 197, 246, 272, 292
Ronettes, 52, 115
Rory and the Hurricanes, 38

Rosen, Robert, 377
Rowe, Dick, 66
Rubber Soul, 135–39, 143–44
Rubin, Jerry, 347–48
"Run for Your Life," 136–37
Russell, Bertrand, 151

Salewicz, Chris, 386
Saltzman, Paul, 232
Sandbrook, Dominic, 277n
Sander, Ellen, 213
Sartre, Jean-Paul, 44, 60
Saturday Night Live (TV show), 366–67
"Save the Last Dance for Me," 257
Schopenhauer, Arthur, 162
Schwartz, Francie, 253, 263, 267
Seaman, Fred, 369, 373, 377
"Searching," 385
Seekers, 138
Sehgal, Parul, 344
Seiwell, Denny, 339
Sellers, Peter, 74
"Sexy Sadie," 235, 261
Sgt. Pepper's Lonely Hearts Club Band, 7, 162, 183, 188, 198–202, 204, 207–15, 220–21, 226, 245, 255, 261, 265, 268
"Sgt. Pepper's Lonely Hearts Club Band," 162, 209–10, 375
Shadows, 49, 66–67, 79, 90, 110, 122
Shakespeare, William, 2, 36, 41, 158
Shankar, Ravi, 280
Shapiro, Helen, 87
Sheff, David, 260, 375–76
"She Loves You," 2, 92–94, 96, 99–100, 190n, 215, 254, 280, 358
Sheridan, Tony, 55, 57, 63, 317
"She Said She Said," 182, 283
"She's Leaving Home," 162–63, 210
Shevell, Nancy, 267
Shirelles, 52
Sholin, Dave, 376
Shotton, Pete, 20, 25, 35, 110, 166–67, 207, 236, 249–50, 264–65
Shout! (Norman), 381
"Silly Love Songs," 365
Simon and Garfunkel, 272

Simone, Nina, 136
Sinatra, Frank, 27–28, 128, 139, 232
Singing Sound '63 (concert), 94
Slick, Earl, 374
Smith, Arlene, 53
Smith, Bill, 35
Smith, George, 14–16, 68
Smith, Howard, 331
Smith, Mimi Stanley (John's aunt), 13–17, 26–27, 32, 38, 54, 79, 81, 118, 141, 158, 182, 193, 265
Smith, Norman, 135, 138
"Some Other Guy," 111, 312
"Something," 309
Some Time in New York City, 347, 352
Spector, Phil, 312, 319, 322, 350
Spelter, Jacky, 169
Stamp, Mr. Justice, 330
"Stand by Me," 357
Stanley, Anne (John's aunt), 13, 15
Starkey, Maureen (Ringo's wife), 150, 220, 232–33
Starr, Ringo, 2–3, 42, 48, 85, 91, 101–2, 110, 112, 116–18, 123, 125, 129, 133–34, 139, 144, 152, 155, 159–60, 164, 169, 172–73, 176, 179, 183–84, 195–99, 205–6, 216–22, 231–33, 244, 251–52, 256–57, 260–61, 264, 271–77, 282, 288–89, 292–94, 297, 300–302, 305–9, 311, 314–17, 322, 324, 327, 332–33, 350, 353, 358, 369n, 376, 381, 384
joins Beatles, replacing Best, 80–83
quits and rejoins Beatles, 260–61
wife and family, 150, 219, 232
Steele, Tommy (Tommy Hicks), 37
Steinbeck, John, 41
Stewart, Eric, 381–82
Stockhausen, Karlheinz, 152, 160, 197
Stoller, Mike, 29
Storm, Rory, 35, 38, 42–44, 48, 80
"Strawberry Fields Forever," 70, 145, 180–85, 188–93, 201–2, 224, 266, 274, 384
"Suicide," 24
Sullivan, Ed, 99–101

Summer of Love (Martin), 199n
Sunday Night at the London Palladium (TV show), 92–93
Supremes, 176
Sutcliffe, Millie, 67, 68
Sutcliffe, Stuart, 31–32, 36–37, 40, 42, 44, 47–48, 53, 56, 59, 67–68, 153, 165
Symposium (Plato), 387

Talented Mr. Ripley, The (Highsmith), 62
Talking Heads, 374
Taylor, Alistair, 63, 65, 217–18, 253
Taylor, Derek, 204, 236–37, 244, 256, 299, 322, 361
Teenager's Turn (TV show), 67
"Tell Me What You See," 132–33
"Tell Me Why," 18, 104
Tempest, The (Shakespeare), 191
Temple, Shirley, 210
"Tequila," 205
"Thank You Girl," 97
Thank Your Lucky Stars (TV show), 86
"That'll Be the Day," 31
"Things We Said Today," 132
Thomas, Dylan, 41
Thrillington, Percy (Paul's pseudonym), 352
Through the Looking-Glass (Carroll), 223
Tibetan Book of the Dead, The, 156
"Ticket to Ride," 115–19, 126, 128, 158–59
"Till There Was You," 69–71, 144, 280
Times of London, 105
Tolstoy, Leo, 145
"Tomorrow Never Knows," 156–63, 177–78, 204, 215
Tonight Show, The (TV show), 244
"Too Many People," 328, 330
Top Hat (film), 171
Town & Country magazine, 245
Tug of War, 385
"Twenty Flight Rock," 20
"Twist and Shout," 89, 156

"Two of Us," 240–41, 274, 280–81, 284–85, 345
Two Virgins, 259

Unforgettable (Paul's mixtape), 149
Unger, Art, 175, 179

van Syoc, Gary, 352
Vaughan, Sarah, 128
Velvet Underground, 24, 247
Venus and Mars, 361, 365
Vietnam War, 151, 164, 245
Vincent, Gene, 26, 40, 103, 385
Vollmer, Jürgen, 44, 60–61
Voorman, Klaus, 44, 68, 322, 332

"Wait," 132, 138
Waits, Tom, 328
"Walking on Thin Ice," 376
Walley, Nigel, 32
Walls and Bridges, 350, 358–59, 362
Wangberg, Eirik, 328
"Watching the Wheels," 374
Weber, Erin Torkelson, 340
"We Can Work It Out," 78, 132–39, 144, 198, 200, 336n, 384n
Weiss, Nat, 246
Weissleder, Manfred, 67–68
Welch, Bruce, 122
Wenner, Jann, 110, 314, 322–23, 328, 332, 380
"What'd I Say," 41, 45, 48, 112, 258
"Whatever Gets You thru the Night," 350, 360, 362
"What Goes On," 138
"What You're Doing," 163
"When I'm Sixty-Four," 24, 190n, 210
White, Andy, 82
White Album, 235, 251–52, 255–56, 260–62, 265–66, 271–73, 295, 308, 359
White Heat (Sandbrook), 277n
Who, 138, 143, 350
"Who's Lovin' You," 52
"Why Don't We Do It in the Road," 260, 384

Wilde, Oscar, 36
Wild Life, 336, 341–42
Williams, Alan, 37–38, 40, 47–48
Williams, Tennessee, 36
"Will You Love Me Tomorrow," 53, 58
Wilson, Brian, 171, 190
Wings, 146, 336, 351–52, 361, 365–68, 373, 378, 381, 387
Wings at the Speed of Sound, 365, 367
Wings over America, 367
Winner, Langdon, 213
"With a Little Help from My Friends," 205
With the Beatles, 96
"Woman," 374
Wonder, Steve, 151, 357, 381
Wood, Leonard, 75
Wooler, Bob, 47–51, 58–61, 86, 110–11, 223, 230
"Word, The," 137, 158
"Working Class Hero," 342
Wycherley, Ronald (Billy Fury), 37
Wynette, Tammy, 128

"Yellow Submarine," 176, 182
Yellow Submarine (film), 212, 225–26
"Yer Blues," 233, 235
"Yesterday," 121–29, 139, 142–43, 146, 158, 166, 171, 263, 324, 331–33, 341, 365
Yoko Ono/Plastic Ono Band, 322
"You Can't Catch Me," 304
"You Can't Do That," 104
"You Know My Name (Look Up the Number)," 302
"You Never Give Me Your Money," 302–4
Young, La Monte, 247
"You Really Got Me," 112
"Your Mother Should Know," 213, 227
"You've Got to Hide Your Love Away," 131
"You Won't See Me," 133, 136

ABOUT THE AUTHOR

Ian Leslie is an acclaimed journalist and author whose books on human psychology, communication, and creativity include *Conflicted*, *Curious*, and *Born Liars*. He has written for the *New York Times*, the *New Statesman*, the *Economist*, the *Guardian*, and the *Financial Times*. He is also the author of the influential newsletter *The Ruffian*. Leslie lives in London.

CELADON
BOOKS

Founded in 2017, Celadon Books, a division of
Macmillan Publishers, publishes a highly curated list
of twenty to twenty-five new titles a year. The list of
both fiction and nonfiction is eclectic and focuses
on publishing commercial and literary books and
discovering and nurturing talent.